ROUTLEDGE LIBRARY EDITIONS: INTERNATIONAL SECURITY STUDIES

Volume 20

SUPERPOWERS IN ECONOMIC DECLINE

SUPERPOWERS IN ECONOMIC DECLINE

U.S. Strategy for the Transcentury Era

RICHARD COHEN AND PETER A. WILSON

LONDON AND NEW YORK

First published in 1990 by Crane Russak, a member of the Taylor & Francis Group

This edition first published in 2021
by Routledge
2 Park Square, Milton Park, Abingdon, Oxon OX14 4RN

and by Routledge
52 Vanderbilt Avenue, New York, NY 10017

Routledge is an imprint of the Taylor & Francis Group, an informa business

© 1990 Taylor & Francis New York Inc.

All rights reserved. No part of this book may be reprinted or reproduced or utilised in any form or by any electronic, mechanical, or other means, now known or hereafter invented, including photocopying and recording, or in any information storage or retrieval system, without permission in writing from the publishers.

Trademark notice: Product or corporate names may be trademarks or registered trademarks, and are used only for identification and explanation without intent to infringe.

British Library Cataloguing in Publication Data
A catalogue record for this book is available from the British Library

ISBN: 978-0-367-68499-0 (Set)
ISBN: 978-1-00-316169-1 (Set) (ebk)
ISBN: 978-0-367-71159-7 (Volume 20) (hbk)
ISBN: 978-0-367-71166-5 (Volume 20) (pbk)
ISBN: 978-1-00-314958-3 (Volume 20) (ebk)

Publisher's Note
The publisher has gone to great lengths to ensure the quality of this reprint but points out that some imperfections in the original copies may be apparent.

Disclaimer
The publisher has made every effort to trace copyright holders and would welcome correspondence from those they have been unable to trace.

SUPERPOWERS in ECONOMIC DECLINE

U.S. Strategy for the Transcentury Era

Richard Cohen and Peter A. Wilson

CRANE RUSSAK
A Member of the Taylor & Francis Group
New York • Bristol, PA • Washington, DC • London

USA	Publishing Office:	Taylor & Francis New York, Inc. 79 Madison Ave., New York, NY 10016-7892
	Sales Office:	Taylor & Francis Inc. 1900 Frost Road, Bristol PA 19007-1598
UK		Taylor & Francis Ltd. 4 John St., London WC1N 2ET

Superpowers in Economic Decline

Copyright © 1990 Taylor & Francis New York Inc.

All rights reserved. No part of this publication may be reproduced, stored in a retrieval system, or transmitted, in any form or by any means, electronic, electrostatic, magnetic tape, mechanical, photocopying, recording or otherwise, without the prior permission of the copyright owner.

First published 1990
Printed in the United States of America

Library of Congress Cataloging in Publication Data

Cohen, Richard 1946–
    Superpowers in economic decline / Richard Cohen and Peter Wilson.
       p.   cm.
    Includes bibliographical references.
    ISBN 0-8448-1624-8. — ISBN 0-8448-1625-6 (pbk.)
    1. United States—Armed Forces—Appropriations and expenditures.
    2. Soviet Union—Armed Forces—Appropriations and expenditures.
    3. United States—Economic conditions—1981–   4. Soviet Union—
Economic conditions—1976–   I. Wilson, Peter A., 1928–
II. Title.
UA23.C585   1990
330.947'085—dc20   90-32080
                                                                             CIP

For our children

Contents

List of Figures vii

List of Tables ix

Acknowledgments xi

Chapter 1. Introduction 1

Chapter 2. Soviet Economic Decline and Its National Security Implications—Reasons and Responses 9
      Economic Decline: The Reasons 11
      Economic Decline: And the Response 21
      The Soviet "Economic Dimension of Security Vulnerability" 30

Chapter 3. Whither the Soviet Threat? 43
      The Andropov Coalition: A Reaction to Economic Decline and Its Alarming Security Implications .. 45
      Gorbachev's Mission: Reversing the Long Cycle Decline and Forging a "Minimal Line of Security" 56
      Why Moscow Must Cut Defense Spending 66
      The Future Soviet Threat 82

Chapter 4. Economic Constraints on U.S. National Security Spending—Reasons and Responses 102
      Why The U.S. Economy has Faltered 105
      U.S. Postwar Policy: Responding to the Inflation/Output Dilemma While Meeting the Challenge to Payments Balances 119
      The U.S. Economy: Cyclical Structure and Intercyclical Retreat, 1959–82 124
      Washington Confronts the "Economic Dimension" 137

Chapter 5.	Taking Stock of the "Reagan Revolution"	153
	A Supply-Side Effort to Reverse the Economic Slide	154
	A Revolution in National Security Accounts	172
Chapter 6.	The Defense Investment Dilemma of the 1990s: Contemporary or Transcentury Weapons?	182
	Transcentury Weapons: Components and Costs	183
	The Cost Explosion in Contemporary Forces	190
Chapter 7.	Conclusion: Expanding the Scope of U.S. National Security Policy	194
	The Economic Policy Component: A Cycle of Adjustment	195
	The Defense Investment Component: Pursuing Advantages and Opportunities	199

Appendices 206

    Appendix A—U.S. Government National Security Outlays, FY1940–88

    Appendix B—U.S. External Balances, 1946–88

    Appendix C—National Security and Transfer Payments as a Percent of GNP, FY1940–88

    Appendix D—National Security and Transfer Payments as a Percent of U.S. Government Outlays, FY1940–88

    Appendix E—National Defense Investment and Procurement as a Percent of U.S. National Defense Expenditures, FY1962–88

Notes 215

Bibliography of Data Sources 258

Selected Bibliography 260

Index 267

About the Authors 276

List of Figures

Figure 1.1 The long-term decline in superpower and ally economic growth rates
  (a) Soviet and CMEA-Six NMP growth, *3*
  (b) U.S. and non-U.S. OECD GNP/GDP growth, *3*

Figure 2.1 Long-term Soviet economic performance
  (a) Soviet national income growth, 1966–2000—official Soviet vs. Aganbegyan's estimates and projections, *10*
  (b) The Soviet long cycle, *10*

Figure 2.2 Stalin's economic reforms and the accelerated rise in factor input costs, *13*

Figure 2.3 Forces contributing to the rising costs of Soviet labor, 1961–80, *19*

Figure 2.4 Forces behind Soviet economic growth, 1961–80, *22*

Figure 2.5 The Soviet policy response to faltering economic performance, *25*

Figure 2.6 Moscow's national security cost and its disposition toward the "Economic Dimension of Security Vulnerability," *32*

Figure 3.1 Lines of growth and Soviet security, *57*

Figure 3.2 The rise and fall of Soviet GNP and labor productivity growth rates, 1985–88, *67*

Figure 3.3 The rise of the Soviet government budget deficit under Gorbachev, *70*

Figure 3.4 U.S. and USSR estimates of Soviet defense spending and their impact on the portion of defense spending Moscow is prepared to cut, *85*

Figure 3.5 Alternative Soviet threat futures—short and long term, *91*

Figure 3.6 Range of Soviet defense spending in the short term, 1989–95, *95*

Figure 4.1 Long cycle in postwar free world economy—Average annual GDP growth rate, *105*

Figure 4.2 Primary commodity price movements, 1958–88, *107*

Figure 4.3 Intercyclical changes in hourly wage growth rates in manufacturing for G-7 economies, *108*

Figure 4.4 Intercyclical changes in consumer inflation rate in world and developed sector, *108*

Figure 4.5 U.S. real national defense spending through the last three spending regimes and the estimated costs of constructing an effective Eurasian conventional deterrent, *141*

Figure 4.6 Strategic forces total obligational authority (1945–86) transformations in the contemporary national security spending regime and the costs of strategic superiority, *145*

Figure 5.1 Developed sector inflation rate increase from Phase Two trough Phase Three peak in last four business cycles, *168*

Figure 5.2 Improvement in the U.S. merchandise trade balance and the degree of dollar depreciation in Phase Three of the last four business cycles, *169*

Figure 5.3 Cumulative size of external balance deterioration from 1980 level to 1988 as percent of cumulative size of growth in national defense outlays from FY80 level to FY88, *173*

Figure 5.4 Reagan administration estimates vs. probable real U.S. defense spending in the 1990s, *179*

Figure 6.1 Growth in unit cost of weapons systems, *190*

List of Tables

Table 2.1   Percent of key primary commodity sectors in total Soviet investment, *16*

Table 2.2   Forces behind the rising cost of capital in the Soviet economy, 1961–80, *21*

Table 3.1   Continued descent of the Soviet economy, 1981–85, *52*

Table 3.2   Rising cost of the Soviet empire, 1981–85, *54*

Table 3.3   Bright and dark sides of Soviet economic performance in 1986, *61*

Table 3.4   Rising costs of USSR national security in 1986, *62*

Table 3.5   Insufficiency of Gorbachev investment program, *68*

Table 3.6   How the Soviet consumer has suffered under Gorbachev, *72*

Table 3.7   Sectoral investment patterns under Gorbachev, *74*

Table 3.8   Deterioration in Soviet non-socialist trade under Gorbachev, *75*

Table 3.9   Stubborn costs of empire, 1986–88, *77*

Table 4.1   Intercycle rise in capital costs and decline in the G-7 real gross fixed capital formation growth rate, *109*

Table 4.2   Intra-developed sector economic performance differentials over the last four business cycles
 (a) GDP growth rate, *115*
 (b) Merchandise trade balance, *115*
 (c) Consumer inflation, *115*
 (d) Central government fiscal deficit as percent of GNP, *116*

Table 4.3 Phasal evolution of the U.S. economy through the first three free world economy business cycles
    (a) Phase One, *126*
    (b) Phase Two, *126*
    (c) Phase Three, *127*
    (d) Phase Four, *127*

Table 5.1 The Reagan supply-side initiative: missed objectives, *156*

Table 5.2 The price of U.S. disinflation in the current business cycle, *158*

Table 5.3 Phase One—The explosion of U.S. financial imbalances, *160*

Table 5.4 Phase Two—A retreat in U.S. economic performance, *162*

Table 5.5 Phase Three—A safe haven, *165*

Table 5.6 Fall and rise of U.S. national defense outlays since the Vietnam War peak, *174*

Table 5.7 Fall and rise of defense investment and procurement from the Vietnam War peak, *175*

Acknowledgments

Several people helped bring this book into being. The authors would like to thank Richard Foster, editor of *Comparative Strategy* journal, for providing opportunity and encouragement to write the two articles on which this book is based; Frederick Leykam, president of the Washington Defense Research Group, for the opportunity to do much of the research that underlies it; and Laura Chasen Cohen for her help with both its substance and its form.

Peter Wilson would also like to thank his colleagues at the RAND Corporation and the MITRE Corporation for discussions over the years that stimulated his thinking on the transcentury defense environment.

Any mistakes of fact or judgment are, of course, the authors' own.

Chapter 1

Introduction

During the transcentury period (1990s and early twenty-first century) a factor long divorced from national security planning—economic performance—will inspire radical alterations in the security environment of the United States. If that environment is defined by the intensity of the foreign threat and the resources available to meet that threat, the impact on it of prolonged superpower economic decline became shockingly evident in 1989. The threat posed to the United States by the Soviet Union and its alliance system—a threat that has dominated U.S. national security planning since the late 1940s—commenced a remarkable retrenchment as economic pressures compelled the first contraction in Soviet real national defense spending since the 1950s and set the stage for a startling descent in Communist party power in Eastern Europe and, as a result, in the military credibility of the Warsaw Pact. At the same time, after four years of negative real growth in budget authority for U.S. national defense, the Bush administration was forced under severe budgetary pressure to accept further defense spending cuts deep into the 1990s.

The forces unleashed by the decline in superpower economic performance will confront U.S. strategy in the coming decade with unique opportunities to dramatically enhance security, as well as with new and alarming instabilities. If U.S. strategy is to seize the opportunities and preempt the maturation of new instabilities, it will have to expand beyond traditional horizons to address the central relationship between national security and economic performance.

Aside from imports, it is a nation's domestic economy that defines the quantity and quality of resources available for national security purposes. Quantitatively, the economy affords the national security sector factor inputs in the form of primary commodities, "raw" labor, and capital, and qualitatively, it provides science/research, technology, and labor skills. The ability of either of the superpowers to generate sufficient quantitative and qualitative inputs to produce an expanding national security output has thus been called into question by the secular decline in their economic performances.

Since the 1960s, the most revealing indicator of national economic health—real economic growth—has decelerated for both superpowers. In the Soviet Union, the National Material Product (NMP) produced—roughly equivalent to Gross National Product (GNP) minus services—growth rate has contracted in each successive five-year plan (FYP) beginning with the Seventh FYP (1961–65), save for a transitory recovery in the Eighth (1966–70) (see Fig. 1.1a). In the United States, the GNP growth rate plummeted in the 1970s from its 1960s average and did not recover in the 1980s (see Fig. 1.1b).

This pattern of faltering economic performance has not been restricted to the superpowers but has extended to their alliance systems. Over the last three decades, the evolution of the average of the NMP growth rates for the six East European members of the Soviet-centered trading bloc, the Committee for Mutual Economic Assistance (CMEA), has roughly paralleled that of the Soviet Union, while the economic growth rate of the non-U.S. component of the Organization for Economic Cooperation and Development (OECD), comprising nations overlapping the U.S. alliance system, has descended in tandem with that of the United States (see Fig.1.1a and b).

The "Economic Dimension of Security Vulnerability"

When portrayed graphically, these NMP/GNP trendlines describe the downward slope of an economic long cycle. Failure to reverse the descent has exposed both superpowers (and their alliance systems) to a growing "economic dimension of security vulnerability." In future lower economic growth environments, attempts to sustain or increase rates of growth in national security expenditures would require further lowering of already declining factor input growth rates for the civilian economy. The result: by sustaining or increasing recent historical rates of growth in national security expenditures, the deterioration in economic growth rates would be aggravated. In turn, this would mean poorer quantitative and qualitative resources available for national security in the future. A superpower that encounters a growing "economic dimension of security vulnerability" could suffer a gradual erosion of its strategic competitiveness, an erosion that, if unchecked, would at some point translate into a downgrading of its deterrent and warfighting potential and, ultimately, the end of its superpower status.

The dilemma posed to a superpower experiencing a growing "economic dimension" is that if it "races against time" and increases or merely sustains recent rates of growth in national security expenditures, it must sacrifice

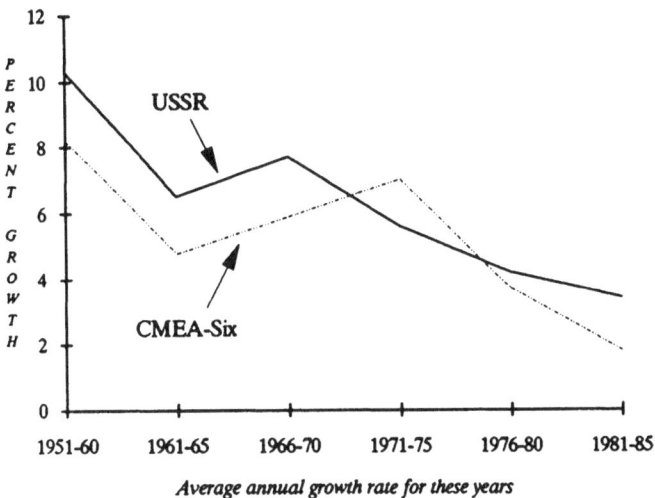

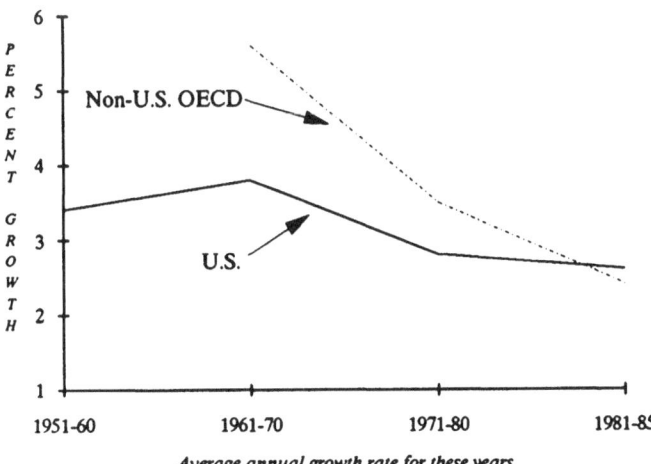

Figure 1.1. The long-term decline in superpower and ally economic growth rates. *Source:* (a) "Soviet Economic Performance: The Recovery That Was Not," *PlanEcon Report,* Vol. 2, no. 7 (17 February 1986) (for USSR); *PlanEcon Reports,* Vol. 2, nos. 15–16, 9, 8 (21 April 1986, 3 March 1986, 24 February 1986) (data compiled from each for Hungary, East Germany, and Czechoslovakia); *PlanEcon Report,* Vol. 2, no. 24 (13 June 1986) (for Bulgaria); *Plan Econ Report,* Vol. 2, no. 11 (17 March 1986) (for Poland); *PlanEcon Report,* Vol. 2, no. 10 (10 March 1986) (for Romania; includes a 4.0 percentage point reduction in reported Romanian NMP growth due to inflated figures). (b) Executive Office of the President, *Economic Report of the President, 1989* (Washington, DC: U.S. Government Printing Office, 1989) (for U.S.); *OECD Economic Outlook: Historical Statistics, 1960–87* (Paris: OECD, 1989) (for non-U.S. OECD).

long-term strategic competitiveness, whereas if it "buys time" and reduces the rate of expansion or cuts its national security spending as a means of avoiding an aggravated descent in economic growth rates or as part of a plan aimed at reversing economic decline, it confronts sacrifices in short-term security.

Both superpowers have, in fact, been laboring under the strain of a growing "economic dimension of security vulnerability" since the inception of the descent in their economic growth rates. National perceptions of security vulnerability driven by economic factors have, however, often been distorted by the penchant of each superpower's political-military establishment to view such vulnerabilities as relative ones. Measured in GNP, the U.S. economy is nearly twice the size of the Soviet economy and enjoys a huge technological edge. Technological improvement accounts for twice as much of economic growth in the United States as in the Soviet Union, and according to the U.S. Central Intelligence Agency (CIA), in 1988 for seven selected advanced manufacturing technologies, the U.S. held a development lead of 7–12 years.[1] From Moscow's perspective, its economic vulnerability in the superpower competition appeared as one of a relative insufficiency of economic resources, especially qualitative inputs.

On the other hand, in the Soviet Union the state owns and distributes the vast majority of economic resources, countenancing only a small private sector with almost no market determination over resource distribution, whereas in the United States the federal government controls a smaller share of economic resources and distributes an equally small share. Further, U.S. government budgetary policy is determined in a process that maximizes the influence of private, nongovernmental interests; in the Soviet political system such influences are minimized. As a result, from Washington's viewpoint, its economic vulnerability in ensuring national security has been perceived as an excess of claims on national resources when compared to the Soviet Union. The advantage of Soviet national security accounts in accessing resources is reflected in Moscow's ability to devote 15–17 percent of its GNP to national defense, compared to 5–6 percent in the United States.[2]

Attempted Remedies

No matter these perceptions of economic vulnerability, by the late 1970s the underlying forces threatening the strategic competitiveness of both superpowers—the deepening decline in national economic health and the consequent expansion of the "economic dimension of security vulnerability"—had breached the limits of tolerance. As a consequence, in the 1980s both Soviet and U.S. policymakers were driven to undertake high-risk initiatives to reverse worsening economic trends and thereby close the "economic dimension."

In the Soviet Union, the Communist party apparatus under Leonid Brezhnev came under increasing attack from national security professionals and the economic intelligentsia for the failing Soviet economy. Some, lead by Marshal Nikolai Ogarkov, drew a stark connection between negative economic performance and future Soviet security.[3] Through a series of political successions, those promoting radical initiatives to revitalize the domestic economy have come to power.

Since the ascension of Yuri Andropov to the general secretaryship, debate over how best to reverse economic momentum has assumed center stage, and under Mikhail Gorbachev, the Soviet government has indicated willingness to endure political risks in order to revive the economy. If not in the minds of the Soviet people, the party, and the state bureaucracy, then at least for Gorbachev and his associates as well as for many who resist his approach fearing the inherent risks, turning around the decline in economic performance has taken on the proportions of a life-and-death struggle in which the relationship between economic health and national security is intensely felt.

Of less drama than Gorbachev's initiatives, a high-risk effort to revive U.S. economic performance was attempted by the Reagan administration at the beginning of the 1980s. Reagan's supply-side economic formula was targeted to increase personal savings and investment as a means of reviving sagging U.S. productivity and, hence, GNP growth rates. As advertised, the supply-side tax cuts were to produce a sufficient increment to economic growth to afford substantial advances in national security expenditures. Implied in the Reagan program was a recognition that a reversal of the 1970s plunge in U.S. national security expenditures could not be accomplished at the expense of an aggravation of the U.S. "economic dimension of security vulnerability."[4] On the contrary, it could only be sustained if U.S. economic growth trends were reversed and the "economic dimension" eliminated.

The Emerging National Security Challenge

By the close of the decade, the results of the 1980s superpower economic measures would seem to have produced trends favorable to the United States. The threat emanating from the Soviet Union and its alliance system was in retreat. The forceful Soviet power projection that dominated the second half of the 1970s, culminating in the invasion of Afghanistan, came to a halt and underwent retrenchment, while closer to home Moscow acceded to a de-Communization of Eastern Europe. Further, the Gorbachev regime's preoccupation with economic revitalization combined with the failure of early efforts to accomplish it produced pressures for a real reduction in Soviet national security expenditures of some magnitude. Indeed, a number of observers were sufficiently impressed by the swell of these events to forecast the imminent demise of the Soviet threat.

At the same time, for most of the 1980s the United States was afforded enough economic prosperity to underwrite a large increase in resources devoted to national security. From FY81–FY87, real national defense outlays advanced by 5.2 percent a year and the share of national defense outlays devoted to defense investment (procurement, RDT&E, and military construction) grew each year, producing the strongest period of accelerated investment in the U.S. defense sector since the Korean War.[5]

There is a great temptation to linearly extend these trends and the comfortable national security environment they imply into the future, especially when comparing them to the not too distant past of the 1970s when Soviet military power and its projection were advancing while U.S. national security expenditures were plummeting. Underlying reality and not transitory trends suggest, however, a highly dynamic future U.S. security environment—one in which fully realizing the potential for enhanced security will require imagination and hard work. In the changing U.S. security environment lie historic opportunities for improvement, but also the potential for setbacks. The Soviet threat may well recede under the weight of the "economic dimension" facing Moscow, providing the United States unprecedented openings for reducing the challenge to its security, but these same economic pressures undermine governability throughout the Soviet Empire, thereby keeping alive the possibility for the reassertion of deeply rooted institutional and historical impulses for a reinvigorated, albeit economically constrained, national security effort. At the same time, the United States will enter the 1990s chilled by a recognition that the Reagan initiative produced only an illusion of prosperity and with unsustainable financial imbalances accumulated over three decades that are certain to place downward pressure on national security outlays and inflame free world economic tensions.

Indeed, contrary to what 1980s trends appear to suggest, U.S. policymakers will confront a formidable national security challenge in the 1990s, one for which the stakes will have been raised by a potential transcentury revolution in weapons technology.[6] Looming on the horizon of the next century are a variety of militarily adaptable technologies whose deployment could rapidly devalue contemporary superpower deterrent and warfighting capability. So radical are these potential changes that they may equate with the revolution in warfare wrought by nuclear weapons and long-range ballistic missiles, and if exploited, these systems will extend the battlefield to space and blur the distinction between nonnuclear and nuclear forces while complicating today's strategic balance. The ability of either superpower to gain asymmetric advantages in the deployment of these weapons systems would have staggering consequences for the other.

To assure U.S. national security in the transcentury era, U.S. strategy faces an integrated set of economic, diplomatic, and defense investment tasks. It must:

- Seek domestic and international economic policy adjustments able to support a revitalization of the U.S. economy and the elimination of the "economic dimension" by the end of the 1990s.
- Exploit the opportunities provoked by the decline of the Soviet economy and fast expanding Soviet "economic dimension" to eliminate those military asymmetries in contemporary forces that have been most threatening to U.S. security since the inception of the Cold War.
- Devise a defense investment strategy that ensures the deterrent value of U.S. military forces—whether efforts to eliminate contemporary force asymmetries succeed or fail and in the shadow of a possible transcentury weapons revolution. Further, it must do so with far less resources devoted to national defense than in the 1980s and with rapidly rising unit costs for contemporary defense machinery on the verge of taking a huge bite out of the force structure.

The failure to craft a strategy to navigate this course during the 1990s could by the end of the decade mean a further expansion in the U.S. "economic dimension of security vulnerability," leading to a U.S. retreat from global security objectives and a weakened capacity to compete in the twenty-first century.

Success would result in a U.S. economy fit to ensure competitiveness in the transcentury weapons arena if called upon to do so, and would bring the elimination of the post-World War II military imbalance most threatening to U.S. security—Soviet preponderance in central Europe—as well as a substantially reduced global threat regime in which the weight of deterrence would shift from contemporary force structure to R&D and industrial mobilization potential, at enormous savings.

* * *

Our purpose is to assess the parameters of the national security environment the United States is likely to face in the future in order to evaluate alternative U.S. national security strategies for the 1990s. The task requires estimates for the evolution of the Soviet threat and of constraints on U.S. national security expenditures. To arrive at these estimates, certain questions must first be examined. Driven by the central role superpower economic performance will play in defining the future U.S. national security environment, these questions must extend beyond the domain traditionally limiting such investigation to include:

- What are the causes of the long-term economic decline of both superpowers and what has been the nature of the policy initiatives that, up to this point, have failed?
- What has been the historical disposition of each superpower toward the dilemma posed by the "economic dimension of security vulnerability"?
- What has been the effect of recent policy initiatives—those of the Andropov-Gorbachev regimes and the Reagan administration—on each superpower's economic performance and on its "economic dimension of security vulnerability"?

Answers to these questions are indispensable for identifying alternative Soviet threat futures for both the short and long terms as well as for assessing the magnitude of future constraints on resources for U.S. national security.

Further, the national security environment to which the United States must respond involves a difficult defense investment dilemma. Beyond a decline in investment resources in the 1990s, the U.S. defense sector faces the prospect of rapidly rising unit costs for the production and maintenance of contemporary forces and of addressing costly transcentury weapons. In order to evaluate U.S. defense investment options in the transcentury era, we must also ask:

- What are the components and costs of transcentury weapons and what are the implications of rising unit costs for contemporary forces?

Chapter 2

Soviet Economic Decline and Its National Security Implications
Reasons and Responses

The regime of Mikhail Gorbachev confronts a Herculean task—a task that, should it meet with failure, would have profound strategic consequences for the Soviet Union. Since the early 1960s, all leading Soviet economic indicators have suffered marked deterioration, save for a brief recovery in the second half of the 1960s. When plotted out, the trend line representing the evolution of growth rates of Soviet national material product (NMP) produced over successive five-year periods beginning with the 1961–65 Seventh Five-Year Plan (FYP) reveals a Soviet economy moving on the downward slope of an economic long cycle.

If this trend line were to be drawn out into the not too distant future, the Soviet Union would be mired in a prolonged economic recession (see Fig. 2.1a). Indeed, according to a number of leading Soviet economists—foremost among them Abel Aganbegyan—Soviet NMP growth rate trend lines derived from official Soviet data understate both the pace at and depth to which Soviet economic performance has descended (see Fig. 2.1a).[1]

The upward slope of the modern Russian long cycle commenced in the aftermath of the depression into which the country's economy had fallen during World War I and the subsequent period of War Communism (1920–22). Reconstruction of the wartorn economy during the life of the New Economic Policy (NEP) from 1922–27 allowed for a rapid acceleration in economic growth—but growth that gave rise to severe domestic economic imbalances. Following a period of transition (1928–32) marked by lower economic growth rates during which Joseph Stalin's economic reforms were implemented, the Soviet economy once again enjoyed an acceleration in economic growth rates associated with the upward slope of the long cycle (see Fig. 2.1b). This ascent was blunted only as a result of periodic surges

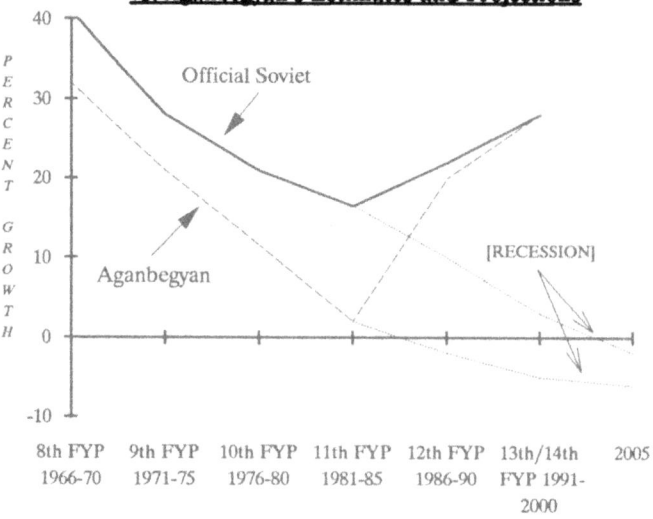

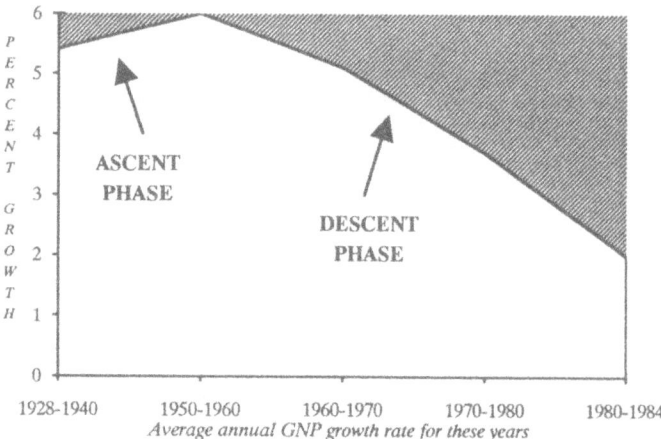

Figure 2.1. Long-term Soviet economic performance. *Source:* (a) Abel Aganbegyan, *The Economic Challenge of Perestroika*, ed. Michael Barratt Brown, trans. Pauline M. Tiffen (Bloomington: Indiana University Press, 1988), p. 2 (for official Soviet and Aganbegyan); authors' projections (for prolonged depression). (b) Paul R. Gregory and Robert C. Stuart, *Soviet Economic Structure and Performance*, 3rd ed. (New York: Harper and Row, 1986), p. 325.

in national defense spending—in 1937–38 in response to a qualitative advance in the Eurasian threat embodied in Nazi Germany and Imperial Japan and from 1951–54 in response to the Korean War and the consequent militarization of the Cold War—and as a result of war devastation in World War II (1941–45). In periods of more relaxed national defense spending and in the absence of war—in the years from 1933–36, in 1939–40 (the era of the Hitler-Stalin Pact), in the 1946–50 period of post-World War II reconstruction, and from 1956–60 during the Sixth Five-Year Plan—the ascending slope of the long cycle was in evidence.[2]

But beginning in the years from 1961–65 and continuing through to the present—save for the transitory 1966–70 recovery—the Soviet economic growth rate, while still positive, has decelerated in each successive five-year period. As suggested in Fig. 2.1a, the Herculean task that the Gorbachev regime has set for itself is the reversal of this trend line.

ECONOMIC DECLINE: THE REASONS

What has caused the dramatic descent in Soviet economic performance since the early 1960s? Soviet economists have pointed with much chargrin to what they refer to as an "extensive mode" of economic development gripping their economy—a mode in which economic growth primarily results from the integration of ever larger magnitudes of factor inputs, that is, primary commodities (land), "raw" labor, and capital, into the economy. Soviet economists and political leaders have often referred to the need for a transition to an "intensive mode" of economic development in which economic growth is the result of a process in which the magnitude of factor inputs required to produce a unit of output is reduced. In this mode, growth is fostered by the introduction of superior technologies, labor skills, and managerial efficiencies into the economic process. In the "intensive mode" of development, the economic system provides incentives for technological change and penalizes its absence, whereas in the "extensive mode," incentives promote immediate output at the expense of technological change.

The economic long cycle is a natural consequence of development in the "extensive mode." The upward slope of the cycle is produced as low cost, abundant factor inputs are mobilized into the economy, prompting an acceleration in the rate of growth of output. The cycle peaks when the costs of factor inputs rise as their supply status moves from relative abundance toward scarcity. As factor input supplies tighten and their costs mount, a prolonged descent in economic growth rates is set in motion.

The downward slope of the cycle can be reversed only by reducing the magnitude of factor inputs required to produce a unit of output sufficiently to restore relative abundance or by acquiring new sources of factor inputs, either through scientific/technological discovery or through imports (or conquest).

In the modern Russian long cycle, the early evolution of the economy during the life of the NEP proceeded within the confines of extensive development characteristic of traditional economies. Eventually, an inadequate supply of capital reflected in a Russian industrial base unable to meet the demand generated from a revitalized rural economy produced an inflationary "scissors crisis." Stalin's economic reforms were in part aimed at overcoming the national shortage in industrial fixed capital through forced development of the heavy industry sector and were also geared toward building an industrial mobilization base for a modern national defense capability.[3] They involved three crucial elements:

- Organizing the Soviet economy toward the end of maximizing immediate output.
- Forcing a huge transfer of resources from agriculture and personal consumption to heavy industry/defense.
- Radically centralizing the planning and administration of the national economy toward the end of ensuring the achievement of the first two objectives.[4]

While this set of economic reforms was able to reawaken the ascent phase of the long cycle, the prize was won at an immense cost. By speeding up the process of extensive development (done by maximizing immediate output) and by disinvesting in two factors of production—primary commodities (agriculture) and labor (personal consumption)—to support investment in another—capital (heavy industry), Stalin's reforms triggered a steeper descent on the downward slope of the cycle. Maximization of immediate output accelerated the pace at which factor input markets tightened, sparking a more rapid rise in costs, while sectoral disinvestment in agriculture and personal consumption prompted an early and aggravated decline in agricultural and labor productivity, thereby exacerbating the rise in primary commodity and labor costs. Finally, the advent of a heavily centralized economic planning and administrative apparatus served to blunt the pace of technological and related changes, reducing the prospects for relief in the rise of factor input costs that could be provided by improved economic efficiencies.

Indeed, the entrenched forces propelling the Soviet economy into decline can be systematically traced to the rise in cost of each factor of production impelled by the three elements in Stalin's economic reforms (see Fig.2.2).

CORE FEATURES OF THE STALINIST ECONOMIC SYSTEM

	Maximization of Immediate Output	Radical Centralization of Planning and Administration	Sectoral Disinvestment
PRIMARY COMMODITIES:	Rapid Depletion of: -- European USSR Energy and Raw Material Reserves -- Arable Land	High Degree of Raw Material/Energy Intensity	Depressed Agricultural Productivity
LABOR:	Underemployment	High Degree of Labor Intensity	Low Levels of Labor Discipline and Morale, and Labor Shortages
CAPITAL:	Overamortization	Rising Capital/Output Ratio	Primitivization

Figure 2.2. Stalin's economic reforms and the accelerated rise in factor input costs

The Rising Cost of Primary Commodities

Maximization of immediate output. Since the early 1960s, the Soviet primary commodity sector (raw materials, energy, and agriculture) has suffered from a dramatic rise in costs resulting from a depletion of both European USSR raw material and energy reserves and arable land.[5] In both cases—raw materials/energy and agriculture—the rise in costs has been exacerbated by a systemic commitment to maximizing immediate output.

One result is that raw material/energy extraction, transportation, and refinement costs have skyrocketed, placing a major burden on the Soviet economy. By the 1976–80 period, the cost of extracting a barrel of oil in the Soviet Union had risen by more than twofold from what it had been in the 1966–70 period, and two-thirds of Soviet energy now came from the Ural Mountains and areas to the east—an immense distance from the nation's industrial centers in the European USSR—adding unusual costs in the form of rail and pipeline transport networks.[6] Moreover, with the depletion of European USSR reserves has come a decline in the quality of raw material and energy resources, provoking a shocking leap in refinement costs. In 1950, for example, enrichment was required for only 37 percent of iron ore; by the 1980s, this figure had risen to 87 percent. As a result, whereas in the 1966–70 period it cost 62 rubles per ton of iron ore in capital expenditures, by the 1980s this cost had risen to 102 rubles.[7]

Since the early 1960s, the Soviet Union has been engaged in a costly struggle to maintain its arable acreage by resort to large inputs of resources to extend its inland water system. Indeed, by the early 1950s the Soviet economy had already run up against limits to continued reliance on extensive development in its agricultural sector. Nikita Khrushchev sought to break those limits through a "virgin lands" program targeted at reclaiming unproductive acreage.[8] The short-run success of the program measured in greater agricultural output turned to disaster in the early 1960s as the productivity of reclaimed land collapsed. And by the 1970s the slow contraction of the Caspian Sea (a development precipitated by the ecological impact of 1930s water projects) was generating a contraction in arable acreage in the eastern Ukraine and western Kazakhstan.[9]

Systematic hostility to technological change. In addition to an acceleration in the rise in primary commodity costs caused by the Stalinist system's emphasis on immediate output, the creation of a huge economic planning and administrative apparatus resulted in a collection of economic incentives hostile to technological change. Thus, while supplies of raw materials/energy were more rapidly consumed, offsetting activity that would yield a reduction in the volume of raw materials/energy required per unit of output was constrained. As a result, the degree of raw material and energy intensity in the Soviet economy is today unmatched in the developed world. The USSR's energy consumption per unit of GNP is 20 percent higher than that of the United States, 40 percent higher than that of the European Community, and 60 percent higher than Italy's. Further, in the 1970s when the worldwide cost of energy rose dramatically, the units of energy consumed per unit of GNP declined in the West while rising in the USSR. And by the 1980s the Soviet economy consumed 25 percent more metal per unit of output than did the U.S. economy and 50 percent more per unit of national income.[10]

Moreover, Soviet agriculture is notorious for its inefficient use of inputs. The absence of efficiency is demonstrated by the fact that while the USSR produces 55 percent of the per capita real product of the United States, equivalent to that of Italy, Spain, and Venezuela, these latter countries devote only 20 percent of their national investment to the production and distribution of food. The USSR, on the other hand, devotes 33 percent of its investment resources to food production and distribution—the equivalent of Thailand, the Philippines, and Portugal, whose economies produce only 25 percent of the per capita real product of the United States.[11] The inefficiency of Soviet collectivized agriculture is further evidenced by the fact that although only 3–4 percent of agricultural acreage is privatized, that acreage produces 20 percent of the nation's agricultural output.[12]

The costs of sectoral disinvestment. From 1928 to 1953 Soviet agriculture suffered through a period of intense disinvestment, which depressed agricultural output during the 1930s and undermined the sector's recovery during the post-World War II reconstruction.[13] The aftershocks of disinvestment have plagued the performance of Soviet agriculture ever since.

The lack of investment in agricultural infrastructure, especially rural transport and storage, during the 1930s and 1940s produced an agricultural complex that has wasted large volumes of inputs, fertilizer in particular, as well as food output. Disinvestment also spawned ecological problems indicated in the challenge to arability. To address these, the Soviet economy has had to incur growing costs in the form of ever increasing investment in the agricultural sector since the late 1950s.

The rising costs in the Soviet primary commodity sector have yielded:

- A declining output growth rate in agriculture and energy since the late 1950s.[14]
- Increased sectoral fragility facilitating a series of deep recessions in agriculture and energy. Soviet agriculture suffered severe output recessions in 1963, 1972, 1975, and 1979–81, while energy experienced a pronounced output contraction in 1984–85.[15]
- Output levels for key primary commodities—grain and petroleum—

that peaked in the 1970s–1980s. The Soviet Union enjoyed its peak year for grain output in 1978; since that time, grain output has not surpassed its 1978 level and his averaged far below it.[16] Petroleum output, which recovered in the second half of the 1980s from a mid-decade recession, appeared by the end of the decade to have reached a stubborn plateau.[17]

- A huge advance in the percentage of total Soviet investment resources devoted to the primary commodity sector (see Table 2.1). Clearly, the output growth rate of and the various sectoral recessions within the primary commodity sector would have been worse were it not for a diversion of investment resources to it. Supplementing this diversion of investment resources has been a rise in food imports. By the early 1980s, food imports came to represent 2.25–2.50 percent of national product.[18]

The Rising Costs of Labor

Maximization of immediate output. The Stalinist system's emphasis on maximizing immediate output prompted a more rapid exhaustion of another factor input—labor. Just as the Soviet economy has depleted its raw material/energy and arable land resources, it has rapaciously consumed its potential workforce by insisting on the full employment of its labor resources. While the Soviet economy has enjoyed the short-term benefit to economic growth of high rates of workforce participation, its full employment objectives have fostered serious underemployment. The absence, until recently, of unemployment has been an obstacle to labor mobility and, as a result, to supply-side adjustment. In any economy, such adjustment requires a regular

Table 2.1
Percent of Key Primary Commodity Sectors in Total Soviet Investment
(Percent Share)

	1959-65	1966-70	1971-75	1976-79
Agricultural Investment	16.5%	17.2%	20.1%	20.2%
Oil/Gas Investment	11.6%	12.9%	13.8%	17.4%

Source: Stanley H. Cohn, "Sources of Low Productivity in Soviet Capital Investment," in *Soviet Economy in the 1980s: Problems and Prospects,* Part 1, selected papers submitted to the Joint Economic Committee of the U.S. Congress (Washington, DC: U.S. Government Printing Office, 1983).

purge of inefficient labor skills and capital and, hence, periods of increased unemployment.

The damaging impact of a Soviet systemic bias in favor of full employment is reflected in the bloated size of the agricultural workforce, which as a share of the total workforce—20.0 percent—is far higher than in developed economies.[19]

Systemic hostility to technological change. Just as the system of centralized planning and administration spawned a raw material/energy intensive economy, it has produced a labor-intensive one. With sluggish technological change compared to developed economies, the Soviet economy has produced a severely underskilled workforce—one that remains dominated by manual labor. Close to 70 percent of agricultural and 50 percent of industrial/construction labor is still manual.[20]

The costs of sectoral disinvestment. In conjunction with agricultural disinvestment, Stalin's reforms mandated a process of disinvestment in personal consumption as both the light industry and housing sectors were deprioritized. To sustain labor productivity in the face of depressed levels of personal consumption, the Stalinist system resorted to a regime of labor discipline targeted at curbing absenteeism and enhancing job performance. But in the absence of a national crisis around which the workforce can be readily mobilized, labor productivity is difficult to maintain unless workers are provided an incentive in the form of improvements in personal consumption—a phenomenon that Stalin's successors were forced to confront.

During the post-Stalin 1950s, a debate emerged within the Soviet leadership over how best to improve the condition of the Soviet consumer, pitting those favoring efforts to boost agricultural output against those preferring to emphasize the need to resuscitate light industry.[21] Although periodic forays weighted toward the former objective were launched in the aftermath of the high levels of consumption austerity suffered during the Korean War, rates of growth of per capita personal consumption followed the slope of the long cycle on its downward course.[22]

The plight of the Soviet consumer is stark when measured against the status of the American consumer. By 1980 the Soviet consumer per capita consumed 48.7 percent of the food, 46.7 percent of the footwear/clothing, and 20.2 percent of the home furnishings of his counterpart in the United States. Further, these quantitative comparisons do not take into account the qualitative superiority of American over Soviet consumer goods, and even while consuming less food and footwear/clothing than in the United States, the consumer in the USSR devoted 65 percent of his expenditures to these items, compared to 27–40 percent in the West. In addition to the scarcity of goods, the Soviet consumer is confronted with a highly inefficient distribution system as the members of the average household spend 1.9 hours each day standing in queues.[23]

The deterioration in Soviet personal consumption growth underlies a decline in workforce morale—a decline that became even more aggravated beginning in 1976. Symptomatic has been the drop in the Soviet birth rate and the simultaneous rise in the death rate. Since the mid-1970s, the birth rate has been undercut by a turn to abortions and an increase in infant mortality. The death rate has been boosted by a decline in male life expectancy, largely the result of a rise in fatal industrial accidents in most cases attributed to the effects of alcohol use. By 1980, 30 percent of the male workforce in towns and cities were counted as chronic alcoholics.[24]

Disinvestment in the workforce has resulted in one that is reproducing itself at a decelerating pace. By the mid-1970s Soviet planners could foresee the prospect of labor shortages. Whereas the Soviet workforce grew by 24.2 million in the 1970s, its projected growth in the 1980s was just 6.0 million. Underlying the shrinkage in the growth rate of the potential labor force has been the deterioration in the Soviet population growth rate. After advancing by 1.34 percent per year from 1959–70, the Soviet population grew by 0.92 percent from 1970–79 and is projected to rise by just 0.5 percent from 1985–95. In the 1960s, Soviet planners anticipated a total population of 340–350 million by the end of the century; by the middle of the 1980s, it was clear that the Soviet population by the year 2000 would be far smaller, approaching only 300 million.[25]

The net effect on the Soviet economy of the rising cost of labor has been:

- A retreat in the factor growth rate of labor (see Fig. 2.3) and labor shortages, which began to surface by the second half of the 1970s. To meet this problem, Soviet authorities have resorted to employment of retirees, housewives, and students, a method that assures lower productivity due to the lower skill levels of these substitutes.
- A decline in the growth rate of labor productivity (see Fig. 2.3). The decline in the Soviet labor productivity growth rate has been matched by that of per capita personal consumption, suggesting the central role the latter has played in prompting the behavior of the former. The deterioration in labor productivity growth has also been fostered by the onerous systemic obstacles to supply-side adjustment that inhibit labor mobility and therefore the pace at which the skill level of the workforce has been upgraded.

The Rising Cost of Capital

Maximization of output. The Stalinist system's goal of maximization of output, which has led to a more rapid depletion of the supplies of the first

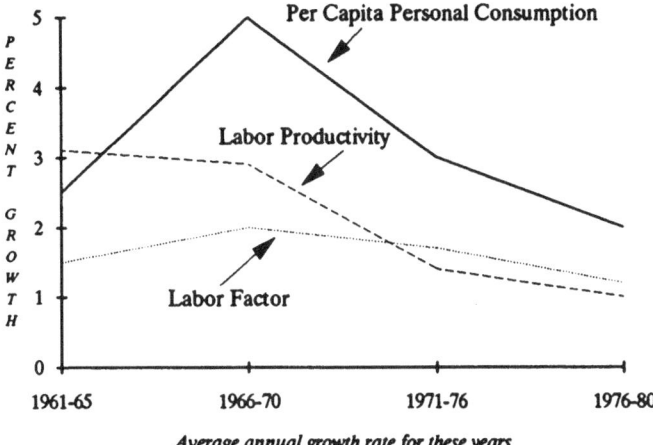

Figure 2.3. Forces contributing to the rising costs of Soviet labor, 1961–80. *Source:* Laurie Kurtzweg, "Trends in Soviet Gross National Product," in *Gorbachev's Economic Plans*, Vol. I, study papers submitted to the Joint Economic Committee of the U.S. Congress (Washington, DC: U.S. Government Printing Office, 1987) (for factor and labor productivity growth); Central Intelligence Agency and Defense Intelligence Agency, "Gorbachev's Economic Program: Problems Emerge," report submitted to the Subcommittee on National Security Economics of the Joint Economic Committee of the U.S. Congress (13 April 1988) (for per capita personal consumption).

two factors, primary commodities and labor, has also done so for the third—capital. The more rapid consumption of fixed capital resulting from emphasis on maximizing short-term output has accelerated the pace at which these assets have depreciated, while at the same time it has pressured the Soviet economy into exploiting its fixed capital assets beyond their natural retirement age, yielding an overamortized capital stock. (The Soviet Union retires its nonresidential plant stock at a 1.5 percent rate, the United States does so at a 3.3 percent rate, and the Federal Republic of Germany at a 3.7 percent rate. The Soviet Union retires producer durables at a 4.1 percent rate, the United States does so at an 8.5 percent rate, and the FRG at a 10.2 percent rate.)[26]

The combined impact of the accelerated depreciation and overamortization of Soviet plant and equipment has produced a less productive and more obsolete stock of capital.

Systemic hostility to technological change. The systemic obstacles to technological change resulting from the central planning and administrative apparatus' commitment to short-term output goals underlie the negative rates of productivity growth in Soviet capital and a rising capital to output ratio since the early 1960s. By 1980 the Soviet economy lagged 15–20 years behind the West and Japan in the level of its civilian technology, and the increment to GNP growth derived from technologically induced productivity gains was less than half that enjoyed in the West.[27]

In addition to suppressing improvements in the level of sophistication of technologies embodied in capital, the system of central planning and administration has persistently produced lower rates of capital put in use.[28] The length of time required to construct and begin to operate new plant in the Soviet Union far exceeds that in the West.

The costs of sectoral disinvestment. The negative consequences of disinvestment in agriculture and personal consumption during the 1930s and 1940s, which became visible during the 1950s, prompted Soviet leaders to consider reinvestment in both sectors. But while in the 1960s and 1970s investment in sectors linked to personal consumption such as light industry and housing continued to lag, investment in agriculture accelerated. The diversion of investment resources to agriculture escalated during the 1970s when it was joined by another critical primary commodity sector—energy—as one prioritized for investment resources.

The gradual transformation in Soviet investment priorities during the 1960s and 1970s served to undermine the capacity of the Soviet economy to generate higher rates of future capital investment by siphoning off investment resources from manufacturing.[29] By the mid-1970s, a process that can only be described as "economic primitivization" was afoot. The share of total investment resources devoted to low technology extractive industries was growing rapidly, while the share going to the manufacturing sector fell. Because the Soviet light industry sector was small and already depressed, sacrifices had to be made by the machine tool and other producer goods industries. In addition to undermining the ability of the Soviet economy to replace its capital stock, the transformation in investment priorities further constrained the pace of technological advance by diverting investment resources into lower technology areas.

The net result of the rising cost of Soviet capital has been:

- A long-term contraction in the investment growth rate, starting in the 1960s, paralleled by a fall in the factor growth rate for capital (see Table 2.2).
- A contraction in the productivity of capital (see Table 2.2), driven by low levels of technological improvement in the civilian economy and exacerbated by the effects of "overamortization" and "primitivization."

Hence, the source of the Soviet economy's long-term descent has indeed been its adherence to an "extensive mode" of economic development—and one whose negative implications for long-term economic performance have been exacerbated by the three central features of the Stalinist economic sys-

Table 2.2
Forces Behind the Rising Cost of Capital in the Soviet Economy, 1961–80
(Percent Growth)

	1961-65	1966-70	1971-75	1976-80
Total Investment Growth Rate	7.3%	5.5%	4.3%	4.3%
Capital Factor Growth Rate	8.8%	7.4%	8.0%	6.9%
Capital Productivity	N/A	-2.2%	-4.6%	-4.4%

Source: Laurie Kurtzweg, "Trends in Soviet Gross National Product," in *Gorbachev's Economic Plans,* Vol. I, study papers submitted to the Joint Economic Committee of the U.S. Congress (Washington, DC: U.S. Government Printing Office, 1987) (for total investment and capital factor growth); Central Intelligence Agency and Defense Intelligence Agency, "Gorbachev's Economic Program: Problems Emerge," report submitted to the Subcommittee on National Security Economics of the Joint Economic Committee (13 April 1988) (for capital productivity).

tem. While under an "extensive mode" of development factor input costs are certain to rise, the advent of the three Stalinist initiatives accelerated the pace at which factor input costs climbed. The result has been a prolonged and steep drop in both factor input and factor productivity growth rates, which in turn has produced a descent in the Soviet GNP growth rate (see Fig. 2.4).

ECONOMIC DECLINE: AND THE RESPONSE

Since the death of Stalin and the end of the Korean War, the Soviet leadership has been engaged in periodic efforts at first to deter the imminent descent and later to reverse the downward movement of economic growth rates. By the beginning of the 1980s, these efforts had left a long trail of failure: they were either insufficient to fulfill their objective or so politically intolerable to the Soviet establishment that they were abandoned—or both.

Importantly, each Soviet government initiative to deter or reverse the economic decline was provoked by a profound disturbance affecting one of the three factors of production, while the substance of many of these efforts was aimed at challenging one of the three core elements of the Stalinist economic system.

Even prior to the beginning of the Korean War, one of the features of the Stalinist system—disinvestment in agriculture and personal consumption—had begun to take its toll. By 1950 the Soviet economy had experienced a

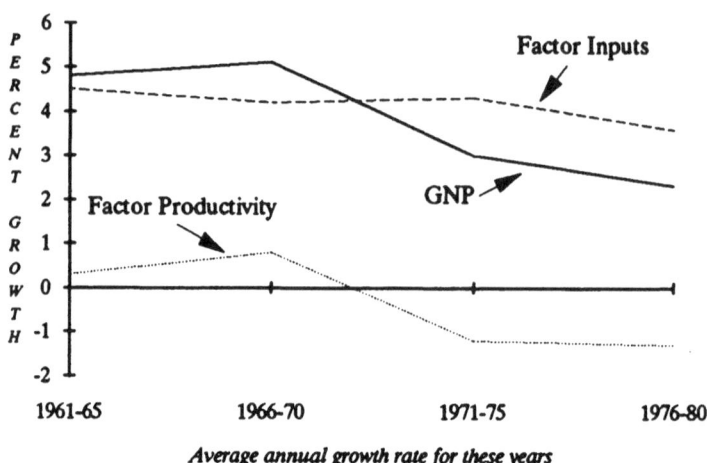

Average annual growth rate for these years

Figure 2.4. Forces behind Soviet economic growth, 1961–80. *Source:* Laurie Kurtzweg, "Trends in Soviet Gross National Product," in *Gorbachev's Economic Plans*, Vol. I, study papers submitted to the Joint Economic Committee of the U.S. Congress (Washington, DC: U.S. Government Printing Office, 1987).

substantial recovery from its devastated World War II status. National income had nearly doubled from what it had been in 1945 and was 60 percent larger than it had been in 1940, prior to the outbreak of World War II. Even more vigorous was the rebound in industrial production, which, by 1950, had grown to more than 70 percent of its 1940 size. In agriculture, however, continued slow investment in the postwar period resulted in dangerous output weaknesses. In the years from 1928–32, the share of total Soviet investment devoted to agriculture was 15.5 percent; during the war, from 1941–45, the percentage shrank to just 9.3 percent. Agricultural output, which by 1945 had fallen by 60 percent from what it was in 1940, had barely recovered to its prewar level by 1950. Worse, grain output, which in 1945 registered just 50 percent of its 1940 level, had still not recovered to its prewar level five years later. In addition to agriculture, light industry output experienced a far weaker postwar recovery than did heavy industry. Whereas producer goods (i.e., heavy industry) output had risen to 100 percent above its prewar level by 1950, light industry output was only 20 percent higher that year than it had been in 1940.[30]

The onset of the Korean War provoked a further diversion of resources to defense and heavy industry at the expense of agriculture and personal consumption. And as in 1937–38 when the ascent phase of the economic long cycle was depressed as a result of accelerated spending on national defense, economic growth rates enjoyed during the 1946–50 postwar reconstruction period fell.[31] This time, however, the fragility of the agriculture sector and the questionable sustainability of labor productivity under conditions of severe personal consumption austerity were more worrisome than in 1937–38. What Soviet leaders feared was that faltering agricultural output and withering labor productivity could foster a permanent turn to lower GNP growth rates.

Changing Soviet Resource Distribution Priorities

From Stalin's death in 1953 until the mid-1960s, disturbances in agriculture and the workforce derivative of disinvestment provoked a series of major government initiatives. While in between, Soviet leaders fell back on "extensive mode" means to relieve these pressures, the period was bracketed by leadership efforts aimed at reversing the resource distribution priorities of the Stalinist system (see Fig. 2.5). In both instances, the reversal became intolerable to the Soviet political-military establishment, leading to the fall of the regimes pursuing this goal.

The first move toward new resource distribution priorities occurred in 1953–54 in the wake of Stalin's death and in the midst of poor economic performance prompted by the costs of the Korean War. A program associated with Gregorii Malenkov sought to reduce defense and heavy industry spending for the purpose of freeing resources for expanded investment in light industry and agriculture. Under the program, light industry investment was to be front-ended with the aim of producing immediate improvements in consumer goods for the urban workforce while investment in agriculture was to have a longer term payoff.

The challenge to Stalin's resource priorities incited a hostile response from the heavy industry/national defense complex, one that would be capitalized on by Nikita Khrushchev as he rose to the forefront of the opposition to Malenkov's proposed deep cuts in heavy industry and defense.[32] Khrushchev's alternative for relieving stress in agriculture and personal consumption represented a cost-free illusion, which, because it did not greatly disturb the existing regime of resource priorities, was more palatable to Communist party conservatives and the representatives of heavy industry and defense. In opposition to Malenkov's long-term plan for agricultural recovery, Khrushchev proposed a short-term quick-fix in the form of a "virgin lands" program, a resort back to extensive means for breaking the constraints on agricultural output in which land reclamation concentrated in Central Asia was to add to the nation's stock of arable land.[33] In January 1955, Khrushchev won a decisive victory for his "extensive mode" solution to systemic ills when Malenkov was forced to step down as chairman of the Council of Ministers.

Over the course of the Sixth FYP (1956–60), the Soviet economy resumed its movement on the ascent slope of the economic long cycle. As in 1939–40, lower defense spending—this time prompted by Malenkov's earlier initiative producing a small post–Korean War military demobilization—contributed to an improvement in Soviet economic performance. Supporting the acceleration of the economy from 1956 to 1960, Khrushchev's "virgin lands" program, once enacted, resulted in a short-term boost in agricultural output.[34]

But despite economic indicators suggesting a revival of the Soviet economy from its Korean War doldrums—indicators of a magnitude sufficient to prompt Khrushchev to predict even greater advances in the 1960s—telltale signs pointing to the imminent transition of the Soviet economy onto the downard slope of the long cycle surfaced in 1959–60. In 1959 Khrushchev's quick-fix "extensive mode" solution to the effects of disinvestment in agriculture came apart as output in recently reclaimed marginal acreage collapsed. Fast on the heels of a mini-recession in agricultural output in 1959, labor discipline weakened as urban workers rioted in response to inflation and consumer goods shortages.[35]

During the 1961–65 Seventh FYP, disturbances related to effects of earlier disinvestment in agriculture and personal consumption were of even greater consequence, as they led the Soviet economy into the descent phase of the long cycle. During these five years, growth rates of virtually all key Soviet economic indicators tumbled from their peak performance in 1956–60.[36] The period was also marked by the first post–Korean War large-scale Soviet agricultural recession, in 1963. Far greater than the mini-recession of 1959, this one was also sparked by a collapse in output in newly reclaimed virgin lands, and the deep recession in agriculture created the foundation for a sharp erosion in labor discipline.[37] Further, it was during the 1961–65 period that raw material/energy costs commenced a slow rise—a development anticipated by Khrushchev in the late 1950s when he first proposed exploitation of Siberian energy resources.[38]

Khrushchev's first response to this set of challenges came in 1959–60 when he promoted a larger "extensive mode" solution in the form of an even greater "virgin lands" program. The dimensions of the 1963 crisis and the irrefutable failure of his solution to the agricultural problem forced Khrushchev to seek an alternative in 1963–64. In essence, Khrushchev retreated back to the Malenkov formula for transforming Soviet resource priorities, including a reduction in funding for defense and heavy industry in order to increase investment in agriculture/personal consumption. Unlike Malenkov's program, however, Khrushchev's initiative was weighted toward investment in agriculture as opposed to light industry.

Nevertheless, as was the case for Malenkov, tampering with the resource priority regime set in train by Stalin's reforms met with a hostile institutional reaction from the heavy industry and national defense sectors. And as in

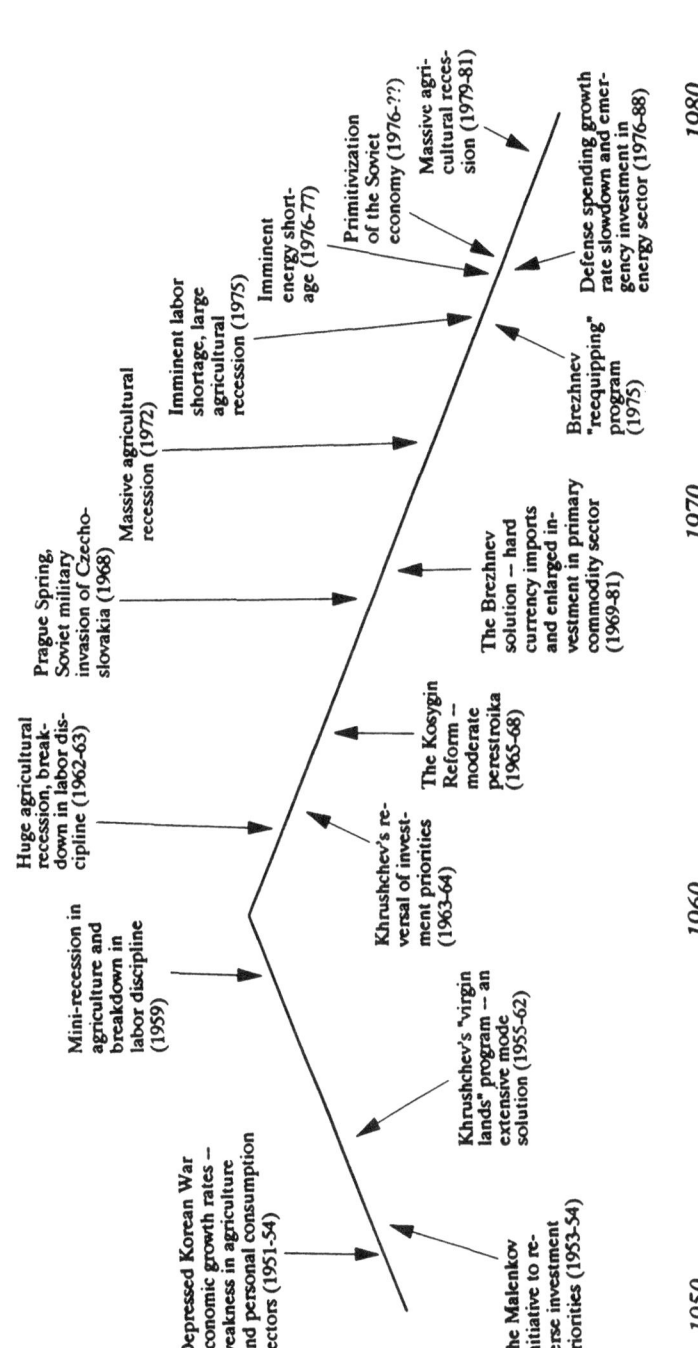

Figure 2.5. The Soviet policy response to faltering economic performance

1953–54, these forces formed the core of support, in conjunction with Communist party conservatives, for an alternative to Khrushchev.[39] In late 1964, Khrushchev was toppled by the same generic political combination that he had once led against Malenkov and was replaced by the regime of Leonid Brezhnev and Alexei Kosygin.

Tinkering with Economic Centralization

Consensus in the new regime was predicated upon a partial reversal of Khrushchev's heretical resource priority regime. The intolerable aspect of it—the assault on heavy industry/defense investment—was excised. Indeed, the new regime supported a dramatic acceleration in Soviet defense spending.[40] However, the severe stress in agriculture and personal consumption from 1961–65 could not be ignored and therefore, on a smaller scale than envisioned by Khrushchev, enlarged resources for these sectors were endorsed. In its early stages, the Brezhnev-Kosygin government wandered into a set of resource priorities—"guns and butter"—that, although politically sensible, left open an economic question of no small significance: where were the resources to come from?

Some of the tension provoked by the new set of resource priorities was relieved during the 1966–70 Eighth FYP by a small recovery in Soviet economic performance from its 1961-65 dive. The higher output growth rates in the years from 1966–70 were in part attributable to the absence of a deep recession in the agricultural sector such as had occurred in 1963 and to the salutary impact on the civilian economy of zero real growth in national defense spending in 1964–65, a result of Khrushchev's final programmatic initiative. But Soviet economic indicators in the 1966–70 period still grew at a slower pace than in 1956–60 and the new regime therefore came under pressure to improve output growth and create a durable foundation for reversing the momentum of the long cycle.

Having rejected "extensive mode" solutions such as the "virgin lands" program and having veered from reversing the priority status of heavy industry/defense, the new regime proposed to reinvigorate the economy by attacking another of the Stalinist economic system's curcial elements—the centralization of economic planning and administration—in an effort to transition development strategy onto an "intensive" footing. Just as disinvestment in agriculture and personal consumption and disturbances in the Soviet economy derivative of those distortions dominated leadership concerns from the death of Stalin to Khrushchev's ouster, systemic hostility to technological change prompted by the Stalinist system's other two features—centralized economic planning and administration and the maximization of immediate output—became the central economic issue for the leadership following Khrushchev's departure (see Fig. 2.5). And just as Malenkov's assault on systemic values met with rejection, the first post-Khrushchev assault was also repudiated. As in the earlier case, it too was followed by an economic solution devoid of any hostility to the elements of the Stalinist system.

The effort to push the Soviet economy into an "intensive mode" of development through reform of economic planning and administration was associated with Kosygin.[41] Efforts to decentralize economic decision making were promoted through the 1965 Kosygin reforms and subsequent 1967 price reforms—reforms that, in aggregate, represented a moderate version of perestroika. In essence, the reform package was an effort to simulate the indicators that influence economic intercourse in a market economy while masking the controlling hand of the central planner and administrator.

To support "perestroika," Kosygin pushed for a more widepsread retreat from Khrushchev's resource priorities by arguing that light industry and not agriculture be the recipient of the lion's share of investment diverted to sectors having suffered from disinvestment. This set of investment priorities in fact represented a restatement of those once associated with Malenkov. Kosygin argued that the difficulties in agriculture were not correctable through greater resource inputs but through tinkering with the structure of agricultural planning and administration.

The foundation for Kosygin's approach began to crumble quite early as, in response to two mini-recessions in agriculture in 1965 and 1967, Brezhnev sponsored a moderate version of Khrushchev's agricultural investment program and did so at the expense of light industry.[42] Brezhnev's victory on this question set the stage for a more decisive defeat of Kosygin's policies. The economic reform process in the USSR provided room for a broader reform effort among the East European Communist economies. In 1968 the political aftershocks of "radical perestroika" in Czechoslovakia were viewed as unacceptable in Moscow. In the wake of the Soviet military suppression of reform in Czechoslovakia, Brezhnev, supported by a consensus in the Soviet establishment, moved to reverse the momentum of perestroika—in both its moderate Soviet and radical East European forms—in a process that spanned the years from 1968–72.[43]

In place of perestroika, the new means for overcoming technological stagnation that Brezhnev chose to promote was an approach that failed to antagonize any of the three principles of the Stalinist system—increased imports. Through a process of East-West detente, the Brezhnev regime came to bank upon hard currency imports from the West (primarily from Western Europe).[44] An enormous improvement in Soviet hard currency imports was facilitated in 1974 by the rise of gold and oil prices (60 percent of Soviet hard currency exports by the end of the 1970s were accounted for by petroleum), which boosted the Soviets' hard currency terms of trade. The terms of trade gain alone translated into a hard currency windfall of $50 billion from 1973–80, a windfall that was converted into machinery imports.[45] This program was not restricted to the USSR. With Eastern Europe also forced to abandon economic reform, it was persuaded to seek an advance in hard currency machinery imports as a way to contest the downward movement of the long cycle.

Perhaps with fewer illusions but with no less confidence, Brezhnev could look to the 1970s as Khrushchev had once looked to the 1960s—as a period of economic renewal. Buoyed by his extensive mode "virgin lands" solution and the accelerating economic performance from 1956–60, Khrushchev's confidence had rested on grounds similar to those bolstering Brezhnev, who could point to higher economic growth rates in the years 1966–70 and the prospect of greater hard currency imports in the coming decade.

But like Khrushchev, Brezhnev found his lofty expectations hurtling back to earth. From 1971–75 the growth rate of most Soviet economic indicators fell sharply from their 1966–70 levels, and although not as precipitous as the drop experienced from the 1956–60 to the 1961–65 period, the absolute growth rates of most indicators in the years from 1971–75 were below those of 1961–65.[46] The Soviet economy had resumed its march on the downward slope.

Leading the decline in economic performance (as it had in the 1961–65 period) was agriculture. In 1972 and 1975 the Soviet economy suffered from two mammoth agricultural recessions—recessions that occurred despite the diversion of a greater share of investment resources into agriculture.[47] While costs in agriculture continued to climb, the Soviet economy in the 1971–75 period began to feel the jump in costs of other components of the primary commodity sector—raw materials and energy. Compounding this, the economy was laboring under the largest and longest interval of accelerated spending growth in national defense in the postwar period, from 1966–75.

In addition to advancing his hard currency import program as an answer to the renewed descent in Soviet economic performance, Brezhnev responded by meeting the rising costs in the primary commodity sector. While ever greater investment resources were directed at agriculture (supplemented by large food imports), the Brezhnev regime publicly contemplated large-scale investments in Central Asian raw materials and energy.[48]

Further, by 1975 the regime could foresee the imminence of labor shortages, and in response Brezhnev initiated actions that, although less politically offensive than perestroika, were nonetheless challenging to the commitments of the Stalinist system. To address the coming labor shortage he relaxed pressures for maximization of immediate output in order to reequip Soviet industry with marginally superior technologies.[49] The paltry reequipping measures turned out to be more trouble than they were worth. Because output growth rates contracted in response to reduced pressure for immediate output, the reequipping effort aggravated economic shortages while the increment to capital productivity was inconsequential. Equally disappointing was the impact on Soviet capital productivity of difficult to digest Western machinery imports.

Absent an effective response to rising factor input costs, the Soviet economy plunged into a free fall from 1976–80. Over that period, the USSR suffered a shocking decline in labor productivity growth, a decline paralleled by a severe drop in personal consumption growth. The Brezhnev regime's commitment to the "butter" half of its "guns and butter" program never amounted to much as investment in light industry was continuously depressed and the increased investment in agriculture yielded little discernible payoff. In addition, high rates of government investment in the primary commodity sector and defense added a burden to personal consumption by producing inflationary pressures felt by Soviet consumers in the form of rising hidden inflation (that is, by rising consumer goods prices presumably inspired by quality improvement when no such improvement had taken place) as well as in forced personal savings prompted by chronic shortages in consumer goods. The acceleration in these two consumer sector ills in 1976–80 coincided with marked evidence of a ratchet down in workforce morale: rising rates of worker absenteeism, industrial accidents, on-the-job intoxication, abortions, and declining health.[50]

Also, the rise in the share of investment resources devoted to the primary commodity and defense sectors ensured a declining share for others. By 1976–80 heavy industry was taking a hit as its portion of total investment fell. The rise in total Soviet investment going to primary commodities in tandem with the decline in the share accounted for by manufacturing (heavy and light industry) represented a dynamic contrary to that traditionally associated with economic progress. Indeed, by 1976–80 the Soviet economy was becoming "primitivized" in a process that ensured ever weaker future growth rates in capital goods output and, hence, a deeper quandary over where to distribute scarce capital resources in the future.

Beginning in 1976–77, the rates of growth in both Soviet real defense spending and procurement were reduced, and it is difficult to contemplate this development having not resulted from leadership concern over the harsh economic consequences of escalating defense costs from 1966–75. Nevertheless, whatever relief the civilian economy received from the slowdown in the defense spending growth rate was quickly offset by new turbulence in the primary commodity arena. In 1977 the Brezhnev regime projected the imminence of an energy crisis, one that would require a major diversion of resources into that sector. That year, huge sums of investment resources were newly dedicated to developing Siberian energy reserves.

THE SOVIET "ECONOMIC DIMENSION OF SECURITY VULNERABILITY"

During the post-Stalin 1950s when the Soviet leadership moved to deter the transitioning of the economy onto the downward slope of the economic long cycle and over the course of the 1960s and 1970s when that leadership undertook efforts to reverse the decline, it was confronted with a policy dilemma of ever greater magnitude caused by the peculiar relationship that evolved between national defense spending and the downward trajectory of economic growth rates.

Soviet national defense consumes large volumes of factor inputs—primary commodities, "raw" labor, and capital—that otherwise would be employed in the civilian economy. In addition to these quantitative inputs, the defense sector removes from civilian economic use qualitative factors—research, development, and engineering, as well as labor skills. These qualitative factors may be embodied in capital inputs consumed by national defense or disembodied in the form of defense sector research, development, and engineering and military training. It can be argued that the gross cost of national defense to the civilian economy is larger than its net cost since the defense sector returns qualitative factors such as technologicial spinoffs from defense R&D and labor skills fostered by military training back to the civilian economy. While such paybacks are relatively small compared to total national defense costs under any circumstances, they are infinitesimal in the Soviet Union where technology transfer from the defense to the civilian economy is minimized for security reasons and where military training expenditures that are low compared to the NATO countries add only an inconsequential skill increment to the workforce.

Further, for a superpower such as the Soviet Union national defense spending, although predominant, represents only one component of a broader range of national security costs, some of which function in direct support of the national defense sector, such as the space program and foreign intelligence, while others, such as foreign economic and military aid and large or prolonged trade surpluses and trade subsidies, function to maintain the Soviet alliance and global influence system.

In the ascent phase of the economic long cycle, sharp or sustained rises in the rate of growth of national defense spending (and broader national security costs) in 1937–38, 1941–45, and 1951–54 served to depress economic growth rates. When national defense and related spending was cut absolutely—in 1922–27 during the New Economic Policy (NEP) and 1946–50 in the postwar demobilization—or when the rate of growth in such spending declined as in 1939–40, economic growth rates reestablished their upward momentum. In the descent phase of the cycle, however, the relationship between national security costs and economic performance assumes a different character, one that confronts policymakers with a different range of potential consequences.

By increasing or even maintaining the existing rate of growth in national security costs during the descent phase of the economic long cycle, one does more than depress economic growth rates; one accelerates the growth rate decline. Pursuit of such a course suggests a trade-off in which the policymaker, in order to maintain short-term strategic competitiveness, accepts the risk of a deterioration in long-term competitiveness. Since national defense spending and the full range of accounts associated with national security depend upon the quantity and quality of inputs from the civilian economy, an accelerated decline in economic performance must at some point serve to degrade national security assets. Alternatively, the policymaker may decide to sacrifice short-term competitiveness in order to avoid an accelerated economic decline and more rapid erosion in long-term strategic competitiveness by reducing the rate of growth in national security costs, or may go further and cut absolutely short-term national security costs as part of an effort to reverse the descent in economic performance.

These policy choices represent the range of possible responses to the dilemma posed by the "economic dimension of security vulnerability"—a dimension that emerges as a consequence of the descent phase of the economic long cycle. For the Soviet Union, these policy choices first surfaced in the wake of Stalin's death in 1953, at which point the prospects for an enduring retreat in economic performance confronted the nation's leadership.

The "dimension" represented a constraining variable on actual Soviet national security costs, defining for the Soviet leadership a set of possible resource distribution alternatives and their short- and long-term national security consequences. Decisions over the allocation of resources for the national security effort were dominated by another variable—the external threat—and Soviet national security costs can be seen to have evolved through a series of distinct threat regimes (see Fig. 2.6). One such regime coincided with World War II—from 1941–45—and the rise of a security threat to the existence of the Soviet Union emanating from its Eurasian peripheries in Nazi Germany in the West and, to a lesser extent, Imperial Japan in the East. The national security response, almost totally contained in the national defense account, was immense as national security spending rose to consume an inordinate percentage of GNP.

With the defeat of the Axis powers, the threat that motivated the World War II national security cost regime vanished, providing for a transition to a new regime associated with the postwar demobilization. Symptomatic of the absolute contraction in real national security costs associated with this regime, Soviet military forces were reduced from ten million to two and one-half million men.[51] This defense retrenchment freed an enormous volume of factor inputs as well as R&D and labor skills that would otherwise

National Security Cost Regime	Soviet Defense Spending	The Costs of Empire	Disposition Toward the "Dimension"
World War II 1941-45	War: Rapid rise as % of GNP, advance to 10 million man armed force		
Post-War Demobilization, 1946-50	Demobilization: Severe reduction as % of GNP, decline to 2.5 million man armed force	New alliance system, net economic asset (1946-55)	
Contemporary National Security Cost Regime, 1951-??	Korean War Period: 1951-54 -- Accelerated spending, rise to 6 million man armed force, reinforce Euro-theatre conventional superiority		Malenkov Initiative -- deep "Buy Time" (1953-54)
	Post-Korean War Period: 1955-58 -- Decline as % of GNP, reduction in size of armed forces, building mobilization base for strategic nuclear program	Extension of Empire costs to Third World neutrals; costs become small net liability	Khrushchev-Malenkov -- moderate "Buy Time" (1955-58)
	Accelerated Spending: 1959-63 -- Rise as % of GNP, procurement phase in strategic nuclear forces and no visible cut in Euro-theatre force funding	Exchange of China for Cuba and Vietnam as costly non-East European allies	Failed Detente -- "Race Against Time" (1959-63)
	Khrushchev Retrenchment: 1964-65 -- Zero growth in national defense spending		Khrushchev -- deep "Buy Time" (1964-65)
	Accelerated Spending: 1966-75 -- Rise as % of GNP -- Surge to strategic parity; -- modernize Euro-theatre force, build new force structure for Sino-Soviet border; -- build power projection capability	Expansion of Empire costs, 1971-75 Eastern Europe trade subsidy rises Advance in military subsidy to allies and neutrals in global theatres	Brezhnev -- "Race Against Time" (1966-)
	Spending Slowdown 1976-88 -- slowdown in rate of growth of defense spending, stable as % of GNP, more radical slowdown in procurement growth	Rapid Expansion of costs (1976-85), growing trade surplus to Eastern Europe, rising military-related subsidy to allies and neutrals in global theatres	Effort to restrain "Race Against Time"

Figure 2.6. Moscow's national security costs and its disposition toward the "Economic Dimension of Security Vulnerability"

have been consumed in the national defense sector for civilian economic use and contributed to the strong postwar Soviet economic recovery.

Despite movement to a lower cost national security regime in the years from 1946–50, the Soviet Union sought to extend its national security perimeter deep into its Eurasian peripheries. To effect this, Moscow successfully supported the expansion and consolidation of allied Communist party control throughout Eastern Europe early in the 1946–50 period, and at the end of the period consolidated an alliance with a victorious Chinese Communist party.[52]

The often forceful expansion of the Soviet alliance system in Eurasia triggered resistance from the United States and its new allies, giving rise to the Cold War. Then in the middle of 1950 the expansionist momentum of the Soviet alliance system spilled over to the Korean Peninsula, provoking the outbreak of a "hot" local war, which inspired the militarization of the Cold War from 1951–54. As a result of the new military threat posed by the U.S. alliance system to continued expansion and consolidation of recently won gains in Eurasia, Soviet national security costs became associated with a new threat regime, one that has persisted to the present. From 1951–54, Soviet national defense spending grew dramatically, as indicated by the doubling of Soviet military forces to six million men.[53]

Meeting the Challenge of U.S. Strategic Superiority

It was the economic consequence of this rise in national defense expenditures that first confronted the Soviet leadership with the dilemma posed by the "economic dimension of security vulnerability." At the same time, the leadership faced a qualitative escalation in the foreign threat.

During the 1930s, prior to the mass purge of leading figures in the Soviet professional military in 1937–38, Soviet military doctrine came to hinge upon the creation of a military force in the Euro-theatre sufficient to successfully conduct "deep operations" far in the enemy rear, a force of sufficient size and speed to thrust aggressively through the enemy's frontline defenses and envelop it (a doctrine first developed and later employed by the German military). While actual Soviet capability fell short of that required to realize doctrinal objectives during the 1930s, the doctrine itself was abandoned by Stalin late in the decade in favor of a closer-in defense.[54] The failure of Stalin's doctrinal approach in the early phases of World War II led to a de facto reconstruction of the Red Army along force structure lines indicated in the earlier doctrine. As a result, in the wake of the defeat of Axis military forces, the USSR emerged with a Euro-theatre military force of sufficient quantitative and qualitative charateristics to approach meeting earlier doctrinal objectives (even after having undertaken a large-scale military demobilization).[55] Conventional force preponderance in the Euro-theatre supplied Moscow with important leverage in the forced expansion of its alliance system in Eastern Europe after World War II. During the Korean War the Soviet Union augmented its Euro-threatre forces, ensuring continued conventional dominance, but the deterrent and coercive value of this force had been severely undermined by the time the war ended.

The United States responded to the reinforcement of Soviet military supremacy in the Euro-theatre over the 1951–54 period by exploiting its technological advantage to build a decisive edge in nuclear weapons and their transoceanic means of delivery.[56] The United States used its strategic superiority to offset its and its alliance system's conventional arms disadvantage in the Euro-threatre by extending its deterrence to that theatre. If Moscow chose to exercise its Euro-threatre advantage, Washington pledged to exercise its strategic advantage. To give credibility to this threat, the United States increased its forward conventional presence in Western Europe and in the Far East (a theatre attack on either front would rapidly involve American military forces), where it had extended its strategic nuclear umbrella (i.e., Japan).

Faced with the challenge posed by the "economic dimension of security vulnerability" and the rise of American strategic nuclear superiority, the post-Stalin leadership offered contradictory responses. Malenkov's policies contemplated a sacrifice of short-term Soviet strategic competitiveness in order to avoid a permanent transition of the Soviet economy to lower economic growth rates by redirecting resources from national defense into personal consumption and agriculture. By seeking deep cuts in real defense spending and a major post–Korean War military demobilization, Malenkov's answer to the challenge involved acceptance of American strategic supremacy over a prolonged period while Soviet economic health was restored. A new policy of "peaceful coexistence" with the United States and its alliance system was articulated for the purpose of moderating the rate at which the foreign threat expanded as Moscow consolidated its postwar Eurasian political empire at the cost of marginal concessions.[57]

Malenkov's deep "buy time" response to the dilemma posed by the "economic dimension" was opposed by others, who offered a range of alternative responses. A consensus of the opposition formed in support of Khrushchev. Although not objecting to some degree of post-Korean War military demobilization, Khrushchev strongly opposed Malenkov's deep cuts in defense. Simultaneously, he promoted a program to meet the threat posed by U.S. strategic supremacy.[58] The policy consensus associated with Khrushchev did not disregard the long-term consequences of the economic dimension and therefore did not adopt a "race against time" effort to catch up with the United States by increasing or even sustaining the rate of growth of defense spending that had evolved during the Korean War. Instead, this consensus accepted a small contraction in defense spending from 1955–58, during which time it fell as a percentage of GNP from 12.1 percent to 9.1 percent.[59] Nevertheless, Khrushchev did force through the least expensive preprocurement phase of a crash program for development of Soviet strategic forces. Even this level of resources required a sizable change in priorities within the national defense sector away from general purpose forces to new strategic accounts. As a result, the level of personnel in the Soviet military built up during the Korean War was reduced.

The marginal contraction in Soviet defense spending from 1955–58, like the retrenchment in 1939–40, took enough pressure off the civilian economy to help revive economic growth rates from their lower Korean War period levels. This occurred even though a portion of the savings won from the national defense sector never made it to the civilian economy, being absorbed instead by other components of the national security account. Functioning as an adjunct to the national defense sector's strategic force spending, the closely related Soviet space program began to grow at an accelerated pace. The program involved development of rocket boosters critical to the creation of intercontinental ballistic missile (ICBM) delivery systems.

However, because of its behavior in subsequent decades, the rise in the cost of the Soviet empire that emerged over the 1955–58 period presents a more important story. Earlier, from 1946–55, the Soviet alliance system had in aggregate represented a net economic asset to the Soviet Union. But from 1955 on, it became an ever larger net liability. The foundation for alliance system contributions to the Soviet economy in the years following World War II lay in the colonial economic relationship established between the economies of Eastern Europe and the USSR under Stalin. During that period Moscow was supported by a trade subsidy from Eastern Europe (i.e., Eastern Europe's exports to the USSR were often below the world market price), and even more important, Moscow received $14 billion in unrequited transfers from its new allies—a sum equivalent to that of the U.S. Marshall Plan for Western Europe.[60] Over the first 10 years of the postwar period, economic transfers from Eastern Europe to the Soviet Union outweighed total Soviet economic transfers to its new East Asian allies China and North Korea, which took the form of military and economic aid and loans to finance trade deficits with the USSR.

In the aftermath of Stalin's death and in the context of depressed economic growth and strained social peace in Eastern Europe, Moscow's economic relations with its European allies were decolonialized. By 1956 net economic transfers from Eastern Europe to the Soviet Union had ceased—unrequited transfers ended and Moscow began to accumulate small trade surpluses with Eastern Europe.[61] Since Soviet economic transfers to East Asian allies continued, the alliance system had by the second half of the 1950s become a small economic liability.

In addition, new Khrushchev initiatives launched to contest the United States and its allies for influence in global (non-European) theatres, the Middle East in particular, added to the costs of the Soviet empire. Soviet military-economic aid as well as loans to finance trade surpluses surfaced for the first time outside of its alliance system, concentrated in Egypt.[62]

Despite the rise in national security costs outside of national defense, cuts in defense spending from 1955–58 were enough to produce a small contraction in Soviet national security costs and this helped reinvigorate economic performance.

By 1957–58, the relatively small costs associated with construction of a mobilization base for Soviet strategic nuclear forces were about to explode as the process moved forward into the more expensive procurement phase. The Soviet strategic nuclear program was swiftly moving up the ladder from research to deployment, as signaled by the 1957 Sputnik launched and successful ICBM test. And as it moved up, the economic costs of the program rose exponentially.

In the face of the 1959–60 economic turbulence (agricultural mini-recession and breakdown of labor discipline), Khrushchev was of no mind to "race against time" and raise the rate of growth of national defense spending in order to exploit the next phase in the development of strategic nuclear forces. Nevertheless, he was committed to the earliest possible elimination of the American strategic nuclear advantage through deployment of robust Soviet strategic nuclear forces. Building on the earlier 1955–58 intra-defense sector resource trade-off between Euro-theatre and strategic forces, Khrushchev proposed an even more radical transformation in 1959–a reduction in Soviet military personnel by one to two million men, which, if enacted, would have reduced the warfighting and coercive value of Soviet forces in the Euro-theatre. To ensure domestic political support for this policy, Khrushchev launched an effort to pacify the Euro-theatre and global environment as a means for reducing the degree of foreign threat perceived domestically.[63]

With the U-2 incident in 1960, the global environment became less favorable to the tactical detente Khrushchev had sought and with the perception of the foreign threat rising anew, Khrushchev found himself under attack from large segments of the professional military and party conservatives for his proposed conventional defense cuts. Under growing pressure in 1960–61, he was forced to cancel the troop cuts and permit real national defense spending to rise.[64] Then during the ensuing period of international tension that came to a head over Berlin in 1961 and to near-eruption during the 1962 Cuban missile crisis, Soviet defense spending rose rapidly. From 1959–63 the Soviet national defense sector experienced a period of accelerated spending; from 9.4 percent of GNP in 1959, defense outlays rose to 10.7 percent in 1963 as the leadership backed into a "race against time" strategy.[65]

The process of heightened spending growth in the defense sector from 1959–63 not only intersected but exacerbated the transition of the Soviet economy onto the downward slope of the long cycle. The consequent opening of a visible "economic dimension of security vulnerability" during the 1961–65 period spurred Khrushchev in 1963 to respond with proposed cuts in the national defense budget in order to free resources for agriculture and personal consumption and through such investment reverse the trajectory of Soviet economic performance. Following his failed effort to assert parity with the United States in the strategic arena on the cheap—by means of bluff in the Cuban missile crisis—Khrushchev sought to secure support for reduced defense spending by easing the perception of threat through a process of detente encompassing arms control. The cut in defense spending and the broader hints of strategic retrenchment implied in Khrushchev's approach proved to be a decisive factor in congealing a conservative-military alliance (which had been gaining shape since 1959) of sufficient strength to topple him and his "buy time" response to the "economic dimension of security vulnerability."[66]

Moscow's Race Against Time

The new Brezhnev-Kosygin regime moved quickly to reverse Khrushchev's response to the "economic dimension." Indeed, during the 1966–75 period not only was real growth restored to Soviet defense spending after two years of zero growth (1964–65) stemming from Khrushchev's final initiative, but the Soviet defense sector enjoyed its longest and largest period of high rates of spending growth since the formation of the Soviet Union. During this 10-year stretch, Soviet defense spending averaged real growth of 4–5 percent a year while real defense procurement, the principal component of defense investment, rose 4 percent a year. Perhaps lulled by the marginal recovery in NMP growth rates from 1966–70 (a recovery due in part to Khrushchev's constraints on defense spending), the Soviet leadership endorsed a vigorous "race against time" strategy. By 1970 Soviet defense spending rose from the below 10.7 percent of GNP it had registered in 1965 to 12.3 percent of GNP.[67] By 1975 the share of GNP accounted for by the defense sector was even greater.

The Soviet leadership had been stung by the coercive value of U.S. dominance in the strategic arena during the Cuban missile crisis, and it therefore dedicated enormous resources to exploiting the mobilization base in strategic nuclear forces resulting from Khrushchev's earlier efforts in order to quickly build a competitive capability. By the late 1960s/early 1970s, these efforts had won the Soviets effective parity in the strategic nuclear competition, a development codified in the 1972 SALT I agreement.

But Soviet military doctrine, having undergone a major permutation in the late 1950s/1960s in response to the advent of strategic nuclear forces and the Khrushchev regime's prioritization of them, contemplated something more than parity. In essence the new doctrine, which asserted that the next war would be global, dominated by nuclear weapons, and launched as a result of surprise attack, represented the translation of Soviet Euro-theatre doctrine into the strategic nuclear realm and, as a result, the conventionalization of strategic nuclear warfighting concepts.[68] Instead of being structured to deter by means of countervalue, Soviet strategic nuclear forces were to be deployed for counterforce purposes in a doctrine that emphasized nuclear warfighting and war-winning. As with Soviet Euro-theatre doctrine in the 1930s, Soviet strategic nuclear doctrine in the second half of the 1960s and first half of the 1970s outstripped force structure capabilities.

Further, in the second half of the 1960s Soviet doctrine began to be altered. Rejected initially, "limited wars"—primarily of a conventional nature, conducted at a level below the nuclear threshold—were now contemplated.[69] Global nuclear war was now considered most likely to result from an escalation of conflict from the theatre level. This rationale supported an immense rejuvenation and expansion of Soviet theatre forces.

In the Euro-theatre especially, the Soviet defense complex enjoyed a legacy of supportive doctrine and a large force structure, as well as backing from major interest groups. Indeed, opposition to Khrushchev's proposed conventional force cuts centered in the defense complex from 1959–61 was strong enough to succeed in sustaining the priority of Euro-theatre military dominance. So, well before the 1966–75 defense spending surge, a politically powerful web of forces within the Soviet establishment held to the need for military preponderance in the Euro-theatre, and this orientation was strengthened by objective events that emerged in the 1960s. In recognition of the development of a minimal Soviet strategic deterrent and the prospects for enlarged Soviet strategic forces in the future, American policymakers, with their homeland now coming under greater threat and with their strategic forces consequently losing deterrent value, sought ways to confine any future Euro-theatre conflict to the theatre level. As a result, beginning in 1963 the emphasis in U.S. defense expenditures shifted from strategic forces to general purpose forces as political and military leaders supported a doctrinal modification, flexible response.[70] This suggested an expansion and upgrading of NATO Euro-theatre general purpose forces aimed at devaluing the Soviet Euro-theatre advantage.

In addition, following a deterioration in Sino-Soviet relations from 1960–66, the Soviet Union took steps to militarize its Chinese border in order to construct a new theatrewide deterrent and coercive capability.[71] With the Sino-Soviet border clashes of 1969, the Soviet military build-up on the border with China escalated, resulting in a Soviet force of 500,000–1,000,000 men armed with modern military equipment by the early 1970s.

Hence, from 1966–75, U.S./NATO commitments to improve Euro-theatre forces and the militarization of the Sino-Soviet conflict increased the dimension of the threat perceived by the Soviet Union on its Eurasian peripheries, and this helped spark a large augmentation and modernization of Soviet Eurasian theatre forces. By 1969 the momentum of these events impelled further alterations in Soviet doctrine as leading military officials proposed the combined employment of nuclear weapons and classic conventional weapons while promoting the need for Soviet forces to fight under both nuclear and nonnuclear conditions.[72]

Finally, in addition to the Euro-theatre (and, by the early 1970s, the Eurasian theatre), Soviet doctrine came to sanction military action in a new array of theatres—"global" theatres. Interest in competing with the West for influence in these theatres had been established in the mid-1950s with Khrushchev's authorization of Soviet military and economic support for nonaligned states and national liberation movements. The 1966–75 process of accelerated defense spending included the construction of a capability to project military power well beyond the USSR's peripheries in support of its global alliance and influence system. As with the sizable upgrading of Soviet Euro- and Eurasian theatre forces, the foundation for expanding Soviet force structure to include transoceanic theatre power projection capabilities is found not only in the evolution of the subjective preferences of the Soviet political-military establishment but in a series of objective developments that unfolded during the decade of the 1960s, in particular, the U.S. military intervention in Southeast Asia and the 1967 Middle East war. By the first half of the 1970s, an effective Soviet power projection capability was on its way to completion.[73]

At the same time that the advance in national defense costs from 1966–75 served to augment the size and quality of Soviet force structure, other costs associated with the national security account began to take off. While expenditures for the Soviet space program continued to mount over this period, even more significant was the rise in the cost of the Soviet empire, a cost that showed substantial growth in the first half of the 1970s.

Central to the rise in the expense of maintaining the Soviet empire has been the increasing economic fragility of the Soviet Union's East European allies. Beginning in 1961–65, the CMEA-six in aggregate experienced the same decline in the growth rate of key economic indicators as the Soviet Union, a process that was mildly reversed in 1966–75 due to the benevolent impact of economic reform in Czechoslovakia, Hungary, and Bulgaria. However, with the crushing of the reform movement in Eastern Europe—from the Czechoslovakia military repression of 1968 to the abandonment of the New Economic Mechanism (NEM) in Hungary in 1972—the economic performance of the CMEA-six was undermined. In an effort to sustain economic growth, Eastern Europe joined the USSR in seeking large-scale machinery imports from the West. While providing some short-term relief, this approach left these economies, especially Poland, Romania, and Hungary, with a new economic vulnerability in the form of sizable hard currency debt.

For the same reason that the Soviet Union was able to escape rising hard currency debt despite growing hard currency imports—the commodity composition of its trade—it began to incur the burden of ever larger trade subsidies to and surpluses with Eastern Europe. From 1956–70 the net cost to the Soviet economy resulting from cumulative trade subsidies to Eastern Europe was relatively minor. Beginning with the leap in primary commodity prices led by petroleum in 1974, Soviet trade subsidies to and surpluses with Eastern Europe started to grow at a breathtaking pace.[74] The Soviet Union's hard currency terms of trade advantage with the West produced a hard currency windfall, but its terms of trade advantage with Eastern Europe translated into an enormous subsidy to these economies, which bloated Moscow's trade surplus with them. The trade subsidy came to represent losses to the Soviet economy in potential hard currency imports it could have secured if its export surplus with Eastern Europe had been transformed into hard currency gains.

As with Eastern Europe, Soviet net economic transfers to its non-East European allies grew only slowly from 1956–70. Savings generated from the retrenchment in Soviet economic relations with China were easily consumed by increasingly expensive Cuban and Vietnamese allies. Further, Soviet economic transfers in support of its influence in global theatres, although having grown (especially for Egypt and Syria) and extended beyond earlier concentration in the Middle East, did not increase dramatically over the same period.

But in 1971–75 perturbations rose in the character and size of Soviet economic intercourse with its non–East European allies and the broader developing world—perturbations that pointed to an explosion in the future cost of empire.[75] Over that period the mix of Soviet aid to both allied and nonaligned Third World countries changed, with a large share taking the form of military aid.[76] Later in the 1970s Soviet aid and, particularly, military aid to the developing sector soared in conjunction with Soviet moves to expand its alliance system in global theatres, a process that saw Moscow exploit its newly won power projection capabilities. In addition, Soviet arms exports rose as a percentage of total Soviet exports to the Third World. While this development reflected the early stages of a rise in the cost of empire as a substantial portion of Soviet arms shipments from its enlarged production facilities was financed by credit and soft currencies, it also resulted from a new Soviet trade strategy for securing hard currency in the Third World.

By 1976–80, the employment of a "race against time" strategy from 1966–75 involving accelerated national defense spending and a smaller but nonetheless visible advance in the cost of other components of the national security account (especially the maintenance of the Soviet empire) had intensified the deceleration in the Soviet economy. After falling at a brisk pace from 1971–75, Soviet economic indicators plummeted from 1976–80. Perhaps the most telling blow delivered to the Soviet economy by the 1966–75 "race against time" strategy was the depletion of capital resources, a development that helped plough the Soviet economy into primitivation. During those years, the share of defense machinery in total Soviet producer durable goods output rose from 20 to 40 percent.[77]

It appears that the slide of the economy that began in 1975–76, combined with the ever growing investment demands (starting in 1977) of the primary commodity sector led by energy, played a role in the decision of the Soviet leadership to slow the rate of growth of defense spending and procurement. After advancing at a 4–5 percent real rate from 1966–75, Soviet defense spending slowed to a 2–3 percent average yearly growth rate from 1976–80. Despite the lower growth rate, the share of defense spending stabilized at 15–17 percent of GNP. Avoiding an acceleration in the economic decline, the slowdown in defense spending growth freed no resources for a possible effort to turn around the direction of the economy. Revealing the leadership's growing sensitivity to looming capital shortages, the defense procurement average annual growth rate dropped from 4 percent in the years 1966–75 to 1 percent from 1976–80.[78]

The component of Soviet national defense to absorb the preponderance of the spending and procurement growth rate reduction was strategic nuclear forces.[79] While there is some reason to believe that the disproportionate contraction in the growth rate of strategic force spending was the result of transitory factors (including technological difficulties in the development of strategic forces and a cyclical slowdown in strategic force modernization), it is probable that economic constraints forced Soviet leaders and defense planners to make choices in defense spending and procurement. In this context it may be more than coincidental that the reduction in the procurement growth rate for Soviet strategic rocket forces was soon followed by Brezhnev's 1977 Tula Doctrine in which parity was identified as Moscow's objective in the strategic nuclear realm.

However, as occurred in the transition from the 1946–55 period to 1955–58, savings generated from lower rates of defense spending growth did not all leave the national security sector. Indeed, from 1976–80 costs associated with maintaining the security of the Soviet empire skyrocketed. This meant that the decline in the growth rate of aggregate national security costs from 1966–75 to 1976–80 was substantially smaller than the decline in the rate of growth of national defense spending.

In the 1971–75 period Moscow began to absorb the cost of its higher trade subsidies to and surpluses with Eastern Europe; these costs mushroomed from 1976–80 as the full impact of the 1973–74 oil price rise was absorbed. (The USSR and its East European allies developed a sliding five-year average for oil prices to determine its intrabloc trading price, a system that had the effect of pushing the bulk of the price hike into the 1976–80 period.) Moreover, the expansion of interest payments on East European hard currency debt and Eastern Europe's dedication to pursuing hard currency imports persuaded the CMEA-six to exchange high quality exports for hard currency, leading to a deterioration in the quality of exports destined for the USSR.[80]

In addition to the rise in its trade subsidy to the economies of Eastern Europe, Moscow experience a similar explosion in the costs of maintaining its non-East European allies and its influence in global theatres. The leap in these costs were intimately tied to the momentum and structure of the earlier surge in Soviet national defense spending. The employment of new military power projection capabilities in global theatres—Angola, Ethiopia, Indochina, and Afghanistan—from 1976–80 not only began to generate costs in the form of combat consumables (i.e., fuel, ammunition, and defense machinery spent in combat) but an escalation in foreign military-economic aid, especially to allies Cuba and Vietnam. Of Soviet economic aid to Cuba form 1960–79, over half came during the last four years, and of economic aid to Vietnam from 1955–80, more than half came during 1976–80. Of even greater magnitude, Moscow-sponsored military intervention from Angola to Afghanistan sparked a radical rise in Soviet military aid to its non–East European allies. The rise in Soviet military aid to its allies active in global theatres was complemented by a sharp increase in military aid to nonaligned Third World nations. More than 50 percent of Moscow's military aid to both sectors from 1955–79 occurred from 1975–79.[81]

In addition to the boom in Soviet foreign aid, Soviet trade surpluses with the Third World continued to rise, fueled by an ever growing Soviet arms trade surplus. By the 1970s, arms exports accounted for 55–60 percent of Soviet exports to the developing world and more than half of this was financed by soft means.

Chapter 3
Whither the Soviet Threat?

With the dawning of the 1980s, the Soviet leadership was confronted with an intimidating set of objective challenges: not only had the Soviet economy persisted on the downward slope of the economic long cycle but the angle of descent had sharpened, and following the course of the economy, the "economic dimension of security vulnerability" had expanded.

In facing the long cycle, the Soviet leadership could see only rising costs in recession-prone primary commodity sectors, imminent labor shortages, a demoralized workforce, and a process of economic primitivization certain to aggravate capital shortages. The rates of growth of both factor inputs and productivity were spiraling downward, taking the GNP growth rate with them. Such conditions would worsen the "economic dimension," compromising national security.

Already, the expanding "dimension" had forced the Brezhnev regime to cut the rate of growth of defense spending while the pressures of economic primitivization helped produce an even greater retrenchment in defense procurement. Perhaps more worrisome than these retreating quantitative indicators, the Soviet national defense sector faced paltry improvements in critical qualitative inputs—technology and labor skills. True, Soviet national security investment since 1966 had won parity with the United States in the strategic nuclear sphere, secured preponderance in the Euro- and broader Eurasian theatres, and underwritten a breakout into global theatres, but to assure these gains, Moscow would have to sustain high levels of national security investment. The costs of maintaining an enlarged global empire would be difficult to control in light of an unstable social peace in Eastern Europe provoked by declining economic performance (e.g., Poland 1980) and new Third World allies under military pressure (e.g., Afghanistan, Angola, Cambodia, Nicaragua, and Ethiopia). Further, faltering improvement in qualitative inputs boded ill for Moscow's future competitiveness in the fast-approaching high technology military environment of the twenty-first century.

The gravity of these objective conditions should have prompted a reversion to a "buy time" strategy, one in which short-term national security costs were reduced in order to mount an effort to reverse the accelerated economic decline and thereby ensure longer term strategic competitiveness in a technological environment endowed with greater security risk. But for most of the 1980s, the Soviet leadership did not reduce the rate of growth in national defense and broader national security costs and failed to mount an effective effort to reverse the movement of the long cycle.

Countering the pressure from objective factors were subjective ones, which have deep institutional and cultural roots in the Soviet political-military establishment. Since it first sensed the imminent transition of the economy to the downward slope of the long cycle and the consequent opening of an "economic dimension of security vulnerability," the Soviet leadership has been prone to "race against time"—in 1959–63 and 1966–1975—and has demonstrated marked intolerance for "buy time" strategies, as indicated in the ouster of Malenkov (1955) and Khrushchev (1964). Even in response to the dramatic widening of the "economic dimension" in the years from 1976–80, the best the Soviet leadership could muster was a small slowdown in the rate of growth of national security costs. Further, the political-military leadership has shown an equal level of intolerance for any challenge to the values of the Stalinist economic system, as demonstrated by the departures of Malenkov and Khrushchev for undermining Stalinist resource priorities and the downgrading of Kosygin in favor of Brezhnev for the former's advocacy of moderate perestroika.

These conservative subjective biases were even widespread among those who rose in opposition to Brezhnev's policies at the end of the 1970s. The Andropov coalition included "race against time" proponents such as Ogarkov and Gregorii Romanov as well as many hostile to any real test of systemic economic principles, including Yegor Ligachev and Victor Chebrikov. Indeed, Andropov's strategy (implemented in 1983) for reversing the trend line in Soviet economic performance represented a marriage of "discipline" directed at the bureaucracy and workforce most vigorously promoted by his conservative allies and a moderate form of perestroika. Gorbachev, during the initial phase of his leadership in 1985–86, sought to extend these initiatives while offering a third—a program for reversing primitivization by increasing the rate of growth of investment in producer goods, a program that was hardly objectionable to Andropov conservatives. It was upon these three policy initiatives that his regime stood when it projected a reversal of the long cycle and the elimination of the "economic dimension" in the 1990s, producing a Soviet Union fit for strategic competition in the transcentury environment.

It was the failure of this program that radicalized Gorbachev (1986–88), prompting him to assert a form of perestroika threatening to the Stalinist system's commitment to centralized planning and administration and to the maximization of immediate output. This effort met with significant institutional and psychological resistance, which in turn provoked Gorbachev to escalate with glasnost/democratization campaigns. But Gorbachev's effort to undermine subjective resistance to radical perestroika has met with only limited success.

By 1988–89 the results of the Gorbachev program had not only failed to reverse long-term economic trends, they had, in fact, worsened them, leading to an inflationary budget deficit and personal consumption and civilian sector investment shortfalls. By the end of the decade, the Gorbachev leadership would have no means available to tackle these new challenges other than sharp cuts in national security costs.

THE ANDROPOV COALITION: A REACTION TO ECONOMIC DECLINE AND ITS ALARMING SECURITY IMPLICATIONS

The precipitous fall of the Soviet economy and its stark implications for Soviet strategic competitiveness began to incite a vocal opposition to the Brezhnev regime's management of the economy over the 1978–82 period, an opposition whose numerous strands created the political foundation for KGB director Yuri Andropov's ascension to the general secretaryship upon Brezhnev's death late in 1982. Importantly, the opposition was generated from two sources: those in the Soviet political-military establishment most sensitive to the plight of the Soviet economy (economic think-tank analysts, planners, and managers sympathetic to the earlier Kosygin and East European reforms) and others focused on Soviet domestic or foreign security such as segments of the KGB and the professional military.

A consensus among these varied forces evolved that argued that a significant effort was required to revitalize the Soviet economy and that this effort would be critical for future Soviet security. Further, any new campaign to reverse the economic long cycle could no longer rely upon extensive means, especially in the face of palpable factor input shortages, but would have to depend on a recovery in Soviet factor productivity. And each of the three components of the eventual Andropov coalition (economic reformers, the KGB, and Red Army professionals) could point to economic models in which their particular means for reviving productivity had appeared to work during the course of the 1960s and 1970s. In fact, the key point differentiating the various forces within the coalition centered about the desired means for reviving the Soviet economy—some favored forms of perestroika that in varying degrees challenged systemic commitments while others emphasized discipline, a means that in no way contradicted the basic tenets of the Stalinist economic system.

The heirs of the Kosygin and earlier Liberman reforms of the 1960s promoted forms of perestroika that proposed varying levels of economic decentralization (including a broader introduction of markets and private ownership) as a means for breaking down institutional hostility to rapid technological change. The dimensions of reform preferred by these forces ranged from moderate perestroika modeled on the simulation tactics of the Kosygin and 1967 price reforms to more radical versions that threatened to go beyond market simulation, such as those represented in the Novosibirsk model associated with Abel Aganbegyan, former director of the Novosibirsk Institute of Organization and Economics of Industrial Production. Experiments involving a handful of enterprises in Novosibirsk, centered about far-reaching decentralization of economic decision making over enterprise wages, investment, and production levels, yielded dramatic productivity improvements.[1] In addition to promoting the broader application of such reforms, the Novosibirsk group argued for reducing the power of the middle bureaucracy in order to enhance the degree of autonomy of local economic decision makers as well as for privatization of the service sector.

The protests of the economic intelligentsia against Brezhnev's management of the economy were echoed within circles associated with domestic security forces, including the KGB. During the 1970s, figures linked with security institutions in the Transcaucasus region—Eduard Shevardnadze, the chief of the regular police in Georgia, and Geidar Aliyev, the director of the KGB in Azerbaijan—toppled local party leaders through anticorruption campaigns to assume the dominant political positions in their respective republics. The economic initiatives pursued by both yielded growth rates over the 1970s superior to those in the Russian republics.

Aliyev's Azeri model was predicated on an intense discipline campaign aimed at removing corrupt and ineffective administrators—a policy that ran contrary to Brezhnev's "trust in cadres" orientation which represented a relatively permissive personnel policy charged with restoring confidence in a nomenklatura shaken by Khrushchev's repeated resort to personnel changeover. Shevardnadze, too, relied upon anticorruption sweeps as a means of enforcing discipline over the Georgian elite. But unlike Aliyev, Shevardnadze dressed over his discipline campaigns with populist public relations including widescale use of television and well-publicized visits to the shop floor (tactics later to be employed by Gorbachev).[2]

Expressing a more critical difference, Shevardnadze's program for revitalizing the Georgian economy went beyond discipline. From experiments first launched in the Abasha region of Georgia in the 1970s, a program for the effective privatization of agriculture modeled on earlier Hungarian reforms was sanctioned for all of Georgia in 1981 by Moscow.[3] The Brezhnev regime's authorization of an agricultural reform program antithetical to its own and one that explicitly challenged commitments to centralized planning and administration was a bitter pill, but one that it was forced to swallow when the Abasha success was measured against the failure of Brezhnev's own high cost agricultural policy.

Another force to vocally react to Brezhnev's economic failures was the professional military. Beginning in 1976, Soviet defense forces had to accept a ratcheting down in the growth rate of defense spending and procurement while at the same time they could foresee little future relief as the economy moved into a tailspin. An intense squeeze in the producer goods sector was unfolding, encouraged by the process of primitivization, and the technology gap with the West was widening. Tension between the professional military led by chief of staff Ogarkov and the Brezhnev regime over the erosion of quantitative and qualitative inputs to the national defense sector reached a boiling point in 1982 following the embarrassing performance of Soviet military technology in the Bekaa Valley. Late that year, Brezhnev was forced to confront a hostile group of senior military officers on these issues.[4]

Although the professional military offered no explicit cure for the Soviet Union's economic ills, one can decipher a close kinship between the approach associated with future Ogarkov ally Grigorii Romanov, the party chief of Leningrad until 1983 when Andropov summoned him to Moscow to oversee heavy industry/defense for the Central Committee Secretariat, and that of Aliyev.[5] Romanov had reconstructed Leningrad's economy in the 1970s so that, like Georgia, Azerbaijan, and the more limited Novosibirsk experiment, it outperformed the Russian republics as a whole. The Leningrad model emphasized labor and nomenklatura discipline, the effect of which was to be positively reinforced through a system of rewards based on performance, and it was specifically hostile to light industry investment, favoring heavy industry and defense. As such, the Romanov resource priority regime was opposed to those associated with the Kosygin and Novosibirsk models.

Lurching Toward a "Buy Time" Strategy: The First Timid Steps

The combined impact of mounting pressure from these three forces—economic reformers, the KGB, and defense professionals—and the crisis in the economy exacerbated by the pronounced agricultural recession and domestic transport breakdown of 1979–81 put the Brezhnev regime increasingly on the defensive in its last two years. During this period Brezhnev was forced to retreat on the centerpiece of his program for reversing the long cycle—hard currency machinery imports—and to give credibility to alternatives that carried with them a threat to systemic economic commitments. In 1982 Soviet hard currency earnings began to weaken as petroleum export volume contracted while earlier, in 1981–82, Eastern Europe's hard currency payments balances collapsed, precipitating an unusually large drop in that sector's hard currency imports. With Moscow's ability to secure hard currency imports weakening and its allies' plight reminding it of the uncertainty of long-term stability in this trade, and with the years of substantial Western machinery imports having no discernible impact on the economy, Brezhnev was forced to acquiesce to criticism of his principal policy initiative. During the early 1980s a consensus emerged in the Soviet leadership that the USSR should turn more to reliance on indigenous technological inputs.[6]

In 1981 the Soviet press initiated a "learn from Hungary" campaign at the same time that Shevardnadze was permitted to expand his Hungarian style agricultural reforms in Georgia. This was followed by Brezhnev himself promoting the "learn from Hungary" theme, pointing especially to Budapest's agricultural reforms. Brezhnev's declining authority in agricultural matters—a sector whose investment status he had championed since the mid-1960s—was in evidence in the 1982 Soviet Food Program in which criticism was leveled at the heavy investments that had been made in the sector in the past while moderate decentralization of procurement and output targets was promoted.[7]

The more pronounced economic slide of 1976–80 had also opened wide the "economic dimension of security vulnerability." Already beginning in 1976 the Brezhnev regime was forced to slow the rate of growth in another of its prized sectors—national defense. And by the end of the decade, it was under pressure to contain the sharply rising costs of empire. Following the full engagement of Soviet forces in Afghanistan in 1980–81, the Soviet surge into new global theatres that had commenced in 1974 in Angola came to a halt. Further, the Brezhnev regime was under pressure to contain the costs of its current involvements, prompting a Soviet effort to foster a reduction in tensions in Asia, which could help facilitate consolidation of Soviet-allied power in Afghanistan and Indochina at minimal economic and political cost. To encourage this endeavor, Brezhnev was forced to take initial steps to ease tensions with China—another bitter pill.[8] In October 1982, Soviet entreaties ultimately led to the reopening of Sino-Soviet border talks.

In addition, pressure began to mount for a reduction in Soviet economic subsidies to Eastern Europe to be secured through a decline in Soviet trade surpluses with the CMEA-six and an upgrade in the quality of East European exports to the USSR.[9]

Just as Brezhnev's rhetorical retreat on the economy bore no meaningful changes or improvement, his regime's fledgling efforts to contain the costs of empire faltered in the face of worsening objective conditions. The war in Afghanistan triggered a burst in the cost of combat consumables. At the same time, the breakdown of social peace in Poland in 1980-81 as well as recession conditions aggravated by hard currency balance of payments crises in several East European economies created domestic political conditions so fragile that Moscow was forced to back off from any effort to reduce the level of its economic subsidy to the region.

The degree of discontent in the Soviet political-military establishment with economic trends upon Brezhnev's death was signaled by Andropov's appointment to the general secretaryship over Brezhnev protege Konstantin Chernenko. During his year and a half in office, Andropov sought to expand upon the meager momentum for change generated in Brezhnev's reluctant retreat by articulating a program for reversing the descent of the Soviet economy that relied upon the two themes—discipline and perestroika—promoted by forces within his coalition. These programmatic themes were to reemerge in 1985 as the bulwark of Gorbachev's initial solution to the Soviet Union's economic sickness following a brief Chernenko interlude in 1984 in which efforts were made to weaken them.

During the Andropov era the greatest headway was made in the implementation of his discipline campaign, which combined labor discipline initiatives with anticorruption measures charged with shaking up a lethargic nomenklatura and weeding out resistant Brezhnev holdovers. The labor discipline campaign gained a high media profile and was targeted to reduce absenteeism and "correct poor work habits."[10] Winning an even higher public profile was Andropov's anticorruption campaign, which cleansed the bureaucracy of an array of Brezhnev associates while taking aim at the entrenched party position of others, most notably Politburo member Victor Grishin, chairman of the Moscow party.[11] By the fall of 1983 as Andropov's health was failing, he delegated to Gorbachev and Ligachev the task of drawing plans for the first large-scale party purge of the post-Brezhnev period, which was to include 20 percent of the Central Committee.

In contrast to the vigorous advance of his discipline campaign, the moderate version of perestroika sought by Andropov met with aggressive and open resistance from the Brezhnevite bureaucracy. By March 1983 it was already clear that Andropov's meek reform package would face a stiff challenge in the Central Committee. Until June leading allies of Brezhnev surfaced to oppose the planned reforms, and at the June 1983 Central Committee gathering, Andropov's reform package was accepted on an experimental basis but was still criticized by such figures as Chernenko. By that fall, opposition administrators typified by Gosplan chairman Nikolai Baibakov were decrying the need for economic change, arguing that the economy was performing well.[12] The busy opposition had managed to deflate the momentum of the experimental reforms.

Even less progress was made in the arena of privatizing the Soviet agricultural and service sectors, indicating that the 1980s Soviet reform movement, contrary to those that had earlier evolved in China and Hungary, was placing urban sector perestroika ahead of agricultural/service sector privatization. Privatization of the service sector only reached the discussion stage within the party while agricultural privatization received only a brief public airing at the December 1983 Central Committee Plenum on agriculture.

Nor did the Andropov regime's efforts to contain the growth of national security costs make practical headway. National defense spending continued to advance at a 2–3 percent real rate, and forces within the Andropov coalition led by Ogarkov sought to accelerate it. Similarly, the Andropov regime met with little success in managing the rising costs of empire. As the Afghanistan war intensified, its cost rose, while Soviet economic and trade subsidies to Cuba and Vietnam (still militarily enmeshed in Africa and Indochina, respectively) swelled. Further, the economic-political fragility of Eastern Europe exposed in 1981–82 made it difficult for the new Soviet leadership to cut its trade surplus with the CMEA-six, despite the fact that Moscow's trade subsidy to Eastern Europe began to drop in 1983 when world oil prices began to fall.[13] In fact, the region's economic condition had so deteriorated that, led by East Germany, it was encouraged by Moscow to seek additional Western imports to help relieve sectorwide resource stress.

Although generating no short-term payoff, the Andropov regime did pursue an activist effort to improve relations with China—a goal that eventually might contribute to a reduction in Soviet national security costs in both global theatres and the Eurasian theatre (i.e., the Sino-Soviet border). Following Brezhnev's modest warming toward China climaxing in his 1982 Tashkent speech, border talks between the two powers resumed in October 1982. In March 1983, soon after Andropov assumed office, the pace of improvement in Sino-Soviet relations quickened as the second round of border talks produced an agreement to double trade and resume technical cooperation. Then in the summer of 1983 Andropov pressed for even greater progress by publicly offering to halt the growth of Soviet SS-20s in Soviet Asia.[14] Suggesting the seriousness of Andropov's intention to advance Sino-Soviet relations, Mongolia and Vietnam—Soviet allies bordering China—began to demonstrate growing unease. After publicly cautioning Ulan Bator and Hanoi about his intention to pursue his China policy, Andropov dispatched Aliyev to Vietnam to pressure the Hanoi leadership to support the new Sino-Soviet dialogue (similar discussions were held with the Mongolians).[15]

During the interlude marked by the succession of Chernenko, even the marginal progress won by Andropov—albeit progress yielding little economic relief to the staggering Soviet economy—in his labor discipline, perestroika, and China initiatives weakened.

While Chernenko permitted the experimental Andropov economic reforms to proceed, they were given no additional impetus. Further, spokesmen for the Novosibirsk model who during the Andropov period made public calls for a drastic reduction in the power of the middle bureaucracy came under attack in the Soviet press. Discussions of privatization in the service sector came to a halt, and at the October 1984 Central Committee Plenum on agriculture, the dominant policy themes were elaborated by Chernenko ally Nikolai Tikhonov and Chernenko himself. Both revived Brezhnev's high-cost agricultural program, arguing for major land reclamation efforts and greater investment in costly Siberian water diversion projects.

In addition to slowing the already weak Andropov momentum for perestroika, the Chernenko interlude saw the steam taken out of the Andropov discipline campaign. Chernenko continued to mouth the rhetoric associated with the 1983 labor discipline and anticorruption campaigns, but no new initiatives were launched and the purge of the Brezhnevite bureaucracy stopped.

Moreover, in the one national security arena where Andropov's initiatives made some progress—relations with China—the new Chernenko government moved to place obstacles in the way of further improvement. In the spring of 1984, the first serious indication of a retreat in the Soviet Union's China policy emerged when the planned trip to China of Soviet Sinologist Ivan Arkhipov was suddenly canceled. By that summer Chernenko himself had commenced a series of verbal assaults against Beijing.[16] This was followed in the fall by an extensive diatribe in the Soviet journal *International Life* that amounted to an indictment of the Chinese 1984 "decision" to launch a program for radical perestroika in the urban industrial sector (the piece clearly had domestic political targets in mind as well).[17] Chernenko also relaxed the pressure on Vietnam and Mongolia, as Vietnamese Defense Minister Van Tien Dung was given a public forum to attack China while in Moscow. Of note, Dung was subsequently disinvited to East Germany and treated poorly in Hungary for his Moscow remarks, indicating that allies of the Andropov coalition retained political strength in Eastern Europe.[18]

Indeed, Chernenko sought a shift in Soviet East European policy. While the new regime resurrected the forceful rhetoric associated with Soviet desires to reduce its economic subsidy to Eastern Europe (in the wake of a CMEA-six economic recovery in 1984) to no practical effect, it used the June 1984 CMEA meeting to emphasize Moscow's new opposition to deeper economic ties between Eastern Europe and the West. More specifically, the Chernenko regime reversed Andropov's earlier encouragement to East Germany to seek closer economic ties with West Germany.[19]

The Meager Results

Over the course of the 1981–85 period, the Soviet leadership made no tangible progress in reversing the downward trend of the economy, as the alterations in Soviet economic and national security policy initiated during the Andropov era were of such little consequence as to have at best a small and fleeting impact on economic performance. Thus, despite the enormous drop in the Soviet GNP growth rate from 1971–75 to 1976–80, the GNP growth rate continued to decelerate in 1981–85 (see Table 3.1).

The deterioration of the Soviet primary commodity sector continued. Although escaping an agricultural recession, the 1981–85 period saw agricultural and grain output growth rates fall well below 1970s peaks, and in 1984–85 the Soviet economy was jolted by a large petroleum sector recession (see

Table 3.1
The Continued Descent of the Soviet Economy, 1981–85
(Average Annual Percent Growth)

	1976-80	*1981-85*
NMP Produced	4.2%	3.4%
Grain Output (mmt, Annual Average)	205 mmt	189 mmt
Primary Energy Production	4.2%	2.6%
Per Capita Personal Consumption	2.0%	0.8%
Labor Productivity	1.0%	1.2%
Investment	3.9%	3.4%
Capital Productivity	-4.4%	-4.2%
Factor Growth	1.2%	0.7%
Factor Productivity	-1.2%	-1.0%
GNP	2.3%	1.9%

Source: "Soviet Economic Performance: The Recovery That Was Not," *PlanEcon Report,* Vol. 2, no. 7 (17 February 1986) (for NMP); Folke Dovring, "New Directions in Soviet Agriculture," *Current History* (October 1987) (for grain output); Central Intelligence Agency and Defense Intelligence Agency, "Gorbachev's Economic Program: Problems Emerge," report submitted to the Subcommittee on National Security Economics of the Joint Economic Committee (13 April 1988) (for per capita personal consumption, capital productivity, factor growth, factor productivity, and GNP); Jochen Bethkenhagen, "Commentary," in *Gorbachev's Economic Plans,* Vol. 1, study papers submitted to the Joint Economic Committee of the U.S. Congress (Washington, DC: U.S. Government Printing Office, 1987) (for primary energy production); Laurie Kurtzweg, "Trends in Soviet Gross National Product," in *Gorbachev's Economic Plans* (for investment).

Table 3.1). The faltering performance of the primary commodity sector continued to make it a magnet for investment resources, especially in 1985 when emergency resources were diverted to the failing petroleum industry.[20] Further, while the Soviet economy began to feel the pinch of anticipated labor shortages, the rate of growth of per capita personal consumption continued to decline, ensuring that any recovery in labor productivity generated by means of labor discipline would have no staying power. And indeed, this was the case with respect to Andropov's labor discipline initiative. Although experiencing a short-lived improvement in 1983–84, labor productivity gains faltered in 1985 (a development exacerbated by the Chernenko regime's lax disposition toward labor discipline). Finally, capital shortages continued to squeeze the rate of growth in Soviet investment; coupled to this, the high rate of growth in primary commodity sector investment ensured that the process of primitivization that had commenced in earnest in the 1976–80 period would persist.

As a result, from 1981–85 the Soviet economy experienced sharply negative factor productivity growth just as it had from 1976–80, at the same time that the rate of growth of factor inputs slowed (see Table 3.1). Hence, the 1981–85 GNP growth rate fell below that of 1976–80.

As Soviet GNP growth decelerated, the rate of growth in Soviet national security costs matched its 1976–80 performance. Within the national security sector the component accounting for the majority of costs—national defense—continued to experience 2–3 percent real growth, and some in the U.S. intelligence community calculated that the rate of growth of defense procurement actually increased to 2–3 percent a year from 1982–84 after advancing by just 1 percent a year from 1976–81 (see Table 3.2).

At the same time, most elements contributing to the costs of the Soviet empire accelerated from 1981–85, led by losses in combat consumables precipitated by Moscow's military engagement in Afghanistan, a cost that was hardly visible from 1976–80. Also, Moscow continued to support the employment of Cuban and Vietnamese military forces abroad, insuring that Soviet economic aid and trade subsidies required to help consolidate its beleaguered alliance system in the developing world would grow at a rapid pace. Indeed, the cost of such transfers from 1981–85 was greater than their cumulative cost from 1954–1980 (see Table 3.2). The Soviet Union's economic aid and trade subsidies to the nonaligned developing world also grew vigorously in the first half of the 1980s as its trade surplus with this sector continued to climb. Finally, the Soviet trade surplus with the CMEA-six rose in the first half of the 1980s (1981–85). This was reflected in the advance in the Soviet trade surplus with all socialist countries, of which the CMEA-six accounts for over 80 percent.

However, some observers saw an easing in the costs of the Soviet empire in the later stages of the 1981–85 period.[21] Most of the savings were seen

Table 3.2
The Rising Cost of the Soviet Empire, 1981–85

	1976-80	1981-85
National Defense Spending (% Growth, Annual Average)	2-3%	2-3%

	1978-80	1981-85
Trade Balance with Socialist Sector (Billion Rubles) (Annual Average)	2.4	3.5

	1954-80	1981-85
Total Economic Aid and Trade Subsidy to Non-East European Allies (Billion Rubles)	20.4	29.7
Total Economic Aid and Trade Subsidy to Non-Aligned (Billion Rubles)	9.3	6.8

	1976-80	1981-85
Trade Balance Average With Third World (Annual Average, $Billion)	3.2	3.4

Source: Central Intelligence Agency and Defense Intelligence Agency, "Gorbachev's Economic Program: Problems Emerge," report submitted to the Subcommittee on National Security Economics of the Joint Economic Committee (13 April 1988) (for national defense spending); *PlanEcon Report*, Vol. 5, nos. 6/7 (17 February 1989) (for trade balance with Socialist sector); Carol Fogarty and Kevin Tritle, "Moscow's Economic Aid Programs in Less-Developed Countries: A Perspective on the 1980s," in *Gorbachev's Economic Plans*, Vol. 2, study papers submitted to the Joint Economic Committee of the U.S. Congress (Washington, DC: Government Printing Office, 1987) (for aid and trade subsidy to Third World Socialist allies and to non-aligned Third World); Marie Lavigne, "Soviet Trade With LDCs," in *Gorbachev's Economic Plans*, Vol. 2 (for trade balance with Third World).

to derive from a drop in the Soviet trade subsidy to Eastern Europe—a development that had nothing to do with Soviet East European economic policy, having been driven by the drop in world oil prices from 1983–85. Because intrabloc oil prices were higher than world oil prices during this time, Moscow suffered no loss in hard currency earnings from its oil exports to the CMEA-six. At the same time its trade subsidy to Eastern Europe shrank, its terms of trade with the CMEA-six continued to advance. The USSR was consequently able to win an even greater improvement in its import volume growth rate from Eastern Europe than it had in the second half of the 1970s, whereas its export volume to that sector barely grew. But the relief to Moscow generated by these circumstances would prove to be transitory, as from 1986–88 the advance in the volume of Soviet imports from Eastern Europe would come to a halt while the volume of Soviet exports to Eastern Europe would begin to grow.

In the years from 1981–85, any possible Soviet leadership desire to reduce aggregate national security costs ran up against a series of hostile objective conditions that tended to exacerbate the perception of threat. Most critical was the fact that the U.S. national defense sector began in 1981 to experience a period of accelerated spending growth. In conjunction with the largest peacetime refurbishing of U.S. national defenses since the Korean War, other U.S. actions launched in 1983 challenged advantages that Moscow had accumulated as a result of its 1966–75 acceleration in defense spending and the employment of the fruits of that effort in Euro- and global theatres in the second half of the 1970s. In the Euro-theatre the United States, in unity with its NATO allies, began deployment of intermediate-range missiles—the Pershing II mobile ballistic missile and the Gryphon ground-launched cruise missile (GLCM)—at the end of 1983 in an effort to devalue earlier Soviet Euro-theatre nuclear advantages won with deployment of the SS-20. In global theatres where the Soviet Union had expanded its influence in the second half of the 1970s, the United States, through a new "Reagan Doctrine," committed itself to indirect military support of indigenous forces hostile to Soviet allies. The existence of organized forces in opposition to the consolidation of political power by Soviet allies in these theatres and the U.S. willingness to militarily equip them raised the cost to Moscow of securing its empire. This was especially the case in Afghanistan. The renewed employment of direct U.S. force in a global theatre—in Grenada in 1983—further raised the perceived threat to Soviet interests. Finally, the U.S. promotion of the Strategic Defense Initiative in 1983 indicated an American desire to exploit its technological edge in the arena of transcentury weapons, which in this case had the explicit objective of devaluing Soviet strategic nuclear forces.

Hence, Moscow could perceive a heightened threat in all spheres—strategic nuclear, Euro-theatre, and global theatre. It may be no coincidence that it was within this environment that Ogarkov made a strong pitch for an acceleration in Soviet national defense expenditures, a move that by the summer of 1984 had breached the tolerance of most in the civilian leadership, bringing about his demotion.

In Eastern Europe, too, objective conditions had emerged making it more difficult to reduce national security costs. The deterioration in the region's economic performance from 1976–80 continued unabated from 1981–85, heightening political frailty. The breakdown of the social peace had gone to such extremes in Poland that Moscow found it acceptable to sanction a proto-Bonapartist solution as the only effective means for maintaining political control.

GORBACHEV'S MISSION: REVERSING THE LONG CYCLE DECLINE AND FORGING A "MINIMAL LINE OF SECURITY"

In early 1985 Mikhail Gorbachev assumed the general secretaryship of the Communist party of the Soviet Union (CPSU) upon the death of Chernenko. He inherited a Soviet economy slipping badly under the pressure of a recession in the energy sector and a renewed retreat in labor productivity. The response of the new leadership was to revive and expand upon the twin domestic programmatic themes ushered in during Andropov's brief reign—the multitargeted discipline campaign and moderate perestroika. To those components of the Andropov coalition's prescription for Soviet economic ills, Gorbachev added a third—an investment program charged with reversing the destructive process of economic primitivization. In addition to these domestic policy initiatives, the Gorbachev regime reasserted earlier feeble attempts to contain the rising costs of the Soviet empire launched in the first half of the 1980s—the effort to reduce the size of the Soviet economic subsidy to Eastern Europe and the pursuit of more normal relations with the Soviet Union's primary theatre adversary in East Asia, China.

Predicated on these initiatives, the Soviet leadership forecast a reversal of economic decline and sharp improvements in NMP growth rates in the 1990s, fueled entirely by a reversal in the performance of Soviet factor productivity (see Fig. 3.1). The three successive five-year plan projections from 1986–2000 for Soviet NMP produced suggested in the Gorbachev plan also represented levels of economic performance consonant with the elimination of future procurement stress in the Soviet national defense sector, as well as with technological improvement in the Soviet economy providing a support base able to offer the entire national security sector higher quality inputs of capital and labor. The projections of future Soviet NMP growth offered by Soviet officials as a result of the Gorbachev plan represented an "optimal line of security" for the Soviet Union; in reality, a more modest "minimal line of security" would be acceptable to Soviet leaders.

What would be unacceptable is economic stagnation or, worse, a continued decline along the downward slope of the long cycle. Such conditions would lead to a further widening of the "economic dimension of security vulnerability" indicated in the gap between the line of minimal security and stagnant or declining Soviet NMP growth rates (see Fig. 3.1).

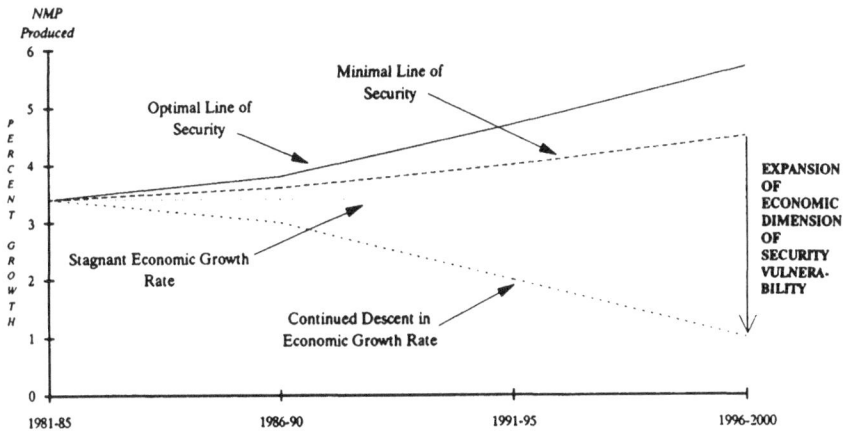

Figure 3.1. Lines of growth and Soviet security

At stake in the success or failure of the Gorbachev initiatives would be the USSR's ability to sustain rates of growth in defense procurement and, accordingly, in defense machinery output as well as the technological and workforce skill base to remain competitive in a future high technology strategic environment. Also in question would be the security of the newly expanded Soviet empire.

By the end of the 1980s, this baseline Gorbachev program in conjunction with several significant adjustments launched in 1987–88 was clearly locked onto a road to failure. Indeed, the obstacles to future success created by the elements of the program itself had forced a substantial retreat in the implementation of its principal features. By the end of the 1980s, the Soviet leadership was forced to face squarely the dilemma posed by the "economic dimension": any prospect for a sustainable reversal in the decline of the economy and for durable transcentury strategic competitiveness would require as a first step a mammoth contraction in national security costs during the first half of the 1990s.

Working From the Andropov Inheritance

Gorbachev, like Andropov, was forced by the immediate emergency conditions in the Soviet economy to give priority to a discipline campaign in order to win quick, positive results. Throughout 1985, the new Soviet leader stressed that the restoration of labor discipline was the critical factor in overcoming the shortfalls in economic output experienced in the first quarter of the year. Well-publicized government exhortations to the workforce were supported by government actions. Following a drive to restore responsibility to the workplace through an effort to curb rampant absenteeism, the new regime unveiled what would be the centerpiece of its labor discipline program in May 1985—an antialcoholism effort to significantly cut liquor consumption.[22]

Gorbachev personally resorted to the populist public relations tactics successfully employed by his ally and new Politburo member Eduard Shevardnadze in Georgia in the 1970s—wholesale use of television and regular informal appearances before groups of "ordinary people" in order to build trust between the new regime and the labor force. Populist public relations merged with an assault on the bureaucratic residue of Brezhnev conservatism. Behind an anticorruption campaign that had stagnated during the Chernenko period, Gorbachev targeted a broad sweep of the party and government bureaucracy, drawing first blood in the energy ministries. The cleansing of the government ministries crescendoed in October 1985 in a ministerial reform involving the creation of a number of superministries in key economic areas including machine building, energy, and agriculture.[23] This coincided with the purge of the most formidable Brezhnev holdovers in the ministerial bureaucracy, Nikolai Tikhonov, chairman of the Council of Ministers, and Nikolai Baibakov, chairman of Gosplan. Under a cannonade of press exposures, the escalating anticorruption campaign had over 1985–86 cleansed the Politburo of Brezhnevites Tikhonov, Grishin, and Dinmukhamed Kuneav as well as Ogarkov ally and potential Gorbachev rival Romanov.

Breaking down the Brezhnev-linked resistance in the economic ministries was central to the implementation of the other two components of Gorbachev's domestic program. Just as the old-line bureaucrats waged a vigorous effort to contain the most modest form of perestroika during Andropov's stewardship, they did so again when Gorbachev sought to reinvigorate and expand Andropov's reforms. At the June 1985 Central Committee session, Gorbachev assailed the economic mistakes made during the 1970s and 1980s, the period of Brezhnev dominance.[24] Unmistakably, the new Soviet leader was referring to the abandonment of the Kosygin-led reform process of the second half of the 1960s at the insistence of Brezhnev. In this context, Gorbachev announced an acceleration in the implementation of the Andropov reforms, which by 1985 had come to apply to just 12–15 percent of Soviet industrial output.[25] Gorbachev set new targets for the reforms. By 1986 they were to apply to 50 percent and by 1987 to 100 percent of industrial output. Concentration on urban sector market reforms in 1985–86 put Gorbachev's challenge to the systemic commitments of the Stalinist system on the same track as Andropov's, one distinguished from earlier reforms in Hungary and China where rural sector privatization gained early emphasis. In 1985–86, agricultural and service sector privatization remained relegated to the experimental phase in areas of the USSR with earlier experience in such reforms, Estonia and Georgia.

The third and only new component of the Gorbachev domestic economic package was one that both elements of the Andropov coalition, the proponents of "discipline" and of perestroika, could support—a front-ended effort to reverse economic primitivization. This Gorbachev initiative called for a visible rise in the Soviet investment growth rate, especially early in the Twelfth FYP, combined with a substantial shift in the distribution of investment resources back toward the manufacturing sector and in particular its high technology areas, including machine tools, electronics, computers, and robotics (the latter two sectors being immature and small).[26]

Even more activist than in their opposition to the expansion of the Andropov reforms was the Brezhnevite ministerial bureaucracy to this proposal. As early as June 1985 at the Central Committee meeting, Gorbachev made public a burgeoning dispute between his office and Gosplan over the draft FYP for 1986–90. In ordering the Gosplan to rewrite the FYP, Gorbachev made it clear that at the center of the conflict lay the Gosplan's opposition to higher investment growth rates and the changes in investment distribution proposed in his plan. The dispute was exacerbated by the emergency investments required to stabilize the failing energy sector, which had the effect of inflating the size of planned short-term investment. By September 1985, the contest over investment growth and allocation targets had reached a climax with the ouster of Gorbachev's two chief antagonists in the dispute, Tikhonov and Baibakov.

The Gorbachev regime's initial disposition toward the "economic dimension" differed little from that of Andropov. The national defense and related sectors were not confronted with new cost constraints and were accordingly permitted to expand at the high end of recent rates of growth (real growth in the national defense sector averaged close to an annual 3.0 percent in 1985–86).[27] At the same time, efforts that had earlier produced little practical gain were revived to contain the expanding costs of empire.

As was the case from 1981–85, the Soviet Union pursued no new military adventures in global theatres. At the same time, with renewed vigor Moscow applied pressure to its East European allies to take actions that would reduce the trade subsidy the USSR was forced to absorb. A fledgling East European economic recovery built upon an improvement in West European markets, a further expansion in sectoral hard currency debt, and better weather conditions created a context more conducive to an intense Soviet effort to reduce its East European economic burden. In 1985 the Gorbachev regime launched a vocal campaign aimed at improving East European exports to the Soviet Union, with East German and Czechoslovakian machine tools and electronics and Hungarian and Bulgarian food, footwear, and clothing exports receiving special attention. Further, Eastern Europe was encouraged to participate in the development of the Soviet extractive sector, and toward this end technical agreements were secured with Poland and East Germany. Finally, Moscow made a more determined effort to reduce its trade surplus with the region by constraining its raw material and energy exports, with Bulgaria becoming the special focus of this program in 1985.[28]

While seeking to reduce the dimensions of Eastern Europe's drag on the Soviet economy, the new regime took steps aimed at positively advancing the region's economic performance. Early in 1985 Moscow reversed Chernenko's moves to restrain Eastern Europe's economic ties with the West by encouraging East German economic relations with West Germany. Later in 1985 and throughout 1986 and early 1987 as Gorbachev made personal appearances at all of the Communist party conferences of the CMEA-six, Eastern Europe was gently coaxed to take the road of perestroika at a pace acceptable to each nation.[29]

The Gorbachev government also reversed the stagnation that had settled in in Sino-Soviet relations as a result of Chernenko's obstructionism. Even while Chernenko lay incapacitated in late 1984, efforts commenced to rejuvenate Andropov's drive for a Sino-Soviet detente, as Moscow renewed pressure on Mongolia to become more accommodating in its relations with China. The once canceled Arkhipov visit to Beijing finally took place, and in July 1985 an agreement was reached with China on a huge five-year trade package.

The Radicalization of Gorbachev's Program: Perestroika, Glasnost, and the "New Thinking"

From 1986–88, the Gorbachev regime's response to both the long cycle decline of the Soviet economy and the widening "economic dimension of security vulnerability" underwent increasing radicalization, and this had the effect of altering in important ways several of the components of its original program. This radicalization in Soviet policy was prompted by recognition that the set of initiatives that characterized the new regime's policy in 1985 and 1986 would be insufficient to assure an enduring reversal in Soviet economic performance.

After barely growing in 1985, the Soviet economy did stage a recovery in 1986, but one based on a frail set of conditions (see Table 3.3). Critical to this rebound was a rise in labor productivity, a phenomenon that had also occurred in 1983–84 as a result of the Andropov discipline campaign. But as close advisers to Gorbachev knew and warned publicly during the course of 1986, without a recovery in the per capita personal consumption growth rate, the 1986 advances in labor productivity would meet the same fate as Andropov's. Ominously, in 1986 per capita personal consumption growth turned sharply negative. Further, in addition to the short-term advance in labor productivity, the 1986 economic spurt rested upon output recoveries

Table 3.3
The Bright and Dark Sides of Soviet Economic Performance in 1986

	1981-85	1985	1986
THE BRIGHT SIDE:			
GNP % Growth	1.9%	0.7%	4.0%
Labor Productivity % Growth	1.2%	1.4%	3.7%
Grain Production (mmt)	189.0 mmt	191.7 mmt	210.1 mmt
Primary Energy Production % Growth	2.6%	2.9%	4.4%
THE DARK SIDE:			
Per Capita Consumption % Growth	0.8%	0.8%	-1.5%
Energy Sector Investment % Growth	7.6%	13.6%	7.9%
Non-Socialist Terms of Trade % Growth	0.8%	-1.4%	-22.7%

Source: Central Intelligence Agency and Defense Intelligence Agency, "Gorbachev's Economic Program: Problems Emerge," report submitted to the Subcommittee on National Security Economics of the Joint Economic Committee (13 April 1988) (for GNP, labor productivity, and per capita personal consumption); Jochen Bethkenhagen, "Commentary," in *Gorbachev's Economic Plans,* Vol. I, study papers submitted to the Joint Economic Committee of the U.S. Congress (Washington, DC: U.S. Government Printing Office, 1987) (for primary energy output); *PlanEcon Report,* Vol. 5, nos. 6/7 (17 February 1989) (for grain production, energy sector investment growth, and non-Socialist terms of trade).

in agriculture and energy from earlier recession levels, and the latter recovery required enormous inputs of new investment while the former reflected a return to better weather conditions. Both sectors therefore remained fragile and susceptible to volatility in their levels of output.

Soviet hard currency terms of trade collapsed with the gigantic fall in world oil prices in 1986. The year before, Moscow was forced to increase hard currency borrowing by a large sum ($5.0 billion) in order to make up for shortfalls in petroleum export volume provoked by the recession in the Soviet energy sector. In 1986 the drop in oil prices, combined with the depreciation of the dollar against currencies of economies from which the Soviets drew the largest share of hard currency imports (Western Europe), forced another large ratchet up in Soviet hard currency borrowing, and still hard currency imports tumbled.[30] So, at the same time that the 1986 domestic economic recovery rested on unstable grounds, external conditions less favorable to the Soviet economy erupted.

In the midst of highly vulnerable economic circumstances, what frustrated Gorbachev most was the seeming absence of any positive effect from his program of moderate perestroika. Neither was the economy receiving relief from cost constraints in the national security sector. National defense spending grew at the high end of the 2–3 percent range established from 1976–85 and defense procurement advanced more rapidly than the lethargic 1 percent growth rate of the 1976–81 period (see Table 3.4).

In addition, the Soviet Union's trade surplus with the CMEA-six rose in 1986 from its 1985 level even though Moscow's trade subsidy to Eastern Europe fell victim to the 1986 plunge in world oil prices (see Table 3.4). Although intrabloc oil prices were now substantially higher than world prices,

Table 3.4
Rising Costs of USSR National Security in 1986

	1981-85		1986
National Defense Spending (% Growth)	2-3 %		3.0%
	1984	1985	1986
Trade Balance With CMEA-Six (Billion Rubles)	1.9	1.1	2.5
Terms of Trade With Socialist Sector (% Growth)	23.5%	1.3%	-1.4%
Import Volume From Socialist Sector (% Growth)	41.0%	7.6%	0.0%
Export Volume To Socialist Sector (% Growth)	5.0%	1.0%	5.7%
Trade Balance with Third World Socialist Allies ($Billion)	1.7	1.7	2.1
Trade Balance With Third World, Aggregate ($Billion)	4.2	2.5	6.7

Source: Central Intelligence Agency and Defense Intelligence Agency, "Gorbachev's Economic Program: Problems Emerge," report submitted to the Subcommittee on National Security Economics of the Joint Economic Committee (13 April 1988) (for national defense spending); *PlanEcon* Report, Vol. 2, no. 14 (7 April 1986) (for 1984); *PlanEcon Report*, Vol. III, no. 16 (17 April 1987) (for 1985 and 1986 trade balance with CMEA-six, Third World Socialist allies Vietnam, Cuba, Mongolia, North Korea, and Laos, and Third World aggregate); *PlanEcon Report*, Vol. 5, nos. 6/7 (17 February 1989) (for terms of trade with Socialist sector, export volume to Socialist sector, import volume from Socialist sector).

they were beginning to fall as, in 1986, Eastern Europe's terms of trade with the USSR began to improve. Most ominous for Moscow, the growth in its import volume from the CMEA-six ground to a halt as its export volume to these countries picked up. For a Soviet Union looking to win improvement in its real trade balance with its allies, this could not have come at a worse time.

The early Gorbachev years also saw increased military efforts to win political consolidation in Afghanistan, Angola, and Nicaragua, and this was reflected in 1986 in rising costs for combat consumables. Finally, Soviet trade surpluses with developing sector allies as well as with nonaligned developing nations rose (see Table 3.4).

During the course of 1986, Gorbachev made clear that he would reject the approach of one wing of the Andropov coalition for dealing with domestic economic uncertainties—those seeking a broader and more intense discipline campaign—and instead endorsed the alternative of the other, a more radical economic perestroika, one that threatened to break the limits of simulation and challenge long-held commitments of the Stalinist system. To undermine institutional and psychological resistance to radical perestroika, Gorbachev undertook equally threatening political reforms through a campaign of glasnost and democratization.

This more radical and high risk Gorbachev approach to reversing the long cycle launched in 1987–88 was complemented by transformations in the Soviet response to the "economic dimension." Cautiously, Moscow, through "new thinking" in national security affairs, set in train a process in which short-term national security concessions became conceivable as a means for constraining national security costs.

Throughout 1987–88 the perestroika contemplated by the Soviet government moved closer to that embodied in the Novosibirsk model, and over the course of this period economists associated with the tenets of that model—Aganbegyan, Leonid Abalkin, and Oleg Bogomolev—rose in influence as Gorbachev advisers.

At the 27th Party Congress in February 1986, Gorbachev revealed his unease with the economic program defined in 1985. While stating that proposals for a stronger discipline campaign to involve larger personnel purges had been rejected as a solution to the inadequacy of the 1985 program, Gorbachev pointed to the preferred areas of change—including greater enterprise autonomy, reduced central planner interference, factory self-sufficiency, reform of the price system, enhancement of the consumer sector, and collective farm control over output above quota—that would be required to restore the Soviet economy.[31] Although a wide ranging debate ensued within the leadership during the course of 1986, radical reforms were neither agreed to nor enacted. The Gorbachev leadership had to satisfy itself with incremental victories: the authorization of greater quality control standards for industry, factory self-financing to cover five ministries in 1987 (this was to be expanded to cover 60 percent of industrial output in 1988), and a new and more liberal system of wage determination.[32]

Incrementalism in the radicalization of perestroika came to an end at the June 1987 Central Committee Plenum, where key proponents of radical perestroika—Gorbachev confidant Alexander Yakovlev and Nikolai Slyunkov—were promoted to the Politburo while Aliyev, whose Azeri reforms represented a model of the "discipline" alternative, was retired. More important, the session adopted a radical reform package slated to be fully implemented by the beginning of the next five-year plan in 1991.[33] When in place, the package as advertised would foster a severe drop in the share of total national spending accounted for by the government to 30 percent and would heavily marketize determination of retail prices by 1991 and wholesale prices by 1992. The huge government subsidies, especially for food and fuel (which if sustained would undermine any effort to increase the role of markets in determining the production and distribution of resources), were targeted to be substantially reduced. Bankruptcy and unemployment—essential in market processes—were to be permitted. If implemented, the program would result in an enormous contraction in the influence of central planners and administrators in the allocation of resources.

Indicative of continued adherence to prioritizing urban market reform over rural/service sector privatization, the regime only later supplemented the June 1987 program with new laws to expand the private sector in services and agriculture. Cooperatives formed within the service sector would be permitted to function privately, and in agriculture the introduction of land leasing and brigade level profit retention (reforms similar to the Chinese "contract responsibility system" initiated in 1979) would at least theoretically permit the spread of the family farm.[34]

To overcome entrenched resistance to radical perestroika and shock the population out of its inertia, Gorbachev forces undertook an effort to expose the negative results of, and thereby discredit, the Stalinist system. The glasnost campaign commenced in the fall of 1986 with the exposure of a number of social problems. From that meager beginning, it expanded through the vehicle of an increasingly liberated Soviet intelligentsia and media to focus on the plethora of misdeeds and failures of the Stalinist system with respect to the Soviet economy, social system, and national security in the past and present.[35] In conjunction with the loud and persistent glasnost initiative, individual victims of the Stalinist system were rehabilitated, including contemporary dissidents such as Andrei Sakharov and earlier foes of Stalin himself such as Nikolai Bukharin.

The Gorbachev leadership also sought to constructively maneuver the new energy in what had become a sizable anti-Stalinist popular movement against resistance to radical perestroika through a companion initiative to glasnost:

democratization. In June 1987 Gorbachev first introduced the idea of democratizing the Soviet political structure. That summer he won agreement in the Central Committee for multicandidate elections to be held at the local and regional level of the Communist party. These elections were held in the spring of 1988. In the summer, Gorbachev won further ground at the June Communist Party Conference by gaining agreement for a strengthened Soviet presidency and multicandidate elections to a new Soviet parliament.[36]

In conjunction with the radicalization of the Soviet regime's domestic policies, national security affairs underwent a transformation with implications for future national security costs. In June 1987 Foreign Minister Shevardnadze called for a new openness—glasnost—in foreign policy. In the wake of Shevardnadze's intervention, public criticism surfaced assaulting past Soviet foreign policy behavior. Under the rubric of the "new thinking," several crucial foreign policy actions of Stalin and Brezhnev came in for heavy criticism. In the case of Brezhnev, the two most prominent targets of attack were the deployment of the SS-20s and the Soviet invasion of Afghanistan, the former symptomizing the excesses of the Soviet drive for Euro-theatre preponderance and the latter, for global theatre advantages through the exercise of military power projection.[37]

The broad parameters of the "new thinking" as it has evolved have included several important themes for future guidance in Soviet national security affairs. Confrontation between East and West, especially in the military sphere (that is, relating to the strategic nuclear and Euro-theatre realms) is to be reduced.[38] The competitive relationship between East and West in global theatres that persisted in earlier Soviet incarnations of "peaceful coexistence" was also to decline as Soviet support for Third World liberation movements was to be downgraded. The pacification of the Eurasian and global theatres issuing from such a policy was to produce a security environment more conducive to planned domestic economic and political changes.

Indeed, even prior to the emergence of the "new thinking," the Gorbachev regime had launched a series of forays aimed at reducing the rate of growth of economic resources devoted to national security in ways that might involve some degree of sacrifice to perceived Soviet security interests. The reversal of earlier Soviet policy established during the 1981–85 period in response to the U.S./NATO introduction of intermediate-range missiles in Western Europe, and the ensuing Intermediate-Range Nuclear Forces (INF) agreement in 1987 which required the dismantling of the Soviet SS-20 force, pointed to a new flexibility in Soviet security policy. The subsequent Gorbachev rush to promote arms control initiatives affecting the strategic nuclear and Euro-theatre spheres indicated an intention to further reduce national security costs, albeit at the least possible sacrifice to Soviet national security.[39]

Evidence of the "new thinking" was also present, well before the official launching of the initiative, in Gorbachev's effort to reduce the cost of Soviet security in global theatres and in the Asian component of the Eurasian theatre. In Vladivostok in July 1986, Gorbachev detailed a new Soviet Asia policy that incorporated a series of concessions to Beijing unthinkable during the Brezhnev years, including Soviet recognition of Chinese border claims on the Soviet-Manchuria border (this territorial dispute was the subject of the 1969 Sino-Soviet border clashes) and a symbolic withdrawal of Soviet troops from Mongolia and Afghanistan.[40] Detente with China might not only facilitate a drawdown of Soviet forces on the Sino-Soviet border at no cost to Soviet security; it might also enhance the prospects for a political solution in global theatres (i.e., Afghanistan and Indochina) in which the economic costs of securing the Soviet alliance system had been high. During 1988–89, the Soviet Union withdrew its forces from Afghanistan and actively sought political solutions in Cambodia and Angola, moves that could lead to a reduction in the cost of empire.[41]

WHY MOSCOW MUST CUT DEFENSE SPENDING

The practical economic impact of the Soviet government's turn to radical perestroika (supported by glasnost and democratization) and the "new thinking" in the national security arena, combined with the implementation of a labor discipline and investment program, was less than impressive. Despite the recovery in the Soviet GNP growth rate in 1986, the economy continued its long cycle descent during the life of the Twelfth FYP, as in 1987–88 the economic growth rate plummeted down to levels experienced during the leaner of the Brezhnev years (see Fig. 3.2). Moreover, by that time the Gorbachev program had resulted in two highly disturbing economic developments: output shortfalls that undermined all prospects for meeting future plan targets for personal consumption and investment and a dramatic expansion in the government fiscal deficit sufficient to quicken the pace of inflation. The deficit/inflation problem in particular emerged as a primary concern of the Soviet leadership—one of enough intensity to force a retreat in all three of the Gorbachev regime's domestic economic initiatives.

The Failure of the Gorbachev Economic Program

Perhaps most predictable was the failure of the Gorbachev labor discipline campaign to generate sustainable results. It was the contraction in the labor productivity growth rate in 1987 that led the Soviet GNP growth rate down from its 1986 level (see Fig. 3.2). As economists associated with the tenets of the Novosibirsk model were warning in 1986—the year in which an im-

Figure 3.2. The rise and fall of Soviet GNP and labor productivity growth rates, 1985–88

provement in labor productivity boosted the GNP growth rate—labor productivity gains derived from discipline campaigns tend to be short-lived unless they are supported by an improvement in per capita personal consumption. But from 1986–88, no such recovery in Soviet personal consumption transpired. In fact, the general condition of the consumer worsened as he was forced to confront growing shortages, especially of food and light industry products, while inflation in consumer goods prices (especially of the hidden variety) accelerated. Little had been done by the Gorbachev government to contest this process, as from 1986–88 the marginal share of light industry in total Soviet investment continued to decline and Soviet agricultural output failed to surpass stubborn plateaus. After closing in on peak output levels reached in the 1970s under hospitable weather conditions in 1986–87, Soviet grain output faltered anew in 1988.

Beyond contributing to a meager Soviet output growth rate in 1987–88 and the consequent emergence of insufficient resources to meet future plan targets, the Gorbachev labor discipline campaign helped generate an unusual rise in the government fiscal deficit. In June 1986, at a special Central Committee session on alcoholism, agreement was reached to cut official sales of liquor by one-third. The drop in legal sales of alcohol caused a major loss in government revenues (these retail sales having been a prominent source of government revenues), contributing to the rise of an inflationary budget deficit.[42]

While the Gorbachev labor discipline campaign faltered, the new regime's investment program yielded less than satisfactory results. As was the case for the labor discipline campaign, the new investment program appeared to make progress in 1986. The heightened investment growth rate goals for industry and for targeted sectors within it—machine tools and electronics—were met.[43] Nevertheless, whereas investment in the industrial sector advanced quickly, industrial output grew less vigorously and was particularly poor in the producer goods sectors given the highest priority in the Gorbachev program (see Table 3.5). One of the reasons for the failure of the industrial sector to meet output targets in 1988 was the low rate of investment put in use.

Further, the improvement in future Soviet capital productivity anticipated as a result of the Gorbachev investment program was undermined by the quality of technology invested. The deterioration in Soviet hard currency terms of trade and the economic fragility of Eastern Europe resulted in no improvement in imports of higher quality technological inputs from 1986–88. Moscow was instead forced to rely on indigenous lower quality technologies during its investment drive. Moreover, shortfalls in projected output growth forced the Soviets to rely on older technologies embodied in inventories, as inventories contracted over this period to help meet investment goals.[44]

While the Gorbachev investment initiative has failed to spur levels of industrial output consonant with plan targets and is unlikely to support future targets because of its relatively poor technological content, it, like the labor discipline campaign, has functioned as a principal driver behind the spiraling Soviet budget deficit. From 1985–88 the government accelerated the rate of growth in its outlays in order to meet planned levels of investment.[45]

Radical perestroika, too, made contributions to the maturation of the new economic impediments—output shortfalls and inflation—confronting the Soviet leadership, as the program of quality controls launched in 1987 depressed output (because poor quality goods were no longer counted as output) while the wage reform package also enacted that year led to inflationary wage increases that became particularly acute in 1988.[46] Perhaps more im-

Table 3.5
Insufficiency of Gorbachev Investment Program (Percent Growth)

	1981-85	1986	1987	1988
Fixed Investment In Industry	4.2%	8.4%	5.7%	4.6%
Industrial Output	3.7%	4.9%	3.9%	3.9%
Capital Put In Use	3.0%	5.9%	6.8%	0.8%

Source: PlanEcon Report, Vol. 5, nos. 6/7 (17 February 1989).

portant, the radical reforms had little positive impact on the Soviet economy. By 1988 leading figures associated with the Novosibirsk model were publicly acknowledging the failures of radical perestroika. In March, Aganbegyan bemoaned the continued drag on the Soviet economy of health, housing, and food supply problems, and Nikolai Schmelev of the USA-Canada Institute followed by reporting that the reform program had resulted in no change for the average citizen.[47] At the June Central Committee session, Abalkin agreed that the economic reforms were not working, pointing to the faltering economic growth rates, a growing technology gap with the West, and worsening supplies of consumer goods.

The apparent ineffectiveness of radical perestroika had several causes. The first was that the critical components of the program were not to be implemented until the early 1990s, and were they to succeed, their positive results would not be felt for some time thereafter. In addition, emphasis on urban market reforms which require a long gestation period served to downgrade the importance of rural/service sector privatization, the components of perestroika that in the cases of China and Hungary were responsible for early and meaningful improvements in output growth and living standards.[48] Finally, radical perestroika and its allied political reforms threatened to sweep aside political and economic systemic principles and replace them with centrifugal forces—with political and economic forces independent of the Communist party and central government—capable of ushering in economic imbalances and political instability (i.e., inflation, unemployment, and income differences, as well as nationalist and labor disturbances). These threats inspired institutional and psychological resistance to the implementation of radical economic and political reforms.

Of note, the one factor that the radical reform process challenged most was discipline, the vehicle for reversing the Soviet economic decline favored by a substantial force within the Andropov coalition. Beginning in earnest following the June 1987 political success of the Gorbachev reform policy, these interests within the party and government displayed visible hostility to the reform process. Although the preponderance of institutional resistance to radical reform has been directed at its political components, both market reforms and private ownership have been publicly challenged. Yegor Ligachev, for instance, openly warned of the pernicious influence of market reforms, while in early 1988 Gorbachev had to overcome heated opposition in the Politburo to win approval for a law allowing private cooperatives in the service sector. But stipulations in the subsequent service sector law provided local party officials enough maneuvering room to constrain the pace of service sector privatization, and by 1989, as scores of profitable private ventures began to surface, the government moved to increase taxes on private incomes.[49]

Gorbachev in Retreat:
Defining an Interim Economic Approach

By the end of 1988, the Soviet leadership was under immense pressure to find the resources with which to alleviate the impact of output shortfalls and to close the inflationary budget deficit. Failure to approach targets for personal consumption or investment would only ensure further weakening of labor and capital productivity and result in ever larger output shortfalls. Failure to reduce the budget deficit would unleash inflationary forces demoralizing to the workforce, making it impossible to consider implementation of the core elements of urban market reform, which in themselves threaten to accelerate inflation.

Of most concern to Soviet leaders was the growth of the government budget deficit. When Gorbachev inherited the leadership of the Communist party in 1985, the government deficit was just 2.6 percent of GNP, and over the 1981–85 period it averaged 2.4 percent. But by 1988 the government budget deficit reached 8.8 percent of GNP, having averaged 7.9 percent from 1986–88 (see Fig. 3.3). Indeed, by 1988 the Soviet government fiscal deficit was equivalent to that of the United States in dollar terms.

Compounding this problem, the growth in nominal wages was far in excess of advances in labor productivity, intensifying inflationary pressures.[50] Supporter of the Novosibirsk model Oleg Bogomolev estimated Soviet inflation in 1988 to have been 5–7 percent, far above the official government

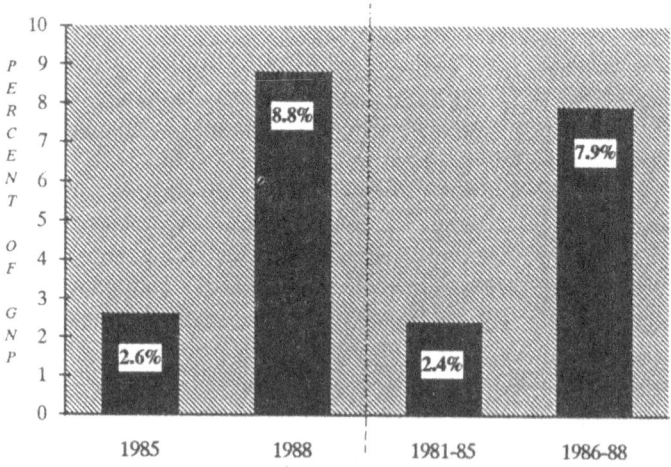

Figure 3.3. The rise of the Soviet government budget deficit under Gorbachev. *Source:* Central Intelligence Agency and Defense Intelligence Agency, "The Soviet Economy in 1988: Gorbachev Changes Course," report submitted to the Subcommittee on National Security Economics of the Joint Economic Committee of the U.S. Congress (14 April 1989).

figure of 0.9–1.5 percent, while private Western analysts estimated it to have reached 6–8 percent.[51]

Following growing debate within the government, it was decided to take emergency steps to contain burgeoning inflationary forces by means of reducing the size of the government deficit. In addition, to avoid a further acceleration of inflation the core elements of radical perestroika—retail and wholesale price reform—were postponed indefinitely, and it was decided that the state would continue to dominate in the consumer sector in 1989 and 1990 in order to ensure sectoral output goals.[52] In support of the anti-inflation campaign, the central government was also to monitor wage growth to make certain that the excessive increases in wages that occurred in 1988 would not be repeated.

Radical perestroika was but one component of the Gorbachev program to find itself in decline as a result of the need to contain inflation. Both the labor discipline and investment initiatives also underwent alterations in order to generate budgetary savings and reduce resource stress. More specifically, some improvement in government revenues was expected to result from the scaling back of the anti-alcoholism campaign, as by the end of 1988 the leadership acceded to new increases in the government production of alcohol.[53] The Soviet investment growth rate, which will have averaged 5.0 percent a year from 1986–90 and much lower in 1989–90, is targeted to continue to grow at a slower pace (1–3 percent) from 1991–95. The area that was to make substantial sacrifices to accommodate the lower investment growth rate was state investments concentrated in large water projects. In 1989 these projects were to be cut by 7.5 billion rubles.[54]

But the pull-back in all components of the Gorbachev economic program would, if successful, still be insufficient to close the budget deficit and reduce resource stress. Therefore, the critical phase the Soviet economy and economic reform process entered into in 1989 focused on the ability of the government to identify new resources whose contribution could relieve immediate inflationary pressures as well as output shortfalls. However, when turning to the sector traditionally gone to by Soviet leaders to reduce resource stress—personal consumption—there arose a further complication.

During the years 1986–88, the per capita Soviet personal consumption growth rate continued its long-term decline. The weakness of growth in personal consumption was also reflected in the status of retail sales during the Gorbachev period (see Table 3.6). In addition, the deprioritization of personal consumption by the Soviet government was reflected in the declining share of light industry investment. From 1986–88 the percentage of total investment accounted for by light industry dropped below its level during the late Brezhnev years, and over the Gorbachev era of economic stewardship the growth rate of investment in light industry has lagged behind total investment.

Table 3.6
How the Soviet Consumer Has Suffered Under Gorbachev (Percent Growth)

	1981-85	1986-88
Per Capita Personal Consumption	0.8%	0.3%
Retail Sales Turnover	2.6%	1.5%

Source: Central Intelligence Agency and Defense Intelligence Agency, "The Soviet Economy in 1988: Gorbachev Changes Course," report submitted to the Subcommittee on National Security Economics of the Joint Economic Committee of the U.S. Congress (14 April 1989) (for per capita personal consumption): *PlanEcon Report*, vol. 5, nos. 6/7 (17 February 1989) (for retail sales turnover).

Devastating to the hopes of a sustainable recovery in Soviet economic performance, Soviet labor productivity continued to follow personal consumption growth down. While additional transfers of resources out of personal consumption to compensate for output shortfalls or to close the government budget deficit would accelerate the decline in labor productivity, even maintenance of the status quo would ensure a continued deceleration, a development that would eliminate the prospects for reversing the long cycle decline.

Alarm over the slide in workforce morale and labor discipline forced the Gorbachev leadership to promote a new, costly economic package. At the end of 1988, the government decided to take steps to quickly improve the lot of the consumer. In the short term, imports of consumer goods from the West were slated to rise. In addition to reviving consumer morale, Soviet leaders hoped that Western consumer goods sold at marked up prices would help to fatten government revenues and reduce inflationary pressures by absorbing a portion of forced personal savings. Bolstering the immediate relief offered by imports, the leadership decided to increase investment in light industry. Investment in food processing was targeted to grow by 46 percent (meat and dairy processing by 60 percent) and the light industry sector in aggregate by 30 percent in 1989.[55]

Reducing New Imbalances: The Search for Resources

While earlier Gorbachev domestic economic policy initiatives were either being disassembled (the antialcoholism campaign) or put on hold (radical perestroika), a new policy formula was gravitating to the fore, one remarkably similar to that proposed by Malenkov and Kosygin where emphasis was placed on infusing resources into light industry in order to win immediate improvement in the living standards of the urban workforce. The key question, however, was how to pay for it, especially when the Soviet government had simultaneously dedicated itself to cutting its fiscal deficit and was also under pressure to make up for earlier output shortfalls. When one turned to the remainder of the civilian economy—the primary commodity sector and producer goods—as potential spheres from which to gain these resources, one found little maneuvering room.

Over the course of the 1960s and 1970s the share of investment accounted for by the primary commodity sector grew forcefully, helping to precipitate the process of economic primitivization. Indeed, one element of the Gorbachev program for reversing the process of primitivization called for a reduction in the percentage of total Soviet investment going to primary commodity production. But depressed investment in this sector runs grave risks, especially when considered in light of the historical frailty of Soviet agriculture and energy output. A reduction in investment resources in either could spark a damaging sectoral recession.

The fragility of these sectors was indicated by their performance from 1986–88. Despite optimal weather conditions, Soviet grain output still failed to breach the peak reached in 1978. After hitting 210.1 and 211.1 million metric tons (mmt) in 1986 and 1987, respectively, grain output dropped back to 195 mmt in 1988. And this performance fell well below the 253–260 mmt target originally set in 1985 as part of the Gorbachev Twelfth FYP. Further, the share of total Soviet investment accounted for by agriculture already declined over the 1986–88 period (see Table 3.7), and in 1989 the largest chunk of planned cuts in state investment were set to come in agriculture-related water projects.

Even though the share of total investment accounted for by agriculture declined during the Gorbachev years, the share accounted for by the primary commodity sector as a whole did not. To reverse the deep energy recession of 1984–85, the new Gorbachev government was forced to accelerate the pace of investment in it. As a result, the rate of growth of investment in energy surpassed that for the entire economy (see Table 3.7).

The increase in energy investment was an essential ingredient in the subsequent recovery in energy output, especially petroleum. In 1986–87 the energy sector rally was sufficient to push output levels above earlier peaks. Despite this strong rebound, petroleum production stabilized at its 1987 level in 1988, and while energy and oil output has grown since the inception of the Gorbachev regime, so has the rate of growth in domestic consumption of energy. Moreover, severe losses in Soviet hard currency terms of trade forced Moscow to increase the volume of its petroleum exports in order to prevent a catastrophic decline in hard currency earnings. With domestic and foreign demand for Soviet energy showing no sign of abatement, high levels of investment in the sector will have to be sustained in order to avoid the risk of new output shortfalls.[56]

The precarious status of the agricultural and energy sectors indicates that

Table 3.7
Sectoral Investment Patterns under Gorbachev

	1981-85	1986-88	1987-88
Total Investment --			
All Sectors	3.5%	6.5%	5.3%
Personal Consumption --			
Light Industry	1.8%	2.5%	1.6%
Primary Commodities --			
Agriculture	1.1%	3.7%	2.3%
Fuels	5.9%	8.7%	9.1%
Oil Extraction	9.2%	10.3%	10.6%
Producer Goods --			
Machinery & Equip.	2.1%	5.9%	4.9%
Machine Building	4.0%	4.9%	1.1%

Source: *PlanEcon Report*, Vol. 5, nos. 6/7 (17 February 1989).

a reduction in the rate of growth of investment in either would run the risk of triggering output recessions—recessions that would have disastrous consequences for the entire economy.

With investment in the primary commodity sector an unacceptable candidate to pay the costs of fiscal deficit reduction, earlier output shortfalls, and increased expenditures for personal consumption, there remains but one large domestic civilian sector left to tap—producer goods. This sector suffered during the process of primitivization and it was Gorbachev's particular policy contribution in 1985 that sought to reverse the process by concentrating investment anew in producer goods.

Nonetheless, even before the end of 1988 it appeared that the Gorbachev initiative to reverse the process of primitivization had weakened. From 1986-88 the rate of growth of total Soviet investment surpassed that for machinery and equipment, including the critical machine-building sector (see Table 3.7). By 1988 the machine tool sector's share of total Soviet investment had fallen back to where it was in 1982-83, and the commitment of resources to the war on economic primitivization was clearly faltering. To cut further into the rate of growth of investment in producer goods would bury all hope of reversing the process of primitivization in the short term and with it the prospects for quickly reversing trends in Soviet capital productivity.

A final component of the Soviet civilian economy—one that lies outside the domestic sphere—which the Soviet leadership might turn to in order to obtain needed resources is hard currency trade. But during the Gorbachev period Moscow's non-socialist terms of trade have collapsed (see Table 3.8). In 1986 world oil prices tumbled, staging only a marginal recovery since then, and beginning in 1985 the U.S. dollar underwent a prolonged depreciation against the currencies of Western Europe. While the USSR's oil exports earn dollars, the economies of Western Europe account for 80 percent of its hard currency imports.[57] Moscow's terms of trade with its leading source of hard currency imports, Western Europe, consequently fell at a breathtaking pace.

To compensate for terms of trade losses, Soviet non-socialist export volume grew energetically while its non-socialist import volume contracted sharply (see Table 3.8). Even with a huge surplus in net export volume, Moscow's hard currency trade surplus in nominal terms fell, spurring rapid growth in its net hard currency debt.

Further, the Soviet hard currency trade balance in 1986–87 was supported by an agricultural recovery that eased the requirements for imports. Indeed, the drop in agricultural imports accounted for the majority of the fall in hard currency import volume. But in 1988 Soviet agricultural imports grew once again as domestic farm output weakened. From an estimated 28 mmt in 1987, grain imports advanced to 42–45 mmt in 1988.[58]

Soviet hard currency manufactured imports will continue to be constrained by the variable nature of agricultural import requirements and by the question mark placed on hard currency export earnings due to the volatility of oil prices. In addition, Moscow's net hard currency borrowing, which rose perceptibly in 1985–87, grew less vigorously in 1988–89, suggesting that

Table 3.8
Deterioration in Soviet Non-Socialist Trade under Gorbachev

	1985	1986	1987	1988
Non-Socialist Terms of Trade % Growth	-1.4%	-22.7%	8.2%	-18.5%*
Non-Socialist Exports % Growth	-10.8%	15.5%	5.6%	7.7%*
Non-Socialist Imports % Growth	0.0%	-14.3%	-2.8%	2.9%*
Hard Currency Debt, Net $Billions	$15.7	$21.7	$26.4	$27.3*

* Estimate

Source: PlanEcon Report, Vol. 5, nos. 6/7 (17 February 1989) (for non-Socialist terms of trade, export growth, and import growth); Central Intelligence Agency and Defense Intelligence Agency, "The Soviet Economy in 1988: Gorbachev Changes Course," report submitted to the Subcommittee on National Security Economics of the Joint Economic Committee of the U.S. Congress (14 April 1989) (for hard currency debt net).

Soviet leaders have rejected any notion of borrowing their way out of their current dilemma.[59] Within the context of continued depressed levels of hard currency terms of trade, the Soviet Union is unlikely to turn to Western imports to solve its problems.

Limits to Reducing the Costs of Empire

With the primary components of the civilian economy in no position to absorb the costs of the economic program arrived at by the Gorbachev leadership at the end of 1988, Moscow came under pressure to shift its focus to the national security arena in search of economic savings. As it did, the Soviet government confronted the dilemma posed by the "economic dimension of security vulnerability" with a greater intensity than at any other time in the post-Brezhnev era.

Examination of the status of Soviet national security accounts in 1989 indicated that any future effort to reduce the costs of empire—the smaller component of national security costs—would face hefty obstacles. Since Gorbachev's ascension to power, the Soviet leadership's attention to these costs has grown. In its early stages, the new regime pressured its allies to improve the efficiencies of their economies, a policy that, if successful, would permit Moscow to diminish its foreign economic transfers at no risk to Soviet national security. Beginning in 1987, however, the leadership shifted focus under the impetus of the "new thinking" to the pursuit of economic savings through a contraction in Soviet and allied foreign combat activity— a venture that carried with it tangible risks to national security. The two-pronged effort to diminish the economic burden of empire has thus far generated uninspiring results and, because of the economic and political weakness of many Soviet allies and Moscow's lingering interest in the political consolidation of its alliance system, the prospects for generating meaningful economic savings from the empire appear remote.

Particularly intractable has been the status of Soviet trade with the CMEA-six. Although Moscow's nominal trade balance with its East European allies improved in 1987–88, this came as a result of a plunge in its terms of trade with Eastern Europe (see Table 3.9, which shows a large drop in Moscow's terms of trade with its socialist trading partners, of which trade with the CMEA-six comprises the largest share). So, while Moscow has seen its trade subsidy to Eastern Europe collapse, it has been unable to translate this into any tangible economic gain as Soviet import volume from socialist economies has slipped and export volume to these economies has climbed (see Table 3.9).

Prospects for any headway in the Soviet real net export balance with Eastern Europe appear minimal. Economic growth in the CMEA-six since the

Table 3.9
The Stubborn Costs of Empire, 1986–88

Trade Balances:	1985	1986	1987	1988
CMEA-Six (Billion Rubles)	1.1	2.6	0.1	-0.4
Non-CMEA-Six Socialist Allies (Billion Rubles)	1.7	2.1	2.2	2.2
New Allies Afghanistan/ Nicaragua (Billion Rubles)	0.5	0.8	0.8	0.9
Third World Aggregate ($Billion)	2.5	6.7	7.9	6.9

Socialist Sector: *(Annual Average Percent Growth)*	1980- 85	1985- 88
Terms of Trade	23.5	-12.1
Export Volume	5.0	8.6
Import Volume	41.0	0.7

Source: *PlanEcon Report*, Vol. 3, no. 16 (17 April 1987) (for trade balances in 1985–86); *PlanEcon Report*, Vol. 5, nos. 13/14 (7 April 1989) (for trade balances 1987–88); *PlanEcon Report*, Vol. 5, nos. 6/7 (17 February 1989) (for Socialist sector terms of trade, export volume, and import volume).

sector's 1984 economic recovery has been weak, as Eastern Europe, like the USSR, has continued its descent along the downward slope of the economic long cycle. At the same time, the financial condition of some of these economies (Poland, Hungary, Bulgaria) have worsened as the region as a whole experienced a renewed rise in its net hard currency debt.[60]

Not only did the economic health of Eastern Europe grow more precarious in the 1980s, so did its political condition. Throughout the region economic stagnation ignited a precipitous deterioration of the social peace, compelling Moscow to make ever greater concessions on its political influence in order to avoid unrestrained instability. By the end of the decade, Soviet leaders accepted what most Western observers had only recently viewed as unthinkable: the abandonment of the "Brezhnev Doctrine" as successful counterrevolution against Communist governments spread throughout the region.

From acceptance of a proto-Bonapartist solution in Poland early in the decade, the Soviet Union sanctioned the existence of a political entity independent of the Communist party—the Solidarity labor movement—and acquiesced to its entrance into the Polish government. In Hungary, the rejuvenation of the reform movement led to the elimination of the Communist party in name as well as agreement to pursue a multiparty political system.[61]

Thus, even before the shocking collapse of Communist party dominance in two of Eastern Europe's most reform-resistant regimes, East Germany and Czechoslovakia, and the bloody removal of Ceausescu in Romania, Soviet leaders had in principle acceded to multiparty political systems in Eastern Europe and non-Communist participation in the region's governance. The remarkable disintegration of Communist rule in these three former bastions of Stalinist orthodoxy did, however, reveal the rapid tempo at which social peace in the area was eroding, and it is this erosion that lies behind the loss of Moscow's influence. Economic weakness and the new political realities it has helped to foster made Eastern Europe a more difficult acount for Moscow to wrench resources from at the end of the 1980s than it had been at the beginning of the decade.

Economic and in some cases political fragility create similar difficulties with respect to Moscow's non-East European allies. Despite much public discussion, Soviet pressure on non-CMEA-six allied economies to improve economic efficiency and thereby allow for a reduction in Moscow's foreign economic transfers has produced no apparent results. The Soviet Union's aggregate trade surplus with Cuba, Vietnam, Mongolia, Laos, and North Korea has continued to rise during the Gorbachev years (see Table 3.9); further, trade surpluses with two of its newest clients, Afghanistan and Nicaragua, have risen as well (see Table 3.9).

The weakness of almost all Third World economies allied to the Soviet Union makes it difficult to envision how Moscow's economic transfers to them could diminish without risking a deterioration in the social peace, which in some cases is already severely frayed.

A more promising target than trade surpluses is Soviet foreign assistance. Not insignificant cuts in foreign aid might be anticipated from the firm application of the "new thinking." Already, the withdrawal from Afghanistan has won Moscow savings in the form of reduced losses in combat consumables. The withdrawal of Cuban forces from Africa and Vietnamese forces from Cambodia should add further savings in the form of lowered Soviet aid to Cuba and Vietnam. (In the 1976–80 period aid to both countries swelled as they became involved in foreign military actions.)

However, economic savings secured through a withdrawal of Soviet and allied military forces from foreign combat suggests potential sacrifices in Soviet national security. Demonstrating concern for its security interests, Moscow has already transferred a portion of the savings it gained from its withdrawal from Afghanistan into increased military aid to the Kabul government.[62] Soviet behavior up to the end of 1989 suggests it will weigh carefully the potential security losses from risking the political consolidation of its allies against the economic gains derivative of pacification in global theatres.[63] Real constraints will therefore persist on both the pace and the degree of Soviet retrenchment in these theatres, and this will put strict limits on the size of economic savings to be anticipated from such a process.

Even more forceful than the rise in Moscow's trade surplus with its non-East European allies has been the advance in its surplus with the developing sector (see Table 3.9). The principal cause of this huge jump in the Soviet trade surplus with the developing world was a drop in agricultural imports. At the same time, Moscow's trade surplus with the developing sector continued to be driven by an enormous arms trade surplus of over $8.0 billion a year.[64]

One obvious means by which Moscow could bring down its trade surplus with the developing world would be to reduce its arms exports—exports that embody valuable capital and labor inputs. But a segment of Moscow's arms sales generates badly needed hard currency, while other sales that are financed by softer means have become a primary vehicle for Moscow to secure influence in global theatres. Large volumes of Soviet arms sales to the developing sector also support scales of efficiency that serve to reduce production costs in the Soviet national defense sector.

Turning to the National Defense Sector

The poor prospects for diminishing the cost of the Soviet empire meant that the success or failure of efforts to restrain inflationary forces and refurbish the consumer sector—objectives considered essential if economic reform was to proceed in the future—would depend upon whether the Soviet government could generate enough savings from the remaining component of its national security account: national defense and the closely related space sector.

Through 1988 there was little evidence to suggest a meaningful retrenchment in national defense. Although the most recent CIA estimates of Soviet defense spending imply that there may have been a small slowdown in its growth rate in 1987–88, over the Gorbachev years as a whole defense spending in real terms grew within the range experienced from 1976–85 and at a pace faster than GNP. Over the 1986–88 period, the rate of growth of Soviet defense procurement appeared to surpass the 1.0 percent it averaged from 1976–81, putting additional pressure on the availability of civilian producer durables, though this slight advance in the pace of defense procurement probably reflected the movement of the procurement cycle and not a secular rise.[65] Indeed, the performance of the national defense sector under Gorbachev's direction was up to that point in the "business as usual" mode, as the behavior of key defense spending indicators followed patterns established from 1976–85.

Although Gorbachev moved aggressively on a range of arms control fronts, the momentum of the "new thinking" did not produce unilateral curbs on the growth of the Soviet national defense sector. In 1986–87 the new regime demonstrated the utmost caution in devising means for gaining economic savings in this sphere. Substantial efforts in the past to unilaterally cut defense spending—Malenkov's moves in 1953–54 and Khrushchev's in 1963–64—provoked a conservative-military political alliance of sufficient strength to topple the governments of both leaders. Aware of the fate of these predecessors, Gorbachev first sought to win economic savings in the defense sector by focusing on its least sensitive areas. Beginning in 1987 meager savings were gained through a more austere operations and maintenance budget for the navy, reflected in a curtailment of naval maneuvers.[66] At the same time, a second program involving little political risk was launched to improve efficiency and reduce waste in the defense industries, and at the beginning of 1988 the ministries associated with the defense industries were given greater responsibility for the production of consumer goods.

If any savings at all were won as a result of these measures, they did not leave the defense sector, as its real rate of spending growth continued at recent levels. More auspicious than the apprehensive government moves to reduce defense costs was the enormous changeover in the leadership ranks of the professional military.[67] From 1986–88, not only were the defense minister and chief of staff replaced by younger and less politically formidable officers, but virtually all of the leading marshals closely associated with the evolution of Soviet doctrine and force structure from the mid-1960s through the 1970s were moved aside. In addition to Marshal Ogarkov who was demoted in 1984, such figures as Marshal Victor Kulikov (commander in chief of the Warsaw Pact Forces) and Admiral Sergei Gorshkov were retired. The transition to a less potent set of leading military officers represented a downgrading of the political standing of the professional military. Further, since Soviet Defense Minister Dmitri Ustinov's death in late 1984, the defense minister has not been a full member of the Politburo, as had been the case during the Brezhnev period.

As the political status of the professional military waned, Gorbachev moved to assert the role of the civilian leadership in military affairs. Beginning in 1987, with the introduction of civilians into the military doctrinal debate, a rationale was created that could allow for a substantial reduction in future Soviet defense spending. New concepts such as "nonoffensive defense" and "reasonable sufficiency," which have yet to be operationally defined, seemed to suggest important changes in Soviet defense doctrine, changes that propose a Euro- (Eurasian) theatre balance in which theatre asymmetries are reduced or removed and reaffirmation of the Brezhnev Tula Doctrine in the strategic nuclear arena.[68]

The marked deterioration in Soviet economic performance and the threat of an inflationary budget deficit energized the regime's sluggish effort to find ways to reduce national defense costs. At the June 1988 Party Conference, the leadership arrived at a consensus that the Western threat was now in decline (an assessment not without objective support, considering the peaking of the U.S. defense build-up and an increasingly benign American administration disposition toward U.S.-Soviet relations) and that the enormous sums of economic resources the defense sector had consumed over the years had weakened the economy and, therefore, Soviet long-term national security.[69] Certain weapons systems such as the SS-20 were not only identified as a waste of resources but as harmful to national security. Criticism of decisions to invest in such systems, decisions that had been generated within the military-industrial complex, produced a further consensus on the need for improvements in the Soviet military based on qualitative and not quantitative grounds, to be achieved through a decision-making process in which the civilian leadership would gain greater voice in defense investment issues. Hence, economic and political (i.e., the impact of Soviet weapons decisions on the status of East-West relations) considerations would, in the future, be given increased weight in the process of deciding on which weapons to develop and deploy.

In January 1989 Gorbachev would confirm that in parallel with the consensus of the Party Conference a government commission had been formed to find ways to reduce national defense spending without damaging Soviet national security. Shortly thereafter, Gorbachev told visiting members of the Trilateral Commission of the defense commission's recommendations: Soviet defense spending was to be cut by 14.2 percent and procurement by 19.3 percent over a two-year period (later clarified to be over a three-year period: 1.5 percent by 1989, 7.0 percent by 1990, and 14.2 percent by 1991).[70]

The commission's proposals appeared to advocate a defense retrenchment of some substance. Even before the January 1989 revelations Gorbachev, in a December 7, 1988, United Nations speech, announced a planned unilateral reduction of 500,000 military personnel and 10,300 tanks along with the withdrawal of other conventional weapons from the European, East-Asian, and southern theatres. Of the 500,000 military personnel to be cut, 240,000 would come from the Euro-theatre (including four divisions from East Germany and one each from Hungary and Czechoslovakia) and 200,000 from the Sino-Soviet border area (including four ground divisions and all Soviet air forces from Mongolia).[71]

When added to the savings in combat consumables resulting from the Soviet withdrawal from Afghanistan and the abandonment of future modernization of medium and long-range mobile missiles in the Eurasian theatre won through the INF Treaty, the U.S. Central Intelligence Agency estimated that the unilateral conventional force cuts in Eurasia, if enacted, would provide Moscow one-third to one-half of the reduction in defense spending Soviet leaders said they intended to enact from 1989 to 1991.[72]

Where else might the Soviet leadership turn to meet its targets for cutting defense spending?

Three areas of Soviet defense and related national security spending in particular recommend themselves for future trimming. First and probably most desirable from Moscow's perspective would be to generate defense savings by means of arms control, a mechanism that provides for little to no loss in national security. Theatre-wide conventional arms reduction in Eurasia through a Warsaw Pact–NATO accord on conventional forces in Europe (CFE) and Sino-Soviet agreements as well as strategic nuclear arms reduction through U.S.-USSR agreements could reduce the Soviet force structure sufficiently to produce future savings through a diminished bill for force structure modernization and maintenance.

During 1988, Soviet defense officials led by Defense Minister Dmitri Yazov launched public criticism of the waste in defense RDT&E.[73] Research and development programs involving a low level of qualitative advance as well as those in exotic high technology areas with low probability of employment began to be questioned. Soviet defense R&D, which since 1975 has grown far faster than the defense sector itself, was promoted as a prime candidate for spending cuts.

Finally, beginning in the 1989 election campaign Boris Yeltsin keynoted an assault on the Soviet space program that was later picked up by advisers close to Gorbachev. Yeltsin proposed a five–to seven-year freeze in spending on space. Later, former director of the Soviet Institute for Space Research Raold Sagdeyev, a close Gorbachev adviser and promoter of reduced defense spending, argued that the Soviet space program is too large—several times the size of NASA—and has been distorted by the interests of the defense establishment. According to Sagdeyev, the failure of the Phobos-2 mission to Mars earlier in 1989 raised public concern over the Soviet space program and the Soviet version of the space shuttle represents an unnecessary waste of economic resources.[74]

THE FUTURE SOVIET THREAT

By the beginning of 1989 the Gorbachev leadership was engaged in replacing its original economic prescription with a new one aimed at correcting the poisonous economic imbalances that emerged during its first four years in office. Cuts in national defense spending were promoted as a means for reducing the government's inflationary budget deficit and for financing a consumer goods expansion, both essential for fostering confidence and vitality in a workforce suffering acute demoralization. Looking remarkably like the economic medicine once offered by Malenkov and Khrushchev, the regime's new interim economic program also closely resembled the policy that had won a revitalization of the Chinese economy in the early 1980s in which economic resources were diverted from national defense (and in the case of China, from heavy industry) to support improvements in living standards. The focus of economic reform had shifted from a frontal assault on the Stalinist economic system's commitment to a centrally planned and managed urban industrial sector (radical perestroika) to another element of the system—its peculiar resource priorities.

For the short term—the first half of the 1990s—the Soviet leadership would now be involved in a crucial struggle not to reverse but to simply neutralize the downward movement of the economic long cycle so that in the long term—post-1995—it might return to an effort to win an enduring reversal of economic trends through radical perestroika. Critical to whether Moscow would be successful in its short-term program and therefore be in a position to prosecute what had now become a longer term project—radical perestroika—was, first, whether it would succeed in removing from the national defense sector the targeted resources, and second, whether the size of the planned defense sector cut would be adequate to correct current economic imbalances, whether the resources could be delivered in time to relieve the impact of the imbalances, and whether the resources gotten from national defense would be sufficiently fungible to be fully absorbed into the civilian economy.

Answers to these two sets of questions will be a principal determinant of the size of the security threat Moscow poses to the United States not only in the short term, but in the long term as well. At the beginning of 1989 three plausible short-term Soviet futures existed, based on three modes for managing Soviet national defense spending:

- "business as usual" in which the rate of expansion of the Soviet national defense effort remains within the range of its recent historical levels;
- "moderate cuts" in defense spending which are insufficient to stop the downward movement of the economic long cycle and, hence, the expansion of the "economic dimension";
- "deep cuts" in defense spending which are necessary to any effort to improve short-term economic performance and thereby provide the foundation for renewed Soviet attempts at "radical perestroika."

By the middle of 1989 evidence was fast accumulating that Soviet defense spending had transitioned from a "business as usual" to a "moderate cuts" mode, and by the close of 1989 Soviet leaders were under pressure to move quickly to "deep cuts."

Short-Term Soviet Threat Futures

Business as usual. Real cuts in the Soviet national defense sector are certain to incite resistance in the defense complex and among conservative forces within the Communist party, especially when the cuts begin to take a toll on either force structure or the pace of modernization. The Soviet political-military establishment has in its past reaction to Malenkov's deep cuts, to Khrushchev's Euro-theatre cuts in 1959 and defense retrenchment in 1963-64, and even to Brezhnev's defense spending slowdown in the second half of the 1970s (i.e., the early 1980s Ogarkov-led rebellion of the professional military), as well as in its stance during extended periods of surges in defense spending—1951-54 (the Korean War), 1959-63, and 1966-75—demonstrated an unmistakable bias against diminishing defense's priority status. Therefore, even if real savings should be won through agreement to cut specific components of force structure, there appeared little guarantee at the beginning of 1989 that savings gained from Gorbachev's unilateral cuts would be wrenched from the defense sector and transferred to the civilian economy.

Indeed, at the very beginning of the current Soviet defense retrenchment initiative in 1989 a series of developments emerged that raised questions as to whether Gorbachev could deliver the defense sector from its pattern of "business as usual." Both Soviet government and military officials reported defense and related sector spending levels to be substantially smaller than Western experts (and, in some cases, Soviet officials) had estimated.[75] Following a long search for the size of national defense spending as part of the glasnost effort, Soviet government officials identified defense spending in 1988 to have reached 77.3 billion rubles, a figure representing only 9 percent of GNP. This figure was far lower than CIA estimates, which placed 1988 Soviet defense spending at 15-17 percent of GNP, or 128.8-146.0 billion rubles. Accordingly, the reported Soviet defense budget represented only 53-60 percent of the CIA estimate (see Fig. 3.4). Even if the restrictions on the components of the Soviet defense effort indicated by General Sergei Akhromeyev in his testimony before the House Armed Services Committee in 1989 are taken into account, U.S. estimates of Soviet defense spending still exceeded those of the Soviet government by a wide margin (by measuring the more restricted elements of Soviet national defense spending that Akhromeyev argued the Soviets used in computing their defense budget, U.S. estimates still showed 1988 defense spending to have surpassed 100 billion rubles).[76]

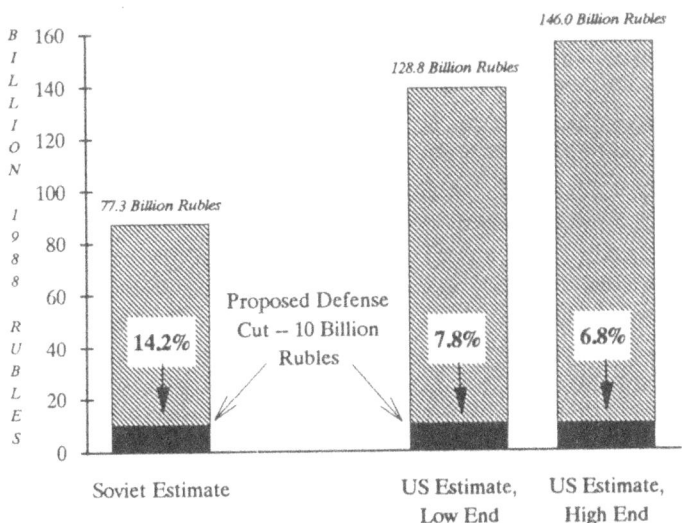

Figure 3.4. U.S. and USSR estimates of Soviet defense spending and their impact on the portion of defense spending Moscow is prepared to cut. *Source: PlanEcon Report*, Vol. 5, nos. 6/7 (17 February 1989).

The practical importance of Soviet government low-balling in these estimates is that it reduced the dimension of the projected contraction in Soviet defense spending implied in Moscow's earlier 14.2 percent reduction target, since 14.2 percent of the Soviet's estimate is substantially smaller than 14.2 percent of the CIA's (see Fig. 3.4). The advertised 14.2 percent cut in the Soviet figure turns into a contraction of just 6.8-7.8 percent of the CIA figure. This means that the savings generated from the Soviet withdrawal from Afghanistan (estimated by Soviet officials to be 5 billion rubles a year) and those from the unilateral cuts in conventional forces announced by Gorbachev were all that would be required to meet the 14.2 percent reduction target, whereas in the earlier CIA estimate these savings (in conjunction with those won as a result of the INF Treaty) would have only accounted for one-third to one-half of those required to meet the 14.2 percent target.[77]

It further appeared that other official Soviet defense and space program expenditure estimates made in the more open atmosphere of glasnost fell around 40 percent short of U.S. and private Soviet assessments. For instance, Soviet accounting of military personnel and tank production reported in 1989 was close to 40 percent below Western estimates, and the spending figure for the Soviet space program was about 40 percent below that suggested by Gorbachev adviser Sagdeyev.[78]

Moreover, official Soviet estimates of defense spending reported in 1989 provided evidence to indicate that while underestimating actual spending, these calculations would also serve to overstate the magnitude of the future defense retrenchment. According to Gorbachev, Soviet defense spending failed to grow in 1987–88; the CIA reported, however, that it continued to advance at a 3 percent pace. (Even the most recent CIA revisions show that Soviet defense spending in 1987–88, although growing more slowly than initially thought, still made positive advances).[79]

When announced in early 1989, this numbers game in which the Soviet military establishment undoubtedly played a large role undermined confidence that even the moderate cuts in Soviet defense spending embraced by the leadership would actually transpire. It further implied that there were limits to what Moscow would be prepared to sacrifice unilaterally in national defense programs to win economic relief and that what had been agreed to up to that point by Soviet leaders—withdrawal from Afghanistan and Eurasian conventional force cuts—represented the upper, not the lower, limit.

Moderate cuts. Over the course of 1989 it became increasingly evident that the Gorbachev leadership had successfully moved defense spending out of the "business as usual" and into the "moderate cuts" mode. Late that year the CIA acknowledged that Moscow would reduce its real defense spending by 1.5 percent in 1989 in accord with earlier announced targets. Further, the U.S. intelligence community reported that Soviet tank and warship production had contracted and that Moscow had complied with its own force structure reduction goals first spelled out in Gorbachev's 1988 U.N. speech.[80]

Even if the Soviet leadership succeeds in the full implementation of planned moderate cuts—thereby escaping any return to "business as usual" defense spending growth—it would still confront a series of awesome obstacles. Will the transfer of resources from the national defense sector to the civilian economy occur in time to stop and be of sufficient size to overcome the erosion in the social peace? If the leadership should fail in either the timing or the magnitude of this effort, the contraction in the Soviet defense sector and the sacrifices made in national security will have gone to waste.

The acceleration in the pace at which Soviet social peace and labor discipline broke down in the first half of 1989 pointed to the need for emergency transfers of economic resources from national defense to the consumer sector. Soviet economists warned that inflation was fast accelerating in 1988 and early 1989, and throughout the USSR shortages of food—inciting public warnings in the new Soviet parliament of a future famine—were complemented by shortages of basic nondurable consumer goods such as soap and toothpaste.[81] The economic decline had picked up such fury that Boris Yeltsin publicly warned of a prospect for revolution within two years and reform economist Schmelev declared that the Soviet economy was headed for a crash within two to three years.[82]

The disastrous consequences of rising inflation and growing consumer goods shortages could be witnessed on streets and in factories. Over the course of 1989 labor discipline crumbled, and as it did it threatened to set off a crushing self-expanding process in which falling labor productivity would beget larger output shortfalls, which in turn would beget a further deterioration in labor productivity. In 1988 the Soviet crime rate rose by an astounding 32 percent, according to official estimates, while labor disturbances picked up pace, crescendoing in the unprecedented coal miners strike that swept western Siberia and the Ukraine in the summer of 1989.[83] Also, growing economic tensions either ignited or exacerbated nationalist disturbances in Central Asia, the Transcaucasus region, and the Baltic states (public demonstrations and other forms of organized nationalist protest surfaced in Moldavia, Byelorussia, and the Ukraine).[84]

The strain of this breakdown in discipline not only sent conservatives in the Andropov coalition into a heightened state of mobilization against the "excesses" of political and economic reform; it also put pressure on the Gorbachev leadership to contain the challenge of the labor and nationalist upsurge with promises of large and imminent improvements in the living standards of the workforce and the republics. In response to the ethnic violence in Uzbekistan, Moscow was persuaded to commit itself to the creation of 200,000 new jobs in the region in 1990 to ease the pressures of unemployment, and Gorbachev himself in the midst of government acquiescence to a range of demands from striking coal miners announced a quick-fix $16 billion package for consumer goods imports.[85] Gorbachev, however, was careful to put no time constraints on his new promise.

Despite this intensifying pressure on the government to speed up delivery of higher living standards, it remained questionable whether the proposed cuts in national defense and the program for enlarging the output of consumer goods linked to these cuts would be of sufficient size to improve the consumer's lot.

Although a series of other measures (increased government alcohol sales and cuts in state investment) were authorized to bring down the government budget deficit, national defense would have to make an important contribution. Yet the cut in the defense budget envisioned over the years 1989–91 represented only 0.9 percent of Soviet GNP while the Soviet budget deficit in 1988 was 8.8 percent of GNP (this figure is the CIA estimate; official Soviet estimates have put the deficit at only 6.2 percent of GNP, a drastic underestimate, and private Soviet economists put it much higher). Moreover, part of the 10 billion ruble cut in defense spending was already targeted to pay for increases in light industry investment.

More important, the resource transfers contemplated by the Soviet leadership in 1989 failed to account for any shift to the rural sector. Essential to a rise in Soviet living standards in the short term is a rejuvenation of agriculture. In the case of the Chinese economic recovery in the first half of the 1980s, the earlier improvements in the Hungarian economy under the NEM, and even the Soviet economic recovery during the NEP, it was rural revitalization that dominated. But prospects for such a development in the Soviet economy were bleak. Over the 1986–88 period the share of Soviet investment resources devoted to agriculture declined, and in 1989 the preponderance of cuts in state investment were targeted at areas related to agriculture. More significantly, the kind of resource transfers to the rural sector that permitted the incentives associated with privatization of agricultural production to work in China and Hungary and in the USSR during the NEP were not even under consideration. For this reason, a 1989 U.S. Department of Agriculture restricted analysis foresaw the Soviet agricultural reforms falling short of expectations in terms of output improvement. In particular, avoidance of price reform that would permit food prices to rise and thereby enhance the purchasing power of the Soviet farmer guaranteed weak supply-side results.[86]

Finally, while under greater pressure to meet immediate consumer demands and with the size of government resource commitments to enhance living standards of questionable dimension, the Soviet leadership faced a third obstacle: the uncertain fungibility of national defense resources. Clearly, raw materials, intermediate goods, and some producer goods consumed by the defense sector are highly fungible with respect to the civilian economy. The degree of fungibility declines, however, when turning to defense sector plant and equipment and personnel, a factor that may be crucial to the success Moscow enjoys in converting defense resources to civilian use. A major component of 1989 Soviet plans for improving light industry output rested on conversion of defense plant and equipment. In 1988 the Soviet defense industries produced about 40 percent of civilian goods. By 1991 this share was slated to rise to 50 percent and by 1995, to 60 percent.[87] Since most of the conversion of defense factories was weighted toward light industry, much of the regime's hopes for improving personal consumption were based upon a changeover from defense to consumer goods products (from tanks to toothpaste), a changeover whose feasibility was questionable.

Another area in which questions of fungibility promise to be substantial is the reintegration of military personnel, and especially retired officers, into the civilian workforce. Failure to accomplish this task would not only increase the number of unemployed, it might well create another disgruntled interest group free to engage in mischief.

Deep cuts. By the close of 1989 the transition to a "moderate cuts" regime had failed to ease the decline in Soviet economic performance. The government budget deficit continued to mount as a percentage of GNP, fueling a ratchet up in inflation as consumer goods shortages worsened. The deal the government had worked out earlier in 1989 with striking workers and recalcitrant republics was fast falling apart, threatening a renewed acceleration in the deterioration of the social peace in 1990. At the same time, Gorbachev's economic policy failures, once combined with the breakdown of discipline, breathed life into a conservative-counterreform backlash. And these developments unfolded in the ominous shadow of collapsing Communist party influence in Eastern Europe, itself a result of a breakdown in the social peace. In response, the Soviet leadership offered a refined economic package at the end of 1989. Before the Congress of People's Deputies, Prime Minister Nikolai Ryzhkov detailed a new five-year plan in which consumer goods output was to grow at a pace far greater than contemplated earlier in the year. In the same breath, the Prime Minister proposed a more extensive retreat from radical perestroika than had been previously spelled out. Further, Yegor Ligachev articulated to the Congress the government's rejection of any serious privatization of the rural sector.[88]

With a resuscitation of rural energies based on the Chinese or Hungarian models squelched, to where would the regime turn to support its proposed 12–18 percent annual growth in consumer goods output and new rigorous budget deficit reduction targets? A portion of these resources were to now come from a large retrenchment in heavy industry investment, indicating that in addition to radical perestroika another of Gorbachev's earlier economic initiatives—his de-primitivization investment program—was savaged in the new economic approach. But even a large assault on heavy industry investment would be far from sufficient to satisfy the government's new economic goals. By the end of 1989 Gorbachev and his associates were under maximum pressure to win much larger savings from the defense sector.

Earlier in 1989 Nikolai Ryzhkov identified a program for "deep cuts" in national defense to be completed by 1995, cuts whose magnitude would be a necessary condition for a tangible advance in Soviet living standards.[89] The targeted $33^1/_3$–50 percent reduction in current defense spending based on the Soviet estimates of such spending represented the equivalent of 20–30 percent of the CIA's low-end estimate of Soviet defense spending and 17.6–26.5 percent of the high-end estimate. Such a cut would be equivalent to 3.0–4.5 percent of GNP.

This level of deep cut would require going well beyond the reduction in force structure the Soviet leadership had acceded to by late 1989. While marginal savings might be wrung from cutbacks in defense R&D and the Soviet space program, the majority of savings required to meet Ryzhkov's targets would have to come from force structure. Here, decisions already made within the leadership indicate that the only acceptable context for accomplishing such cuts would be a material reduction in the foreign threat secured either through arms control or through independent and mutual force structure reductions between NATO and the Warsaw Pact, the U.S. and the USSR, and/or China and the USSR.[90]

Unwilling to make further large unilateral cuts in force structure beyond those to which it has already committed itself out of fear of the national security consequences, the Gorbachev leadership will be under unusual pressure to obtain substantial arms control results.

Long-Term Soviet Threat Futures

The three national defense spending options available to Soviet leaders at the beginning of 1989 not only defined a range of plausible short-term Soviet threat futures but also a spectrum of longer term ones. Ironically, the long-term threat futures that involve objective conditions most inhospitable to a sustained or heightened Soviet national security effort—continued descent of the economic long cycle and a widening "economic dimension of security vulnerability"—are those that tend to stimulate political forces most prone to promote Moscow's historical biases of hostility to "buy time" and sympathy for "race against time" responses to the "economic dimension." Similarly, the long-term threat futures that entail objective conditions most conducive to a surge in Soviet national security activity—a respite from or a reversal in the downward movement of the economic long cycle and the elimination of the "economic dimension"—coincide with the maturation of new political forces whose subjective preference would be to downgrade the status of national defense. The former long-term threat futures flow from either the "business as usual" or "moderate cuts" alternatives while the latter requires that "deep cuts" be followed in the short-term (see Fig. 3.5).

Pursuit of the "business as usual" course in the early 1990s would have resulted in an accelerated decline in Soviet economic performance and an erosion in living standards. By 1995 the Soviet leadership would have been in no position to renew its program of radical perestroika. Indeed, the acceptance of a "business as usual" approach to Soviet defense spending would have required the downgrading of Gorbachev and the de facto rise to political dominance of a conservative-military coalition. While this institutional resistance was highly visible in 1988–89, it demonstrated less willingness to take the form of opposition than similar political combinations in 1953–54 and 1959–64. The grave objective economic reality of today has made the preferred policy response of these forces to the "economic dimension" less plausible than in the 1950s and 1960s. Their relative weakness removed any obstacle to the transition of Soviet defense spending to a "moderate cuts" mode in 1989.

If the "business as usual" course had been pursued in the early 1990s, the continuation of recent rates of growth in Soviet defense spending would

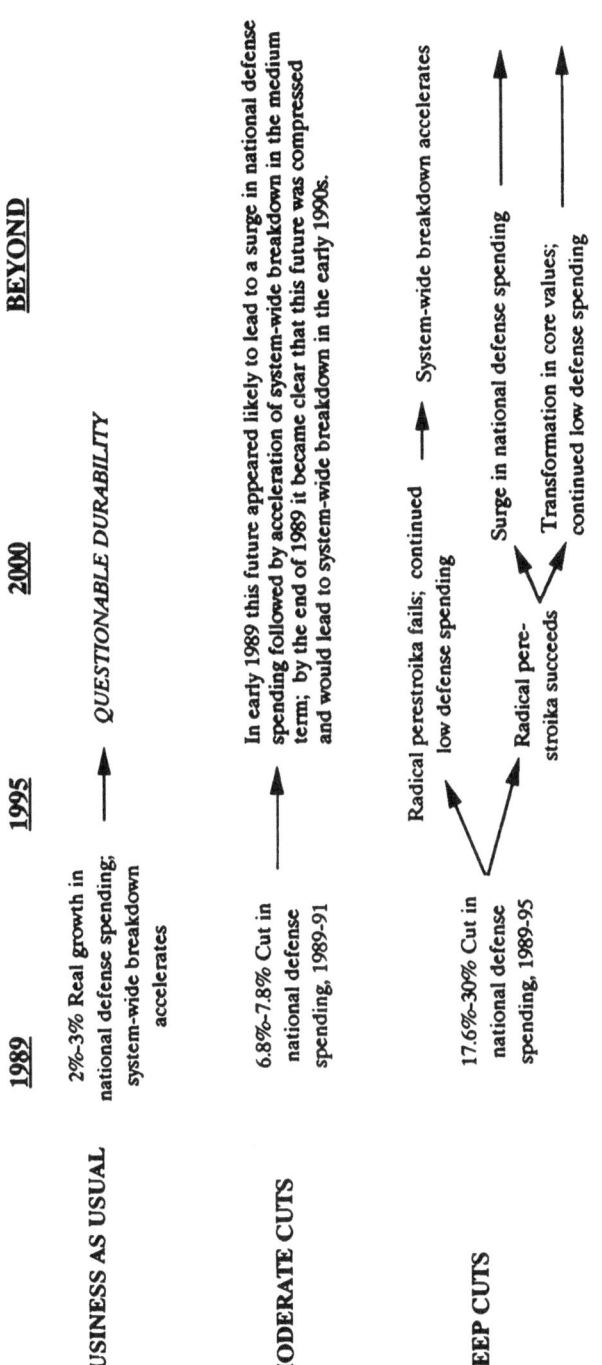

Figure 3.5. Alternative Soviet threat futures—short and long term

have sparked a steep slide in living standards and would consequently have accelerated the pace of erosion of the social peace. Under the guidance of Andropov conservatives, Moscow's most likely response would have been to emphasize the restoration of order. This in turn would have increased the political standing of Soviet security forces—the military and the police—as these forces were called upon to reinforce weakened Communist party/central government authority.[91] The seeds for a heightened political status for Soviet security forces were already visible in their role in quelling nationalist disturbances in Georgia, Armenia, Azerbaijan, and Uzbekistan in the late 1980s. These forces represent that component of the Soviet establishment most sensitive to national security interests and therefore biased toward maintaining resource commitments to national defense. Their growing influence in the determination of Moscow's response to the "economic dimension" would have served to support continuation of historical rates of defense spending growth. An attempt to carry a "business as usual" approach into the long term would, however, have been of highly questionable durability, as it would have accelerated the descent of the economic long cycle, widened the "economic dimension," and brought to the Soviet Union a collapse of the social peace similar to that experienced in Eastern Europe by the early 1990s.

If the Soviet defense budget should endure from 1989–91 the "moderate cuts" presently under way but nothing deeper, Soviet leaders would be unable to raise living standards meaningfully. The Soviet economy would, as in the "business as usual" case, suffer continued decline in the early 1990s, undermining all plans to relaunch radical perestroika. Unlike in the "business as usual" case, however, the Soviet national security sector would have made a substantial sacrifice, yet one that would not have resulted in the promised reversal of economic trends. Indeed, the "economic dimension of security vulnerability" would have widened. Such conditions would inspire a more activist opposition similar in constitution to those that toppled Malenkov and Khrushchev, one that might seek to restore losses suffered by the national defense sector as a result of the defense spending retrenchment.

Although a conservative-military opposition may be subjectively inclined to promote a surge in the national defense sector, any such move would be constrained by objective conditions far different from those that confronted Soviet leaders from 1959–63 and 1966–75. Domestic resource constraints in the 1990s will be immeasurably greater and the U.S. threat significantly smaller (no longer being one of strategic superiority and operating under resource constraints of its own) than in earlier periods when Moscow decided to "race against time."

Hence, whatever defense spending surge might result from the ascendance of a conservative-military coalition in the mid-1990s would be weak and of limited durability when measured against the three post-World War II periods of accelerated Soviet defense spending (1951–54, 1959–63, 1966–75). No matter how small, such an effort would accelerate the pace of economic decline and drive down living standards, igniting a disintegration of the social peace. The collapse of discipline would prompt a central government response. As in the "business as usual" case, any effort to restore order would carry with it a rise in the influence of those forces most sensitive to security interests—the military and the police—and by the middle of the 1990s they might find support for a restoration of order in a radicalized nationalist reaction among the Russian population rather than simply a revival of the Stalinist wing of the Communist party. Already, symptoms of such a popular movement are in evidence among Russian nationals living in rebellious non-Russian republics.[92]

At the beginning of 1989 it was conceivable that "moderate cuts" in Soviet defense spending could be translated into enlarged consumer goods output sufficient to prevent a social explosion in the early 1990s. "Business as usual," on the other hand, would have made it impossible for Moscow to avoid an East European fate. But the deterioration in the Soviet economy intensified during 1989 and a breakdown in the social peace was only averted by promises of immediate improvements in living standards which later failed to materialize, while within the CMEA-six rebellions against Communist party rule struck. Together, these developments have served to compress the Soviet Union's future. The "long-term" future for the "moderate cuts" course by which time it would lead to social catastrophe is no longer the mid-1990s, but tomorrow, the same time frame as for the "business as usual" approach.

Just as for "business as usual," a "moderate cuts" mode, if sustained, would translate into the demise of Gorbachev's program of radical perestroika, eliminating all prospects for a durable reversal in Soviet economic trends in the long term. It would also mean continued economic descent in the short term, which threatens East European-style social disorder and perhaps an East European fate for the Soviet Union. Central to any policy capable of avoiding these results—of creating a foundation for the reintroduction of radical perestroika in the long term and avoiding a catastrophic collapse of the social peace in the short term—would be "deep cuts" in the national defense sector. Following such a path, although a necessary condition for the success of the regime's interim economic program, may not be sufficient. The 1989 decision by the People's Congress to thwart privatization in the agricultural sector will under any circumstances make Moscow's effort to quickly raise living standards extremely difficult.

If a "deep cuts" approach should succeed in neutralizing the downward movement of the economic long cycle in the early 1990s, the long-term Soviet threat future will be shaped by whether Moscow succeeds in the implementation of radical perestroika. If successful, it will have forged the conditions for a reversal in the trajectory of economic trends, creating the foundation for a new long cycle that would commence with an ascent phase, at the same time eliminating the Soviet "economic dimension of security vulnerability." If the leadership should fail in this endeavor, the Soviet economy would resume its long-term decline after a brief respite and the "economic dimension" would once again widen. In this context it is noteworthy that whereas socialist regimes have managed to effect the transitional program that the Soviet leadership has defined for itself in the short term—the Soviet NEP, the Hungarian NEM, and the Chinese Readjustment—none has succeeded in managing a radical perestroika of the urban/industrial sector.

Failure to implement radical perestroika and the subsequent resumption of economic decline would be unlikely to spur enough political pressure to win an acceleration in national defense spending in this "deep cuts" scenario. Unlike conditions associated with the "moderate cuts" approach, the inability to accomplish radical perestroika would have come after a period in which the Gorbachev interim economic program raised living standards for important segments of the Soviet population. A successful interim policy would create new interest groups, including a remoralized workforce, local governments (especially those of the non-Russian republics) with enhanced economic power, and urban sector entrepreneurs whose interests are better served by constrained national defense budgets. The devolution of economic and political power to these forces, especially to the republics, would profoundly alter Moscow's capacity to command resources for national defense and would supply the reform leadership with a committed political base with which to withstand counterreform pressure.

The greatly diminished Soviet long-term threat that would come from the combined effect of a successful interim economic program and failed radical perestroika could also result from successful urban/industrial reform. Such a development would mean the coalescing of new interest groups hostile to rising national security costs—a process that could foster an enduring transformation in Soviet core values. If such a transformation should not transpire, however, Moscow would be in a position to surge in its national defense program in the early twenty-first century, free of the dilemma posed by the "economic dimension." Unlike conditions set off by continuation of recent historical rates of growth or an acceleration in national defense spending in the first half of the 1990s, a surge in defense spending following successful radical perestroika would be sustainable. The prospects for such a surge, however, would depend on the ascendance of a major external threat since a Soviet regime fresh from economic success would be unlikely to shift resources back to national defense without provocation, and the prospects for the emergence of a heightened transcentury military threat to the Soviet Union from the United States, China, or Western Europe (i.e., a unified Germany) are limited by economic realities and by the decline of the Soviet threat perceived by these nations over the 1990s implied in a "deep cuts" scenario.

Implications for Force Structure and Doctrine

The range of prospective Soviet defense spending levels implied in the three short-term defense spending approaches available to Soviet leaders at the beginning of 1989 was so great that it pointed to widely varying possibilities for the size of Soviet defense forces by the year 1995 (see Fig. 3.6). The course followed from this array of defense expenditure futures would have profound influence on Soviet force structure and doctrine into the long term. At stake in the early 1990s is whether the imbalance that has undergirded the superpower military competition since the onset of the Korean War—Soviet preponderance in the Euro-theater—will or can be sustained.

Business as usual. The ascendance of "business as usual" defense spending levels in the first half of the 1990s would have meant little real change in either Soviet force structure or doctrine. Although there would have been considerable rhetorical emphasis on the new doctrine of "nonoffensive defense," reality would have presented a Soviet force structure in the Euro-theatre that would have done little to reduce the threat perceived by the Western military planner, as no meaningful cuts would have occurred in the ground and air elements of the Soviet armed forces beyond those announced by Gorbachev in December 1988.

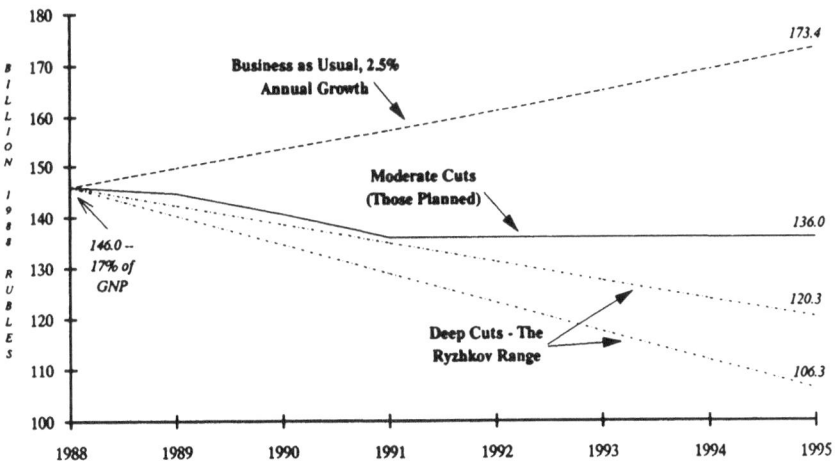

Figure 3.6. Range of Soviet defense spending in the short term, 1989–95

Consistent with "business as usual" spending levels, most major contemporary weapons programs would have continued to be developed and procured on a rigorous schedule. Such a development would have reflected the biases of the military cadres who oversaw the post-Khrushchev maturation of the Soviet military machine.

Even if the Soviet defense establishment were able to retain for itself much of the savings won through the unilateral cuts and the evacuation of the Soviet military from Afghanistan and thereby sustain recent rates of defense spending growth, its ability to prosecute a strong contemporary weapons defense investment strategy would be challenged by an increasingly steep rise in the unit costs of defense machinery. The cost and difficulty of maintaining a vigorous modernization effort across the spectrum of weapons systems have become more apparent with the heightened scrutiny given military industries under glasnost. This has led to public acknowledgment of significant delays associated with development problems in a number of high technology contemporary weapons programs. Further, there is evidence that the Soviet defense industry has found the transition from R&D prototype to reliable mass production extremely difficult—not surprising since the contemporary generation of advanced weapons relies on mastery of complex computer hardware and software, precisely the area of deficiency throughout the entire Soviet economy.[93]

The natural rise in the unit costs of defense machinery exacerbated by technological difficulties ensures that to maintain effective modernization efforts in the Euro-theatre and strategic realms even at the high end of plausible short-term Soviet military spending levels, sacrifices in other components of force structure would be necessary. Given these pressures it is possible that some unilateral cuts could occur in the Soviet navy and Air Defense Forces (PVO).

Even in a "business as usual" environment, the Soviet navy would be uniquely vulnerable. Given the Eurasian theatre ground/air bias of the Soviet high command, the navy is a plausible victim during any internal "budget wars." Further, there seems to have arisen a broad consensus within the Soviet political-military establishment that much of the global surge during the Brezhnev era carried too high a price tag, and with Admiral Sergei Gorshkov's death, the navy lost its most successful doctrinal and fiscal advocate. Under Gorshkov's successor, Admiral Vladimir N. Chernavin, a submariner, the Soviet navy has refocused its efforts on satisfying the basic mission of "homeland defense," an approach that has led to concentration on building a smaller number of high technology warships while reducing the force structure of the older fleet.[94] Most striking has been the cutback in conventionally powered submarines over the course of the 1980s. The process of structural surgery on the Soviet navy would be likely to continue even under the most favorable budgetary conditions.[95]

Nearly as vulnerable as the navy in this scenario would be the PVO with its vast array of obsolete radars and surface-to-air missile sites. Even under hospitable budgetary circumstances, the PVO would be under pressure to move to a smaller and higher technology force. This suggests that a number of radars, surface-to-air missile sites, and manned interceptor squadrons would not be replaced.[96]

Consistent with the philosophy of a status quo Soviet defense investment strategy, the effort to modernize contemporary forces would not be compromised to support a massive program to construct a mobilization base for transcentury weapons. Nevertheless, sufficient resources would still be available at "business as usual" levels of spending to permit a transcentury weapons program large enough to remain competitive with the United States.

Moderate cuts. If Soviet defense spending should contract over the 1989–91 period and persist at this lower 1991 level through the 1991–95 FYP as indicated in the "moderate cuts" alternative future, the defense investment strategy identified with the "business as usual" approach would become unfeasible as resource stress within the military sector would force a reduction in the overall size of Soviet armed forces.

It appears that Gorbachev won significant support within the ranks of the professional military for the "moderate cuts" option over the course of 1987–88. The acquiescence of important segments of the defense establishment, especially among the new generation of military technocrats, to retrenchment implies the emergence of an approach to force structure and related defense investment strategy different from that promoted by those who managed the modernization of Soviet defense in the Brezhnev era. Many among the new generation of the Soviet high command may in fact be prepared to subject force structure to a severe restructuring. Although holding to the cardinal objective of their predecessors—Soviet preponderance in the Euro-theatre—the new generation of defense planners may be prepared to cut down the existing force structure in the Euro-theatre in order to replace it with one able to compete more effectively in a transcentury military environment.[97]

Central to such an effort would be a successful conclusion of the START negotiations as well as a CFE agreement leading to moderate reductions in NATO and Warsaw Pact forces. Through START, Moscow would seek to moderate the pace of nuclear force modernization while undermining any residual support in the United States for deployment of SDI technologies. From the perspective of the Soviet leadership, a CFE agreement that allows for a substantial U.S. and Soviet presence in central Europe would be attractive. The Soviet military would be able to preserve some forward presence in the key military states of the northern tier—Poland, East Germany, and Czechoslovakia—a condition critical to the maintenance of a viable command relationship with East European armies now under pressure to come under greater national control. Further, a CFE agreement of modest dimensions would provide domestic and international cover for a restructuring of the Soviet armed forces.

Although the operative public strategy under such circumstances would be "nonoffensive defense," the aim of the military reduction would be to facilitate the evolution of a "leaner and meaner" Soviet force posture. To effect such a defense investment strategy, Soviet defense planners would first accelerate some of the trends that would also be evident in the "business as usual" strategy. Both the Soviet navy and PVO would undergo radical surgery, while the production of high technology contemporary weapons would be cut back moderately. The most severe cuts would fall on the production of contemporary armored fighting vehicles, especially the main battle tank, and this would be consistent with the public diplomacy of "nonoffensive defense" as well as with a doctrinal shift within the Soviet armed forces away from quantity to quality.[98]

It is worth noting that the new generation of Soviet military leaders may feel quite comfortable with the end of the operational supremacy of the main battle tank in land warfare. Ironically, a CFE agreement could facilitate a transformation in the nature of combined arms warfare not unlike the result of the Washington Naval Agreement of 1922 for naval warfare. That agreement led to the destruction or conversion of large numbers of battleships, the supreme "offensive" naval platform of that era. Not fully understood by the participants in that arms control and disarmament treaty was the role that it played in encouraging major navies to move to a new generation of naval technology—the aircraft carrier and the long-range submarine.[99]

A similar process could unfold during the 1990s if the Soviet military takes advantage of the pause in the competition in contemporary weapons to restructure its armed forces with the aim of developing technologies to enable it to intervene rapidly in central Europe. A successful restructuring would require significant investment in construction of a transcentury weapons mobilization base as well as continued heavy investment in a select group of contemporary weapons. While the funding status of the main battle tank would be downgraded, classes of weapons associated with the "third revolution" in warfare would be favored, requiring hefty investments in advanced reconnaissance, surveillance, and target acquisition (RSTA) platforms and their associated precision guided munitions (PGM) systems.[100] The objective of this restructuring in turn points to a Soviet interest in assuring that a moderate-size military presence remain in Eastern Europe after a CFE agreement and that a strong command, control, communications, and intelligence (C^3I) infrastructure be maintained there to allow for a rapid return of Soviet ground and air combat units. One of the Soviet worries about a reduced military presence in Eastern Europe is the encouragement it would provide for neutralization. Currently the Soviet military relies heavily on the tight integration of the command structure of its forces with the national armies of the northern-tier countries of the region both to meet a hypothetical conflict with NATO and to ensure political loyalty.[101] One of the prices Moscow would have to pay for a CFE agreement is greater maneuvering room for the armies of its allies to move back under national control—a development whose prospects have risen sharply with the recent collapse of Communist political power in Eastern Europe. (Of course, a CFE agreement would also reduce the U.S. military presence in Europe and especially in West Germany).

It has become increasingly apparent to many in the Soviet military leadership, especially among the new generation in the wake of their combat experience in Afghanistan, that the nineteenth century style mass mobilization army based on conscription has become unwieldy and inefficient, and that contemporary and future warfare requires highly trained and motivated personnel. The transition of Soviet force structure in the Euro-theatre contemplated by those promoting a restructuring would demand better trained and educated personnel but would also require fewer of them as the magnitude of standing forces would be sharply reduced.[102] The smaller force would permit higher unit outlays for personnel while also easing demographic stress on the quality of troops by ensuring that high technology and quality combat units could remain predominantly Slavic if not Great Russian.

Deep cuts. Were such a "moderate cuts" defense investment strategy to be followed in the first half of the 1990s and were the Soviet economy to be revitalized, Moscow would be in a position to exploit a transcentury weapons revolution at the beginning of the next century. The problem, however, is that for the Soviet economy to have even a chance to escape its long-term decline, the defense sector would have to incur a reduction in funding far greater than that contemplated in the "moderate cuts" alternative. Indeed, the military implications of deep cuts on the scale proposed by Ryzhkov are profound. In essence, the Gorbachev regime will have embarked, if such cuts are enacted, upon a road analogous to that on which China's Deng Xiaoping set forth at the beginning of 1980—a road along which military modernization becomes clearly subordinated to economic renovation.

Central to a "deep cuts" Soviet defense spending future would be the successful negotiation of a CFE agreement leading to a radical reduction in NATO and Warsaw Pact force structures. These deep reductions would allow for only a U.S. and Soviet residual "token covering force." In acceding to a mammoth drawdown of Soviet armies from Eastern Europe, Moscow would have to accept the prospect of intensified pressure for East European neutralization, including the reunification of Germany. And in the wake of the recent political shocks within Eastern Europe, the Soviet high command would face a drastic change in the Warsaw Pact as a result of a radical CFE agreement. As East European armies move under greater national control, Soviet forces, having departed en masse, would have no hope of return in the absence of a new world war. At maximum, Soviet leaders might hope that Eastern Europe would maintain a military relationship with the Soviet Union not unlike Finland's (i.e., strict neutrality). But Moscow might be forced to accept the adoption of the Swedish/Austrian model involving increasing security ties between Eastern Europe and the countries of the European Community.

In this defense spending alternative future, the Soviet high command would be confronted with the near impossible task of designing a force structure and a defense strategy within the Ryzhkov funding constraints. For the Euro- and East Asian theatres, ground forces would have to be radically restructured, and recent evidence suggests that if such a restructuring were to evolve, the smaller Soviet ground forces would be organized into brigade and corps elements, optimized for defensive operations in selected regions such as the Sino-Soviet and Transcaucasus borders.[103] In such circumstances it would be likely that a much smaller force having less mechanized and armored maneuver elements than do contemporary forces would be maintained as a central strategic reserve. Given the prospects for domestic strife within the USSR, the Soviet leadership may welcome an elite air transportable force capable of reinforcing the Ministry of the Interior's troops.[104]

The PVO would be likely to suffer a dramatic retrenchment while tactical aviation would be cut in half. The Soviet navy would be savaged in this scenario, and in the most extreme case its mission could be reduced to a continental defense. Given the increased threat of space-based RSTA and long-range strike systems to surface warships, Soviet defense planners may conclude that further large-scale investment in a smaller fleet of expensive high technology surface ships represents a cost/benefit dead-end. Radical solutions in which the bulk of naval investment is focused on further improvements in submarines, long-range aviation, and space-based C^3I at the expense of the next generation of surface ships are conceivable in the context of this "deep cuts" strategy.[105]

Even in the context of "deep cuts" in military expenditures the Soviet leadership is unlikely to allow investment in transcentury weapons research and development to atrophy. After all, one of the promises of successful economic reform is that revived economic performance will make the Soviet Union competitive in all spheres with the industrial democracies. But unlike in the "moderate cuts" alternative future, transcentury weapons investment would be consciously skewed to dual-purpose civilian-military technologies, suggesting heavy investment in information processing, telecommunications, advanced materials, robotics, and biotechnology, as well as the continued channeling of sizable resources for the Soviet space program and civilian aerospace sectors.

Central to the "deep cuts" strategy is the belief that near-term threats can be successfully managed by political-diplomatic action and that by the beginning of the next century Moscow will have managed an economic transformation enabling it to respond to the long-term threats that may have matured.

Chapter 4

Economic Constraints on U.S. National Security Spending
Reasons and Responses

The descent of the Soviet economy and the dangerous expansion of Moscow's "economic dimension of security vulnerability" during the last three decades have culminated in pressure for a reduction in Soviet defense spending over the transcentury period. Furthermore, of all the plausible Soviet threat futures, in only one could Moscow enjoy a vigorous and durable national defense expansion, and the prospects for this future seem remote. First, the Soviet Union would have to succeed in the implementation of its interim economic program, then follow that with successful radical perestroika, and finally over this decade-long process undergo no transformation in its core values.

By the end of the 1980s, the momentum of the Soviet economic decline and its implications for Soviet security had already become so stark that they produced a perception of a decisive advantage if not victory for the United States and its allies in the Cold War. This perception was so blinding that it threatened to hide the fact that its source lay not in American strength but in Soviet weakness. The United States, too, had experienced nearly three decades of declining economic performance and a widening "economic dimension of security vulnerability," and it was only because its economy was larger and the descent slower and less precipitous than that of the USSR that by the end of the 1980s its enjoyed a sense of greatly improved security.

But in the 1990s, the United States will also confront an enlarged "economic dimension" and unusual pressure on its national security expenditures. In the absense of a process of economic adjustment involving the entire free world economy, the United States will enter the twenty-first century in no position to refurbish its depleted national security accounts, while facing growing intra-free world economic threats. Further, the Soviet threat, although likely to weaken in the 1990s, may recede at varying paces and to different degrees while also being subject to the possibility of a transitory upsurge.

In the 1990s the U.S. economy will labor under resource stress as it endures a process of adjustment, and the strategy for economic adjustment adopted in the next decade will determine whether and at what pace this resource stress will be relieved. Recognition of the imminent descent of the U.S. economy into a lower GNP growth rate regime has been stifled by the dulling effects of the economic recovery that commenced in 1983. While few observers would declare total victory for the Reagan administration's supply-side program in reversing the deterioration in U.S. economic performance that took place in successive free world economy business cycles since the 1959–67 cycle (through the cycles of 1968–75 and 1976–82), the relatively low U.S. inflation and moderate GNP growth rates enjoyed in the current (1983–??) business cycle have left many with a sense that the decline in U.S. economic health has come to an end.[1] This conclusion seems all the more reasonable since it was during the 1980s that the U.S. economy assumed the burden of a radical expansion in national security expenditures without ill effect in inflation or on economic growth. By the end of the 1980s, as Gorbachev's prescription for Soviet economic ills faltered and Moscow suffered a widening "economic dimension of security vulnerability," Reagan's economic policies appeared to produce some success, perhaps enough to win a minimal line of security for the United States in the 1990s.

Such a judgment suffers, however, from historical myopia. Reagan's measures have, like Gorbachev's, produced economic imbalances that will work to weaken economic growth in the future. Both the Gorbachev and Reagan initiatives resulted in large expansions in central government budget deficits. Paralleling the consequences of leaps in the U.S. government fiscal deficit in the 1960s and 1970s, the rise in the Soviet budget deficit in the second half of the 1980s inspired an intolerable acceleration in inflationary pressures. However, in the 1980s the unusual advance in the U.S. government budget deficit produced no inflationary upsurge.

The U.S. economy's ability to experience large government fiscal deficits without debilitating inflation in the 1980s sprang from two sources. Unlike the Soviets, U.S. economic performance is not forced by an autarkic trade and payments policy into reliance on its domestic factors of production. With an open trade and payments approach, the United States enjoys a free flow of factor inputs across its borders and is therefore inalterably integrated into a larger free world economy that includes the remainder of the developed sector and the non-CMEA developing economies. In the 1980s this permitted the inflationary consequences of the Reagan budget deficits to be exported to the rest of the free world economy through the aegis of unprecedented U.S. trade deficits.

The U.S. economic recovery that began in 1983 was prompted by a massive expansion in the government budget deficit in two successive fiscal years, 1982 and 1983.[2] The government deficit in turn stimulated a powerful rise in U.S. domestic demand.[3] If met by only the stock of domestic factor inputs, this enlarged domestic demand would have triggered a swift jump in inflation as the supply status of factor inputs would have quickly transitioned to relative scarcity. The United States only avoided a recovery-killing inflation by exporting it abroad as U.S. net import surpluses were large enough, once combined with domestic resources, to dash what otherwise would have been a steep increase in inflationary pressures.

The ability of the United States to enjoy 1970s levels of economic growth in the 1980s without inflationary consequences required a second development in addition to enlarged trade deficits: a contraction in the free world economy GDP (gross domestic product) growth rate.[4] If the free world economy in aggregate had sustained its 1970s rate of growth into the 1980s, global inflationary forces would have been produced that would have undermined the U.S. economic recovery in its early stages. Hence, the level of economic growth experienced by the United States in the 1983–?? business cycle required a large drop in the domestic demand growth rate of the rest of the free world—a drop of sufficient dimension to more than offset the rise in that sector's net export surplus with the United States and drag the GDP growth rate of the entire free world economy down.

The peculiar evolution of the U.S. economy during the current business cycle points to the forces that will constrain it in the 1990s. Its deviation from the GDP growth rate pattern of the free world economy as a whole was purchased at the price of enlarged domestic and external deficits, deficits that will function to depress its growth rate in the future.

Because of its failed effort to escape from the bounds of the free world economy's long-term trend line in the 1980s, the U.S. economy faces a business cycle of adjustment that will consume most of the 1990s and one that will be driven by the need to reduce government fiscal and trade deficits. The result: U.S. domestic demand will be under pressure to decelerate and, as a consequence, the U.S. "economic dimension of security vulnerability," whose existence was blurred during much of the 1980s, will come back into focus.

Exploration of the causes of the decline in U.S. economic performance, the policy measures that have evolved in the past to try to reverse this trend, and the biases expressed by the American political establishment in reacting to the "economic dimension" will provide insight not only into what U.S. policy responses to a renewed economic slowdown and a widening "economic dimension" are likely to be in the coming decade, but also what they should be, especially when viewed in the context of the range of plausible short- and long-term Soviet threat futures.

WHY THE U.S. ECONOMY HAS FALTERED

Like the economic growth rate trend line of the Soviet and East European economies, that of the post–World War II free world economy describes a long cycle. After ascending to a peak in the 1959–67 business cycle, the free world economy GDP growth rate has descended in each successive business cycle (see Fig. 4.1). Further, the cause of this retreat in economic performance beginning in the 1968–75 cycle is the same as that which triggered the decline of the European centrally planned economies (CPEs)—a rise in the cost of the factors of production. U.S. economic performance, like all component parts of the free world economy, has been subject to the same forces—rising factor input costs—and has itself experienced a prolonged deterioration. But absent the excesses of the Stalinist system and with an array of intensive mode incentives, the free world and U.S. economies have consumed factor inputs at a less rapacious pace and have engineered more vigorous supply-side adjustment than the European CPE and Soviet economies, and have therefore suffered a milder descent in economic performance.

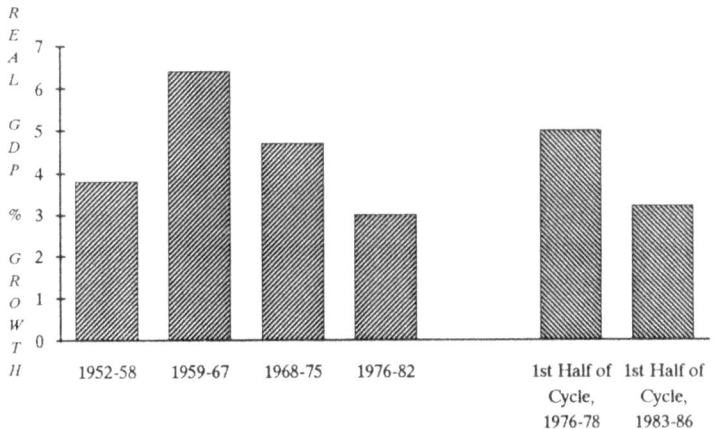

Figure 4.1. Long cycle in postwar free world economy—average annual GDP growth rate. *Source:* General Agreement on Tariffs and Trade, *International Trade, 1985/86* (Geneva: GATT, 1987) (for 1952–85 GDP); General Agreement on Tariffs and Trade, *International Trade, 1988* (Geneva: GATT, 1989) (for 1986 GDP).

The Intercyclical Decline of the Free World Economy

The degree of supply-side adjustment in the free world economy was not enough to prevent the tightening of factor input markets starting in the 1959–67 business cycle, and all of the segments of the free world economy including the United States have had to function within this environment. During the 1959–67 cycle, primary factor input costs—primary commodities and labor—began to accelerate, a development that escalated in the two subsequent cycles. In the first half of the 1960s, the overcapacity in nonfood primary commodity production borne of the high rate of extractive sector investment that had followed the early Korean War speculative price surge began to be breached.[5] From 1968–81, primary commodity prices rose at an extraordinary pace, experiencing moderate increases in the years 1968–70 and 1976–77 and explosive advances in 1972–74 and 1979–81 (see Fig. 4.2). While the price rise was prompted and sustained by tight primary commodity markets, a series of special circumstances, led by political-military instability in the Middle East/Persian Gulf and the assertion of power by the Organization of Petroleum Exporting Countries (OPEC) as well as by periodic food deficits centered in the USSR, incited aggravated increases in petroleum and food prices.[6]

At the same point at which primary commodity markets began to tighten, the economies of the developed sector approached full employment. With the dawning of the 1968–75 business cycle the costs of labor in the free world economy began to accelerate, driven by tight labor markets in the developed world. From the breakdown of Western Europe's labor discipline in the 1968–69 strike wave and the consequent wage explosion of 1969, developed sector nominal wages surged throughout the 1970s, and did so despite a rise in unemployment during the 1976–82 business cycle (see Fig. 4.3).[7] Indirect labor costs also boomed. Starting with an expansion of U.S. income insurance programs with the advent of the Johnson administration's Great Society and an even more vigorous enhancement of government transfer payment programs in Western Europe at the close of the 1960s, this component of developed sector government outlays grew at a startling pace as a percentage of both government outlays and GNP in the 1970s.[8]

The leap in primary input costs confronted the governments of the free world with an increasingly daunting inflation/output dilemma. If accommodated, rising primary input costs would produce higher inflation; if contested, lower output growth. From the 1959–67 to the 1968–75 business cycle, the principal elements of free world economic policy—developed sector macroeconomic (i.e., fiscal and monetary) and international payments policies—became more permissive in response to the jump in primary input costs. One result was that overindebtedness in developed sector government fiscal and developing sector capital importers' current account balances com-

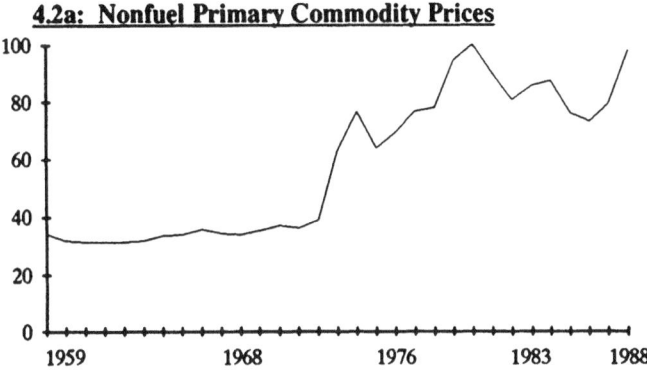

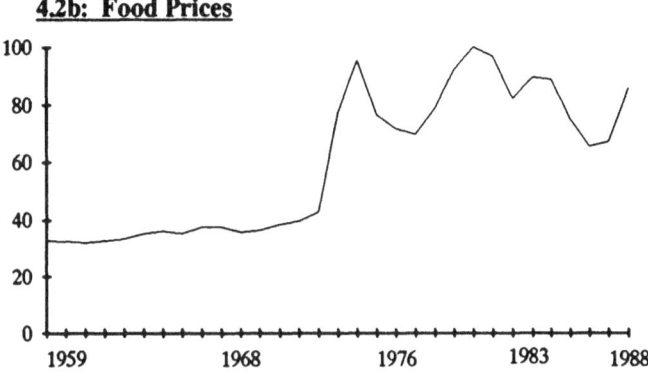

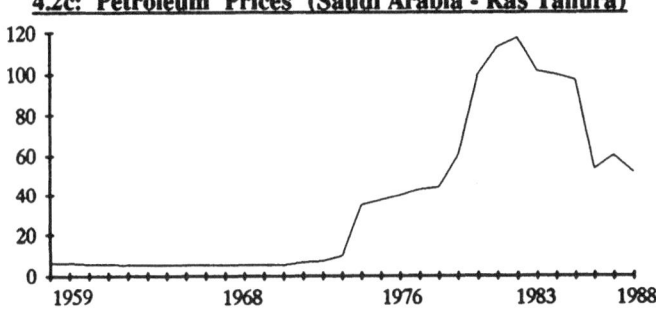

Figure 4.2. Primary commodity price movements, 1958–1988 (index: 1980 = 100). *Source:* International Monetary Fund, *International Financial Statistics, Supplement on Trade Statistics* (Washington, DC: IMF, 1988) (for 1958–85 nonfuel and food prices, and 1958–85 petroleum prices, Saudi-Ras Tanura); *OECD Economic Outlook, June 1989* (Paris: OECD 1989) (for 1986–88 petroleum prices, spot market); International Monetary Fund, *International Financial Statistics, July 1989* (Washington, DC: IMF, 1989) (for 1986–88 nonfuel and food prices).

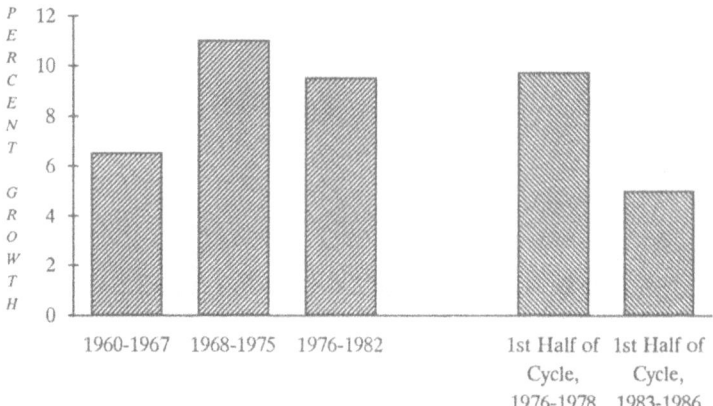

Figure 4.3. Intercyclical changes in hourly wage growth rates in manufacturing for G-7 economies. *Source: OECD Economic Outlook: Historical Statistics, 1960–87* (Paris: OECD, 1989) (for 1968–75, 1976–82, and 1983–86); authors' estimate (for 1960–67). Note: G-7 nations include U.S., Japan, West Germany, the U.K., France, Italy, and Canada.

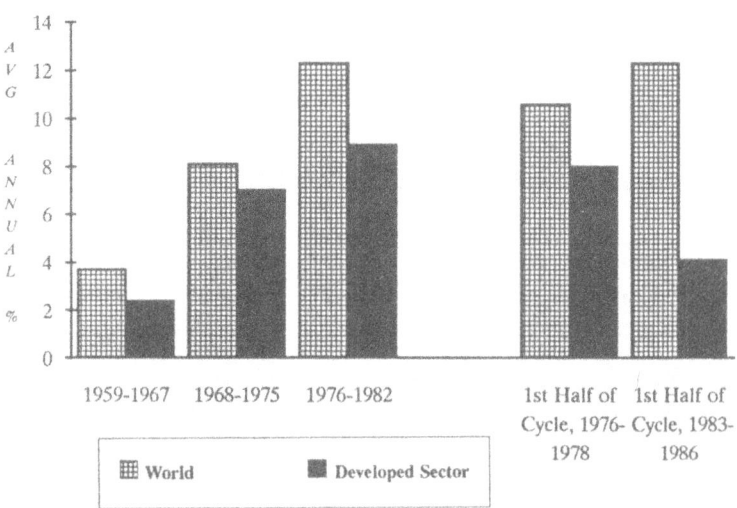

Figure 4.4. Intercyclical changes in consumer inflation rate in world and developed sector. *Source:* International Monetary Fund, *International Financial Statistics Yearbook, 1986* (Washington, DC: IMF, 1986) and *International Financial Statistics, November 1988* (Washington, DC: IMF, 1988).

menced. In both instances, the ratio of deficits to GNP rose visibly from the 1959-67 cycle to the 1968-75 cycle.[9] This, in turn, brought a hefty rise in inflation (see Fig. 4.4).

During the 1976-82 business cycle economic policy became ever more concerned with inflation and overindebtedness. Indeed, by 1980-82 developed sector domestic monetary policy turned decisively constrictive, many large developed economy governments pledged to eliminate their fiscal overindebtedness, and developing sector capital importers were all but shut off from private financing for their current account deficits.[10] As a result, although inflation and sectoral overindebtedness continued to grow during the 1976-82 business cycle, they accelerated at a slower pace than in the 1968-75 cycle, and the free world economy output growth rate therefore slowed, producing a period of stagflation.

The expansion in free world economy financial deficits from 1968-82 served to increase the cost of the third factor of production—capital. The stock of free world savings was drained from investment to finance these deficits while inflation dragged interest rates upward (see Table 4.1). The rise in the cost of capital prompted a decline in the investment growth rate over the course of successive business cycles, which in turn weakened the already slackening process of supply-side adjustment.

By the early 1960s, even before the decline in the investment growth rate, two forces that had enhanced the pace of supply-side adjustment in the 1950s were losing strength. After World War II, the technological advances won through research, development, and engineering activities associated with the war effort, once converted to civilian purposes, produced a productivity shockwave. By the 1960s, the saturation of these technologies combined with a slower pace of advance in contemporary civilian technologies to weaken

Table 4.1
Intercycle Rise in Capital Costs and the Decline in the G-7 Real Gross Fixed Capital Formation Growth Rate (Annual Averages)

	1960-67	1968-75	1976-82	1976-78	1983-86
Interest Rates (U.S. Prime Rate, % Growth)	4.7	7.5	12.1	7.6	10.3
G-7 Real Gross Fixed Capital Formation (% Growth)	6.2	2.9	2.1	5.8	5.1

Source: Executive Office of the President, *Economic Report of the President, 1989* (Washington, DC: U.S. Government Printing Office, 1989) (for U.S. prime rate); *OECD Economic Outlook: Historical Statistics, 1960-87* (Paris: OECD, 1989) (for real gross fixed capital formation).

the technological increment to economic growth. In addition to declining capital productivity growth rates, labor productivity improvement was slowed by a steep decline in developed sector labor mobility. Throughout the decade of the 1950s, high rates of developed sector rural-urban migration and south-north and east-west labor flows within Europe had stimulated hefty advances in labor productivity borne of a rapid upgrade in workforce skill levels.[11] By the 1960s, these flows fell precipitously.

From 1968–82, the slowdown in the free world economy investment growth rate ensured that all prospects for more vigorous supply-side adjustment and avoidance of the downward slope of the long cycle would be unachievable. Further, the free world economy experienced a mild version of economic primitivization as the investment growth rate in the primary commodity sector surpassed that for manufacturing. This phenomenon was reflected within the developed economies where the share of investment in mining and real estate rose relative to manufacturing in both the 1968–75 and 1976–82 business cycles, a pattern that represented a reversal from the earlier postwar period.[12] Primitivization also showed up in the shift in the comparative growth rates of investment in the developed and developing sectors.[13] The latter, with its greater concentration in primary commodities, experienced faster investment growth in the 1968–82 period compared to the 1959–67 business cycle, whereas the latter, with its greater concentration in manufactured goods, saw its investment growth rate slip.

The turn toward a more contractionary macroeconomic and international payments policy at the end of the 1976–82 business cycle was sustained in the current cycle as aggregate developed sector monetary policy remained constrictive, reflected in the persistence of high interest rates. Leading non-U.S. developed economies have successfully slowed and in some cases reversed the earlier pattern of rising government deficit to GNP ratios, and North-South capital flows, which rose with such force in the preceding two business cycles, have slowed to a trickle, forcing a contraction in the current account deficits of developing sector capital importers.[14] The reduction in overindebtedness in the free world economy caused a slowdown in domestic demand and, as a result, in GDP growth; this, in turn, relieved pressure on primary input markets. During the current business cycle, primary commodity prices have fallen and the growth in labor costs has weakened sufficiently to trigger disinflation in the developed sector.

Advances in the pace of supply-side adjustment have in the 1983–?? business cycle been impaired by continued high capital costs, which have contributed to a further retreat in the free world economy investment growth rate.[15] Although difficult to measure, it is virtually certain that the drop in the investment growth rate has prohibited any improvement in the pace at which superior technologies have been invested and at which attendant workforce skills have been upgraded.

Sectoral and National Differences: The U.S. Performance Distinguished

While the United States and other nations comprising the free world economy all confronted the rising cost of factor inputs in the 1960s and 1970s, and while national economic performances have all deteriorated over the course of successive free world business cycles with only periodic deviation, the relative performances of individual nations and sectors have differed. These national and sectoral performance differentials have been prompted by variances in the degree of exposure to fluctuations in primary input costs and to differing national economic policy biases that have arisen in response both to degree of national vulnerability to movements in primary input costs and to national economic traumas caused by the product of rising primary input costs—higher inflation or lower output growth.

Differences in the commodity composition of trade within the free world economy have produced different degrees of vulnerability to primary commodity price fluctuations, while differences in the cost of domestic social peace have yielded different degrees of vulnerability to pressure on labor costs. In turn, variations in sensitivity to primary commodity price fluctuations have induced trade and development policies that differentiate those nations, both exporters and importers, whose commodity composition of trade exposes them more to such fluctuations, while differences in domestic social peace costs have resulted in variances in national wages and government income insurance policies as well as in the pattern of distribution of personal consumption and savings, both of which have contributed to differentials in capital costs. Finally, differing national experiences with the most extreme results of rising primary input costs—hyperinflation or depression—have produced diverging macroeconomic policy dispositions toward the inflation/output dilemma.

The most extreme differentials in economic performance within the free world economy were sparked by the combined impact of rising primary commodity prices and sectoral differences in the commodity composition of trade. From the 1959–67 business cycle through the cycles of 1968–75 and 1976–82, both the external balances and the GDP growth rate of the developing sector improved at an unusual pace while those of the developed economies suffered.[16] Indeed, the terms of trade advantages gained by the developing sector were of such magnitude as to permit its GDP growth rate to delink from the long cycle decline of the free world economy in the 1968–75 cycle.[17]

Further, out of the search by developing economies for means to avoid a repetition of the harsh domestic consequences of the plunge in primary commodity prices during the Great Depression and prolonged soft prices in the aftermath of the Korean War emerged an effective primary commodity producer cartel—OPEC—which, in the tight primary commodity market conditions in the 1968–75 and 1976–82 business cycles, asserted its leverage to effect an unprecedented advance in the terms of trade of petroleum.[18] Accordingly, the external balances and GDP performance of developing sector oil exporters enjoyed remarkable improvement—a development that overwhelmed the positive impact of rising nonoil primary commodity prices for developing sector oil importers whose external balances faltered and whose GDP growth rate was only temporarily spared a sharp contraction as a result of greatly enlarged capital inflows.[19]

In the current business cycle, differences in the commodity composition of trade have combined with a decline in primary commodity prices, led by oil, to produce similar economic performance differentials within the free world economy. This time, developing sector terms of trade losses have been translated into a GDP growth rate that has decelerated more rapidly than that of the free world economy.[20] The pace of decline in this rate has been aggravated by a steep drop in capital inflow.[21]

While the most striking short-term disparities in economic performance within the free world have taken place between the developed and developing sectors and among developing economies, slower moving disparities in performance have emerged among developed economies. It is in contrast to other leading developed economies that the unique evolution of the U.S. economy is best seen.

With the rise of primary factor input costs, differentials in the economic performance of leading developed economies have been driven by two forces: variations in the pace of supply-side adjustment and in the pace of demand-side accommodation. The former have resulted from the combined impact of disparities in national development strategies prompted by unequal degrees of sensitivity to rising primary commodity prices and disparities in national labor costs fostered by differences in social peace costs. Variations in demand-side accommodation derive from differing predispositions toward the inflation/output dilemma triggered by reaction to earlier national economic shocks.

While all leading developed economies are net primary commodity importers, they are so to different degrees. The commodity composition of Japanese and West European imports differs from that of the United States and did so especially in the immediate post–World War II period, with the former economies not only more dependent on imports but on primary commodity imports in particular. Japanese and German sensitivity to primary commodity import exposure was exacerbated following the war by the loss of "special trade arrangements" that had provided each with access to cheap sources of primary commodities.[22] To shield their domestic economies from enhanced exposure to sudden and steep rises in primary commodity prices, the Japanese and West German governments were encouraged to foster rates of growth in private investment above those that market forces would have generated and to steer investment into manufacturing sectors with high export potential.[23]

Although the commodity composition of British and French imports was as concentrated in primary commodities as that of West Germany, the sensitivity of London and Paris to their exposure was dulled by the persistence into the postwar years of prewar "special trade arrangements" with developing sector primary commodity exporters in the sterling and franc zones, respectively.[24] As a result, each nation avoided supply-side initiatives to boost investment in its manufacturing sector.

The United States was driven toward a development strategy similar to that of Britain and France, but for different reasons. It emerged from World War II with a lower import to GNP ratio than other large developed economies, and because of immense wartime import substitution, that rate was lower than it had been when the country entered the war. In addition, because of the strength of domestic primary commodity production, the share of primary commodities in U.S. imports was smaller while its primary commodity exports, especially food, accounted for a significantly larger share of its total exports than was the case for Western Europe or Japan.[25] Over the course of the postwar years, periodic upsurges in world food prices temporarily helped boost U.S. economic performance and have consequently weakened the incentive for U.S. supply-side initiatives targeted at improving the competitiveness of manufactured exports.

The result: from 1948 to 1958, even prior to the rise in primary input costs, intra-developed sector differences in development strategy produced huge differentials in the pace of supply-side adjustment, and this generated West German and Japanese export and industrial production growth rates remarkably superior to those of the United States and the second-tier West European economies (i.e., the United Kingdom, France, and Italy).[26]

The rise in labor costs within the developed sector that commenced in the 1959–67 business cycle sparked a leap in the costs of capital, precipitating a slowdown in the pace of supply-side adjustment throughout the sector. But differences in the costs of social peace led to national differences in the pace at which labor and, hence, capital costs grew. Variances in the cost of capital worked to enhance Japan's advantages in supply-side adjustment as greater social cohesion and a less politically influential organized labor movement than in Western Europe or the United States served to restrain the pace at which wages and government transfer payments rose. In Western Europe even more than in the United States, higher degrees of class division than in Japan and politically powerful organized labor movements produced greater advances in wages and government transfer payments. In addition to the more vigorous transfer of resources to labor from capital in Western Europe and the United States compared to Japan, Tokyo's cost of capital advantages were heightened by large intra-developed sector divergences in the allocation of personal income. Western Europe and, especially, the United States suffered lower personal savings rates than Japan.[27]

More influential than the disparities in the pace of supply-side adjustment for the relative performances of leading developed economies were dissimilarities in macroeconomic policy. Both the United States and the United Kingdom exited World War II obsessed with avoiding a repetition of the economic disaster rendered by the Great Depression. The postwar economic culture of both nations focused on macroeconomic and, especially, fiscal means to counter the pressures for output contraction, building on the institutional reform inherited from the Depression and war years—the New Deal in the United States and the Beveridge System in the United Kingdom. The German economic psyche was scarred by Weimar and immediate post–World War II hyperinflation and, accordingly, developed a postwar economic culture whose anti-inflation macroeconomic policy bias ran counter to those of Britain and the United States.[28] Japan's postwar macroeconomic policy orientation evolved a schizophrenic character—concerned, on the one hand, with inflation, having experienced hyperinflation in the immediate postwar period while being highly exposed to rising primary commodity prices, but fixated, on the other, on producing high rates of GDP growth.

Within the developed sector, the discrepancy in supply- and demand-side economic policy approaches widened over the course of the last four business cycles in response to rising primary commodity and labor costs and an increasingly intense inflation/output dilemma to produce observable differentials in economic performance.

On the foundation of its superior supply-side adjustment, the Japanese economy has outperformed the other leading developed sector economies. Japan's supply-side adjustment advantage derived from the persistent execution of its development strategy and an ability to better pursue a high investment policy as a result of its relatively low capital costs.

Over the course of the last four business cycles the Japanese GDP growth rate decelerated yet remained visibly higher than those of other large developed economies and the developed sector average (see Table 4.2a). Japan's supply-side performance, symptomized by an investment growth rate that has remained higher than that of any other leading developed economy in each business cycle, has supported its GDP growth rate more so than has the degree of supply-side adjustment in any other large developed economy.

In addition to a superior GDP growth rate, Japanese external balances have improved in each successive business cycle to the point where over the current cycle Tokyo's merchandise trade and current account surpluses have been the largest in the developed world (see Table 4.2b). This, too, was sparked by energetic supply-side adjustment, as the improvement in external balances sprang primarily from dynamic export growth.

Table 4.2
Intra-Developed Sector Economic Performance Differentials over the Last Four Business Cycles

4.2a: GDP Growth Rate (% Growth, Annual Average)

	1959-67	1968-75	1976-82	1976-78	1983-86
Developed	5.1	3.9	2.6	4.4	3.3
U.S.	4.4	2.0	2.3	5.5	4.3
Japan	11.7	7.0	4.5	5.1	3.7
FRG	5.7	3.7	2.3	3.8	2.3
U.K.	3.3	2.3	1.2	2.9	3.1
France	5.4 } 5.0 Avg.	4.6 } 3.6 Avg.	2.7 } 2.2 Avg.	4.0 } 3.5 Avg.	1.5 } 2.4 Avg.
Italy	6.4	3.8	2.7	3.5	2.5

4.2b: Merchandise Trade Balance ($Billion, Annual Average)

	1959-67	1968-75	1976-82	1983-87
U.S.	4.5	-0.1	-27.4	-121.3
Japan	0.6	4.6	13.3	64.2
FRG	2.5	10.7	18.2	39.6
U.K.	-0.7	-3.7	-1.0	-8.0
France	N.A. } -0.6 Avg.	-0.3 } -1.8 Avg.	-4.8 } -3.8 Avg.	-6.2 } -5.4 Avg.
Italy	-0.4	-1.4	-5.5	-2.0

4.2c: Consumer Inflation (% Growth, Annual Average)

	1959-67	1968-75	1976-82	1976-78	1983-86
Developed	2.2	7.0	8.9	8.0	4.1
U.S.	1.6	6.2	8.8	6.6	3.3
Japan	4.7	9.6	5.7	7.0	1.7
FRG	2.3	4.7	4.5	3.6	1.9
U.K.	2.9	8.3	13.2	13.6	4.8
France	3.8 } 3.4 Avg.	7.6 } 8.4 Avg.	11.1 } 13.6 Avg.	9.4 } 12.8 Avg.	6.3 } 7.1 Avg.
Italy	3.6	8.3	16.6	15.3	10.2

Sources: (a) IMF, *International Financial Statistics Yearbook, 1986* (Washington, DC: IMF, 1986) and *International Financial Statistics Yearbook, 1988* (Washington, DC: IMF, 1988). (b) IMF, *International Financial Statistics Yearbook, 1986* (Washington, DC: IMF, 1986) and *International Financial Statistics, November 1988* (Washington, DC: IMF, 1988). (c) IMF, *International Financial Statistics Yearbook, 1986* (Washington, DC: IMF, 1986) and *International Financial Statistics, November 1988* (Washington, DC: IMF, 1988). (d) IMF, *International Financial Statistics Yearbook, 1986*, *International Financial Statistics, November 1987*, and *International Financial Statistics, November 1988* (Washington, DC: IMF, 1986, 1987, and 1988, respectively) (for 1959–82); *OECD Economic Outlook, June 1988* (Paris: OECD, 1988) (for 1983–86). Note: Although the 1959–67, 1968–75, and 1976–82 cycles are not directly comparable to the 1983–86 cycle as a result of different data bases, the patterns hold.

Table 4.2 (*Continued*)
Intra-Developed Sector Economic Performance Differentials over the Last Four Business Cycles

4.2d: Central Government Fiscal Deficit as Percent of GNP (Annual Avg. of %)

	1959-67	1968-75	1976-82	1976-78	1983-86
U.S.	-0.8	-1.5	-2.9	-3.1	-4.9
Japan	-0.8	-1.8	-4.3	-4.9	-3.9
FRG	-0.7	-0.2	-2.8	-3.4	-1.4
U.K.	-1.1	-2.1	-4.3	-3.6	-2.6
France	-1.2 -1.6	-0.5 -3.5	-1.6 -6.2	-1.2 -5.7	-3.2 -6.0
Italy	-2.5 Avg.	-7.8 Avg.	-12.6 Avg.	-12.3 Avg.	-12.2 Avg.

Further, whereas Japan's inflation remained relatively high in the 1960s and early 1970s, its constrictive macroeconomic policy response to the first primary commodity price and inflation explosion, hitting at the end of the 1968–75 business cycle, allowed its inflation rate to stay below the developed sector average during the 1976–82 and 1983–?? cycles (see Table 4.2c).[29] Japan's turn in macroeconomic policy intensified in response to the second surge in primary commodity prices and inflation at the end of the 1976–82 cycle as Tokyo pledged—and later fulfilled its promise—to reduce its government deficit to GNP ratio (see Table 4.2d).

Although West Germany's economic performance in the face of rising factor input costs has been superior to that of the developed sector as a whole, both the structure and the relative health of its performance underwent a transformation starting at the end of the 1968–75 business cycle. Until that cycle its GDP growth rate, even while restrained by a relatively constrictive macroeconomic policy, surpassed developed sector averages on the basis of Bonn's more forceful supply-side adjustment (see Table 4.2a). Then in the 1976–82 cycle, both West Germany's GDP growth rate and the pace of its supply-side adjustment retreated as its investment growth rate sank. These developments reflected a decided retrenchment in Bonn's macroeconomic policy at the first signs of the primary commodity price and inflation expansion that surfaced as the 1968–75 business cycle ended and the concomitant sharp increase in domestic labor and, therefore, capital costs.[30]

The macroeconomic policy retrenchment permitted West Germany to maintain a domestic inflation rate lower than the developed sector average while also allowing its external surplus to continue to grow (see Table 4.2b and c). Indeed, over successive business cycles Bonn's external surpluses increased, but in the 1976–82 cycle they came to rest upon soft import growth and not the healthy export growth that had fueled advances in the 1959–67 and 1968–75 cycles.[31] In the current business cycle these trends have continued as, in response to the second surge in primary commodity prices and inflation, Bonn like Tokyo successfully committed itself to reversing its government overindebtedness (see Table 4.2d).

Over the course of the 1959–67 and 1968–75 business cycles, the GDP growth rate of the second-tier West European economies—the U.K., France, and Italy—was lower than that of West Germany despite their more accommodative macroeconomic policies (see Fig. 4.2a). These early GDP differentials resulted from Bonn's superior supply-side adjustment. In the 1976–82 and 1983–?? cycles, the GDP growth of the second-tier economies suffered a severe deceleration as they were forced into a large-scale macroeconomic policy retrenchment. Once combined with the decline in the West German GDP growth rate, this fall pushed Western Europe's economic growth rate well below what it had been in earlier business cycles.

During the 1959–67 and 1968–75 cycles, the economic growth rate of the second-tier West European economies was supported by government fiscal and external overindebtedness greater than that experienced in the developed sector on average (see Table 4.2d). The inflationary pressures of government fiscal overindebtedness, while partially relieved by larger trade deficits, were exacerbated by the high degree of exposure of these economies to rising primary commodity prices and labor costs. As a result, they suffered inflation greater than the developed sector average (see Table 4.2c). Overindebtedness and inflation provoked a growing loss of confidence in these economies, leading to an escalating challenge to the value of their currencies (the franc devaluation of 1959, the onslaught against the pound in 1961, the assault on the lira in 1963, the attack on the pound leading to its devaluation in 1967, the franc devaluation of 1969, and the lira depreciation of 1973). Finally, in response to the first major eruption in primary commodity prices and inflation at the end of the 1968–75 business cycle, the domestic inflation and external deficits of the second-tier West European economies became unsustainable, forcing a decisive macroeconomic policy retreat. At the beginning of the 1976–82 cycle, the pressure on these countries continued as both the pound and the lira came under attack. The more constrictive macroeconomic measures that they adopted tightened further at the end of the 1976–82 business cycle in response to the second wave of rapidly rising primary commodity prices and inflation.

In the current (1983–??) business cycle, the pace of overindebtedness and inflation slackened from what it had been in the 1976–82 cycle. These economies have not only slowed the growth of their fiscal overindebtedness but have experienced a remarkable recovery in their current account balances as a result of a sharp cutback in the rate of growth of imports and have also enjoyed disinflation.

Over the course of the last two free world economy business cycles, U.S. macroeconomic policy has increasingly diverged from that of the remainder of the developed sector. Whereas the latter's policy has turned more contractionary, Washington's has become more expansionary. One result is that while the U.S. GDP growth rate fell below the developed sector average in the 1959–67 and 1968–75 business cycles, it approached it in the 1976–82 cycle and has surpassed it in the current cycle (see Table 4.2a).

In the 1959–67 and 1968–75 business cycles, the U.S. GDP growth rate suffered the same plight as those of the second-tier West European economies: although sustaining a more accommodative macroeconomic policy than West Germany, its GDP growth rate failed to match the West German rate because of the latter's superior supply-side performance. In addition, like the second-tier West European economies, the U.S. expansive macroeconomic policy produced growing government fiscal and external balance deterioration as well as a steeper acceleration in inflation than West Germany experienced from the first to the second cycle (see Table 4.2b, c, d). As a result, the dollar followed the path of the pound, franc, and lira, suffering its first major attack in 1961, succeeded by forceful assaults in 1965 and 1967–68 before succumbing to devaluations in 1971 and 1973.[32]

But unlike second-tier Western Europe, the United States was not pressured into a sustained macroeconomic policy retrenchment as a result of the upsurge in primary commodity prices and inflation at the end of the 1968–75 business cycle. The U.S. economy enjoyed distinct advantages over the second-tier economies, advantages that provided insulation against external pressures, including its much larger size and stock of assets, its smaller internal and external deficits relative to GDP, and the commodity composition of its trade, which offered it better protection against the inflationary pressures of rising primary commodity prices and helped it win a sizable external balance improvement in the midst of the 1973 primary commodity price explosion. (Rising food prices fueled the recovery in the U.S. merchandise trade balance while advancing oil prices prompted a leap in U.S. direct investment income.) As a result, the United States was the last of the leading developed economies to launch more contractionary macroeconomic measures at the end of the 1968–75 business cycle.

In the 1976–82 and 1983–?? cycles, while the macroeconomic policies of the second-tier West European economies and the entire non-U.S. developed sector turned increasingly constrictive, producing a reduction in fiscal overindebtedness in the later cycle, Washington continued on an expansionary course, generating an acceleration in fiscal overindebtedness. This set of circumstances permitted the U.S. GNP growth rate to ascend above the developed sector average, but the economy has had to pay a price in a huge increase in both government fiscal and external deficits. In the 1976–

82 cycle, burgeoning U.S. domestic deficits propelled its inflation rate close to the developed sector average, while the disinflation experienced during the 1983–?? cycle has only come as a result of a spectacular leap in external deficits, one of such magnitude as to send the U.S. net investment balance into a shocking decline. The United States has emerged as the free world economy's largest net debtor in the current cycle, while the creditor status of Japan and leading West European economies (West Germany primarily but also the U.K.) has been amplified.[33] World capital flows, dominated in the 1968–75 and 1976–82 business cycles by North-South flows, are now consumed by intra-developed sector flows as private financing for developing sector debtors has collapsed, to be replaced by foreign financing of U.S. deficits.

The sustainability of U.S. GDP growth rates thus depends on the ability and willingness of the remainder of the free world economy to finance the continuation of the intercylical escalation in U.S. overindebtedness.

U.S. POSTWAR POLICY: RESPONDING TO THE INFLATION/OUTPUT DILEMMA WHILE MEETING THE CHALLENGE TO PAYMENTS BALANCES

Up to the onset of the current free world economy business cycle, American policymakers had long avoided efforts to fundamentally reverse the decline in U.S. economic performance, opting instead for measures to defer the negative consequences of rising factor input costs on short-term economic growth. The product of these policies was an intercylical expansion in the twin evils of overindebtedness and inflation. Intermittent efforts to contest the two led to a series of economic recessions of increasing ferocity, a development particularly disturbing to American economic sensibilities. Seeking to revive U.S. economic health while escaping this exasperating inflation/output dilemma, the Reagan administration reverted back to the initial U.S. government formula for defeating the rising cost of factor inputs: President John F. Kennedy's supply-side tax cuts.

Early Signs of Weakness

While the Reagan initiative came in the midst of a palpable and prolonged decline in U.S. domestic and external performance, Kennedy's, launched some 20 years earlier, came in the wake of economic signs that, although less pronounced than those that greeted the Reagan administration, were nonetheless alarming—a seeming inability to avoid frequent domestic recessions and a decline in post-World War II U.S. external surpluses. The latter developments were encouraged by Washington's rejection of vigorous supply-side adjustment following World War II as U.S. domestic demand gravitated instead toward personal consumption and, following the start of the Korean War, hefty government defense expenditures.

Ironically, what had fostered the U.S. transition from the Great Depression of the 1930s to an expanding economy in the late 1940s and 1950s— an economy able not only to sustain domestic growth but also to export huge volumes of factor inputs to reconstruct wartorn Western Europe and Japan as well as support a global military force capable of containing the Soviet Union—was the massive supply-side adjustment that took place during World War II.

Afforded sanctuary from the destruction in Eurasia, the economy of the United States nearly doubled in size and made enormous productivity gains during the course of the war. This was facilitated by a big increase in the government fiscal deficit (nearly 10 times its average annual size during the Great Depression), which did not trigger undesirable levels of inflation as personal savings were forced up and as the inflationary pressures produced by the component of the deficit that was monetized were constrained by means of an effective incomes policy (wage and price controls).[34] Popular support for the war mobilization made all of this possible. Government policies to drive up savings and check inflation worked to depress personal consumption, but under war conditions, these actions became politically feasible. The high degree of labor discipline, morale, and, hence, productivity stimulated by the war effort made a major contribution to the real economic growth experienced during the war, as did the deep drop in unemployment from depression levels. But the most critical factor inducing high rates of economic growth was the vast expansion of the U.S. industrial base, and especially its high technology segment which sparked improvements in capital and labor productivity, in the latter by forcing an upgrading of workforce skills.

From the end of World War II to the 1959–67 business cycle when factor input costs began to accelerate, the U.S. economy escaped a return to the depression conditions of the 1930s and financed both a global economic recovery and heavy national security costs, and did so while running miniscule government budget deficits and persistent external surpluses.[35] These healthy economic vital signs stand in contrast to the rising government fiscal and external deficits that plagued the economy from the 1959–67 business cycle to the inauguration of the Reagan administration. But despite the appearance of vigor, the U.S. economy over the 1946–58 period experienced disturbing trends. The price of fiscal stability was fragile economic growth as the economy could muster only brief expansions before sinking into recessions of ever greater intensity. And while the United States accumulated positive merchandise trade and current account balances, the size of these surpluses plummeted from their peak in 1946–48 to close to zero in the 1958 recession.

A contributor to these worrisome trends in postwar U.S. economic performance was the absence of aggressive supply-side adjustment, especially when measured against those economies that prioritized such efforts—West Germany and Japan. While the United States experienced a surge in postwar personal consumption encouraged by a consumerist tax code, Bonn enacted supply-side tax cuts and ran continuous budget surpluses that together served to reduce the cost of capital, thereby stimulating higher investment growth rates while constraining personal consumption. Tokyo's postwar tax code elicited high rates of savings, thereby also invigorating investment at the expense of personal consumption. The advantage of West German and Japanese capital costs compared to those of the United States was aggravated by the rise in U.S. national defense spending during the course of the Korean War—defense spending that was sustained at only moderately lower levels after the war compared to the marginal defense outlays of Bonn and Tokyo during the 1950s. At the same time that resources flowed toward personal consumption and national defense in the United States, they gravitated toward investment in West Germany and Japan, causing large intra-developed sector differentials in the pace of postwar supply-side adjustment.

While the lackluster investment performance of the United States weakened noninflationary economic growth and undermined the country's relative competitiveness in manufactured goods trade, other factors played a more direct role in the uninspiring postwar economic performance. First, prior to the 1959–67 business cycle, postwar U.S. macroeconomic policy led by its fiscal component had been highly constrictive as the government sought to produce budgetary surpluses, and it was within this context that U.S. economic growth stumbled. Second, immediate postwar U.S. external surpluses were inflated by short-term special circumstances that were unsustainable, and this meant that the dollar's fixed exchange rate would become overvalued as the bloated surpluses dissipated. Thus, as the weakness of supply-side adjustment from 1946–58 pointed American policymakers in the direction of one instrument for reversing unwanted economic trends, an alternative menu including macroeconomic policy expansion and dollar devaluation offered another.

Although growing government fiscal overindebtedness has characterized the intercyclical evolution of the U.S. economy since the 1959–67 business cycle, postwar policy sought the opposite goal—budget surpluses to reduce the inflated national debt inherited from World War II. In embarking upon the path of budgetary retrenchment following the war, Washington was only following tradition. Sizable expansion in the U.S. national debt had resulted from the Civil War and World War I, and in each case this prompted forceful fiscal retrenchment leading to prolonged periods of government budget surpluses. In fact, fiscal conservatism and government budget surpluses had been the norm for much of pre–World War II U.S. economic history. Peacetime government budget deficits had been registered on only two occasions—in the late 1890s and first few years of the twentieth century as the government helped finance industrial expansion through infrastructure projects, and in the 1930s as a result of the New Deal as policymakers sought to prop up the social peace and economic growth by supporting personal consumption.[36]

In FY1947–49 the U.S. government won annual budget surpluses as a result of a large drop in defense outlays, but in 1949 the economy, after only one year of economic expansion, fell into a recession. In FY50 the United States registered a budget deficit fomented by weaker revenue growth springing from the 1949 recession and from another factor that would boost the deficit in the 1960s and 1970s—the growth in outlays for "payments to individuals." One of the crucial innovations of the New Deal was the establishment of a component of government outlays mandated by law and therefore beyond the bounds of the appropriations process.[37] These "uncontrollable outlays" residing in income insurance programs would rise in high unemployment circumstances to bolster personal consumption and, hence, growth, and they did just that in FY50.

Even with the escalation in national defense outlays over the FY51–54 period associated with the Korean War, the United States averaged very small budget deficits as much as the cost of the war was financed by higher taxes. Soft personal consumption induced by these high taxes left the economy vulnerable to another recession in 1954 when defense spending contracted in the wake of the Korean War.[38] Following the 1954 recession Washington resumed its commitment to fiscal retrenchment, producing two more years of budgetary surpluses in 1956 and 1957. But again after a brief expansion, the U.S. economy fell into recession in 1958.

While U.S. fiscal balances were stabilized from 1946–58, external balances had begun to worsen, a process that would persist through the 1976–82 business cycle (and beyond). The primary cause of the retreat in U.S. external surpluses up to the 1959–67 business cycle was the dissipation of abnormal circumstances that bolstered them immediately following World War II. The war devastation in Western Europe and Japan resulted in postwar output among the developed economies of Eurasia well below prewar levels; to rebuild this sector of the free world economy required large net imports. As a result, the developed economies of North America and the developing sector ran export surpluses with developed Eurasia, with the United States accumulating the largest.[39] Moreover, U.S. external surpluses were enhanced as a result of extraordinary wartime import substitution, which reduced the already low import dependency of the United States.

But both conditions were unsustainable. As the developed economies of Eurasia were revived, they would substitute domestic output for imports, diminishing their import surpluses and consequently the export surpluses of the rest of the world. At the same time, U.S. import dependency was certain to grow as measures fostering wartime import substitution were relaxed and as U.S. domestic demand patterns shifted from defense expenditures to personal consumption. During the 1950s, U.S. external import dependency did increase as Americans developed a taste for foreign consumer goods and as dependency on nonfood primary commodity imports increased.[40]

Together, these two developments worked to lower U.S. surpluses following the immediate postwar period (1946–48), and the retreat in external surpluses was exacerbated by West Germany's growing trade competitiveness. By the end of the Korean War, West Germany had dislodged the United States as Western Europe's largest capital goods supplier while accumulating trade surpluses through the 1958 recession.[41]

Policymaker appreciation of the decline in U.S. external surpluses up to the 1958 recession was undermined by the existence of a "dollar gap" in the immediate postwar period. The current account deficits of the embattled economies of developed Eurasia were not financible by domestic means, and from 1946–48 U.S. official and private capital outflow was insufficient to bridge the "gap." This threatened the postwar recovery as hyperinflation and shortages were pervasive in Western Europe and Japan.[42] These conditions persuaded Washington to take extraordinary action to finance the "gap" by means of government loans and grants through programs such as the Marshall Plan.[43] Since the current account deficit to be financed was greater than the U.S. bilateral current account surplus with these economies, the United States accumulated annual balance of payments deficits for most of the years in the 1946–58 period. With the advent of the Korean War, the means for financing what by then had become a smaller West European and Japanese current account deficit underwent a transformation. Government loans and grants receded in favor of overseas military expenditures mandated by the new U.S. forward presence in Eurasia and by U.S. private capital outflow—the early postwar artifacts of expanding American military and economic power abroad.

From 1948–58, the "dollar gap" underwent a secular contraction and by the later year it had all but vanished. Despite this process, the traumas aroused by the early ascendance of the "gap" once combined with its periodic resurgence worked to blind many observers to its underlying retreat.[44] In 1949 and 1954 the "dollar gap" appeared to reassert itself as economic recession depressed U.S. imports, and in 1951 U.S. external surpluses escalated in response to a decline in imports associated with the peaking of the Korean War mobilization. Finally, in 1956–57 special circumstances produced a jump in U.S. primary commodity exports (a poor harvest in Western Europe and the enactment of a U.S. "surplus disposal program" facilitated higher food exports and the shutdown of Persian Gulf flows of oil due to the Suez crisis prompted a leap in petroleum exports) along with a short-term escalation in the U.S. merchandise trade and current account surpluses.[45] The existence of the "dollar gap" and the fear of its expansion fostered a perception of an undervalued dollar when in fact the underlying contraction in U.S. external surpluses heralded the coming of an overvalued American currency.

THE U.S. ECONOMY: CYCLICAL STRUCTURE AND INTERCYLICAL RETREAT, 1959–82

The Kennedy administration came to office in 1961 mindful of the weaknesses of the U.S. economy and determined to eliminate them. However, its ascendance intersected a new challenge—the early stages of the rise in primary input costs. In the aftermath of the administration's supply-side measures of 1961–62, American policymakers responded to the new economic challenge by reversing the conservative direction of their postwar macroeconomic policy and periodically pressing for a downward adjustment in the dollar exchange rate. The heightened inflation/output dilemma facing Washington as a result of rising primary input costs, and the character and consequences of U.S. policy responses to the dilemma, produced a sequence of four distinct phases that were repeated in each of the free world economy business cycles.

Phases of the Business Cycle

Phase One. The 1959–67, 1968–75, and 1976–82 business cycles all started with a recovery in U.S. economic growth from preceding recessions, and each recovery was stimulated by an expansionary advance in U.S. macroeconomic policy. Within an environment of tight primary input markets, the acceleration in U.S. domestic demand prompted a rise in inflationary pressures (seen in a declining unemployment rate), and this coincided with an expansion in the U.S. government fiscal deficit and in U.S. external deficits as the Phase One recovery in the U.S. domestic demand growth rate repeatedly rushed ahead of that of the remainder of the free world economy to create import growth rate differentials detrimental to the U.S. merchandise trade balance. Over successive business cycles the deterioration in the U.S. government fiscal balance and in U.S. external balances in Phase One became increasingly severe (see Table 4.3a).

Phase Two. Rising inflationary pressures and worsening budget and trade balances in Phase One provoked a policy response from Washington in the first two business cycles. Macroeconomic policy led by government fiscal policy was retrenched, and this resulted in a decline in inflationary pressures and a recovery in the fiscal and trade balances. But the turn to a contractionary policy produced an undesirable side effect—a U.S. recession, whose intensity grew in the second business cycle. In the third cycle, U.S. government policy in Phase Two reflected its growing tilt toward accommodation of rising factor input costs as it was not retrenched. Instead, economic growth was sustained at the price of worsening inflation and budget and trade deficits (see Table 4.3b).

Phase Three. The economic conditions that arose in the second phase of the business cycle confronted American policymakers with a new dilemma: how to revive or, as in the case of the third cycle, sustain economic growth while at the same time winning improvement in external balances. In the first two cycles the U.S. economy had experienced a small advance in its merchandise trade and current account balances in Phase Two, but this was accomplished at the price of depressed imports. In the absence of a cut in imports in the second phase of the third cycle, U.S. external deficits continued to explode. The only way for the United States to enjoy positive economic growth and improve its external balances would be through an export recovery. How to rally U.S. exports thus became the principal question facing Washington in each Phase Three.

After exploring a supply-side solution under Kennedy, U.S. policymakers resorted to a formula of dollar depreciation coupled with pressure for a more expansionist macroeconomic policy among surplus developed sector trading partners as the vehicle for reviving exports. One result of all Phase Three U.S. initiatives has been a rise in the developed sector domestic demand growth rate, and this has served to squeeze primary input markets with sufficient force to trigger more powerful advances in primary input costs and inflation than occurred in the first phase of the business cycle.

In addition, U.S. policy measures launched in Phase Three induced a recovery in U.S. exports. The export boom in turn sparked a rally in U.S. investment, and together these forces inspired resource utilization rates in Phase Three higher than those seen in any other phase of the business cycle (that is, the lowest unemployment rates and the highest industrial capacity

Table 4.3
The Phasal Evolution of the U.S. Economy Through the First Three Free World Economy Business Cycles

4.3a: Phase One of the First Three Cycles

	1959/1959	1967/1968	1975/1976
Government Fiscal Balance ($Billion)	-2.8 / -12.8	-8.6 / -25.2	-53.2 / -73.7
Domestic Demand Growth Rate (%)	0.3 / 6.7	3.0 / 4.7	-1.9 / 6.0
Civilian Unemployment Rate (%)	6.8 / 5.5	3.8 / 3.6	8.5 / 7.7
Import Growth Rate (%)	-2.3 / 17.7	5.5 / 22.7	-5.4 / 26.5
Merchandise Trade Balance ($Billion)	3.5 / 1.1	3.8 / 0.6	8.9 / -9.5

4.3b: Phase Two of the First Three Cycles

	1959/1960, 1961	1968/1969, '70, '71	1976/1977, 1978
Government Fiscal Balance ($Billion)	-12.8 / 0.3, -3.3	-25.2 / 3.2, -2.8	-73.7 / -14.7, -53.6
Domestic Demand Growth (%)	6.7 / 1.4, 2.7	4.7 / 2.6, -0.5	6.0 / 5.5, 4.9
Consumer Inflation Rate (%)	1.7 / 1.4, 0.7	4.2 / 5.5, 5.7, 4.4	5.8 / 6.5, 7.6
Import Growth Rate (%)	17.7 / -3.3, -2.0	22.7 / 8.5, 11.5	26.5 / 22.3, 15.7
Merchandise Trade Balance ($Billion)	1.1 / 4.9, 5.6	-.6 / 0.6, 2.6	-9.5 / -31.1, -34.0

Source: (a) *OECD National Account Statistics 1986* (Paris: OECD, 1987) (for U.S. domestic demand growth, 1959–67 cycle); *OECD Economic Outlook, December 1987* (Paris: OECD, 1987) (for U.S. domestic demand growth in subsequent cycles); Executive Office of the President, *Economic Report of the President, 1989* (Washington, DC: U.S. Government Printing Office, 1989) (for U.S. fiscal balance, civilian unemployment rate, import growth, and merchandise trade balance). (b) Executive Office of the President, *Economic Report of the President, 1989* (Washington, DC: U.S. Government Printing Office, 1989) (for government fiscal balance, consumer inflation, import growth, and merchandise trade balance); *OECD National Account Statistics, 1986* (Paris: OECD, 1987) (for U.S. domestic demand growth in 1959–67 cycle); *OECD Economic Outlook, December 1987* (Paris: OECD, 1987) (for U.S. domestic growth after 1967). (c) *OECD Economic Outlook, June 1988* (Paris, OECD, 1988) (for non-U.S. OECD domestic demand growth in 1968–75 and 1976–82 cycles); Executive Office of the President, *Economic Report of the President, 1989* (Washington, DC: U.S. Government Printing Office, 1989) (for other categories). (d) Executive Office of the President, *Economic Report of the President, 1989* (Washington, DC: U.S. Government Printing Office, 1989) (for interest rates and consumer prices); *OECD National Account Statistics, 1986* (Paris: OECD, 1987) (for domestic demand growth in 1959–67 cycle); *OECD Economic Outlook, December 1987* (Paris: OECD, 1987) (for domestic demand growth and consumer inflation).

Table 4.3 (*Continued*)
The Phasal Evolution of the U.S. Economy Through the First Three Free World Economy Business Cycles

4.3c: Phase Three of the First Three Cycles

	1962/1963, '64, '65	1971/1972, '73, '74	1977/1978, '79, '80
Non-U.S. OECD Domestic Demand Growth Rate (%)	NA/NA, NA, NA	3.9 / 5.3, 7.2	2.2 / 3.2, 4.7
Export Growth Rate (%)	4.0 / 7.2, 14.3, 3.9	1.9 / 14.1, 44.5	5.3 / 17.6, 29.8
Civilian Unemployment Rate (%)	5.5 / 5.7, 5.2, 4.5	5.9 / 5.6, 4.9	7.1 / 6.1, 5.8
Capacity Utilization Rate (%)	81.4 / 83.5, 85.6, 89.5	77.4 / 82.8, 87.0	81.4 / 84.2, 84.6
Government Fiscal Balance ($Billion)	-7.1/-4.8, -5.9, -1.4	-23.0/-23.4, -14.9, -6.1	-49.7 / -59.2, -40.2
Merchandise Trade Balance ($Billions)	4.5 / 5.2, 6.8, 5.0	-2.3 / -6.4, 0.9	-31.1 / -34.0, -27.5
Consumer Price Inflation (%)	1.0 / 1.3, 1.3, 1.6	4.4 / 3.2, 6.2, 11.0	6.5 / 7.6, 11.3, 13.5

4.3d: Phase Four of the First Three Business Cycles

	1965/1966, 1967	1973/1974, 1975	1979/1980, '81, '82
Interest Rates (Federal Funds Rate)	4.07 / 5.11, 4.22	8.73 / 10.5, 5.82	11.19 / 13.36, 16.38, 12.26
Domestic Demand Growth Rate (%)	6.4 / 6.1, 3.0	4.4 / -1.7, -1.9	1.5 / -1.8, 2.2, -1.9
Consumer Inflation Rate (%)	1.6/2.9, 3.1	6.2 / 11.0, 9.1	11.3 / 13.5, 10.3, 6.2

utilization rates). The higher rates of resource utilization spawned surges in U.S. government revenues, which in each Phase Three produced a cylical contraction in the government budget deficit. The leap in U.S. exports also produced an improvement in U.S. external balances. Critical to the recovery in U.S. merchandise trade and current account balances in each Phase Three was the impact of rising primary commodity prices, especially food and petroleum prices. Food deficits centered in the USSR intersected each Phase Three and U.S. food exports boomed as a result. In the second and third business cycles, Phase Three overlapped immense leaps in oil prices provoked by Middle East/Persian Gulf instability and OPEC decisions. Because of the strong position of U.S. overseas investment in the petroleum sector, this development led to unusual increases in U.S. direct investment income (see Table 4.3c).

Phase Four. In response to the escalation in inflation in Phase Three of each business cycle, the United States and the developed sector as a whole have responded with increasingly harsh contractionary macroeconomic policies. But in each case, U.S. fiscal policy has not changed, the full burden of the macroeconomic policy contraction being put on the back of monetary policy. While cooling inflation, these measures have produced U.S. and free world economy recessions of ever greater dimension (see Table 4.3d).

The 1959–67 Business Cycle—Kennedy's Supply-Side Initiative

The 1959 U.S. economic recovery from the 1958 recession was encouraged by a major transformation in the government fiscal balance as it swung from a surplus in FY57 to its largest post–World War II deficit up to that point in FY59. Government revenues stagnated in FY58–59 and domestic spending growth accelerated as the recession compelled a large expansion in uncontrolled "payments to individuals" outlays—a development that would appear in ever greater magnitude at the beginning of each subsequent business cycle—while postwar government macroeconomic policy preferences were relaxed enough to allow for a meaningful rise in discretionary domestic spending.[46]

U.S. domestic demand growth was revived in 1959. The United States encountered, however—in addition to an enlarged budget deficit—both greater inflationary pressures and a deterioration in external balances. The leap in U.S. domestic demand growth was stronger than in the remainder of the developed sector and this yielded intra-developed sector domestic demand and import growth rate differentials harmful to the U.S. merchandise trade balance.

To the fiscally conservative Eisenhower administration and a Congress still infatuated with budget surpluses, the economic imbalances of 1959 were intolerable. In FY60 the U.S. budget moved back into surplus as government revenues rose and spending growth came to a halt with discretionary domestic spending suffering a sizable decline.[47] Supported by a more constrictive Federal Reserve Board monetary approach, the fiscal retrenchment not only produced a budget surplus in FY60, it subdued inflationary pressures and prompted a decline in domestic demand and import growth rates. Because U.S. exports continued to rise in 1960, supported by vigorous West European domestic demand growth, the drop in U.S. imports resulted in an improvement in the merchandise trade and current account balances.[48] However, the unwanted consequences of the contractionary turn in U.S. policy was a recession in 1960.

Even before the rise in factor input costs began to cut into economic performance, the incoming Kennedy administration could detect in 1961 the need for action. What the new administration confronted was not simply the

1960 recession but a U.S. economy that since its recovery after World War II had experienced four recessions in only 14 years. The uninspiring performance of the country's economy extended to its external accounts, as falling current account surpluses were increasingly inadequate to support expanded capital account deficits. This development had, by Kennedy's inauguration in 1961, incited the first full-scale speculative assault on the dollar exchange rate.[49]

To restore value to the dollar, the new administration rejected any effort to cut the capital account deficit by sharply reducing overseas military expenditures and private capital outflows—measures that would have compromised American global power.[50] This meant that a contraction in the balance of payments deficit would have to come as a result of an improvement in the trade balance. But if the Kennedy administration was to revitalize the nation's economic growth, it would have to forego reduced imports as a means of bolstering the trade balance, leaving a recovery in U.S. exports as the only available avenue for restoring health to external accounts. To achieve a revival in U.S. export competitiveness, the new administration rejected the quick-fix solution of a dollar devaluation that would have also reduced the purchasing power of the U.S. currency. Instead, measures were adopted to boost economic growth and exports by means of more rapid supply-side adjustment as new tax measures were enacted to provide incentives for private investment.[51]

To support the supply-side tax package in its quest for improved export competitiveness, the Kennedy administration pursued measures to weaken external barriers to U.S. exports through a series of export enhancement initiatives as well as through a challenge to the new European Economic Community's (EEC) Common Agricultural Policy (CAP). The latter effort was inspired by a growing American fear of the competitive strength of the EEC, and although unsuccessful, it did evolve into the General Agreement on Tariffs and Trade (GATT) multilateral negotiations to liberalize world trade known as the Kennedy Round.[42] Importantly, the price the Kennedy administration was forced to pay for congressional support of its trade initiative was the Long-Term Agreement on Cotton (1962), which sought not to improve U.S. exports but to slow U.S. imports by protectionist means.[53] Over the course of successive business cycles, the strength of this "new protectionism" in the United States and in Western Europe would increase in the first two phases as well as the last phase of each cycle.[54]

As a result of the growth in the government fiscal deficit spawned by Kennedy's tax cuts, the U.S. domestic demand growth rate accelerated in 1962–63, a development echoed in Western Europe where second-tier domestic demand growth also rose.[55] The Phase Three advance in the aggregate developed sector domestic demand growth rate prompted a tightening in free world economy primary input markets. Nonfood primary commodity prices underwent their first significant rise since the beginning of the Korean War and the first of the Soviet Union's major agricultural recessions helped to fuel a steep jump in food prices. Escalating primary commodity prices in turn triggered an increase in free world economy inflation.[56]

In addition to a surge in global and U.S. inflation, Phase Three of the 1959–67 business cycle involved a recovery in U.S. merchandise trade and current account balances. Free world economy domestic demand growth rate differentials favorable to U.S. external balances emerged as a leap in Western Europe's domestic demand growth was reinforced by swelling domestic demand and import growth in the developing sector, made affordable by the first solid post–Korean War recovery in the sector's primary commodity exports.[57] But the U.S. trade recovery of 1963–64 was the result of more than a favorable turn in free world economy domestic demand growth rate differentials. Fully 50 percent was attributable to rising primary commodity exports, especially food.[58]

Indeed, in the wake of the closing of Soviet and broader Eurasian food deficits in 1965, U.S. export growth began to slacken and U.S. merchandise trade and current account surpluses started to weaken, setting off a new round of speculation against the dollar.[59] Of even greater concern to American officials was the acceleration in inflation. In response, in 1966 the Federal Reserve launched a constrictive turn in monetary policy which resulted the following year in a U.S. growth recession.[60] But while the Fed pursued a contractionary course, U.S. fiscal policy remained accommodative, leading to a divergence in direction within the U.S. fiscal and monetary policy mix that would become increasingly extreme in subsequent Phase Fours.

The 1968–75 Business Cycle—Johnson's and Nixon's Permissive Policies

In the 1959–67 business cycle, the U.S. economy escaped the sputtering growth of the 1948–58 period to enjoy a more vigorous and extended expansion. The superior U.S. economic growth performance in the 1959–67 cycle, however, came at the cost of higher inflation and worsening government fiscal and external balances. In the 1968–75 cycle, the U.S. economy faced a dramatic advance in primary input costs, and despite a far more powerful rise in inflation and a more precipitous deterioration in budget and trade balances, economic growth plummeted to below 1959–67 levels, failing, too, to surpass the rates of growth experienced from 1948–58.

In the first phase of the 1968–75 business cycle (that is, in FY68), the U.S. government budget deficit—the largest since the war—registered twice the size it had in FY59.[61] The budget deficit explosion at the beginning of the 1968–75 cycle was aggravated by the "guns and butter" policy adopted by the second Johnson administration. Beginning in FY66, real national defense outlays soared as a result of costs associated with the escalation of U.S. military involvement in the war in Southeast Asia, reaching a peak in FY68.[62] At the same time, Johnson's newly inaugurated Great Society programs extended and enhanced the income insurance expenditures base of the New Deal, driving up the percentage of government outlays that lay beyond the control of the appropriations process. Hence, while in response to the 1967 growth recession the rise in government revenues slowed in FY68, national defense and "payments to individuals" outlays ballooned.

One consequence of the enlarged budget deficit was a forceful rise in U.S. domestic demand growth. Although less pronounced, the fiscal deficits of the leading developed sector U.S. trading partners also rose, spurring a jump in their domestic demand growth. Accordingly, aggregate developed sector domestic demand experienced a resurgence in 1968 strong enough to put a strain on primary input markets. From 1968–71, the full spectrum of primary commodity prices enjoyed a recovery more intense than that of 1959, while labor costs, signaled by the 1969 West European "wage explosion" and the expansion in developed sector income insurance programs, took off.[63] As a result, the inflationary pressures felt by the U.S. economy in 1968 were more severe than those of 1959.

Also as in 1959, the U.S. domestic demand growth rate recovered more rapidly than that of the rest of the free world economy, producing import growth rate differentials detrimental to the U.S. merchandise trade balance. The U.S. merchandise trade surplus consequently dropped close to zero in 1968. In addition, due to the U.S. involvement in the war in Southeast Asia, military expenditures abroad rose at a staggering rate to threaten a serious expansion in the U.S. balance of payments deficit.

Under pressure of a renewed speculative assault on the dollar, both the legislative and executive branches began to revive the "new protectionist" momentum that had arisen in the early 1960s, this time shifting the focus of attack to Japan. By 1967–68 Japan's earlier supply-side programs were beginning to yield large competitive advantages for its exports and the start of the 1968–75 business cycle intersected the full maturation of Japan's export power, driving Tokyo's bilateral merchandise trade balance with the United States into a surplus in 1968.[64] Whereas the EEC had been viewed as the principal U.S. competitor during the Kennedy administration, this role had transferred to Japan by the time Nixon assumed office.[65]

The jolting rise in U.S. inflation and the erosion in the U.S. budget and trade balances in Phase One of the 1968–75 business cycle induced a response from American policymakers similar to that of Phase Two in the preceding cycle. The U.S. macroeconomic policy retrenchment that began in 1968 and stretched through 1970 would, however, be the last to be launched in Phase Two of a business cycle.

In 1968 following the 1967 devaluation of the British pound, the worsening in U.S. external balances inspired a new speculative challenge to the dollar.[66] In response, the Federal Reserve tightened monetary policy, forcing U.S. interest rates up sufficiently to attract enough foreign capital inflow to produce a balance of payments surplus.[67] While the Fed's tight money policy was sustained through 1969, the Johnson administration and the Congress came to agreement on a meaningful deficit reduction package. In FY69 the United States produced a budgetary surplus, just as it had in 1960.[68] This would be its last.

In addition to a budgetary surplus, the constrictive U.S. fiscal and monetary policy mix produced a rise in the U.S. merchandise trade surplus by 1970 and enough capital inflow to stabilize the dollar while cooling domestic inflationary pressures. But the price the economy had to pay for these positive developments was high—an economic recession in 1969-70 greater in magnitude than that of 1960.

In 1971 the Nixon administration was confronted with the same quandary as was the Kennedy administration 10 years earlier: how to revive U.S. economic growth while at the same time improving external balances. While the Nixon administration did not undertake supply-side measures, it, like the Kennedy administration, oversaw a hefty expansion in the government budget deficit and a consequent rise in U.S. domestic demand growth. In FY71 the government fiscal balance sank, from a surplus two years before, to a deficit almost as large as that incurred in FY68, as the 1969-70 recession produced stagnation in government revenues while expenditures surged ahead despite a decline in nominal defense outlays. The government spending spree in FY70-71 was entirely the result of an explosion in "payments to individuals" outlays.[69]

In addition to the expansion in the U.S. government budget deficit, U.S. monetary policy was eased as part of the effort to push the economy out of recession.[70] The resultant heightened domestic demand rekindled strong growth in imports and a retreat in the merchandise trade balance into its first postwar deficit in 1971, as receding interest rates prompted an exodus of capital from the United States and a widening of the country's capital account deficit. By the middle of 1971, the U.S. economy had exited recession, but at the price of a jump in the balance of payments deficit, a deficit that was igniting a speculative assault against the dollar.[71]

Like Kennedy, Nixon was of no mind to undertake a global retrenchment of American overseas power on the scale that London and Paris had been forced into in the 1950s and 1960s in order to restore stability to their payments balances. Also like Kennedy, Nixon was unprepared to purchase balance of payments stability at the price of economic recession and depressed imports. As in the case of the earlier administration, Nixon's therefore had to design a means for reviving U.S. exports, and by the summer of 1971 it succumbed to the alternative Kennedy had rejected: devaluation of the U.S. dollar, whose exchange rate had by that time become unquestionably overvalued.

On August 15, 1971, Nixon kicked Phase Three of the 1968–75 business cycle into high gear, announcing that dollars could no longer be exchanged for U.S. gold reserves, a measure aimed at freeing U.S. macroeconomic policy from constraints borne of defending the dollar's fixed exchange rate while opening the door for a devaluation of the currency. In conjunction with the latter initiative Washington launched an overtly protectionist 10 percent surcharge on imports, a bargaining chip that would later be exchanged for trading partner acquiescence to dollar devaluation through the December 1971 Smithsonian Agreement.[72]

The burden for maintaining the new Smithsonian parity regime fell to U.S. trading partners, especially those that had accumulated external surpluses such as West Germany and Japan. In order to defend the new parity regime and avoid any further dollar depreciation, Bonn and Tokyo led a process of massive official currency intervention from 1971 through early 1973, which caused their domestic money supplies to swell.[73] Further, to offset losses to GNP in net exports anticipated as a result of the Smithsonian dollar devaluation and yen/Deutsche mark revaluations, Tokyo in particular undertook a mammoth fiscal expansion in 1972.[74]

The purposes and consequences of the Nixon Phase Three initiatives had been to secure a dollar devaluation and a rise in developed sector trading partner domestic demand growth in order to revitalize U.S. exports, which would permit the United States to sustain high rates of domestic demand growth while enjoying improvement in its external balances. In the subsequent Phase Threes, the U.S. government would resort to the same objectives and the same policy formula as had the Nixon administration.

Also in subsequent Phase Threes, the consequences of these measures would be the same as those that evolved from 1972–74. With U.S. domestic demand growth beginning to rise in 1971 and that of the rest of the developed sector escalating even more forcefully beginning in 1972–73, the aggregate developed sector domestic demand growth rate surged with greater strength than it had in 1962–63. This development squeezed already tight primary input markets, and the consequent pressures on primary commodity prices were magnified by Eurasian food deficits, again centered in the Soviet Union as they had been in 1963, and by the assertion of the OPEC oil embargo launched in response to the 1973 Arab-Israeli War.[75] From 1972–74 primary commodity prices experienced their strongest rise in the postwar period, and this produced the biggest runup in global and U.S. inflation of any in the modern era, while most economies highly exposed to primary commodity imports saw their external balances collapse.

Importantly, aside from West Germany whose relatively low inflation supplied its exports unusual advantages, the U.S. economy was among the few developed economies to experience a marked improvement in its external balances in 1973. As in 1963–64, this recovery was driven by an export boom that spawned, as in the previous cycle, a rally in U.S. nonresidential fixed investment. With rising exports and investment, the United States again enjoyed its lowest unemployment and highest industrial capacity utilization rate of any point in the business cycle, and these higher rates of resource utilization fostered a leap in government revenues and a decline in the budget deficit.[76]

As in 1963–64, the boom in U.S. exports was enhanced by the commodity composition of U.S. trade, as the growth in U.S. agricultural exports in 1973 above recent rates equaled the size of the improvement in the U.S. merchandise trade balance.[77] Further, the size and structure of U.S. direct investment abroad contributed strongly to the current account balance advance as U.S. direct investment income shot up in 1973 and 1974 with the rise in primary commodity and especially petroleum prices.[78]

With much greater intensity than in 1966–67, the upsurge in global inflation inspired a macroeconomic policy retrenchment throughout the developed sector in 1974–75. While the contractionary turn in Washington's macroeconomic policy was more intense than in the preceding business cycle, it too was restricted to monetary policy, and although it was more moderate than that of the remainder of the developed sector, it nevertheless led the United States to experience its deepest postwar recession up to that point.[79]

The 1976–82 Business Cycle—Carter Prescribes the Same Medicine

In the 1976–82 business cycle, national macroeconomic policy biases among the leading developed sector economies exerted themselves as governments responded differently to the heightened inflation/output dilemma provoked by the leap in global inflation that had confronted them during Phase Three and the deep recession in Phase Four of the preceding cycle. Led by fiscal policy, the U.S. economic approach remained expansionist as it gave priority to economic growth while the rest of the leading developed economies became less accommodative out of fear of inflation or rising external deficits.

The permissive U.S. fiscal policy in the 1976–82 cycle allowed the U.S. GNP growth rate to maintain its 1968–75 cycle level but at the cost of an egregious worsening in budget and trade deficits. In contrast, a less accommodative macroeconomic policy among other leading developed economies—i.e., Japan and West Germany—led to a decline in their GNP growth rates and an improvement in their external balances.[80]

As in 1959 and 1968, the Phase One rebound in U.S. economic growth in 1976 was supported by an enlarged U.S. government budget deficit. In FY76 the deficit reached a new postwar peak, rising to three times its size in FY68.[81] In FY75–76 U.S. government revenue growth slowed as a consequence of recession; outlays, however, driven by "payments to individuals," mushroomed. The consequent recovery in U.S. domestic demand growth, in conjunction with higher domestic demand growth in the rest of the developed sector, served to tighten primary input markets, just as happened in 1968–70. In 1976–77 primary commodity prices underwent a mild upswing, rekindling global inflation.[82]

Also as in 1968, the more dramatic advance in domestic demand in the United States compared to the rest of the free world economy produced import growth rate differentials harmful to the U.S. merchandise trade balance. But the deterioration in the U.S. trade balance was more severe in 1976 than in 1959 or 1968 as domestic demand and import growth rate differentials grew larger.[83] At the same time that U.S. macroeconomic policy performed as it had in earlier Phase Ones to promote a rise in U.S. domestic demand, the macroeconomic policy of the non-U.S. developed sector turned more cautious, leading to a less vigorous rise in domestic demand and imports in these countries.

In Phase Three of the 1968–75 business cycle, West Germany was exposed to what its macroeconomic policy bias fears most—high rates of inflation—while Japan's vulnerability to high priced primary commodity imports prompted a huge jump in that nation's domestic inflation and a collapse in its external surplus. The second-tier West European economies saw inflation surge at home, their external balances fall into deep deficit, and their currencies come under speculative attack. These jolts inspired a meaker macroeconomic policy expansion in 1976 among these economies than had been seen in 1968.

The decline in the U.S. trade balance in 1976 reawakened the "new protectionist" momentum, and again Japan became the target as its exports to the U.S. rose by 40 percent that year.[84] Western Europe, with a higher unemployment rate at the beginning of the 1976–82 cycle than at any time since the immediate postwar period and with constrained domestic demand growth, joined in the "new protectionist" upsurge.[85]

In contrast to 1960 and 1969, in 1977 Washington did not respond to rising inflationary pressures and faltering fiscal and external balances with a macroeconomic policy retrenchment. Instead, macroeconomic policy remained accommodative in the second phase of the 1976–82 business cycle, and as a result the United States avoided a recession while growing at a marginally slower pace than in 1976. But also as a consequence of a continued expansionist macroeconomic policy, inflationary pressures mounted, the fiscal deficit declined but was not eliminated, and external balances deteriorated. The slide of the United States into deeper merchandise trade and current account deficits in 1977–78 was exacerbated by another development that had been absent in the second phase of the 1959–67 and 1968–75 cycles: a weakening West European domestic demand growth rate. In 1960 and 1969, an acceleration in West European domestic demand growth boosted U.S. exports, and this had helped to bolster the advance in U.S. external balances. But in 1977 Western Europe's economic and import growth rates fell, providing no new support for U.S. exports.[86]

By as early as 1977, the newly inaugurated Carter administration was forced to confront the same policy challenge as had the Kennedy and Nixon administrations before it. But because of the absence of recession in the second phase of the 1976–82 business cycle, the new administration did not have to manage a revival of U.S. economic growth; it simply had to develop a means for sustaining it. In order to do so, Carter could not achieve the second component of Phase Three economic objectives—a recovery in external balances by means of import compression. Again, as in the Kennedy and Nixon periods, the Phase Three improvement in U.S. external balances could be won only through a rally in exports.

The Carter administration's formula for sustaining growth while improving exports represented the equivalent of Nixon's involving dollar depreciation and a promotion of macroeconomic policy expansion abroad. However, in the context of the floating exchange rate regime that had replaced the Smithsonian fixed parities, dollar depreciation was made considerably easier than it had been for Nixon. Talking the dollar down in 1977 and the first half of 1978, the Carter administration was only adding to existing market pressure against the U.S. currency.[87] Compared to Nixon, Carter could focus more energy on the second objective of getting surplus trading nations—Japan and West Germany—to adopt more permissive macroeconomic policies.[88]

In 1977–78 the dollar succumbed to a prolonged depreciation. As in 1972, the effort to stem it by currency intervention led by Tokyo and Bonn caused an acceleration in their domestic money supply growth. But reflecting the new caution in the fiscal and monetary policy mix of U.S. developed sector trading partners, the Phase Three monetary and fiscal expansion in Western Europe and Japan was weaker than in the preceding cycle, and as a result, the rise in the domestic demand growth rate of the non-U.S. developed sector in 1978–79 was smaller than in 1972–73.[89]

Nonetheless, sustained domestic demand growth rates in the United States and the mild increase in West European and Japanese rates were enough to trigger a rise in the developed sector domestic demand growth rate as in Phase Three of the 1959–67 and 1968–75 business cycles, and this in turn served to tighten primary input markets. From 1979–81 the free world economy experienced another upheaval in primary input costs, led by a rise in primary commodity prices, rivaling that which had transpired from 1972–74.[90] The magnitude of the primary commodity price recovery was even less justified than that of 1972–74 by the pressure generated from growing developed economy demand. Even more than in the earlier cycles, the runup in primary commodity prices owed its vitality to special circumstances: the eruption of another large Soviet-centered food deficit in 1979, a series of threats to Persian Gulf political stability (the fall of the Shah of Iran, the Soviet invasion of Afghanistan, and the Iran-Iraq war), and something that did not exist in earlier Phase Threes—a highly speculative market driven by the shock of the 1972–74 price advance and resulting fear of another like it. No matter its speculative character, the 1979–81 primary commodity price rise fueled a new upsurge in global inflation.[91]

Moreover, as in 1963–64 and 1973, U.S. external balances enjoyed a recovery in 1979, albeit one not as strong as the previous two, and, like its predecessors, one that rested upon a boom in U.S. exports. Rising U.S. resource utilization rates resulting from the export and related investment rally underwrote a decline in the government fiscal deficit, as similar circumstances had done in earlier Phase Threes.[92] The U.S. merchandise trade balance advance relied strongly on the vitality of U.S. primary commodity exports, especially agricultural exports which bounded above recent rates of growth, while the U.S. current account balance improvement owed more to an explosion in U.S. direct investment income than it had in 1973.[93]

But with even greater intensity than in 1974, the furious rise in global inflation fomented a developed sector macroeconomic policy retrenchment that resulted in the most severe postwar recession, which hit in 1981–82. In this policy transformation, the United States joined the remainder of the developed sector, but as in 1966 and 1974, the full burden for the shift in policy fell to monetary measures as U.S. fiscal policy remained unchanged.[94]

WASHINGTON CONFRONTS THE "ECONOMIC DIMENSION"

The weakening of U.S. economic performance at the beginning of the 1968–75 business cycle confronted American leaders with an "economic dimension of security vulnerability," just as the Soviet economy's deterioration in the first half of the 1960s forced an "economic dimension" upon the Soviet political-military establishment. Even though the United States enjoyed a distinct advantage in that its economy was quantitatively and qualitatively superior to that of the USSR and therefore suffered a less severe descent, its national security accounts underwent disinvestment during the 1970s—

just at the time when Moscow was experiencing an explosion in its national security expenditures impelled by the unprecedented peacetime surge in defense spending from 1966–75 and the forceful expansion of its global empire in the second half of the decade.

The disparity in the national security efforts of the superpowers lay in their contrasting responses to the dilemma posed by the "economic dimension." Whereas Moscow's instinct was to "race against time," squeezing its civilian economy and especially its personal consumption component in favor of larger national security expenditures, the United States de-funded its national security effort in order to shield personal consumption from the full impact of declining output growth rates.

Despite a deep drop in national security spending, the U.S. economy exited the 1970s in a worsened condition as savings in national security accounts failed to support more vigorous supply-side adjustment. Instead of engineering a successful "buy time" strategy, U.S. fiscal policy during the Nixon, Ford, and Carter administrations had sponsored a dangerous waste of time. As a result, the new Reagan administration inherited an immense burden. In addition to a faltering economy and a widening "economic dimension," it confronted an underfunded national security effort that, when contrasted to Moscow's dynamic military expansionism, appeared to be inspiring theatre and strategic asymmetries.

U.S. National Security Accounts and Spending Regimes

Like that of the Soviet Union, the U.S. national security effort has evolved within the bounds of economic constraints. As a superpower, the United States has assumed unusual national security costs, costs that, although dominated by national defense, also include some that support defense, led by space exploration, and others that enhance alliance system security, including economic and military aid. These national security measures consume quantitative and qualitative economic inputs that otherwise would be absorbed into the civilian economy, and the means by which their transfer to the national security sector is financed suggest a variety of ways in which the burden of national security costs are felt.

National defense, space exploration, economic aid, and security assistance represent outlays of the U.S. government, and as such they may be funded by means of taxing the private economy. If tax revenues are not sufficient to fund these outlays and they therefore induce government fiscal deficits, the deficits may be financed in a number of different ways that each entail specific economic penalties. Government fiscal deficits may be monetized, in which case the national security costs that underlie them will have provoked a rise in inflation. Alternatively, they may be funded by borrowing from the domestic stock of savings, prompting pressure for higher interest rates and, hence, capital costs, and enlarged future government interest outlays on the national debt. Finally, government fiscal deficits may draw upon foreign savings and be financed through foreign borrowing, in which case the funding of national security accounts would engender pressure for higher domestic interest rates in order to attract foreign capital and would require future repayment in the form of capital outflow.

In addition to vying with the private economy for access to factor inputs, U.S. national security accounts have had to compete with other segments of government outlays—discretionary domestic spending, "payments to individuals," and net interest—for resources.

From the end of the World War II to the inauguration of the Reagan administration in 1981, the real rate of growth in U.S. national security outlays came under continuing pressure from one or more of the undesirable economic consequences associated with their financing. In the late 1940s and 1950s, Washington's commitment to elimination of fiscal deficits combined with a desire to avoid excessive taxation to restrain the rise in national security costs, while in the 1960s a more permissive fiscal policy unleashed larger deficits and inflation, which provoked an anti-inflation backlash and a budgetary retrenchment, including a cut in national defense spending, in FY69.[95] Then in the 1970s, in the face of rapidly rising inflation and an explosion in "payments to individuals" outlays, national security accounts were severely squeezed.[96]

In addition to government outlays, the size of U.S. national security costs has been influenced by the behavior of U.S. goods and services trade and financial capital balances with the remainder of the world. Indeed, several forms of national security outlays—unrequited transfers such as economic and military aid and overseas military expenditures—represent segments of U.S. international transactions. These cross-border flows of resources, although accounting for only a tiny portion of U.S. international transactions, have a perceptible national security function in that they serve to enhance either the social peace or national defenses of U.S. allies or are a consequence of the forward basing of U.S. military forces.

The other, vastly larger segment of U.S. international transactions is overwhelmingly private and appears to have no direct national security function. Nevertheless, large or prolonged U.S. current account surpluses and capital account deficits can be viewed as a de facto national security cost, since in their absence the social peace and/or national security of American allies might be weakened and as a result, political-economic conditions more hospitable to Soviet expansionism might evolve. At times, the de facto national security dimension of these costs may become explicit, as was the case in the immediate post–World War II period when large U.S. current account surpluses were sanctioned as a critical component of national security policy. At that time the government took emergency measures to finance the current account deficits of its Eurasian allies through unrequited transfers and official capital outflow. Similarly, if the United States were to incur large or prolonged current account deficits and capital account surpluses, its international transactions could be seen to be reducing the immediate economic burden of its national security expenditures.

As was the case for the Soviet Union, economic factors served only to influence the size of the national security effort. Large transformations in U.S. national security spending have been prompted by changes in the character and dimension of the external threat, and in a fashion similar to our analysis of the Soviet Union, we can distinguish the evolution of U.S. national security spending regimes associated with specific threats. Figure 4.5 shows the movement of U.S. national defense spending from a national security spending regime associated with relative isolationism prior to World War II to one identified with the prosecution of that war. The elimination of the Axis threat following the defeat of Germany and the surrender of Japan sparked a new transformation in U.S. national defense spending associated with the demobilization of military forces following World War II.

Although the contemporary U.S. national security spending regime involves elements that first surfaced in the 1947–50 postwar demobilization, it only matured in 1951, with the beginning of the militarization of the Cold War. The huge rise in U.S. national security costs led by national defense spending that overlapped the Korean War generated a new regime predicated on a desire to contain, by military force if necessary, the expansionist threat of the Soviet Union and its alliance system, and this spending regime has continued to the present.

While the assertion of the Soviet threat incited a dramatic escalation in U.S. national security expenditures, the behavior of these expenditures within the contemporary spending regime have been subject to economic constraints. Even before the emergence of the U.S. "economic dimension," the size and structure of U.S. defense spending evolved through distinct pattern periods that involved changes in military force structure and doctrine resulting from the combined impact of stringent limitations on economic resources and permutations in the Soviet threat. Further, balance of payments pressures on the dollar that swelled in the 1960s precipitated restraints on U.S. military expenditures overseas and on private capital outflow—means whereby large volumes of economic resources had been transferred from the United States to the rest of the free world economy from 1951–67.

Then in the period of more intense economic resource stress associated with the opening of a U.S. "economic dimension of security vulnerability" from 1969–80, real U.S. national security costs plummeted. The national defense and space sectors suffered a period of accelerated disinvestment in part as a result of the response of American policymakers to the dilemma

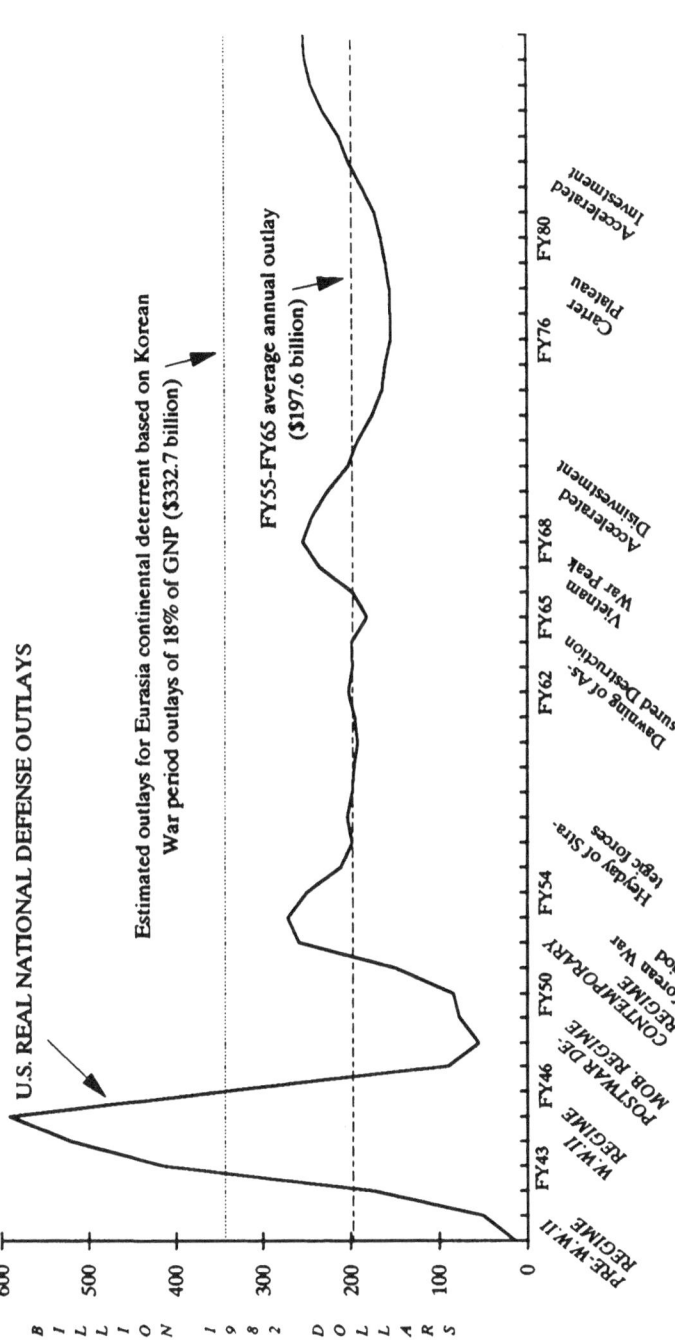

Figure 4.5. U.S. real national defense spending through the last three spending regimes and the estimated costs of constructing an effective Eurasian conventional deterrent. *Source:* Executive Office of the President, Office of Management and Budget, *Historical Tables—Budget of the United States Government, FY90* (Washington, DC: U.S. Government Printing Office, 1989).

posed by the "economic dimension," while elements of U.S. international transactions reflected the beginning of net transfers of economic resources from the rest of the free world to the United States.

Economic Influences on U.S. Military Doctrine and Force Structure, 1947–68

The transition from the World War II (FY43–46) national security spending regime to that of the postwar demobilization (FY47–50) involved an enormous contraction in real defense outlays (see Appendix A). The average annual real outlay for national defense during the life of the demobilization was only 14.6 percent of the average for the war years regime. But whereas the national defense component of U.S. national security outlays shriveled in the FY47–50 period, real government outlays for "international affairs"—involving primarily unrequited transfers in the form of economic and military grants and government foreign loans—rose by 150 percent (see Appendix A). From only 2.4 percent of national security outlays in the World War II spending regime, this component jumped to 28.0 percent during the demobilization spending regime.

The cause of the drop in U.S. national defense spending in the FY47–50 period was the elimination of the Axis power military threat, while the source of the surge in "international affairs" outlays during the FY47–50 regime was the emergence of a new foreign threat: the Soviet Union. Over the course of the demobilization, Moscow sought to expand its defense perimeter throughout Eurasia, instigating the ascension of allied Communist parties to power throughout Eastern Europe in the Euro-theatre, concluding a military alliance with the victorious Chinese Communist party in the East Asian theatre, and physically occupying segments of northern Iran while seeking to pressure and subvert the governments of Greece and Turkey on its southern periphery.

The sudden extension of the Soviet alliance system alarmed policymakers in Washington, inspiring limited measures to contain Soviet expansionism which focused on refurbishing the weakened economies of non-Communist Eurasia. Shortages of factor inputs and uncontrolled inflation ravaged the social peace in Western Europe, creating conditions conducive to the growth of Communist influence, especially in Italy and France, which emerged from the war with large Moscow-allied Communist parties. An aggressive Communist insurgency threatened Greece, and the defeat of the Chinese Nationalists forced the United States to fall back upon a Japan suffering postwar economic instability as its principal East Asian ally. Through such measures as the Marshall Plan, emergency aid to Greece and Turkey under the banner of the Truman Doctrine, and the "reverse course" in U.S. occupation policy in Japan, emphasis was put on economically revitalizing non-Communist Eurasia as the primary means for containing Soviet expansionism, and it is this process that sparked the unusual leap in U.S. government "international affairs" outlays.[97]

From 1947-50 the United States accumulated large capital account deficits caused by abnormal levels of net official outflows, and these were supported by unrequited U.S. government transfers. These U.S. capital account deficits financed the bloated current account deficits of non-Communist Eurasia, allowing these economies to secure sufficient net merchandise import surpluses to ease domestic factor input shortages and inflationary pressures. Indeed, international transactions represented the dynamic component of U.S. national security costs during the demobilization. In addition to sizable capital account deficits, the U.S. registered merchandise trade, current account, and real net export surpluses far larger than those of the prewar period (see Appendix B).

The transformation in U.S. national security spending to a new regime beginning in FY51 was incited by the Soviet-allied military adventure on the Korean Peninsula. Real U.S. national defense outlays rose during the FY51-54 Korean War defense spending period by 203 percent over their average in the postwar demobilization regime (see Appendix A). While a portion of this advance was accounted for by combat consumables associated with the prosecution of the local war in Korea, the majority of the increase went to build a U.S. military deterrent charged with preventing Soviet-centered expansionism in Eurasian theatres.

Even here at the beginning of the contemporary U.S. national security spending regime, the influence of economic constraints was evident. Despite the desire to construct a nonnuclear Eurasian deterrent as outlined in the Truman administration's 1950 NSC-68 memorandum, the costs of fielding such a deterrent were deemed too high.[98] Figure 4.5 shows what such costs would have looked like in relation to actual real national defense outlays from FY51-88 (this assumes that such costs would have amounted to 18 percent of GNP during the Korean War period when national defense spending averaged 12.2 percent of GNP). Absent an effective Eurasian theatre deterrent, Washington turned to its technological advantage in search of a cheaper means of deterring Soviet behavior. By exploiting its lead in nuclear technologies and by investing heavily in a modernized bomber fleet, the United States won unquestioned strategic superiority over the 1951-54 period.[99]

From Moscow's perspective, its role in fomenting the Korean War turned out to be a massive strategic blunder, as the U.S. nuclear weapons arsenal swelled. Defense Department spending on strategic forces rose fourfold in real terms from the postwar demobilization regime to the Korean War period, providing the Strategic Air Command (SAC) with sufficient resources to move out of the propeller and into the jet engine age, and research and development outlays for nuclear weapons doubled (see Fig. 4.6).[100]

The Korean War also spurred the militarization of NATO, which involved the forward deployment of U.S. ground and tactical aviation forces into Western Europe. These forwardly deployed forces were critical to a strategy that linked the deterrent potential of U.S. strategic nuclear forces to the defense of the European members of NATO through an "extended deterrent guarantee" that rested on the proposition that the United States and its European allies could compensate for their military inferiority in the Euro-theatre by fully exploiting the deterrent potential of nuclear weapons technology.[101] Indeed, by the end of the Korean War period, American policymakers sought to extend the deterrent value of their strategic forces beyond Europe (and Japan) to global theatres under a doctrine of massive retaliation whose credibility was to be enhanced through a plethora of new alliances with developing nations.[102]

Both during the upsurge in Korean War defense expenditures and immediately afterwards from 1955-62, the emphasis on strategic forces was not only evident in doctrine but in the distribution of resources within the U.S. defense sector, as strategic forces assumed a position of primacy (see Fig. 4.6) Although U.S. defense spending fell sharply with the Korean armistice, new strategic force spending levels unfolded from FY55-62 that were not only above pre-Korean War levels but even higher than those during the war. With an objective of securing strategic nuclear superiority, the Eisenhower administration sustained high levels of funding for the SAC bomber fleet while initiating a strong R&D program for long-range ballistic missiles. Over the course of the 1950s, the U.S. nuclear arsenal grew at an astounding pace—from 450 first generation fission bombs to 18,000 second-generation fusion and third-generation fission bombs.[103]

The Khrushchev initiative to construct a mobilization base for Soviet strategic forces represented a threat to U.S. strategic superiority. For technical and geostrategic reasons much of the early Soviet nuclear/missile program concentrated on theatre (intermediate-range) aircraft and ballistic missiles designed to put the ring of forward U.S. bomber bases at risk. For Khrushchev and his lieutenants, however, the key to a strategic nuclear "second revolution" in warfare lay in the capacity to radically increase the direct nuclear threat to the United States.[104] In 1957 Soviet successes in the Sputnik launch and ICBM test ended America's sense of relative invulnerability.

Washington's response to this qualitative Soviet challenge to the deterrent value of its strategic forces and the credibility of its doctrine was reflected in the distribution of national defense spending beginning in FY59, when defense R&D outlays more than doubled and continued to expand through FY62, while outlays for general science, space, and technology rose at a staggering pace beginning in FY59.[105] Then, from accelerated

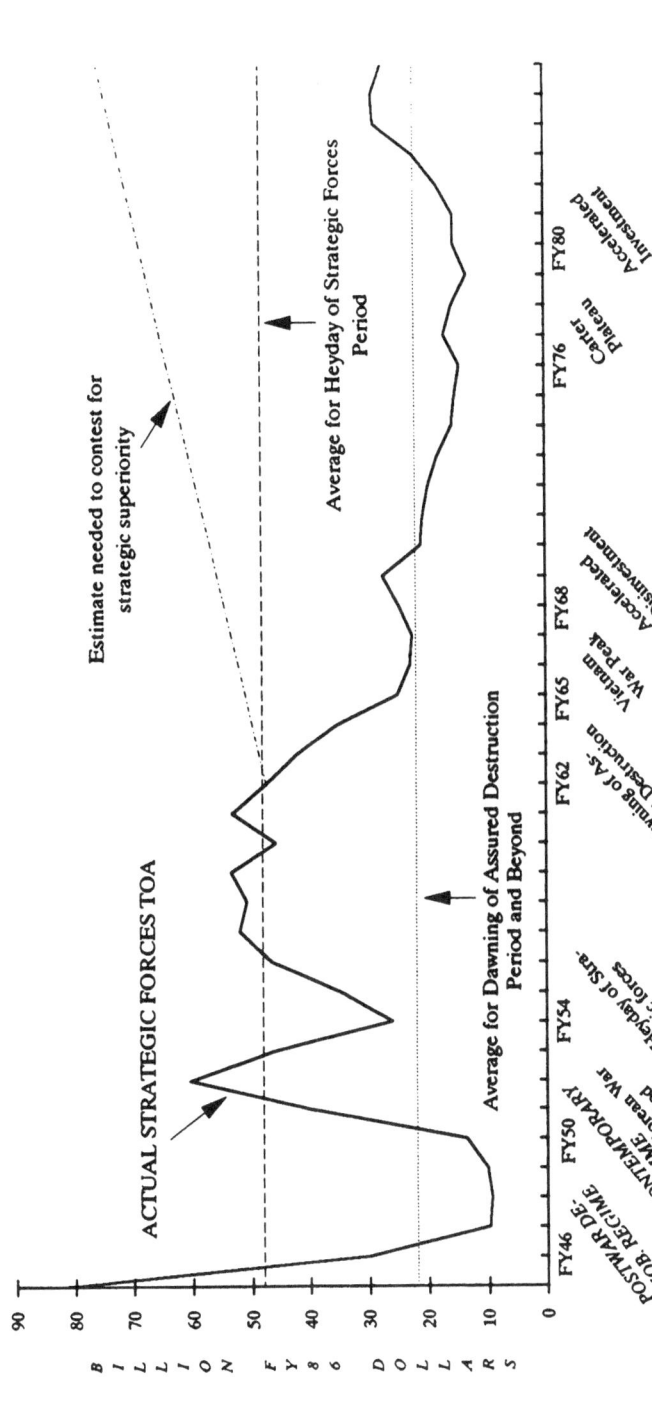

Figure 4.6. Strategic forces total obligational authority (1945–86) transformations in the contemporary national security spending regime and the costs of strategic superiority. *Source*: U.S. Department of Defense, Office of the Assistant Secretary of Defense (Comptroller), "National Defense Budget Estimates for FY87" (Washington, DC: U.S. Department of Defense, Office of the Assistant Secretary of Defense (Comptroller), May 1986)

funding for ICBMs and submarine-launched ballistic missiles (SLBMs) in the second half of the 1950s, the U.S. effort to ensure strategic superiority began to contemplate more expensive damage limitation and counterforce measures in the early 1960s during the first year of the Kennedy administration.[106]

As in the formation of the contemporary national security spending regime during the Korean War period, economic constraints again surfaced to influence changes in U.S. military force structure and doctrine. From FY63–65, DOD total obligational authority (TOA) for strategic forces suffered a mammoth contraction (see Fig. 4.6), and because defense spending in real terms failed to fall over this period, funding for general purpose forces raced ahead.[107] The sudden decline in the share of defense spending accounted for by strategic forces reflected a decision by the Kennedy administration to abandon the effort to sustain strategic superiority, and this was reflected in the advent of an explicit finite deterrent policy known as mutually assured destruction, or MAD.[108] One reason for this turn in U.S. doctrine and defense spending is suggested in Figure 4.6. Identified here are the hypothetical costs of supporting the goal of strategic superiority based upon strategic forces TOA maintaining in FY86 the percentage of total Defense Department TOA it enjoyed over the 1955–62 period. Extraordinary and unsustainable in themselves, these costs would have had to increase by a still greater magnitude in the face of probable Soviet countermeasures.

With the loss of strategic superiority and with an extended deterrent of lessened credibility, U.S. defense planners sought means for restoring value to theatre deterrents. In conjunction with the rise in U.S. general purpose forces funding from FY63–65, a new doctrine of flexible response sought to offset the impact of the reduced value of the extended deterrent by emphasizing the role of theatre-level deterrence in Europe.[109] But any effort by the Johnson administration to de-nuclearize NATO strategy by enhancing the U.S. Euro-theatre nonnuclear capability would face the same economic limitations that undermined the Truman administration's desire, articulated in NSC–68, for an effective conventional theatre deterrent. Further, just as in the case of the Truman administration, the economic infeasibility of a Euro-theatre conventional deterrent confronted by the Johnson administration was exacerbated by a sudden diversion of national defense resources to prosecute a local war in a global theatre. Thus, although NATO accepted a revision of its planning doctrine to "flexible response" which gave greater emphasis to improved nonnulcear forces, serious modernization attempts in this area remained limited.

From FY66–68 the behavior of U.S. defense spending was shaped by an effort to undermine the advance of a perceived Communist threat in a global theatre—Vietnam—through the projection of U.S. theatre force. Real U.S. defense spending during the Vietnam War peak of FY66–68 rose 16.0 percent on average above that of the FY55-65 period to approach the level of real defense spending during the Korean War. And as during the Korean War, the advance in real defense outlays above the FY55-65 average was largely accounted for by the cost of combat consumables associated with the prosecution of the war in Southeast Asia.

While U.S. national defense and related space exploration costs mounted from the FY47-50 postwar demobilization to the contemporary national security spending regime, the cost of U.S. international transactions declined. In the 1950s, U.S. capital account deficits and unrequited transfers fell from their late 1940s peak and the structure of capital outflow changed. The special programs associated with the reconstruction of non-Communist Eurasian economies receded, as by 1950 this sector had surpassed prewar output levels and U.S. grants and loans therefore waned, as reflected in a noticeable decline in U.S. "international affairs" outlays (see Appendix A). Indeed, these outlays did not even begin to approach their FY47-50 nominal levels again until the middle of the 1960s. But in the 1950s, with the revival of world economic growth, U.S. private capital outflow once again surged and overseas military expenditures associated with the enlarged U.S. military presence abroad advanced to compensate for part of the impact of the dive in "international affairs" outlays on U.S. capital account balances.

At the same time that the U.S. capital account deficit contracted, the inflated postwar U.S. merchandise trade, current account, and real net export surpluses also receded (see Appendix B).

In the 1960s U.S. international transactions fell victim, like national defense expenditures, to economic constraints. Inspired by rapid economic growth in Western Europe and initial post-Korean War signs of vigor in primary commodity prices, U.S. private capital outflow accelerated, prompting growing capital account deficits.[110] But while these deficits widened, U.S. merchandise trade and current account surpluses failed to expand, fueling repeated speculative assaults on the dollar (see Appendix B). In essence, U.S. current account surpluses and domestic savings were no longer sufficient to finance domestic investment, the government fiscal deficit, and the expansion of overseas military and economic power. As efforts to revive current account surpluses failed and as the government fiscal deficit expanded, Washington came under pressure to curb the growth in its global power by cutting overseas military expenditures and restraining private capital outflow in order to defend the dollar. Meanwhile, the overvaluation of the dollar showed up in the collapse of real net export surpluses as the U.S. imported more real goods and services than it exported in every year but one from 1958-68 (see Appendix B). The inflated price of the U.S. currency produced a de facto trade subsidy for the United States, allowing it to accumulate positive nominal goods and services trade surpluses while enjoying real goods and services trade deficits.

The Plunge in U.S. National Security Costs, 1969–80

As a consequence of the transition from the World War II to the postwar demobilization spending regime, the competitive position of U.S. national security expenditures declined relative to the remainder of the economy and to other government outlays (see Appendices C and D). After accounting for 34.9 percent of GNP in the FY43–46 regime, national security outlays led by national defense sank to only 7.2 percent of GNP in the FY47–50 period while falling from 86.9 percent to 48.2 percent of U.S. government outlays. The advent of the contemporary U.S. national security spending regime during the Korean War prompted a renewed advance in the relative status of U.S. national security accounts as, led by defense, they jumped to 12.9 percent of GNP and 69.1 percent of government outlays. Then, just as Soviet national security costs dropped as a percent of GNP following the Korean War, so did those of the United States. From FY55–65 these costs fell to 10.6 percent of GNP and 58.1 percent of government outlays. But whereas Soviet national security expenditures started to rise as a percentage of GNP only a few years into the post-Korean War demobilization, those of the United States slowly retreated until the Vietnam War peak in FY66–68. From FY66–68, U.S. national security expenditures advanced from 9.1 percent to 10.8 percent of GNP but failed to rise as a percentage of government outlays, as over this period Johnson's "guns and butter" policy fueled an equally energetic escalation in outlays for "payments to individuals."[111]

From FY69–80, U.S. national security expenditures suffered a shocking transformation in both real magnitude and relative status. Both as a percentage of GNP and of government outlays, they collapsed, falling from 10.8 percent of GNP in FY68 to 5.7 percent of GNP in FY80 and from 52.1 percent of government outlays to 25.9 percent.[112] A prominent contribution to this process was made by the government's response to an expanding U.S. "economic dimension of security vulnerability" that first surfaced during the Vietnam War peak. The spurt in national defense outlays associated with the escalation in U.S. military involvement in the war intersected the opening of the 1968–75 business cycle and the steep rise in primary input costs. In FY68 growing national defense expenditures unleashed a huge increase in the U.S. government budget deficit and a recovery in domestic demand growth, which together provoked an upsurge in inflationary pressures. Hence, in 1968 American policymakers first confronted an "economic dimension" as a jump in the rate of growth of national defense spending precipitated a visible deterioration in economic performance.

In FY69 Washington responded to the emergence of the "economic dimension" by cutting national defense outlays, yielding a hefty slide in national security expenditures as a percentage of both GNP and government outlays (see Appendices C and D). Also, "international affairs" outlays—whose share of GNP and government outlays had swelled beginning in FY62 in response to enlarged U.S. unrequited transfers to South Vietnam—commenced a prolonged contraction in FY66, while U.S. government space expenditures, which rose meteorically beginning in FY59, started a decade-long fall in FY66 (see Appendix A).

The initiation of a long-term decline in U.S. economic performance at the start of the 1968–75 business cycle was joined by perturbations in U.S. international transactions that signaled a transition through which the United States would gradually move from being a net exporter to a net importer of resources. The rise in U.S. domestic demand and import growth in 1968 sparked contraction in the U.S. merchandise trade and current account surpluses, which both sank close to zero, and at the same time the net export deficit in real goods and services spiraled up. In addition, to defend the dollar against renewed assault the United States was forced to register its first post–World War II capital account surpluses in 1968–69 by attracting larger capital inflow through higher interest rates. During the 1970s the transition in U.S. international transactions proceeded, led by a clear sign of the relative decline of American economic power—a 22.2 percent depreciation in the dollar's effective exchange rate.[113]

Over the course of the 1970s, American policymakers did not so much respond to the dilemma posed by the "economic dimension" as attempt to evade it. While rejecting the alternative adopted by the Soviet leadership of sustaining or increasing the rate of growth in national security costs, Washington instead countenanced a decade of sacrifice in national security. But the savings won from national security accounts did not become part of an effort to reverse the long cycle descent in U.S. economic performance in order to create future economic conditions hospitable to an acceleration in national security expenditures. Instead of facilitating higher rates of investment and supply-side adjustment, these savings were diverted to prop up declining personal consumption growth rates and the social peace.

The distribution of U.S. resources in the 1970s reflected economic policy biases borne in the Great Depression, biases that had given rise to New Deal income insurance programs later enhanced by Johnson's Great Society. In the face of rising factor input costs and the higher inflation and deeper recessions of the 1970s, "payments to individuals" outlays spurted ahead even more rapidly than national security costs fell (see Appendices C and D). Accordingly, from FY68–80 U.S. government "payments to individuals" expenditures jumped from 5.9 to 10.4 percent of GNP and from 27.9 to 47.0 percent of government outlays.[114] Further, uncontrollable outlays, of which "payments to individuals" is the largest component, snowballed, accounting for three-quarters of all U.S. government outlays by the mid-1970s.[115]

With Washington unwilling to raise tax rates out of fear of recession or to change the laws affecting transfer payments, budgetary restraint could only be secured by a reduction in controllable outlays—national defense and discretionary domestic spending—and in the hostile economic environment of the 1970s, policymakers were resistant to cuts in domestic programs. Thus, the full burden of deficit reduction fell to national defense, and although the national defense and the related space sectors shrank, the requirements placed on the budget to subsidize personal consumption were so great that the budget deficit widened nonetheless.

The peculiar response of the American leadership to the emergence of the "economic dimension of security vulnerability" was only one factor propelling national security outlays downward. In the late 1960s and 1970s, the U.S. perception of the foreign threat underwent alterations that had the effect of depressing national security expenditures. Of greater impact on defense spending than the Soviet assertion of a detente policy, the U.S. calculation of the political-military risks associated with gaining its objective in the Southeast Asian war prompted a retrenchment in the level of military engagement beginning in 1969. The gradual diminution in U.S. forces devoted to the war and the decline in combat consumable costs helped push national defense spending down.

From its Vietnam War peak in FY68, U.S. national defense outlays in real terms fell by a staggering 36.9 percent by FY76 to well below the average for FY55–65, when defense spending had not been bolstered by the cost of combat consumables. Indeed, in FY76 real defense expenditures were 22.3 percent below the FY55–65 average, and hence the decline cannot be accounted for by the savings won by withdrawal from Vietnam alone.[116]

From FY69–76 the U.S. national defense sector suffered from a process of accelerated disinvestment. As real national defense outlays declined each year, the percentage of total outlays devoted to defense investment (procurement, RDT&E, military construction, and atomic energy defense) also fell each year and therefore sank at an accelerated pace when compared to total defense spending (see Appendix E). Within the sphere of national defense investment, procurement accounted for a preponderance of the contraction: over this period real defense procurement fell by 65.4 percent.[117] Thus, beyond the withdrawal from the local war in Southeast Asia, the burden of the FY69–76 process of accelerated disinvestment was felt in the modernization of U.S. defense machinery—a development that affected both strategic and general purpose forces and, as a result, the competitiveness of the U.S. military in the strategic arena as well as in the Euro- and global theatres.

During this period, the modernization of the American nuclear arsenal was restricted primarily to the deployment of MIRVed (multiple independently targeted reentry vehicle) variants of the Minuteman ICBM and the Poseidon

SLBM.[118] This allowed the United States to raise the number of warheads in its arsenal without approaching launcher limits imposed by the SALT I treaty. At the same time, the size of U.S. nonnuclear general purpose forces continued to shrink and the weapons modernization programs of all four services were virtually terminated. Amplifying the deterioration in U.S. military power during the late 1970s, morale and discipline among the forces began to weaken.

During the years from FY77–80 that overlap the Carter presidency, the hemorrhaging in U.S. national defense spending came to a halt but the sector underwent little real recovery. National defense spending reached a low-end plateau for the contemporary national security spending regime, while defense investment slowly gained a larger share of defense outlays (see Appendices A and E). Inheriting an underfunded national defense sector and promoting the national investment priorities that facilitated earlier defense disinvestment in its initial stages, the Carter administration did nonetheless respond as theatre and strategic asymmetries became more alarming. By the second half of the Carter plateau period, Washington, under pressure from a surging Soviet threat whose projection of power abroad culminated in the military invasion of Afghanistan and from an aggressive anti-American Iranian leadership whose actions made the U.S. ability to project power seem impotent, began to perceive threatening imbalances not only in global theatres but in the Euro-theatre and on the strategic level.

By the late 1970s concerns were rising within Western Europe over the continued build-up of Soviet Euro-theatre forces—most specifically the deployment of the ground mobile continental-range ballistic missile, the SS-20—while considerable public controversy arose in the United States over the status of the strategic nuclear balance and over whether an unfavorable "window of vulnerability" in strategic forces had opened.[119] In reaction to these challenges, U.S. defense spending commenced a small rise and the proportion of defense outlays dedicated to investment grew. These meager increases in resources were devoted to an early revival in U.S. strategic force and Euro-theatre force modernization.[120]

Paralleling the contraction in the U.S. defense and space sectors, slipping U.S. international power was reflected in its balance of international transactions. The failure to constrain domestic demand led by personal consumption and to promote enlarged supply-side adjustment worked to undermine the U.S. merchandise trade balance, which, after suffering its first post–World War II deficit in 1971, endured large and growing deficits in the second half of the 1970s (see Appendix B). Driven by its falling merchandise trade balance, the United States in the 1970s registered several years of large current account deficits (the first since three small ones in the 1950s). To avoid the contractionary domestic economic implications of high interest rates, Washington acquiesced to renewed capital account deficits beginning in 1970 (see Appendix A). As a consequence, unbearable pressure built against the dollar, forcing its devaluation in 1971, while worsening U.S. merchandise trade and current account balances and continued large capital account deficits ensured further dollar depreciation through the remainder of the decade.

Chapter 5
Taking Stock of the "Reagan Revolution"

The Reagan administration entered office with a popular mandate for change. The United States had suffered more than a decade of deteriorating economic performance in which successive administrations appeared impotent in the face of rising factor input costs and their distressing consequences: raging inflation followed by deep recessions and high unemployment. At the end of this period, from 1980–82, the United States experienced its harshest post–World War II recession as the Federal Reserve promoted double-digit interest rates to contest double-digit inflation.

Compounding the new administration's challenges, the faltering economic activity of the 1970s had spawned a widening "economic dimension of security vulnerability" for the United States, and in accordance with the American policy response to the dilemma it posed, national security accounts underwent a harsh contraction—a contraction that by the second half of the 1970s was perceived to have contributed to new theatre and strategic military asymmetries. Even under more hospitable economic circumstances, what would have been required to address these challenges would have been a tall order and one that no postwar American government had been able to fill: a durable period of noninflationary economic growth sufficient to support a swift expansion in national security expenditures.

Although less formidable than the problems confronting the Andropov coalition in the USSR, those inherited by the incoming Reagan administration were no less daunting. To achieve a reversal in the country's long cycle economic descent while addressing threatening military imbalances, the Reagan administration was forced to craft a program that at least in theory would mean a reversal in the resource distribution priorities that had persisted since the opening of the "economic dimension," priorities that found a strong resonance in modern American economic culture. From 1968–80, personal consumption had grown as a share of GNP at the expense of net nonresidential fixed investment, which retreated, and national security expenditures, which plummeted.[1] The "Reagan revolution" rested upon an integrated set of policy measures charged with overturning 1970s resource priorities by advancing the status of economic investment and national security.

A SUPPLY-SIDE EFFORT TO REVERSE THE ECONOMIC SLIDE

To induce noninflationary growth, the Reagan administration resurrected the long dormant supply-side formula of the Kennedy era, proposing huge personal income tax cuts intended to bolster the personal savings rate and thus reduce capital costs along with investment tax credits for business to directly stimulate higher investment growth rates.[2] The higher investment growth rates were to accomplish what they had done for the U.S. economy during World War II and for the West German and Japanese economies in the 1950s and 1960s—inspire higher levels of economic efficiency through a sped-up integration of superior technologies and workforce skills. The resulting leap in productivity growth would underwrite high rates of GNP growth even as factor input growth rates remained weak.

It was further believed that the retardation of government revenue growth caused by the tax cuts and credits would not aggravate government overindebtedness and therefore inflationary pressures since the increment to economic growth stemming from invigorated supply-side adjustment would yield a rise in government revenues large enough to pay for early tax losses as well as for the budget deficit inherited by the new president. Indeed, the anticipated government revenue boom was projected to be so large that it would also finance a steep rise in national security outlays.

In FY82 and FY83 the Reagan supply-side tax measures went into effect, and starting in FY81–82 the U.S. national defense sector enjoyed its longest post-World War II period of uninterrupted real growth (see Appendix A). In 1983 the supply-side tax initiative helped propel the U.S. economy out of recession, and in 1983–84 the U.S. Phase One recovery singlehandedly pulled the free world economy out of negative growth. As real national defense outlays grew by a spectacular 54.2 percent from FY80 to FY88, the U.S. economy enjoyed 1970s rates of GNP growth in conjunction with a retreat in domestic price inflation.

This performance has moved some to suggest that the "Reagan revolution" secured its principal objectives, bringing the long-term deterioration in U.S. economic performance to a close while redressing 1970s military imbalances. But other indicators argue the contrary: that critical goals of the supply-side program were not only missed but imbalances that the program was charged with remedying have worsened, and in some cases dramatically so. Moreover, the supply-side program failed to alter the structural evolution of the U.S. economy through the current (1983–??) free world business cycle. By comparing the U.S. economy's performance and its phasal features during the current cycle to preceding cycles, its continued deterioration during the 1980s comes into stark relief.

The High Price of the Reagan Expansion

Perhaps the most flagrant deficiency in the behavior of the U.S. economy to result from the Reagan supply-side initiative has been the explosive growth in the government fiscal deficit. The intercyclical leap in government fiscal overindebtedness from the preceding to the current business cycle has been the largest in the country's postwar history (see Table 5.1). Administration strategists badly overestimated the revenue increment resulting from the revival of economic growth.

Another missed target of the program points to the source of inadequate economic growth. The largest component of the supply-side tax package was the personal income tax cut. But instead of producing a higher personal savings rate, the tax reductions in fact have coincided with an alarming plunge in that rate. The average U.S. personal savings rate for the current postwar business cycle is lower than that for the other three, and the 1987 rate was the lowest since 1947 (see Table 5.1).[3] Clearly the centerpiece of the Reagan program missed its mark, as the personal income tax cuts did not go to savings but, following on the depressed levels of consumer spending in the 1980–82 recession, went to support a rebound in personal consumption.[4] Inadvertently, the supply-side program turned into yet another subsidy to personal consumption. This unwanted reaffirmation of the priority status of personal consumption was reflected in the fact that in the 1983–?? cycle, the share of GNP that it accounted for continued to rise (see Table 5.1).

The combined impact of accelerating U.S. government overindebtedness and a plummeting personal savings rate resulted in an aggravation of the very condition that the supply-side program was intended to relieve: high capital costs. Over the first two phases of the current business cycle, U.S. nominal interest rates surpassed those of previous cycles while real interest rates remained higher as well (see Table 5.1). High capital costs have undermined the prospects for a revival in economic investment as net nonresidential fixed investment as a percentage of GNP has not risen but has instead continued to fall during the 1983–?? cycle (see Table 5.1).

Perhaps the single most prominent set of figures seized upon by those arguing for the success of the Reagan supply-side initiative has been the improvement in the nonfarm business productivity growth rate in the current

Table 5.1
The Reagan Supply-Side Initiative: Missed Objectives (Annual Averages)

	1959-67	1968-75	1976-82	1983-88
U.S. Government Fiscal Deficit as % of GNP	-0.8	-1.5	-2.9	-4.7
Personal Savings Rate (%)	6.7	8.0	7.1	4.5
Personal Consumption as % of GNP	59.5	61.5	63.3	65.1
	1959-62	*1968-71*	*1976-78*	*1983-86*
Federal Funds Rate (%)	2.8	6.4	6.1	8.6
	1959-67	*1968-75*	*1976-82*	*1983-87*
Net Non-Residential Fixed Investment as % of GNP	3.2	3.6	3.0	2.4
	1959-62	*1968-71*	*1976-78*	*1983-86*
Non-Farm Business Productivity Growth Rate (%)	2.7	1.4	1.7	2.2
	1967	*1973*	*1980*	*1988*
Manufacturing Employment (Million Employees)	19.4	20.2	20.3	19.5

Source: Executive Office of the President, Office of Management and Budget, *Historical Tables—Budget of the United States Government, FY90* (Washington, DC: U.S. Government Printing Office, 1989) (for U.S. government fiscal deficit as percent of GNP); Executive Office of the President, *Economic Report of the President, 1989* (Washington, DC: U.S. Government Printing Office, 1989) (for other categories).

expansion. Over the first two phases of the current business cycle, the U.S. nonfarm productivity growth rate surpassed those registered in the same phases in the previous two cycles, although its advantage over productivity performance in the 1968–75 cycle is due entirely to the negative impact of the Phase Two recession that hit that cycle in 1969–70 (see Table 5.1). Although the advance in the nonfarm productivity growth rate of the current expansion over that of the previous business cycle is unquestionable, it is difficult to attribute this development to the supply-side tax cuts.

That virtually all of the recent productivity advances have come in the manufacturing sector and not the low productivity service sector suggests causes other than the supply-side tax initiative. Since the early 1980s U.S. manufacturing has been subjected to unusual pressures, first as a result of the deep 1980–82 recession and later, the competitive disadvantage of a vastly overvalued dollar. Manufacturing is far more sensitive than service industries to recession and currency misalignment, and under these twin assaults U.S. manufacturing was forced to rationalize its operations in order to survive. Accordingly, in the current business cycle much of the fat in the form of the excessive inventories and bloated management staffs and employment rolls that were carried in the 1970s has been reduced, producing a productivity growth rate spurt that, unlike that induced by technology and skill upgrades, has only a short-term life span. The early 1980s recession and dollar overvaluation also helped to foster a higher gross investment growth rate concentrated in equipment, and this contributed to higher productivity. But in exchange for higher short-term productivity growth rates, the U.S. manufacturing sector has suffered a contraction in size. Whereas over the course of the first three postwar business cycles U.S. manufacturing employment grew, in the current cycle it has fallen (see Table 5.1). And because the net nonresidential investment growth rate has weakened, U.S. fixed capital stock has failed to expand.

Even more deceptive than the performance of U.S. economic growth in the wake of the Reagan supply-side tax measures has been that of inflation. And more than economic growth, the behavior of U.S. price inflation in the 1980s—when contrasted to the volatile price upsurges of the 1970s—has contributed to a sense of economic wellbeing.

In the current business cycle, the intercyclical rise in U.S. price inflation visible in the progression of the past three cycles has come to an end as domestic inflation has fallen from its 1976–82 level (see Table 5.2). Crucial to this development was the unprecedented growth in the merchandise trade deficit, which permitted the U.S. economy to export its inflation to the rest of the free world (see Table 5.2). The trade deficit's explosive growth was triggered by two factors—domestic demand growth rate differentials far less favorable to U.S. external balances than were those in any previous business cycle and a dramatic appreciation in the dollar's effective exchange rate.

The domestic demand differentials were induced by the combined impact of a highly stimulative U.S. fiscal policy (the Reagan supply-side tax cuts and defense spending splurge) and constrictive fiscal policies in the non-U.S. developed sector, abetted by economic retrenchment in the developing sector impelled by balance of payments pressures issuing from depressed primary commodity prices and a drop in foreign capital inflows.[5] The appreciation of the dollar was initially sparked by interest rate differentials brought about by the sharp divergences between the fiscal and monetary policy mix of the United States and that of the remainder of the developed sector.[6] Beyond aggravating the deterioration in the U.S. merchandise trade balance, the dollar overvaluation—far more extreme than any experienced in the 1960s or 1970s—prompted a huge U.S. terms of trade advantage,

Table 5.2
The Price of U.S. Disinflation in the Current Business Cycle (Annual Averages)

	1959-67	1968-75	1976-82	1983-88
Inflation Rate (Dec.-Dec.)	1.8	6.4	8.4	3.6
Merchandise Trade Balance as % of GNP	0.7	0.0	-1.1	-2.9
Net Export Balance as % of GNP	-0.4	-1.0	0.2	-2.4
Capital Account Balance as % of GNP	-0.9	-0.9	-0.3	2.4
Current Account Balance as % of GNP	0.5	0.2	-0.2	-2.7

Source: Executive Office of the President, *Economic Report of the President, 1989* (Washington, DC: U.S. Government Printing Office, 1989) (for consumer price inflation 1959–88, merchandise trade 1959–87, net export 1959–85, current account 1959–87, GNP 1959–85); IMF, *International Financial Statistics Yearbook, 1986* (Washington, DC: IMF, 1986) and *International Financial Statistics, November 1988* (Washington, DC: IMF, 1988) (for capital account 1959–87); "Merchandise Trade: Second Quarter 1989," U.S. Department of Commerce, Bureau of Economic Analysis, August 28, 1989 (for merchandise trade 1988); U.S. Department of Commerce, "Gross National Product: Third Quarter 1989 (Preliminary)" (29 November 1989) (for 1985–88 GNP, net exports); "Summary of U.S. International Transactions: Second Quarter 1989," U.S. Department of Commerce, Bureau of Economic Analysis (12 September 1989) (for 1988 capital account and current account).

which translated into a de facto trade subsidy from the rest of the free world economy. As a result, the U.S. net export balance in goods and services in real terms has deteriorated more forcefully than in nominal terms in the current cycle (see Table 5.2), and the decline in the nominal trade balance therefore understates the degree to which U.S. domestic inflation was exported, since the real goods and services trade balance reflects the magnitude of cross-border transfers of factor inputs.

To finance its enlarged external deficits, the United States was forced to accelerate massively its sale of assets to foreigners. And in the 1980s the vast preponderance of U.S. assets sold to foreigners were debt instruments, with government debt playing a prominent role. Accordingly, the U.S. capital account balance, which had only encountered surpluses in three years prior to the 1980s, experienced large and persistent surpluses during the 1983–?? cycle (see Table 5.2). One effect of annual capital account surpluses has been to drive the U.S. net investment balance from its surplus peak in 1981 into deep deficit in the second half of the 1980s.[7] The sudden transformation of the United States from the developed sector's largest net creditor to the world's largest net debtor has fostered a condition of aggravated overindebtedness in U.S. external accounts, a condition that had already infected the government budget. As the U.S. net investment balance eroded, it caused a tumble in surpluses and, more recently, some quarterly deficits in the U.S. investment income balance, which in turn prompted a more substantial deterioration in the U.S. current account than in the merchandise trade balance.[8]

In addition to the collapse in the U.S. merchandise trade balance and the more egregious deterioration in the net export, capital account, net investment, and current account balances, the ability of the U.S. economy to escape inflation has relied on the same severe drop in the domestic demand growth rate of the rest of the free world economy that has contributed to the plunge in U.S. external balances. If these domestic demand growth rates had not fallen from their 1970s level in the current business cycle, free world economy primary input costs would have resumed their rise, and this would have driven up domestic inflation in the United States.

The Cyclical Evolution of the U.S. Economy Unaltered

The Reagan supply-side initiative was also unable to alter the structure of the evolution of the U.S. economy in the current business cycle and, worse, many of the undesirable characteristics that had marked the economy during particular phases of earlier cycles intensified.

Phase One: Mushrooming twin deficits. Phase One of the 1983–?? business cycle began, as had Phase One in 1959, 1968, and 1976, with a leap in the U.S. government fiscal deficit. But as a consequence of the Reagan tax package and defense spending program, the deficit soared beyond what might have been anticipated from the slowdown in revenues and jump in "payments to individuals" outlays provoked by the 1980–82 recession. The FY83 budget deficit climbed to nearly three times the size of the FY81 deficit (and was also close to three times the size of the FY76 deficit; see Table 5.3).

From the Phase One that began in 1968 to that of 1976, deep divergences emerged among the macroeconomic policies of leading developed economies, and these in turn produced greater intra-developed sector differentials in the pace at which domestic demand accelerated from preceding Phase Four recessions. In 1983–84 U.S. fiscal policy was even more expansionary than it had been in 1976, while the fiscal policies of the other large developed economies had become far more contractionary. Therefore the first phase of the 1983–?? business cycle saw bigger differentials among the domestic demand growth rates of key developed economies than had occurred in 1976.

Once added to a 43.7 percent appreciation of the dollar's effective exchange rate from 1980–84, the huge intra-developed sector differentials in

Table 5.3
Phase One—The Explosion of U.S. Financial Imbalances

	1975/1976	1982/1983	1984
U.S. Government Fiscal Balance ($Billion)	-53.2 / -73.7	-127.9 / -207.8	-185.3
U.S. Domestic Demand Growth Rate (%)	-1.9 / 6.0	-1.9 / 5.1	8.7
Civilian Unemployment Rate (%)	8.5 / 7.7	9.9 / 9.9	7.4
Import Growth Rate (%)	-5.4 / 26.5	-6.6 / 8.6	23.6
Merchandise Trade Balance ($Billion)	8.9 / -9.5	-36.4 / -67.1	-112.5

Source: Executive Office of the President, Office of Management and Budget, *Historical Tables—Budget of the United States Government, FY90* (Washington, DC: U.S. Government Printing Office, 1989) (for government fiscal balance); Executive Office of the President, *Economic Report of the President, 1989* (Washington, DC: U.S. Government Printing Office, 1989) (for other categories).

the behavior of domestic demand resulted in intra-developed sector import growth rate differentials far greater than those of 1976.[9] When the 1983–84 dive in developing sector imports (caused by unusual balance of payments stress) is added, the import growth rate differentials between the United States and the rest of the free world economy reached a staggering level, unparalleled in any previous Phase One. In 1983–84 the United States accounted for 91.1 percent of developed sector import growth and 119.9 percent of world import growth—a performance that towered above the U.S. role in all previous Phase Ones.[10]

The immense import growth rate differentials in the free world economy caused a worsening in the (nominal) U.S. merchandise trade deficit, which went from 1.1 percent of GNP in 1982 to 3.0 percent of GNP in 1984 (see Table 5.3). Because of the unusual terms of trade advantages accruing to the United States as a result of dollar appreciation, the collapse in its real goods and services export balance was even greater, falling from a surplus of 0.8 percent of GNP in 1982 to a deficit of 2.4 percent of GNP in 1984.[11] It was through the vehicle of these Phase One merchandise trade and net export deficits that the United States was able to export its domestic inflation abroad. But in addition to exporting inflation, it also exported GNP growth and jobs, and it was the stimulus of U.S. imports that pulled much of the free world economy out of recession by the end of Phase One. In turn, the remainder of the free world economy, led by its surging surplus economies Japan and West Germany in concert with the United Kingdom, financed the U.S. external imbalances through enlarged capital account deficits.[12] The new U.S. capital account surpluses that began in 1982 were also financed by a radical turnaround in the U.S. capital account balance with the developing sector. The retrenchment in U.S. private sector loans to embattled Third World economies transformed what had once been a large U.S. deficit into a surplus by 1983. The accumulation of capital account surpluses sent the U.S. net investment balance careening downward, approaching zero by the end of 1984.[13]

Phase Two: An abortive U.S. retrenchment and a surge in economic tensions. The depressed levels of domestic demand growth in the non-U.S. free world economy in 1983–84 more than offset the vigorous jump in U.S. domestic demand growth to produce an aggregate free world economy GNP growth rate not only lower than that experienced in 1976 but one that also advanced at a slower pace from the preceding recession. As a consequence of a deeper recession in 1980–82 compared to 1974–75 and a weaker economic recovery in 1983–84 compared to 1976, the pressures on primary input costs were visibly reduced from what they had been in the earlier cycle. Indeed, in Phase One of the current cycle, 1982–83 declines in the volume of OPEC exports provoked a slide in oil prices while nonfuel primary commodity prices showed little vitality, in contrast to their behavior at the beginning of the 1976–82 cycle.[14]

The unusual retreat in primary input costs in Phase One of the 1983–?? cycle permitted the inflation rates of the developed economies including the United States to contract for the first time in any Phase One (see Table 5.4). But while the U.S. economy enjoyed disinflation in 1983–84, a movement for macroeconomic policy retrenchment similar to those that led the U.S. economy into Phase Two in the 1959–67 and 1968–75 business cycles emerged. Still scarred by the draining war against inflation, the Federal Reserve judiciously guarded against its return, tightening monetary policy in the middle of 1984.[15] More importantly, anxiety over the shocking rise in the government fiscal deficit and its consequences for domestic capital costs persuaded the U.S. Congress to enact legislation in 1985—the Gramm-Rudman-Hollings law—charged with enforcing a fiscal retrenchment to end in a balanced budget.[16] Through this legislation Congress sought to impose discipline on itself by mandating automatic across-the-board cuts in the 25 percent of government outlays that remained "controllable" if it failed to produce sufficient budgetary savings through new taxes and/or cuts in "uncontrolled" outlays to meet annual budget deficit targets.

But despite its loud roar and a small bite in the form of a tiny across-the-board sequestration in FY86, Gramm-Rudman fizzled, to be ultimately ruled unconstitutional by the Supreme Court. In FY85 and FY86, the U.S. government fiscal deficit failed to decline (see Table 5.4). Although unable to generate a meaningful fiscal retrenchment, the Gramm-Rudman process did serve as a restraint against further expansionary fiscal measures. In the absence of new fiscal stimulus, U.S. domestic demand growth receded in the second half of 1984, and in Phase Two of the current cycle—1985-86—it dropped substantially (see Table 5.4).

The decline in the U.S. domestic demand growth rate in 1985-86 caused the import growth rate to fall, but in 1985 the U.S. merchandise trade deficit continued to widen as the remainder of the developed sector maintained a contractionary macroeconomic policy and sustained depressed domestic demand and import growth rates (see Table 5.4). By the middle of 1985 the Reagan administration was confronting the same challenge that had tested the Kennedy, Nixon, and Carter administrations before it: how to revive or sustain Phase Two U.S. economic growth while improving U.S. external balances. And like the preceding administrations, Reagan's was forced to seek an answer in a revitalization of exports. In September 1985, Treasury Secretary James Baker orchestrated a policy through the Plaza Accords that the Nixon and Carter administrations had trailblazed, one aimed at securing dollar depreciation and reflationary macroeconomic policy adjustments in the economies of surplus developed sector trading partners.[17]

Beyond the problems addressed by the traditional U.S. Phase Three prescription, the Reagan administration was forced to respond to growing economic tensions in the free world economy—tensions that worsened in the

Table 5.4
Phase Two—A Retreat in U.S. Economic Performance

	1976/1977	1978	1984/1985	1986
U.S. Government Fiscal Deficit ($Billion)	-73.7 / -14.7	-53.6	185.3 / -212.3	-221.2
Domestic Demand Growth Rate (%)	6.0 / 5.5	4.9	8.7 / 3.6	3.7
Consumer Price Inflation (Yr. to Yr. % Growth)	5.8 / 6.5	7.6	43. / 3.6	1.9
Import Growth Rate (%)	26.5 / 22.3	15.7	23.6 / 1.7	9.0
Merchandise Trade Balance ($Billion)	-9.5 / -31.1	-34.0	-112.6 / -122.1	-144.5

Source: Executive Office of the President, Office of Management and Budget, *Historical Tables—Budget of the United States Government, FY90* (Washington, DC: U.S. Government Printing Office, 1988) (for government fiscal balance); Executive Office of the President, *Economic Report of the President, 1989* (Washington, DC: U.S. Government Printing Office, 1989) (for consumer price inflation, import growth rate, merchandise trade balance); Executive Office of the President, *Economic Report of the President, 1986* (Washington, DC: U.S. Government Printing Office, 1986) (for domestic demand growth 1976, 1977, 1978, 1984, and 1985); U.S. Department of Commerce, Bureau of Economic Analysis, "Gross National Product: Third Quarter (Preliminary)" (29 November 1989) (for 1986).

low growth, high unemployment, and soft primary commodity price environments associated with Phase Two. In 1985 intra-developed sector economic friction centered about trade protectionism and North-South economic tensions focused on developing sector foreign debt-related balance of payments difficulties experienced a resurgence, and in both cases the Reagan administration's weak hand was exposed.

The "new protectionism" represents an intra-developed sector malady that has risen in intensity in the United States and Western Europe in each successive business cycle, reaching a fever pitch in the 1980–82 recession. In order to protect increasingly crowded domestic manufactured goods markets from foreign penetration, developed economies have resorted to managed trade through such vehicles as orderly marketing agreements (OMAs) and voluntary restraint agreements (VRAs), and in the high unemployment and low industrial capacity utilization conditions of Phases Two and Four, large manufactured importing developed economies have come under ever greater political pressure from organized labor and business for protectionist relief.[18] The advantage to foreign exporters rendered by acute dollar overvaluation during the 1981–82 period further invigorated the "new protectionist" momentum in the United States, and the profound imbalance in U.S.-Japan merchandise trade once again made Tokyo the primary target.[19] Economic tensions between the two countries reached a crescendo in the recession before being quieted by the positive impact on U.S. unemployment and business activity of the 1983–84 recovery and by a more accommodative Japanese trade policy under Prime Minister Yasuhiro Nakasone. Despite the benevolent impact of the economic recovery, further dollar appreciation and the rapid deterioration of U.S. external balances in 1983–84 ensured that the protectionist momentum would escalate in the harsher economic climate of Phase Two.

At the beginning of 1985, with U.S. economic growth weakening, manufacturing employment contracting, and external deficits growing, the protectionist time bomb exploded as the U.S. Congress launched a multifaceted attack concentrating on Japanese trade practices.[20] While encouraging the Reagan administration to promote its Phase Three Plaza Accord tactic, Congress's wrath (supported by popular sentiment) pushed the administration into a policy retreat that left it hard-pressed to control a dangerous upsurge in the "new protectionist" momentum.

The debt-related balance of payments crisis of the developing sector has become a principal point of tension in North-South relations. Up to Phase Four of the 1976–82 business cycle, worsening current account deficits of developing economies—caused by retreating primary commodity prices in Phases Two and Four of the business cycles and the uneven price rise favoring oil among the spectrum of primary commodities in Phase Three of the 1968–75 and 1976–82 cycles—had been financed by an increasingly accommodative developed sector international payments posture.[21] The forceful retrenchment in that policy among private lenders produced a Third World debt crisis in 1982, one that had been long in the making but gained widespread attention only as a result of the threat to global financial stability prompted by Mexico's near default. The exposed debtors of the developing world concentrated in Latin America and Africa experienced anything but an economic recovery in 1983–84 as faltering primary commodity prices combined with a sharp reduction in capital inflow to force a mammoth import compression and deep recessions.[22] In 1985 the plunge in the U.S. and developed sector domestic demand growth rates prompted a dive in nonfuel primary commodity prices, a fate temporarily avoided by oil prices as a result of OPEC "swing producer" Saudi Arabia's willingness to stabilize the price of oil by swallowing a 25 percent drop in export volume.[23]

By the middle of 1985 the decline in primary commodity prices and contraction in developing sector exports began to threaten new balance of payments crises. In October of that year, the Reagan administration responded with the Baker Plan, authored by the U.S. Treasury secretary, which sought to create a pool of private and public funds to help ease the new balance of payments stress and thereby allow developing sector debtors to enjoy higher levels of domestic demand growth.[24] But the plan met with strong resistance from creditors and debtors alike and, as a result, failed to take shape.

Phase Three: Reaching a safe haven but not before a scare. What finally served to relieve intra-developed sector protectionist and North-South debt tensions in 1987–88 was the onset of Phase Three economic conditions prompted by the Reagan administration's Plaza Accord initiative. As had occurred from 1971–73 and 1977–78 (during previous Phase Threes), the non-U.S. developed economies led by Japan and West Germany intervened to stem the momentum of dollar depreciation, enduring monetary expansions in 1986–87 greater than those in 1977–78.[25] And while developed economies aside from the U.S. maintained their stingy fiscal approach, Tokyo did come forth with a multiyear fiscal stimulus package.[26] By 1987 the rise in non-U.S. developed sector domestic demand growth (see Table 5.5) touched off a recovery in primary commodity prices, and this price recovery of 1987–88 served to ease temporarily developing sector balance of payments stress.[27] Similarly, the recovery in Western Europe's domestic demand growth rate prompted a rise in its resource utilization rate and improved domestic demand growth rate differentials set off a traditional Phase Three rally in U.S. exports, leading to a rise in the country's resource utilization rate, a contraction in the government budget deficit, and a drop in external deficits (see Table 5.5). Lower unemployment and higher capacity utilization rates in Western Europe and the United States as well as a decline in the U.S. mer-

Table 5.5
Phase Three—A Safe Haven

	1962/1963	1964	1965	1971/1972	1973	1978/1979	1986/1987	1988
Non-U.S. OECD Domestic Demand Growth Rate (%)	NA	NA	NA	3.9 / 5.3	7.2	3.2 / 4.7	3.1 / 4.2	5.3
Export Growth Rate (%)	4.0 / 7.2	14.3	3.9	1.9 / 14.1	44.5	17.6 / 29.8	3.8 / 11.4	27.9
Unemployment Rate (%)	5.5 / 5.7	5.2	4.5	5.9 / 5.6	4.9	6.1 / 5.8	7.0 / 6.2	5.5
Industrial Capacity Utilization Rate (%)	81.4 / 83.5	85.6	89.5	77.4 / 82.8	87.0	84.2 / 84.6	79.7 / 81.1	83.2
U.S. Government Fiscal Deficit ($Billion)	-7.1 / -4.8	-5.9	-1.4	-23.0 / -23.4	-14.9	-59.2 / -40.2	-221.2 / -149.7	-155.1
Merchandise Trade Balance ($Billion)	4.5 / 5.2	6.8	5.0	-2.3 / -6.4	0.9	-34.0 / -27.5	-144.2 / -159.2	-127.2

Source: OECD Economic Outlook, June 1989 (Paris: OECD: 1989) (for non-U.S. OECD domestic demand growth rate, 1971–74, 1978–79, 1986–88); Executive Office of the President, *Economic Report of the President, 1989* (Washington, DC: U.S. Government Printing Office, 1989) (for export growth, unemployment, industrial capacity utilization, U.S. government fiscal deficit, U.S. merchandise trade balance, 1962–65, 1971–74, 1978–79, 1986–87, and unemployment and U.S. government fiscal deficit, 1988), "Summary of U.S. International Transactions: Second Quarter 1989," U.S. Department of Commerce, Bureau of Economic Analysis (12 September 1989) (for 1988 export growth and U.S. merchandise trade balance); *Economic Report of the President, 1989* (for first half 1988 industrial capacity utilization) and "Capacity Utilization," Federal Reserve Board Statistical Release (14 November 1989) (for second half 1988 industrial capacity utilization).

chandise trade and current account deficits served, as in previous Phase Threes, to weaken the "new protectionist" momentum.

But in contrast to earlier Phase Threes when the upward spurt in global inflation and the recovery in U.S. external balances began within four quarters of the launch of U.S. Phase Three economic policy measures, these two developments were delayed in the current business cycle, taking more than twice as long to emerge, and this had the effect of worsening tensions within the free world economy.[28] In 1986 primary commodity prices not only failed to rally, they tumbled as Saudi Arabia abandoned its role as OPEC's "swing producer," opening the way for a collapse in world petroleum prices while nonfuel primary commodity prices continued to fall.[29] With its terms of trade diving, the developing sector's foreign debt woes mounted. Also in 1986 the U.S. merchandise trade balance not only failed to improve, it deteriorated at a greater pace than in 1985.[30] In contrast, Japan and West Germany, benefiting from the fall in primary commodity prices and the appreciation of their currencies, enjoyed a further expansion in their external surpluses.[31] The U.S. Congress responded to these developments with a higher pitched demand for "new protectionist" measures, and the Reagan administration followed by launching restrictive trade actions against virtually all of its key trading partners, including Western Europe (over corn, soybeans, and wheat), Canada (over lumber), Japan (over semiconductors), and the newly industrializing economies (over a stronger Multi-Fiber Arrangement secured in August 1986 and targeted to further cut textile imports).

But even more alarming than the growing economic friction within the free world, the delayed appearance of the tell-tale features of Phase Three triggered an unprecedented drop in the dollar's value, one that ultimately sparked financial instability. The failure of U.S. external balances to improve in 1986 and much of 1987 inspired the longest and deepest dollar depreciation of the postwar period.[32] Fearing that further depreciation would lead to a loss in the value of their U.S. investments, private foreign investors began to retrench, setting in train a stubborn bear market in the U.S. currency.[33] Concerned over the prospects for domestic recession due to anticipated losses in net exports, Tokyo and Bonn contested the dollar depreciation through official purchases of dollar assets while lobbying Washington to take actions to stem the slide of its currency. By the end of 1986, the Federal Reserve became concerned that the dollar's drop might run out of control.

In February 1987 the Group of Seven (G-7) resolved their concerns through the Louvre Accords, which represented the functional equivalent of the Smithsonian Agreement of 1971 and the Bonn Summit of 1978.[34] Through the new agreement the leading developed economies committed themselves to bringing the dollar's fall to a halt while shifting the burden for the adjustment of external imbalances to macroeconomic policy. Bonn and, to a greater extent, Tokyo pledged to increase fiscal stimulus (and thereby boost domestic demand growth) and Washington committed itself to tighten domestic monetary policy (to restrain domestic demand growth) if such action became necessary to secure the dollar exchange rate.

But over the first 10 months of 1987 the U.S. merchandise trade deficit continued to worsen, and by the summer the Fed was forced to nudge up interest rates in response to a retreating dollar.[35] Higher interest rates and dollar weakness had already inspired a huge contraction in the U.S. bond market by the time the August merchandise trade report was issued in October. The unexpected leap in the August deficit shattered the market's confidence, convincing it that U.S. interest rates would continue to rise in response to a weakening currency. As a result, stock prices plunged on Wall Street, setting off a shocking global contraction in financial asset prices.[36] Only reluctantly Washington sought to convince nervous financial markets—through the 1987 Congressional-White House Budget Summit—of its intention to adjust by fiscal means, as its Louvre commitment to monetary restraint as a mechanism for managing the dollar exchange rate was abandoned.[37] Ultimately, the only thing that saved the dollar from likely free fall was the belated recovery in the U.S. merchandise trade balance in 1988.

While the Phase Three rise in global inflation and the U.S. merchandise trade balance recovery have taken longer to mature than in earlier business cycles, the magnitude of both phenomena in the current business cycle has been smaller—and the source of these two anomalies is the same.

The later arrival and weaker acceleration in developed sector inflation in the 1983–?? business cycle is the result of a less vigorous Phase Three surge in the aggregate developed sector domestic demand growth rate from its Phase Two trough compared to the 1968–75 and 1976–82 cycles, due to a poorer recovery in the non-U.S. developed sector domestic demand growth rate. Fiscal policy among developed economies other than the United States has been more contractionary during the current cycle than in earlier cycles, and it has remained so in Phase Three. Whereas in all previous Phase Threes the central government fiscal deficit as a percentage of GNP has climbed for major U.S. developed sector trading partners, it has continued to fall in 1987–88.[38]

As a consequence of the comparative weakness in the developed sector's domestic demand growth rate in Phase Three of the current business cycle, primary input markets have come under less pressure than in 1972–74 or 1978–80 and the rise in primary input costs has therefore been weaker as well. More important, the vitality of primary commodity prices in 1987–88 suffered—in comparison to 1972–74 and 1979–81—as a result of a smaller and later arriving agricultural drought (this time centered in North America in 1988) and the absence of sufficient Persian Gulf instability and OPEC power to prompt a speculative rise in oil prices.

The smaller advance in primary input costs reflected in primary commodity prices and developed economy nominal wages in the current Phase Three has caused a smaller jump in developed sector price inflation over its Phase Two trough than occurred in the previous three postwar business cycles (see Fig. 5.1).

The same factors responsible for the weaker inflation performance in the current Phase Three have fostered a poorer U.S. merchandise trade and current account balance recovery. Despite a depreciation in the dollar's effective exchange rate from 1985–88 more than twice the size of that experienced in 1971–73 and more than three times that of 1977–79, it took the merchandise trade balance three times as long to improve in the current Phase Three than in the previous two, and the magnitude of the improvement failed to match that of the previous three Phase Threes, including the U.S. trade recovery of 1963–64 when the dollar had not depreciated. These disparities in performance spring from a later blooming and less vigorous U.S. merchandise export recovery in the current Phase Three compared to previous ones—the result of a smaller advance in the domestic demand growth rate of the non-U.S. developed sector, a weaker developing sector import recovery fostered by a poorer primary commodity price rally and more restricted access to foreign capital, and a significantly weaker acceleration in U.S. agricultural exports in the wake of a less severe Phase Three disruption

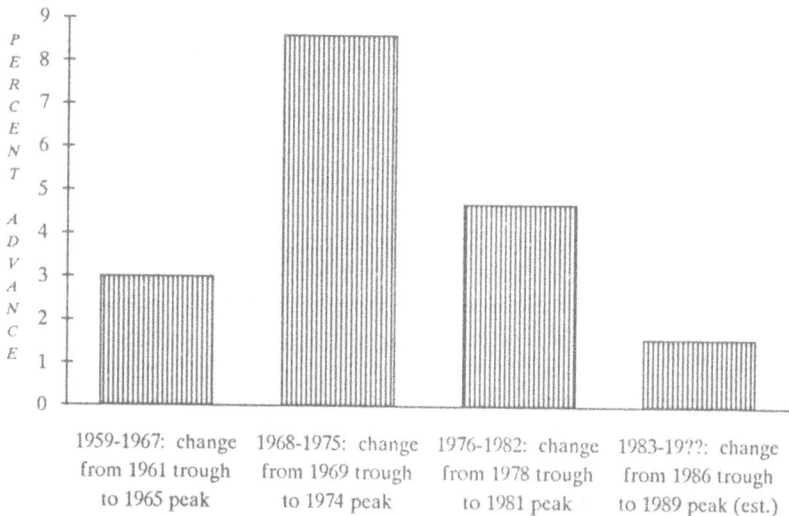

Figure 5.1. Developed sector inflation rate increase from Phase Two trough to Phase Three peak in last four business cycles. *Source:* International Monetary Fund, *International Financial Statistics Yearbook, 1986* (Washington, DC: IMF, 1986) and *International Financial Statistics Yearbook, 1988* (Washington, DC: IMF, 1988) (for 1961–65, 1969–74, and 1978–81 movement in inflation rate); authors' estimate (for 1986–89).

in world agricultural production.[39] Accordingly, measured against total merchandise exports and imports just prior to the Phase Three recovery in the merchandise trade balance, the 1988–first half 1989 recovery was smaller than any of the earlier three (see Fig. 5.2).

Further, whereas the U.S. current account balance gained more ground than the merchandise trade balance during previous Phase Threes (especially the last two), it has improved by less in the current Phase Three. In 1973 and 1979, the U.S. current account balance was bolstered by a large jump in U.S. direct investment income spawned by the dramatic leap in oil prices. With 1987–88 oil prices failing to advance, U.S. direct investment income has barely increased.[40] More important, the United States was a net creditor

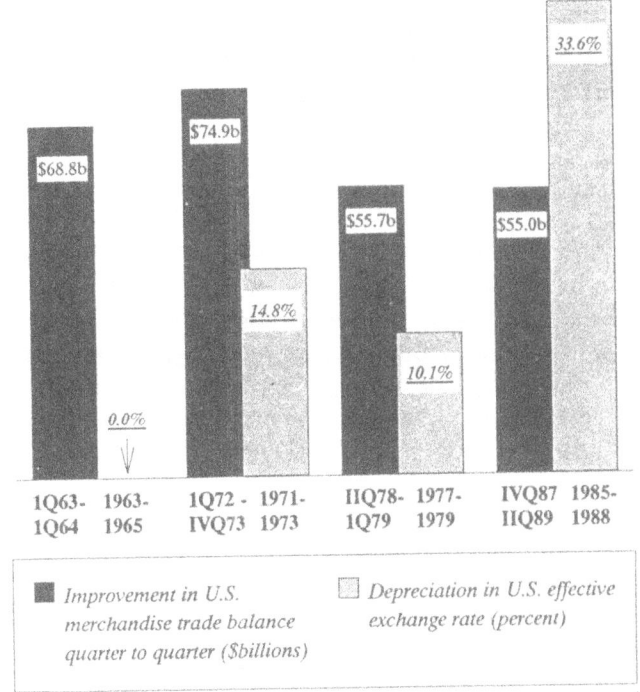

Figure 5.2. Improvement in the U.S. merchandise trade balance and the degree of dollar depreciation in phase three of the last four business cycles. *Source:* International Monetary Fund, *International Financial Statistics Yearbook, 1986* (Washington, DC: IMF, 1986) and *International Financial Statistics, November 1988* (Washington, DC: IMF, 1988) (for 1959–87 U.S. effective exchange rate); U.S. Department of Commerce, Bureau of Economic Analysis, *National Income and Product Accounts of the United States, 1929–82—Statistical Tables* (for 1959–67, 1968–75, and 1976–82 merchandise trade balances); Executive Office of the President, *Economic Report of the President, 1989* (Washington, DC: U.S. Government Printing Office, 1989) and U.S. Department of Commerce, Bureau of Economic Analysis, "Summary of U.S. International Transactions: Second Quarter 1989," BEA 89-41 (12 September 1989) (for current cycle merchandise trade balance).

in 1973 and 1979 while in 1987–88 it was a large net debtor, a turnaround that fomented a huge deterioration in the U.S. investment income balance.[41]

Looking Beyond the Short Term

Economic near-sightedness has a way of perpetuating itself when the short-term picture looks rosy, and in 1989 the relatively comfortable condition of the U.S. economy was enough to persuade some observers that it might never leave the agreeable environs of Phase Three. What has made Phase Three of the 1983–?? business cycle so enticing is the weakness of inflation, especially when compared with its sudden acceleration into the double-digit range in Phase Three of the 1968–75 and 1976–82 cycles. The marginal upswing in inflation suggests that the traditional contractionary macroeconomic policy response associated with the beginning of Phase Four will be mild and that the consequent retreat of economic growth will be small. As a result, the duration of Phase Three will be longer than in the previous two cycles while Phase Four may permit a "soft landing" for the U.S. and free world economies, allowing them to escape a recession.

The longer span of Phase Three in the current business cycle will provide more time during which the U.S. government's fiscal and external overindebtedness will appear to recede without Washington having to administer painful adjustment as the cyclical components of the budget and merchandise trade deficits vanish. It also offers the free world economy a bigger breathing space during which high developed sector resource utilization rates restrain the momentum of the "new protectionism" and revived primary commodity prices soften the Third World debt crisis. Indeed, by 1989 with global stock prices having recovered and with the dollar stabilized and even appreciating, Black Monday seemed a distant aberration.

Further, a "soft landing" in Phase Four of the current cycle would provide an opportunity to escape the aggravation in intra-free world economic tensions that occurred as a result of the sharp drop in developed sector resource utilization rates and in primary commodity prices in the previous two Phase Fours.

The problem, however, is that the plausibility of continued positive economic conditions ends here. The same forces that produced the single factor—weaker inflation—that is making Phases Three and Four of the current cycle seem more hospitable than the previous two have also fostered a relatively weak recovery in U.S. external balances. Accordingly, the U.S. economy will exit Phase Three of this business cycle with extraordinary merchandise trade and current account deficits which, to be financed, will require unprecedented U.S. capital account surpluses and a rapidly growing net investment deficit.[42] In addition, in Phase Four U.S. external deficits and more emphatically the U.S. government fiscal deficit will once again assume the burden of a cyclical component and are thus likely to grow, widening the prospect for financial instability.

Of critical importance, these developments will not only serve to constrain U.S. and world economic growth in the next business cycle, they will demand that the structural evolution of the U.S. economy that persisted through the last four postwar free world economy business cycles be fundamentally altered. While investors would react vociferously against a further deterioration in the U.S. government fiscal and merchandise trade balances, just such deterioration marked the Phase One "take off" of all four previous cycles and has become increasingly aggravated in each successive Phase One. And in each successive Phase One, the economic vigor of the non-U.S. free world economy has come to depend more and more on U.S. import growth—to the point where in 1983-84 the United States assumed the burden of more than 100 percent of world import growth.

While the paralysis of U.S. government fiscal policy in the coming business cycle means that U.S. domestic demand growth will be lower than during the 1983-?? cycle (especially during Phase One), large components of the world economy, led by the developing sector and the CPEs plagued by soft primary commodity prices and foreign overindebtedness, will be unable to offset the retreat in U.S. macroeconomic policy. Only Japan and the surplus economies of Western Europe will enjoy sufficient macroeconomic policy flexibility to expand. But in Phase One of the last two cycles, these economies became increasingly conservative in their approach.[43] If they shun macroeconomic expansion in the coming cycle, lower resource utilization rates in the developed sector and anemic primary commodity prices loom, which will trigger a new round of intra-free world economic tensions. Further, whatever willingness these economies express to sustain more expansive macroeconomic policies in the next cycle will be challenged by a growing inflationary threat caused by an underlying weakening in the supply status of primary inputs. During the 1980s the free world economy's extractive sectors, led by petroleum, experienced disinvestment, while developed sector demographics point to a slowdown in the growth of the potential labor market (especially the skilled workforce).

Beyond intolerance for any expansion in the U.S. twin deficits in the coming business cycle, investors will exert pressure for their reduction. Even though the degree of force they will apply remains uncertain and highly volatile, what is certain is that the perpetuation of the current status of U.S. international transactions in the future will become increasingly unsupportable.[44] Hence, in some form the U.S. economy will endure an adjustment in the 1990s, one that must have at its center a reduction in the U.S. government fiscal deficit.

Lower U.S. economic growth and pressure for fiscal deficit reduction will ensure that during the coming business cycle, the United States will confront an "economic dimension of security vulnerability," and the bias of its leaders and people expressed in the 1969–80 period in response to the opening of the "dimension" suggests that U.S. national security expenditures will erode.

A REVOLUTION IN NATIONAL SECURITY ACCOUNTS

From 1981–88 under the stewardship of the Reagan administration, U.S. national security accounts underwent radical transformations. While most attention has been drawn to the expansion in government national security expenditures—almost wholly the outcome of an unparalleled peacetime advance in national defense outlays—a change nearly equal in magnitude and more revolutionary in its implications transpired in another area. During this period, in all accounts related to international transactions the United States became the world's largest net importer of resources, thus experiencing an astounding turnaround over the postwar period. From 1947–50 the United States sought to enhance its national security by restoring the economies of its Eurasian allies through large merchandise trade, current account, and real net export surpluses as well as unusual capital account deficits; from 1981–88, however, it accumulated huge merchandise trade, current account, and real net export deficits along with unprecedented capital account surpluses, and these resource transfers, largely from U.S. Eurasian allies, supported the rejuvenation of the U.S. national defense sector.

From FY81–FY88 three-quarters of the cumulative growth in nominal national defense outlays above the FY80 level were supported by the cumulative expansion in U.S. goods, services, and financial deficits with the rest of the world that had occurred over the same period (see Fig. 5.3). This means that Americans effectively contributed only one-quarter of the resources accounted for in the cumulative growth of the defense sector during the Reagan period, the remainder having been borrowed from foreigners. If the United States had been left to itself to supply the factors of production and financing for the full national defense expansion, the current U.S. economic recovery would have burned up early in the flames of inflation. Alternatively, to avoid inflation the national defense build-up of the 1980s could have been financed at the expense of the civilian economy through increased taxes or by cutting other outlays, including "payments to individuals," both of which would have weakened the economic expansion. These latter two options would have also involved a major transfer of resources from personal consumption to defense. Because of their harsh implication for economic performance and their penalization of personal consumption,

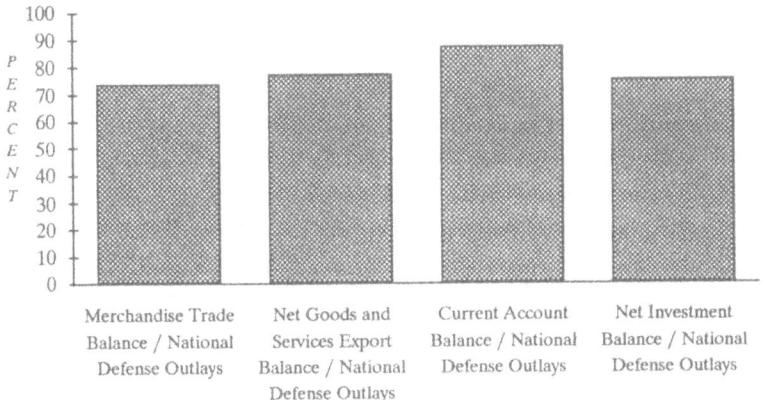

Figure 5.3. Cumulative size of external balance deterioration from 1980 level to 1988 as percent of cumulative size of growth in national defense outlays from FY80 level to FY88. *Source:* Executive Office of the President, Office of Management and Budget, *Historical Tables—Budget of the United States Government, FY90* (Washington, DC: U.S. Government Printing Office, 1989) (for FY80–88 national defense outlays); Executive Office of the President, *Economic Report of the President, 1989* (Washington, DC: U.S. Government Printing Office, 1989) (for 1980 merchandise trade balance, current account balance, net investment balance, and net export balance); U.S. Department of Commerce, Bureau of Economic Analysis, "Summary of U.S. International Transactions: Second Quarter 1989," BEA 89-41 (12 September 1989) (for 1988 merchandise trade balance and current account balance); U.S. Department of Commerce, Bureau of Economic Analysis, "GNP Second Quarter 1989—Advance" (27 July 1989) (for 1988 net export balance); Department of Commerce, Bureau of Economic Analysis, "U.S. Net International Investment Position, 1988" (29 June 1989).

alternatives that would have relied on domestic resources to revive U.S. national defenses would have rapidly lost political support. In effect, what the revolution in U.S. international transactions permitted the Reagan administration to enact was a "guns and butter" policy which, if it had had to rely on domestic resources alone, would have quickly foundered, as had that of the second Johnson administration.

The funding surge in national security accounts was targeted to address the perceived theatre and strategic asymmetries that had arisen in the 1970s and the vast majority of the funding increase took place in the national defense sector. In the FY81–FY88 period, U.S. national defense outlays enjoyed their first postwar peacetime advance as percentages of GNP and government outlays—something that had only occurred previously during the Korean War years of FY51–54 and during the Vietnam War peak in FY66–68. Further, real national defense outlays rose by 54.2 percent from FY80 to FY88, a leap whose magnitude had been surpassed only in the transition from the postwar demobilization regime to the contemporary national security spending regime (see Appendix A). Even the rise in U.S. national defense spending during the Vietnam War did not match that of the Reagan years.

But when viewed in isolation the Reagan defense sector recovery appears more impressive than when seen in the context of U.S. national defense expenditures over the course of the FY69–76 period of accelerated disinvestment and the Carter plateau years of FY77–80. From the Vietnam War defense spending peak to the regime nadir during the Carter plateau, average national defense outlays as a percentage of GNP and of government outlays fell more forcefully than these percentages rose from the Carter plateau to the Reagan period, and while national defense outlays in FY82 dollars jumped to $252.9 billion in FY88, they still fell short of the Vietnam War period peak of $254.8 billion reached in FY68 (see Table 5.6).

Indeed, the primary focus of the 1980s defense effort was to redress the process that had weakened U.S. defenses during the preceding decade—the process of accelerated disinvestment. Hence, as real national defense spending grew each year from FY81–87, the percentage of defense outlays devoted to investment increased each year and the rate of growth of defense investment accordingly accelerated beyond that of defense spending as a whole (see Table 5.7). Further, the procurement component of defense investment, which led the process of accelerated disinvestment from FY69–76, was also the principal ingredient driving the process of accelerated investment from FY81–87 (see Table 5.7). Defense research and development underwent unusual real growth in the 1980s as well, with much of this increase resulting from a rejuvenation of weapons development, an effort directly supportive of short-term procurement.

The Reagan defense build-up was thus concentrated in the modernization of defense machinery, a process that had been paralyzed in the 1970s. As a consequence, it was functionally biased toward contemporary military technologies. Despite the enormous weapons development and procurement

Table 5.6
The Fall and Rise of U.S. National Defense Outlays since the Vietnam War Peak

	Vietnam War Peak FY66-68 Avg.	Carter Plateau FY77-80 Avg.	Reagan Period FY81-88
National Defense Outlays as % of GNP	8.8	4.9	6.1
National Defense Outlays as % of U.S. Government Outlays	44.9	22.7	27.3

Source: Executive Office of the President, Office of Management and Budget, *Historical Tables—Budget of the United States Government, FY90* (Washington, DC: U.S. Government Printing Office, 1989).

Table 5.7
The Fall and Rise of Defense Investment and Procurement from the Vietnam War Peak

	Vietnam War Peak FY66-68 Avg.	Carter Plateau FY77-80 Avg.	Period of Accelerated Investment FY81-87 Avg.
Defense Investment as a % of National Defense Outlays	40.6	34.1	40.9
	FY88	FY80	FY87
National Defense Procurement (Billion FY82 Dollars)	72.5	35.5	71.6

Source: Executive Office of the President, Office of Management and Budget, *Historical Tables—Budget of the United States Government, FY90* (Washington, DC: U.S. Government Printing Office, 1989).

programs of the 1980s, the U.S. effort to overcome the ill effects of earlier defense disinvestment was plagued by the rapidly rising unit costs of new, more sophisticated defense machinery, a phenomenon that hit public consciousness near the close of the decade when the immense unit costs of the B-2 bomber became a cause celebre.[45] American defense planners confronted a force structure that—despite the unprecedented procurement boom—failed to increase, aside from the navy (and by the end of the decade the planned increase in naval vessels was scaled back).[46]

So, while improving the quality of force structure, the 1980s modernization surge made no dent in the U.S. quantitative Euro-theatre disadvantages and even failed to eliminate the principal military asymmetry that the Reagan administration vowed to remedy at the beginning of the decade—the theoretical "window of vulnerability."[47] Secretary of Defense Caspar Weinberger promoted a specific nuclear force investment program that differed from that of the Carter administration; nonetheless, he did not seek to enhance the relative priority of strategic forces. In fact, as a percentage of national defense TOA, strategic force funding (including funding for the Strategic Defense Initiative) increased little compared to its performance in the Carter Plateau period and remained below its average percentage of DOD TOA for the period of accelerated disinvestment.[48] Further, although during the first two years of the Reagan administration elements of the civilian staff at the Department of Defense became enamored of ambitious protracted nuclear war operational requirements, this interest later waned, leaving the U.S. offensive nuclear doctrine inherited from the late 1970s intact.[49] Indeed, in 1982 the bipartisan Scowcroft Commission sponsored by Weinberger to examine the question of future nuclear offensive force modernization concluded that the issue of ICBM vulnerability was overblown, citing the existence of robust U.S. long-range aircraft and submarine-based elements of the strategic triad.[50] Though the remainder of the 1980s, the "window of vulnerability," so much a matter of concern at the end of the previous decade, faded.

Yet despite the failure to right military imbalances identified as most threatening to U.S. national security at the beginning of the Reagan administration, the credibility of the U.S. deterrent grew during the Reagan years. The revival of the national defense sector was paralleled by a series of less costly initiatives that helped reduce the degree of perceived asymmetries in the military arenas in which imbalances had appeared to grow most rapidly in the 1970s—the global and Eurasian theatres.

Although expanding by less than 2 percent a year in real terms, "international affairs" outlays helped underwrite a new Reagan Doctrine in which Washington supplied security and other forms of assistance to insurgent forces active in global theatres where Moscow's empire had extended in the second half of the 1970s, enhancing the threat these forces posed to the ability of weak Soviet allied regimes to consolidate power.[51] In Afghanistan and Angola, the United States discovered the advantages of being on the side of a motivated insurgent force, as the Soviets had in Vietnam. Washington found that it could supply insurgents with sufficient levels of military support— above all, air defense weapons—to frustrate the military power of the Soviet Union in Afghanistan and of Cuba in Angola. The credibility of Washington's challenge to Moscow's expansion into global theatres was reinforced by the use of American military force in the 1983 invasion of Grenada, the first such use of force since the Vietnam War. The later 1986 U.S. air raid on Libya enhanced the perception of renewed American willingness to use limited military force under certain conditions in global theatres. And the U.S. will to push through acceptance of theatre nuclear deployments (the Pershing lls and ground-launched cruise missiles) on the soil of its West European allies and to promote a "zero option" proposal for the elimination of intermediate range missiles in the Euro-theatre led to a galvanization of the NATO alliance around a goal of offsetting Euro-theatre advantages won by Moscow in the 1970s.[52]

During the mid-1980s, perhaps no events more than the Soviet Union's withdrawal from Afghanistan and acquiescence to elimination of its stock of SS-20s through the INF agreement prompted a shift in perception of the superpower balance from the unfavorable asymmetries of the 1970s to the restoration of equilibrium. Reagan's accelerated investment in national defense was a factor in this turn of events, but its precise role remains nebulous. Even more than the 1980s invigoration of U.S. and allied resistance to the earlier Soviet advances in the global and Euro-theatres, Moscow's growing "economic dimension" and its response to it were the crucial factors impelling it to pull out of Afghanistan and sign the INF accord. Similarly, the revolutionary developments in Eastern Europe at the end of the decade owed their emergence to the long cycle economic decline gripping the entire Soviet empire.

An even greater gulf between image and reality than that found in the exaggerated notions of the size and achievements of the FY81–87 process of accelerated investment in the U.S. national defense sector emerged from the Reagan administration's flirtations with transcentury weapons. The bark from the administration's initiatives in this area turned out to be larger than their bite.

Relative to the amount of resources committed to contemporary military technologies and their exploitation, the allotment to transcentury weapons in the 1980s was miniscule. Despite the outcry over the SDI program, real resources devoted to strategic defenses remained smaller in the 1980s than they had been in the 1960s. What was larger was the publicly articulated goal given strategic defenses and the enormous costs associated with future development and deployment. Implied in President Reagan's March 23, 1983, announcement of a national commitment to make nuclear missiles "impotent and obsolete" was a radical revision of a U.S. postwar nuclear doctrine that had grudgingly accepted the argument that offensive nuclear forces would dominate. The lack of a national consensus behind such a transition, serious technical questions associated with its feasibility, and unusual costs required to effect it left the program vulnerable to attack.[53]

Less visible than the Reagan administration's embrace of transcentury weapons in the strategic nuclear realm but equally ambitious were a series of initiatives aimed at promulgating the cause of transcentury weapons and warfighting strategies for nonnuclear forces in both theatre and strategic arenas. Like the SDI program, they too suffered from a credibility gap in which practical reality remained far from articulated goals, as through the course of the 1980s proponents of the U.S. Army's Air/Land Battle and the U.S. Navy's "maritime strategy" found themselves promoting transcentury weapons strategies in the absence of transcentury weapons.

Rejecting its own passive attrition orientation for forces in the Euro-theatre, the army introduced under the banner of Air/Land Battle a new approach that argued for a dynamic and offensive oriented Euro-theatre strategy in the early 1980s. This strategy was to be implemented through the exploitation of 1980s-generation weapons.[54] Later, a high technology spinoff of Air/Land Battle was crafted by the Supreme Allied Commander of NATO, General Bernard Rogers. The concept of Follow On Forces Attack (FOFA) represented an explicit effort to exploit innovations in RSTA and PGM technology anticipated to emerge in the 1990s in order to forge a qualitative counter to the quantitative superiority of Warsaw Pact forces in the Eurotheatre. Unforeseen technical difficulties that drove up the already enormous costs projected for implementation of FOFA have helped to undermine the expected 1990s revolution in weapons technology, and today the "Rogers Plan" remains a primarily a paper one.[55]

Part of the reason for the disproportionate growth in the navy's procurement compared to that of the army and air force in the 1980s was a new "maritime strategy" that postulated the possibility of nonnuclear strategic warfare with the Soviet Union conducted not with transcentury weapons systems but contemporary warships and naval air systems. As defined by its most forceful advocate, former Navy Secretary John Lehman, central to the concept was the idea that the United States should be prepared to fight a protracted nonnuclear global war against the Soviet Union without resorting to the early use of nuclear weapons in the event of a failed nonnuclear campaign in defense of Western Europe.[56]

U.S. National Defense Spending in the 1990s

The U.S. national defense sector enters the 1990s with vulnerabilities. While continuing to suffer from rising unit costs for new defense machinery, it also must spend more on O&M to maintain the more sophisticated—and therefore more costly—inventory of machinery generated during the 1980s period of accelerated investment. At the same time, transcentury weapons programs have been losing credibility, a loss that has contributed to a decline in funding.

Beyond these factors, the U.S. national defense sector has already begun to feel the tremors set off by the need to reduce U.S. domestic and external deficits. Beginning in FY86 real national defense budget authority began to contract, by FY88 the investment component of national defense outlays sank—bringing to an end the period of accelerated investment—and in FY89 and FY90 real defense outlays were projected to fall.[57]

In the 1990s the U.S. economy will suffer greater resource stress than in the previous decade as investor wariness over government fiscal and external overindebtedness undermines GNP growth and steers the American government toward fiscal adjustment. Within this more austere economic environment, the 1980s perturbations in U.S. national security accounts will come under pressure to recede. The mammoth transfer of resources to the United States from the rest of the free world economy reflected in U.S. international transactions will be forced to shrink, while U.S. government national security outlays will be pressed to fall in real terms. Already in the wake of the Gramm-Rudman budget cutting legislation and the plummeting investor confidence that triggered a series of events leading to the fall 1987 Budget

Summit, real budget authority for national defense has fallen. This process in turn produced a continuous retrenchment in outyear real outlay projections for defense over the course of the second Reagan administration (see Fig. 5.4).

The magnitude of the decline in these outyear projections would have been even greater were it not for the impact of Phase Three of the current business cycle, which served to ease the momentum for U.S. government budget and merchandise trade deficit reduction by eliminating the cyclical components of the twin deficits. But political and financial market pressures to cut these deficits are certain to increase in the early 1990s when their cyclical components reemerge. The consequences of these pressures—lower U.S. economic growth and a more contractionary government fiscal policy—will promote an awareness of the U.S. "economic dimension of security vulnerability," which in the 1980s was buried under the seeming success of the Reagan "guns and butter" approach.

Indeed, this reality was acknowledged by the Bush administration when Secretary of Defense Richard Cheney announced late in the fall of 1989 a five-year defense program to begin in FY91 involving annual increases in DOD budget authority lower than the estimated rate of inflation. As recently as the summer of 1989 the White House had been projecting five-year defense spending to grow slightly faster than inflation. In the face of mounting

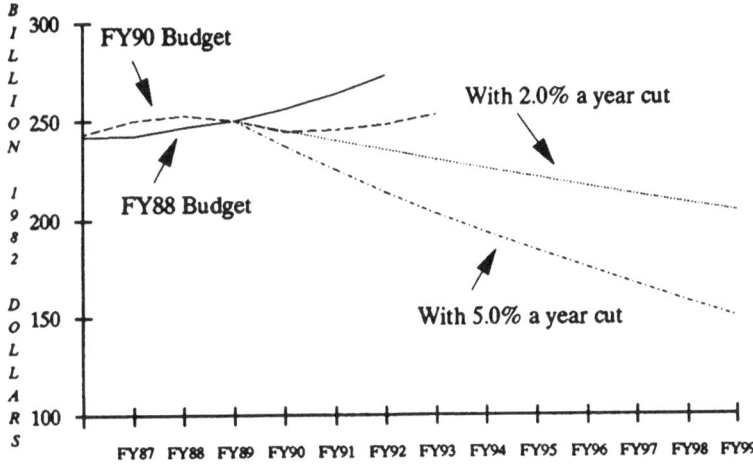

Figure 5.4. Reagan administration estimates vs. probable real U.S. defense spending in the 1990s. *Source:* Executive Office of the President, Office of Management and Budget, *Historical Tables—Budget of the United States Government, FY88* (Washington, DC: U.S. Government Printing Office, 1987) and Executive Office of the President, Office of Management and Budget, *Historical Tables—Budget of the United States Government, FY90* (Washington, DC: U.S. Government Printing Office, 1989) (for changing Reagan administration outyear outlay projections for national defense).

fiscal pressures supported by political changes in Eastern Europe, the administration acquiesced to negative real growth in defense spending into the mid-1990s.[58]

By December 1989 the four services were preparing to make substantial cuts in force structure and contemporary weapons modernization and the Defense Department moved to pare back further development of transcentury weapons. The army proposed cutting two heavy armored/mechanized divisions from Europe and three U.S.-based divisions. M-1 battle tank production was to be terminated and production of contemporary PGMs reduced. The navy's goal of a 600-ship fleet was abandoned and replaced with a new 500-ship target. The Marine Corps was to reduce personnel by 21 percent. Finally, the air force offered up large-scale cuts in its tactical aircraft fleet with the elimination of five fighter wings and a stretch-out in procurement of contemporary aircraft including the B-2 bomber.[59]

The postwar history of U.S. national resource priorities, and even more emphatically their behavior in response to the "economic dimension" in the 1970s, suggests the probable character of the instinctive American reaction to the reappearance of the "dimension" in the 1990s: forces pressing to further raise the relative status of personal consumption will gain ascendancy. Washington will be inclined to protect "payments to individuals" and discretionary domestic spending while avoiding any new taxes that could weaken already fragile economic growth. Postwar history also indicates that U.S. national security accounts will be targeted to bear a disproportionate share of the burden of fiscal adjustment (a tendency that will be intensified by the perception of a retreating Soviet threat) and that the transfer of these savings to personal consumption will ensure a slower pace of new investment and, hence, of supply-side adjustment.

If the U.S. national resource policy of the 1970s is reinvoked in the 1990s, the worst of all possible worlds for national security accounts will have reemerged. Assuring less resources for national security in the 1990s than enjoyed in the 1980s, such a turn of events would also undercut prospects for a rejuvenation of the U.S. economy, as needed advances in the pace of supply-side adjustment will have been avoided, thereby undermining the ability of the nation's economy to support higher national security expenditures at the beginning of the next century.

While U.S. national defense spending will confront a hostile economic environment in the 1990s, both the severity of that environment and the degree to which national defense spending will suffer remain uncertain. Two factors are likely to join in defining the dimensions of the 1990s U.S. national defense retrenchment: the degree to which investors lose confidence in the U.S. economy and the status of the Soviet threat.

Financial markets will not tolerate a further expansion of the U.S. government fiscal deficit, but the degree of pressure they exert for deficit reduction may vary. Accordingly, the plausible range of U.S. government deficit reduction measures could span from moderate efforts like those of the second half of the 1980s to more probable harsher initiatives. At the same time the intensity of the Soviet national defense effort may span from the levels associated with deep cuts as proposed by Ryzhkov to those resulting from a "moderate cuts" defense spending approach. The interaction of these variables defines the extremes of minimal and maximal U.S. defense spending decline for the 1990s within which this spending may range.

The drop in real defense outlays in the 1990s may exceed that experienced in the 1970s. From FY69–79, real defense outlays fell at an annual rate of 4 percent. This period, and more specifically the era of accelerated disinvestment that it included, overlapped the reduction in U.S. force structure in Southeast Asia. In the 1990s the United States could experience a more dramatic contraction in its foward military presence, especially its force structure in the Euro-theatre. Under conditions of maximum plausible U.S. force structure reduction induced by a decline in the Soviet threat (where Soviet defense spending converges on the "deep cuts" defined by Ryzhkov) and by strong pressures to reduce U.S. economic imbalances, defense spending could contract by a maximum 5.0 percent a year over the course of the 1990s. Under these conditions, by the turn of the century U.S. defense spending would be in the process of exiting the contemporary spending regime that has existed since FY51. The lowest plausible annual average outlay contraction for national defense in the 1990s—one compelled by moderate pressure for U.S. economic adjustment and a Soviet national defense effort limited to "moderate cuts"—would be 2.0 percent a year (see Fig. 5.4).

Chapter 6

The Defense Investment Dilemma of the 1990s:
Contemporary or Transcentury Weapons?

During the 1990s the squeeze on U.S. defense investment resources may exceed that experienced in the 1970s, when real procurement fell by more than 50 percent. Under any circumstances, the plausible range of U.S. defense spending in the coming decade will mean an immense drop in defense investment from that enjoyed during the Reagan period of accelerated investment. To what purpose should these limited resources be directed?

An important dilemma faces American defense planners as they move to respond to this question. At the same time that defense investment resources will be shriveling, the unit costs of producing contemporary defense machinery, especially manned combat vehicles, will be surging, as will the operations and maintenance (O&M) expenses associated with more sophisticated defense machinery. Beyond these demands on resources, technological advance has created the possibility for an escalation over the transcentury period to a new range of weapons that in theory could seriously degrade the deterrent and warfighting value of contemporary forces. The asymmetrical deployment of these weapons could provide a superpower with new military operational capabilities that greatly diminish the military worth of opposing forces equipped with contemporary weapons. But exploiting the new technologies would involve a formidable expense. Even prior to facing the staggering costs of production and deployment of these weapons in the next century, a vast investment would have to be made in building the needed research and development base in the remainder of this century.

Within the parameters of meager defense budgets over the coming decade, prioritization of either contemporary or transcentury weapons would mean the near elimination of investment resources for the other. In choosing to emphasize investment in transcentury weapons, defense planners must accept further sacrifices in modernization and force structure beyond those driven by declining budgets and rising unit costs. These sacrifices would have to be weighed against the possibility that failure to invest in transcentury weapons could result in a radical degradation of deterrent and coercive capabilities and a waste of investment in an inventory of contemporary weapons that are rendered obsolete at the beginning of the next century.

TRANSCENTURY WEAPONS: COMPONENTS AND COSTS

PGM/RSTA Warfare

For the last two decades there has been a debate within the U.S. national security community over the prospects for a "revolution" in nonnuclear warfare. The debate has centered around whether guided weapons, now commonly known as precision guided munitions (PGMs), have changed the nature of warfare. In theory, precision guided munitions should allow for the efficient destruction of the full range of ground-, air-, and sea-based targets. Advocates of the transformation believe that PGMs have called into question the current emphasis on the development of ever more costly combat vehicles—battle tanks, fighter bombers, and surface warships.[1] Coupled with improved tactics and theatre-wide reconnaissance, surveillance, and target acquisition (RSTA) systems, it may be possible to inflict heavy losses on an opponent massively equipped with contemporary weapons but unprotected by appropriate countermeasures. The Israeli success against the Syrian air force and ground defense units during the military confrontation in Lebanon in the summer of 1982—often cited as the model application of PGM/RSTA capabilities—suggests this possibility.[2]

Yet there has been considerable skepticism expressed about the extent and prospects for a PGM/RSTA "revolution." The technological challenges to military effectiveness and the economic costs have already retarded this mooted transformation in warfare. The history of technological innovation in warfare is a story of measure and countermeasure, and PGM systems are not immune to this dynamic.

Perhaps the clearest example of the vulnerability of PGMs to countermeasures and therefore to spiraling costs has been the history of the antitank guided missile (ATGM).[3] A process of measure and countermeasure between the developers of ATGMs and the developers of the armored fighting vehicle has produced an escalation in economic costs and military uncertainties. In the late 1950s a first generation of wire guided ATGMs was deployed, leading the heavy main battle tank to be declared "obsolete." In fact, the early performance of these lightweight and mobile guided munitions was so impressive in field tests that Soviet leader Nikita Khrushchev was moved to declare that the main battle tank, the hub of Soviet ground force structure and doctrine, would pass into history as the dominant weapon. Similar views were expressed in the West.[4]

The designers of the main battle tank quickly responded with development of a number of low cost countermeasures, led by short-range optical smoke grenades. By the early 1980s the ATGM designers had countered with a new generation able to function under adverse optical conditions. The battle tank designers responded with new armor concepts, leading to heavier battle tanks. This approach involved a hefty increase in unit costs as the first-line NATO tank rose in weight nearly 30 percent.[5] Most recently, Soviet deployment of "reactive" armor has fueled a further ratchet up in the competition as a "tank panic" within NATO spurred innovations leading to a new generation of ATGMs.

This process which has funnelled rising inputs into ATGMs has been repeated for other varieties of PGMs, as similar measure/countermeasure contests have been under way between the designers of surface-to-air missiles/combat aircraft and antiship missiles/surface ships.[6] The rising unit costs of PGMs have already won them the appellation "golden bullets." Further, many targets can be reconstituted after suffering damage from nonnuclear hits, and this dramatically increases the inventory requirements for PGMs sufficient to carry out a militarily decisive campaign and, therefore, the costs of any PGM revolution.[7]

Contemporary guided munitions as well as the more traditional components of the armed forces already rely on RSTA systems, but the costs of rendering these systems combat capable and insulated from countermeasures promise to be enormous.

A wide array of technologically sophisticated sensors and communications systems has already been deployed, but they have been optimized for peacetime intelligence collection and have consequently been left vulnerable to direct attack. Rendering these systems battleworthy is one of the costly technological challenges facing the United States and the Soviet Union in the RSTA area.[8]

Despite huge and unknown costs and uncertainty over the degree of military effectiveness of PGM/RSTA systems, they hold the promise of an immense payoff. Their advocates believe that it will be possible to deploy transcentury weapons systems capable of significantly attriting contemporary combat vehicles and that the combatant that gains RSTA dominance—even while directing air, ground, and naval forces equipped with contemporary weapons—will gain the advantage.[9]

Space: "The Fourth Dimension" of Warfare

Since October 4, 1957—the Soviet launching of Sputnik—there has been an expansion of the role of space as a zone of military operations. For the last three decades satellites have proven powerful as platforms to conduct RSTA (in fact, earth observation satellites launched the "reconnaissance revolution"), to assist in navigation, and to provide communications relays.

As these developments unfolded, the notion of space as a military sanctuary took hold, legitimized through arms control negotiations between the two superpowers in which space-based reconnaissance was sanctioned as part of the arms control verification regime.[10] But future developments may place the sanctuary status of space under stress, especially during a major conflict.

In the transcentury period, space's most important role is likely to be as a repository for RSTA systems. Developments during the 1990s are expected to enable the information acquired by space-based RSTA platforms to be relayed directly to mobile tactical forces, including aircraft in flight and ships at sea, indicating their future crucial role in directing nonnuclear forces.

In response to this reconnaissance threat, modern combat forces have come to rely increasingly upon camouflage, concealment, and deception measures as well as increased emphasis on the deployment of mobile platforms to frustrate opponents' targeting attempts.[11] Exploitation of space for military purposes could experience a substantial rise in costs in response to such countermeasures. Near-term RSTA initiatives aimed at enhancing reconnaissance and targeting support for nonnuclear forces may include "staring" sensor platforms operating at geosynchronous orbit at altitudes from which continentwide zones and oceans can be placed under continuous surveillance, more sensitive sensors capable of detecting high altitude aircraft and cruise missiles, radar deployed as an all-weather surveillance and target acquisition means, and, by the turn of the century, multispectral sensors tied to increasingly powerful supercomputers and able to resolve subtle target signatures at ground level.[12]

Space-based RSTA systems have a crucial role to play in the strategic nuclear realm as well. Nowhere has the process of mobility and concealment to avert detection been more evident than in the arena of nuclear weapons competition between the two superpowers. The strategic balance, like the nonnuclear balance, will therefore become increasingly less dependent on the quantitative and qualitative characteristics of offensive forces than on RSTA capabilities. For the planner of countermilitary operations against an opponent's nuclear arsenal, the problem of finding "strategically relocatable targets" has already become the central challenge.

The transcentury military exploitation of space also holds out the prospect for an enhancement of navigation aids of potential importance for the economic feasibility of PGMs. Currently, the United States is in the process of deploying an orbital constellation of NAVSTAR satellites, and the Soviets are deploying an analogous system, GLONASS.[13] With the use of low cost inertial platforms and satellite updates, relatively cheap and accurate nonnuclear armed long-range cruise missiles could appear in large numbers, reducing the cost of the prospective PGM "revolution" in warfare.

Further, precise and low cost navigation aids could enhance the military efficiency of all aspects of combined arms operations as accurate position "self awareness" would boost the ability of unit commanders and their superiors to direct mobile forces in highly dynamic battlefield situations.

Another use for space-based systems, though less important than their use for RSTA and navigation, is the exploitation of satellite relays for long-range communications. Currently, both superpowers deploy large constellations of satellite communications systems (SATCOMs) to support theatre and strategic forces. The next generation of SATCOMs will employ narrow-beam communications, probably including laser relays with which submarines could gain access to larger quantities of targeting information.[14] This may allow modern submarines equipped with long-range cruise missiles to attack mobile land targets during the course of a future campaign.[15]

However, even with the possible deployment of laser communications relays, the military role of SATCOMs is likely to remain less significant than space-based RSTA and navigation. Fearing SATCOMs' vulnerability to interference and/or destruction, both superpowers (as well as a number of more technologically advanced lesser powers) have directed investments to a new generation of terrestrially based communications systems.

Space as a combat arena. The enormous theatre and strategic advantages accruing from exploitation of space-based RSTA, navigation, and communications systems by one superpower ensures that for the other superpower the military importance of their degradation would be irresistible. Already satellite relays are susceptible to countermeasures, including electronic interference and high altitude nuclear bursts, while the effectiveness of satellite surveillance has been challenged by camouflage, concealment, and deception. By the end of the 1990s technologies may be deployed that could reduce the military value of satellites by combat means.

Up to now, both superpowers have viewed space as an operational sanctuary, a view reinforced by the mutual acceptance of peacetime space reconnaissance overflights, while both have found space reconnaissance useful during the course of various local conflicts and crises. Until the late 1970s, the demilitarization of space tended to lull the U.S. national security community's appreciation of the potential requirement for combat operations in this arena.

Four factors have caused a shift within the U.S. military over this issue. First, the Soviets deployed a first generation land-based antisatellite (ASAT) capability, with the capacity to threaten the small number of space reconnaissance vehicles that the United States operates at low orbit. Second, recognition has grown that Soviet space-based reconnaissance vehicles, especially those optimized to detect the U.S. surface fleet, could present a grave threat.[16] Third, the U.S. defense establishment has become aware of the prospects for combat in space as the technologies developed for ballistic missile defense (BMD) in the U.S. Strategic Defense Initiative (SDI) program appear equally applicable to space combat/denial. Finally, recognition of the looming revolution in space-based reconnaissance and navigation has emerged, and with it has come appreciation for the fact that these satellites would be a very important target during the course of a future war with the Soviet Union even if the conflict were to remain nonnuclear and contained to Eurasia.[17]

The employment of a wide range of manned and unmanned deep strike weapons will become increasingly dependent upon space-based RSTA and navigation systems, and in response—and as a natural consequence of their investment in improved space launch capabilities and BMD technologies—both superpowers would be under pressure to exploit their mobilization bases for space combat/denial capabilities. The United States is currently developing a rich resource for future ASATs through the SDI program, which has emphasized the development of two classes of interceptors during the 1990s: first, land-based systems—the exoatmospheric reentry vehicle interceptor system (ERIS); second, and more controversial, space-based interceptors.[18]

While the task set for these various interceptors in ballistic missile defense—destroying thousands of missile warheads—appears overwhelming, their use as a credible space combat/denial means provides a less daunting military challenge. In theory, a limited number of ERIS class interceptors in conjunction with improved space object surveillance could be employed as an ASAT system. Farther in the future lies the possibility of deploying a limited number of ground-based free electron lasers as a potent backup to the ERIS interceptor fleet.[19]

The Soviet Union also continues to invest heavily in ballistic missile defense technologies and will have a similar ASAT mobilization base during the 1990s. Further, the Soviet military appreciates the direct application of BMD R&D to enhanced space combat/denial capabilities.[20] Indeed, there are signals that the Soviets have been more concerned about the short-term ASAT potential of the SDI program than with its BMD potential. This concern is consistent with the Soviet military's considerable public commentary on the "third revolution" in warfare in which the combination of RSTA and PGM technologies plays a central role. Since in transcentury warfare gaining information dominance will be the route to operational superiority on the battlefield, destruction of the opponent's space-based "eyes and brains" will be a critical goal.

Unless banned by arms control agreement, both superpowers are likely to have impressive ASAT capabilities by the beginning of the next century. These capabilities would, at minimum, place at risk the low earth orbit satellites of the opposing side and may include high altitude variants of ERIS and space-based directed energy weapons (DEWs) able to target satellites operating at high and geosynchronous orbit.

Should a theatre military conflict involving the superpowers erupt in the transcentury period, these capabilities would create momentum for escalating the terrestrial combat to space, since a counter-reconnaissance campaign would likely unfold in which each side attempts to gain an "information" edge on the battlefield by destroying the opposing side's RSTA satellites. The stakes in such space combat would take on an immediate strategic nuclear dimension, because whichever side gains RSTA superiority during the course of a nonnuclear campaign could also gain a decisive advantage in its ability to acquire and therefore target dispersed nuclear arsenals, creating an enhanced preemptive potential. A second incentive aggravating transcentury warfare's tendency toward escalation arises because the capacity for space combat could involve the homelands of the superpowers as launch facilities for space-based RSTA and navigation systems become high value targets. The vertical escalation from theatre conflict to space would thus imply the threat of a simultaneous escalation from the theatre to the strategic nuclear realm.

The incentives to exploit space-based systems and to attack them ensure that the costs of deploying and protecting one's own capability and constructing counters to one's opponent's will be extremely high, while the military effectiveness of the systems, because of potential countermeasures, is more uncertain. But as in the case of PGM/RSTA warfare, the imbalances that would emerge in both the theatre and strategic realms as a result of asymmetries in exploitation of space-based assets are so large that any superpower that foregoes meaningful investment in these areas would countenance grave twenty-first century security risks.

The Rise of Aerospace Defense?

A third component of the transcentury weapons revolution consists of the technologies that may enhance aerospace defenses. Aerospace defenses have been pursued by both superpowers for the past several decades but rose in visibility with the U.S. Strategic Defense Initiative in the 1980s. The SDI has focused on ballistic missile defense, but transcentury aerospace defense systems may also include aerodynamic defenses applicable to both the strategic nuclear and theatre realms.

While the prospects for BMD are far from the extreme of an astrodome protecting the national homeland from ballistic missile attack as implied in President Ronald Reagan's 1983 proposal for the SDI, in theory asymmetrical deployment of such systems could devalue an opponent's forces sufficiently to alter the strategic nuclear balance and could downgrade the deterrent value of third party nuclear forces.

Although both superpowers continue to invest in BMD, the prospects for effective systems have been fraught with technical obstacles and enormous long-term investment requirements. Recognition of these impediments has already forced alterations in the planning for SDI and has cooled initial Soviet fears of a U.S. breakout in the short term.[21]

Ambitious directed energy weapons programs once central in SDI short-term planning have been stretched out in the face of technological and resource constraints, and the program has shifted priority for late 1990s deployment toward the development of ground- and space-based kinetic energy kill weapons, putting off the deployment of high energy DEWs well into the first decade of the twenty-first century.

Alone, BMD systems are of questionable value when considered in light of the very large aerodynamic attack forces, emphasizing cruise missile technology, that have been deployed by both superpowers. It is now clear that in the strategic realm both the United States and the Soviet Union would have to deploy balanced ballistic missile and aerodynamic defenses to be assured the military benefit of either. Currently, the United States has a modest program, the Air Defense Initiative (ADI), to explore a number of transcentury air defense concepts—a considerable task since both superpowers have already deployed the first generation of "stealthy" cruise missiles.[22]

In addition to use in the strategic nuclear arena, aerodynamic defenses promise to have applications in the theatre realm. By the turn of the century, both superpowers may be deploying a number of mobile DEWs designed primarily to counter sensors and provide local defenses. In the case of air/ground warfare, technical success may warrant the deployment of DEWs to protect ground forces from PGMs, and at sea they could provide surface warships with point defense.

One of the uncertainties about the fate of the large combat vehicle is whether active defense can be devised to raise the "entry price" for any guided weapon attacker. It is possible that the next generation of battle tanks and surface warships may have exploited the defensive value of first generation DEW technology against the guided weapons threat.[23] However, this additional capability would hike still further the unit cost of the next generation of combat vehicles.

THE COST EXPLOSION IN CONTEMPORARY FORCES

Policymakers and defense planners will have to weigh carefully the possible military costs of avoiding substantial investments in transcentury weapons in the 1990s against those for cutting further investment in contemporary weapons. If, during the 1990s, modernization of strategic offensive nuclear forces to provide more secure basing modes and modernization of theatre/conventional forces to overcome obsolescence are foregone and/or unilateral cuts in contemporary force structure are enacted, unfavorable strategic or theatre asymmetries could result.

In these evaluations, the argument for emphasizing investment in contemporary weapons will confront several stiff challenges. The expense of replacing contemporary weapons is rising spectacularly, as are operations and maintenance costs associated with higher quality defense machinery, while the potential for transcentury weapons to dramatically attrite them—especially in the theatre context—makes the durability of the deterrent and warfighting value of modernized contemporary forces less secure.

The next generation of manned combat vehicles is certain to sustain the historical trend of rapid increases in unit costs (see Fig. 6.1). It was the advent of the precision guided munitions era that fueled the process in which each new generation of manned combat vehicle costs a multiple of its preceding generation. This multiplication of unit costs has instigated a process of "structural disarmament" in which the armed forces of the major powers

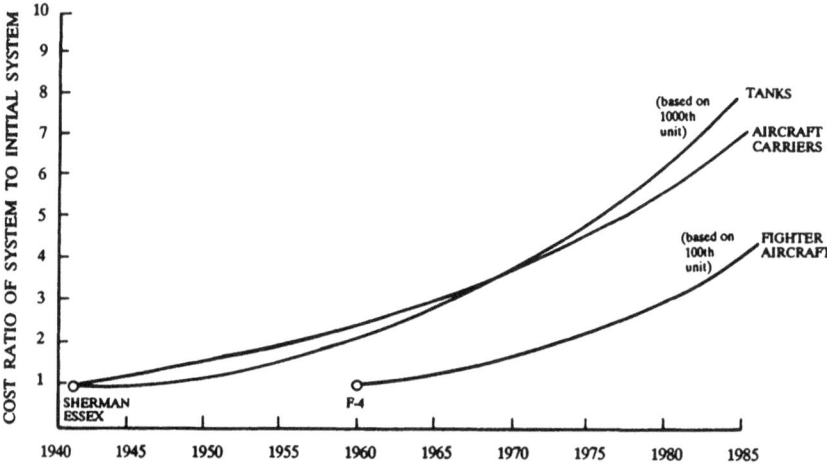

Figure 6.1. Growth in unit cost of weapons systems; adjusted for inflation and quantities. (Reprinted with permission from *Reorganizing America's Defense: Leadership in War and Peace*, ed. Robert J. Art, Vincent Davis, Samuel P. Huntington, Pergamon Brassey's International Defense Publishers, 1985.)

have been compelled to buy fewer and fewer combat vehicles in the face of rising unit costs and finite fiscal resources.[24]

Even with defense outlays rising by more than 50 percent in real terms over the first six years of the Reagan administration, the U.S. military, with the exception of the navy's surface fleet, saw no quantitative expansion in its force structure. The massive increase in capital investment for all four services only provided for a generational modernization of combat vehicles, as defense machinery output did not grow sufficiently to equip the entire force structure (and especially not the reserves).[25] The Soviet Union has not been immune to structural disarmament either. From the second half of the 1970s, constraints on the growth rate of Soviet defense spending have forced a retrenchment in the rate of growth of procurement. Although ground combat vehicle production growth rates remained high, by the mid-1980s there was evidence of a slowdown in the introduction of the next generation of combat aircraft and naval vessels.[26] For the same reasons, Western Europe and Japan are likely to stretch out the procurement of contemporary combat vehicles, while all major military powers will be increasingly forced into preserving force structure through the modification and upgrade of current inventories rather than progressing quickly to the next generation.

Defense planners can only look forward to ever increasing unit costs for combat vehicles. As PGMs and related RSTA systems become more sophisticated, the costs of countermeasures to secure combat vehicles will escalate.

One bruited means for averting this cost explosion and potentially breaking out of the bind of structural disarmament is to develop a variety of robot weapons to carry out combat functions currently performed by more expensive manned vehicles.[27] Today there is a worldwide proliferation of robotized systems in unmanned airborne vehicles (UAV) used for reconnaissance and support. Since the Israeli success during the 1982 air/ground campaign in Lebanon, all major (and some lesser) powers have developed a variety of UAVs, and these penetrating reconnaissance vehicles may soon be complemented by a family of long endurance drones, to be followed by a family of direct attack weapons.[28]

However, like guided weapons, robot combat vehicles are susceptible to new countermeasures, which would necessitate the development of either a new generation of robot weapons—at immense cost—or modular characteristics that allow for incremental upgrades in response to countermeasures without the need to scrap the entire inventory—also an expensive and technologically challenging project. But even before the risks of spiraling costs and diminishing military effectiveness stemming from prospective countermeasures are considered, changeover to robot vehicles implies a significant economic burden, since the costs of constructing production facilities would be enormous.

Hence, with limited prospects for constraining the rising unit costs of defense machinery, the defense planners of both superpowers must accept the fact that even if they maintained recent rates of growth in national defense spending, their force structures would face the prospect of expanding structural disarmament. Contesting this process, they could resort to modifications and upgrades of existing weapons rather than the production of whole new inventories—but this approach would accept a slowdown in the modernization of contemporary weapons.[29]

The 1990s requirements for an adequate R&D effort to support procurement of a transcentury weapons arsenal at the beginning of the next century, if met by either superpower, would be so expensive that they would necessitate an even greater retrenchment in the modernization of contemporary weapons systems and/or cuts in force structure than that driven by "structural disarmament" and budget cuts.

Faced with this dour choice between the alternatives of foregoing contemporary force modernization and/or slashing force structure on the one hand or foregoing transcentury weapons development on the other, what will most influence the attitude of U.S. planners will be the defense investment strategy adopted by the Soviet Union.

The Diffusion of Contemporary Weapons

Of rising significance will be the incremental loss in deterrent and coercive power of U.S. military forces likely to stem from the proliferation of advanced contemporary military technologies and weapons of mass destruction to third parties. In the coming decade, the spread of ballistic and cruise missile technologies in concert with biochemical and nuclear weapons into global theatres—especially the Middle East—may reduce the value of both superpowers' regional power projection capabilities and, consequently, their coercive assets in a region vital to their national interest.[30] Further, the spread of advanced missile technologies and the production base for weapons of mass destruction in this theatre is likely to spawn growing interest in antimissile defense systems. (Already both Israel and Iraq have indigenous antitactical missile programs.)

Pursuit of these technologies will, by the mid-1990s, have made the greater Middle East a more intimidating military theatre for the superpowers, as both will face a rising "entry price" involving the risk of major military losses during a future operation against a regional power. Virtually all existing superpower intervention scenarios into the region will have been undermined. To restore the deterrent and coercive value of their power projection forces in this theatre and thereby sustain existing levels of influence, both superpowers would be under pressure to exploit transcentury RSTA technologies, long-range nonnuclear strike systems, and aerospace defenses. Thus, the spread of advanced contemporary military technologies in global theatres is likely to add momentum to the pursuit of transcentury weapons.[31]

The upgrading of advanced contemporary weapons systems by third parties is even weakening the coercive value of superpower (i.e., Soviet) strategic forces.[32] Of note is the continued modernization and expansion of the nuclear arsenals of the United Kingdom, France, and China. All three will likely become strategic nuclear powers able to support an assured retaliation capability at some point in the 1990s. Further, all three have deployed an array of theatre and transcontinental range nuclear forces to threaten the Soviet Union with multisalvo operations. By the mid-1990s, these three states may be able to hold at risk a portion of the Soviet military theatre forces in the event Moscow were to conduct a major nonnuclear operation in Europe or along the Chinese border. This deterrent threat will be reinforced by the expansion of long-range nuclear forces deployed in more survivable basing modes. The United Kingdom and France will continue to rely primarily on a fleet of ballistic missile armed submarines. China has deployed a more balanced "triad" of mobile land-based missiles, medium-range aircraft, and submarine missile platforms.[33]

Appropriation by third parties of advanced contemporary military technologies, if sustained into the next century, could have a growing impact on U.S. decision making, pushing defense investment strategies in the direction of greater concentration in transcentury weapons. But in the 1990s U.S. decisions over the relative priority of contemporary vs. transcentury weapons investment will be driven primarily by the behavior of the Soviet Union.

Chapter 7

Conclusion:
Expanding the Scope of U.S. National Security Policy

To be successful, a U.S. national security strategy for the 1990s must be unshackled from traditional conceptual limitations to embrace the role of economic performance. From different starting points and at different speeds, the economies of the United States and the Soviet Union have suffered a decline in performance, and with this process has come, for each, a widening "economic dimension of security vulnerability." Critical to any national security strategy the United States adopts for the coming decade will be the approach it takes to its own "economic dimension" and the degree of sensitivity it demonstrates to the strategic implications of the Soviet response to its "dimension." An effective U.S. national security strategy must, we believe, include an economic policy component charged with reversing the long cycle descent of the U.S. economy and closing the "economic dimension" as well as a defense investment segment responsive to a Soviet threat whose intensity and nature will reflect how Moscow reacts to its own "dimension"—and this will have to be accomplished with fewer resources devoted to the national defense sector and especially its investment component than the United States enjoyed in the 1980s.

We believe that our estimates of the future Soviet threat and of the constraints on U.S. resources available to meet that threat recommend a particular strategy for the coming decade, one that seeks to "buy time" through an economic policy that prioritizes domestic investment within the context of a coordinated free world economy adjustment process and a defense investment strategy that raises the status of preparations to compete on the transcentury battlefield.

THE ECONOMIC POLICY COMPONENT: A CYCLE OF ADJUSTMENT

Central to any American effort to reverse the deteriorating health of its economy must be the adoption of a set of national resource priorities that aggressively promotes supply-side adjustment, a set of priorities that in the austere economic environment of the 1990s will clash with the biases of post-Depression American economic culture. Moreover, rejuvenating the U.S. economy in the coming decade will require equally radical adjustments in the policies of U.S. free world trading partners, adjustments that also run contrary to long-held economic policy prejudices. In short, the United States must seek a cycle of adjustment that embraces the entire free world, a cycle that includes:

- A decade-long effort to eliminate U.S. government fiscal and external overindebtedness by means of fundamental changes in macroeconomic and development policy. This will require a more contractionary U.S. government budget strategy and a transition in resource priorities to support more vigorous supply-side adjustment.
- A transformation in the macroeconomic and development policies of U.S. developed sector trading partners. Surplus economies led by Japan and West Germany must entertain more expansionary macroeconomic policies. Also, Japan should reorder its resource priorities toward a greater role for personal consumption and Western Europe toward improved investment.
- An adjustment in the international payments policy of the developed sector toward the end of supporting higher levels of developing sector and CPE imports. This will require the implementation of meaningful debt relief programs.
- Enhanced trade liberalization facilitated by an expansion of the GATT's sectoral purview and the encouragement of trade-creating "special trade arrangements."

Successful implementation of such a cycle would ensure a revival of the U.S. economy by the beginning of the twenty-first century, the elimination of the "economic dimension," and the establishment of an economic foundation able to support U.S. strategic competitiveness in the environment of the coming century. Failure would mean that the U.S. economy would depart this century suffering a continued retreat and a widening "economic dimension," with a national defense sector that, after having contracted during the 1990s, would find it difficult to regain ground at the expense of a faltering civilian economy early in the next century.

Exiting the current free world business cycle, the United States will entertain three alternative resource priority options as it confronts the reassertion of its "economic dimension." The most powerful intuitive response of the American people and political establishment will be to repeat the waste of time folly of the 1970s in which personal consumption accounts were protected at the expense of national security and economic investment. If such measures come to pass again, U.S. national defense expenditures would have to endure the brunt of 1990s U.S. government efforts to reduce its budget deficit while a foundering economy would be in no better position at the end of the decade to support a recovery in defense expenditures. The ability of the United States to compete in a transcentury weapons environment would, in this case, have been compromised.

One alternative to a repetition of the 1970s approach would be to seek to reach the outyear projections of the first FY90 Bush Administration national security budget, which involved a return to positive real growth. To pay for this moderate "race against time" strategy, both personal consumption and economic investment would have to assume the burden of declining output growth rates and fiscal deficit reduction. Aside from a forceful rise in the intensity of the foreign threat—not a likely development, given the range of plausible Soviet responses to its "economic dimension"—a "race against time" strategy would confront enormous political opposition in the coming decade. Moreover, while this set of national resource priorities might win short-term security ground, it would do so at the expense of long-term national security, since the consequent deterioration in investment growth would leave the U.S. economy to enter the next century unfit to support meaningful exploitation of transcentury weapons. By the end of 1989 the Bush administration itself was compelled, primarily by fiscal realities supported by the initial evidence of a decline in Soviet defense spending, to reject this option.

A final set of U.S. national resource priorities for the coming decade would raise the status of economic investment. Financing an acceleration in the pace of U.S. supply-side adjustment while at the same time reducing overindebtedness would place a heavy burden on both personal consumption and national defense. In light of the historical prejudice in U.S. economic policy—especially under low growth conditions—such a set of priorities would face stout political resistance. But compared to the "race against time" option, a well-conceived "buy time" strategy which holds out the prospect of a future economic payoff that would ease the stress on personal consumption has better political prospects. Still, national acceptance of such a strategy would require unusual strength of leadership to overcome the tide of popular resistance.

Under a "buy time" strategy, U.S. economic adjustment would not be restricted to demand-side constraint but would also include a supply-side component financed by a portion of the savings won from personal consumption and national security accounts. To meet such an agenda, domestic spending outlays, especially "payments to individuals," would have to contract in real terms (i.e., grow slower in nominal terms than the rate of inflation) and/or new taxes would have to be levied on personal consumption. By downgrading the traditional status of personal consumption in favor of investment and savings, a more equitable sharing of the adjustment burden will be possible. Although this approach requires a drop in U.S. national defense spending for much of the 1990s, the reversal of the long cycle descent of the U.S. economy made possible through this set of national resource priorities would create the foundation going into the next century upon which to build a technologically advanced defense sector.

Unfortunately, economic investment will find itself in a more hostile domestic environment in the coming decade as the U.S. economy suffers lower domestic demand growth rates than in the 1980s and, consequently, lower rates of industrial capacity utilization. To achieve the desired level of investment a supply-side renovation of the U.S. economy would therefore have to depend on a prolonged export recovery, which in turn would require expanding foreign markets for U.S. goods and services. For this reason, the process of economic adjustment will have to extend beyond the United States to the rest of the free world where, to support higher U.S. export growth, enhanced domestic demand must be stimulated.

The United States will have to reach agreement with its developed sector trading partners for a coordinated cycle of adjustment, one that must include accelerated expansion in the Japanese domestic market and revitalization of Western Europe's domestic demand growth. In addition to sustaining strong domestic demand, Japan will also have to shift its resource priorities away from investment, especially in export related sectors, toward personal consumption. Although the stimulus for enhanced West European domestic demand and, hence, import growth in a cycle of adjustment must come from its surplus economies, the entire region will have to work at reducing overemphasis on personal consumption in favor of economic investment. Unlike in the United States, improved West European supply-side adjustment in the 1990s must rest upon strong regional domestic demand growth enhanced by more vigorous intraregional trade, especially in the wake of the European Community economic integration slated for 1992.

Despite the fact that Japan and the surplus economies of Western Europe will have exited the current business cycle with greater margins of macroeconomic policy flexibility than the United States (since in the 1980s they were able to accumulate large external surpluses while their government fiscal deficit to GNP ratios declined), economic policy prejudices as strong as those in the United States will present stiff impediments to required adjustment. Japan's traditional fears of isolation from access to foreign sources of raw materials and markets and its national affinity for personal frugality make it difficult for it to break with the centerpiece of its postwar economic success—high rates of export-oriented investment. West Germany and the smaller surplus economies of Western Europe have long been guided by an entrenched fear of inflation, and this will work against the macroeconomic policy expansion needed from them in the coming business cycle. Further, the high cost of social peace throughout Western Europe will provoke political resistance to a shift of resources from personal consumption to economic investment.

A durable U.S. export expansion would also be served by a reversal in the developing sector's economic performance in the current business cycle. Central to reviving developing sector imports from their long compression in the 1980s would be a shift in developed sector payments policy that would permit a reduction in the developing sector's investment income deficit and a consequent improvement in its current account balance. What is needed is large-scale debt relief that relaxes immediate balance of payments stress, followed by additional relief that seeks to advance the sector's creditworthiness by reducing the stock of its foreign debt.

A coordinated cycle of adjustment should also consider markets outside of the free world economy—the CMEA and Chinese markets—as ones whose expansion could boost U.S. exports. Coincidentally, the political stabilization of Eastern Europe rests upon whether the region's economies quickly undergo their own versions of radical perestroika, and this would require greatly enlarged capital inflow from the developed economies to finance hard currency imports to the region. If extended to the economies of Eastern Europe, the kind of debt relief needed by the developing sector would permit for an acceleration in hard currency imports. Further, new capital inflow to the region is needed to support the reform process, and increased inflow of private capital would follow successful reform. Such a process, while having important political implications, would have only a limited direct effect on U.S. export performance, since the majority of CMEA hard currency imports originate in Western Europe and the plurality of China's originate in Japan.[1]

Again, as in the case of economic adjustment in the United States and the rest of the developed sector, immense obstacles confront any effort to boost developing sector and CPE imports. Because the free world is likely to experience a lower GNP growth rate in the 1990s compared to the 1980s, any tendency toward improvement in developing sector imports will be weakened by the perpetuation of soft primary commodity prices, a development that will also limit improvement in Soviet hard currency import growth. At the same time, to judge by recent experience, the sweeping debt relief needed in both the developing world and Eastern Europe will be stoutly resisted by private creditors at risk to lose profits, while the creditworthiness of these sectors in the absence of such relief is likely to worsen. Equally important, there will be sizable domestic opposition within developing and East European economies to economic reform centered about privatization and marketization that must accompany any meaningful debt relief or aid package.

Another vehicle for boosting aggregate free world economic performance and U.S. exports is trade liberalization. Such liberalization can be accomplished through expanding the sectoral menu of the General Agreement on Tariffs and Trade (GATT), rolling back the "new protectionism" that surged in the 1980s, and promoting trade-creating "special trade arrangements" such as the U.S.-Canada Free Trade Agreement of 1988 and the planned intra-EC trade liberalization of 1992.[2] But these efforts, too, will confront challenges as pursuit of a broadened GATT and a rollback of the "new protectionism" will run up against increased stress in free world markets resulting from a 1990s slowdown in the world import growth rate. Under such economic conditions, the trade-creating potential of enlarged "special trade arrangements" could be perverted into destructive trade-diverting protectionist blocs.

In addition to determining whether the U.S. and free world economies are able to reverse their long-term negative trends, the success or failure of the coming cycle of adjustment will influence whether and to what degree new threats to U.S. security borne of intra-free world economy tensions retreat or advance. At stake is whether intra-developed sector economic frictions that could test the stability of the U.S. alliance system—frictions focused on the "new protectionism" but also including potentially explosive issues relating to cross-border capital flows (i.e., foreign direct and portfolio investment)—abate or grow to more dangerous levels than experienced in the 1981–82 recession or in Phase Two of the current cycle, in 1985–86.[3] Beyond these intra-developed sector tensions, Washington must be concerned that worsening foreign debt-induced recession conditions in Latin America could incite growing ungovernability and magnify hemispheric threats to U.S. borders posed by illegal drugs and flows of immigrants.[4]

THE DEFENSE INVESTMENT COMPONENT: PURSUING ADVANTAGES AND OPPORTUNITIES

We believe there are compelling reasons for a change in U.S. defense investment strategy in the 1990s. In contrast to the 1980s emphasis given to modernization and maintenance of contemporary force structure, the United States should seek a transition during which emphasis would be given to construction of a mobilization base for transcentury weapons. In the long term, the viability of this course is contingent upon the success of the economic strategy we propose. Only by executing the one resource priority option capable of erasing the "economic dimension of security vulnerability" can the U.S. afford to exploit a transcentury weapons mobilization base during a twenty-first century production and deployment phase. In the short term, the degree to which Washington is able to transition its defense investment priorities will be contingent upon whether and to what extent Moscow is prepared to reduce its defense effort and on how effectively the U.S. exploits the dilemma Moscow confronts in its "economic dimension."

Three lessons to be drawn from the postwar U.S.-Soviet military competition argue for a change in the U.S. defense investment mix. First, since the Korean War it has always been in the U.S. interest to steer the military competition away from the quantitative sphere, where the Soviet defense sector's superior access to resources has helped win it distinct advantages— advantages that have produced a critical asymmetry in the nonnuclear force balance in Eurasia and, most importantly, in the Euro-theatre. In response, the United States tried to move the competition to the qualitative plane where its technological superiority gave it an edge, one that provided it with strategic nuclear preponderance during the 1950s and most of the 1960s. The evolution of the postwar competition has testified to a second lesson, often repeated in the history of warfare: that technologically induced weapons revolutions may yield sudden and shocking military imbalances, as demonstrated by the strategic asymmetries spawned by U.S. exploitation of nuclear weapons and transoceanic delivery systems in the 1950s. The third lesson teaches, however, that the destabilizing effects of these revolutions in weapons technology tend to be transient as nations exploit their scientific and economic potential to respond to new threats. That capacity to respond, however, has become increasingly constrained by weakening superpower economic performance.

Hence, by pushing the future military competition—if there is to be one— into the qualitative, high technology arena while at the same time rejuvenating its economy so that such a shift remains credible, the United States will have ensured against large and unfavorable military imbalances in the transcentury period. Simultaneously, this approach will prod a Soviet Union with an even more formidable economic task (and therefore a lower chance of remaining militarily competitive in a transcentury weapons environment) to shift its defense investment commitments out of the quantitative sphere where it has the advantage. The historical arguments in support of a new U.S. defense investment strategy are reinforced by the combined implications of the fast rising unit costs of contemporary defense machinery and the threat posed to their future military worth by transcentury weapons. These two factors belie the wisdom of a defense program that concentrates excessively on modernizing contemporary force structures.

During this decade, defense planners will be forced to make difficult investment decisions. As structural disarmament continues to eat away at the

Conclusion

pace at which force structure is modernized, the U.S. defense sector will have transited from the halcyon days of accelerated investment to a period of prolonged spending decline. In addition, the rising O&M costs that come with the current generation of combat systems will ensure that the investment component of defense expenditures falls faster than total outlays.[5] Already confronting fiscal pressure, the Bush administration under Defense Secretary Richard Cheney has begun a process of program and force posture cuts. As this process deepens, the degree of trauma to the plans of the military services and their industrial suppliers will grow, and this will activate a powerful inclination among institutional forces to guard their own beleaguered bailiwick at the expense of a more coherent and effective military posture. Laboring under accelerated disinvestment in the 1990s, the U.S. defense sector will tend to pursue an even less cogent approach than the 1980s overemphasis on contemporary force modernization as political clout and bureaucratic self-interest gain greater influence in the defense investment decision making process.[6] To avoid this dangerous drift and to reorient investment strategy instead toward addressing the challenges of the transcentury environment, we believe that U.S. defense investment should be instructed by a set of clear objectives:

- Within the austere budget environment of the 1990s, the United States must secure a vigorous research and development program for transcentury military technologies as well as a heavy investment in dual-use transcentury technologies and a more expansive civilian space program.
- To accommodate the cost of this effort, U.S. theatre forces will have to bear the burden of the 1990s drop in defense spending. The degree to which U.S. contemporary force structure can be prudently cut and/or forego modernization will be heavily influenced by the size and structure of the Soviet national defense effort. This condition is most crucial to the Euro-theatre, where the arms control process and/or developments in Eastern Europe are likely to allow for a drawdown in the size of active force structure and a shift of theatre forces toward reserves.
- It seems certain that what has been at the center of the U.S. military deterrent for the past 40 years—strategic forces—will remain so through the coming decade. Whether or not the START negotiations yield progress, ensuring the value of the U.S. strategic nuclear deterrent will require that its budget be shielded in the hostile fiscal climate of the 1990s.

Reordering Defense Investment Priorities

While through restructuring a number of existing defense programs the United States can begin to slowly reorient its defense investment priorities toward greater emphasis on transcentury weapons, the dimension of any 1990s transition will depend largely on the Soviet response to its "economic dimension." If the Soviet leadership seeks "deep cuts" in defense spending as spelled out by Prime Minister Ryzhkov, Soviet force structure will have to undergo sizable reductions beyond those already announced by Gorbachev. A contraction in Soviet force structure of such magnitude could provide the United States with a unique opportunity not only to eliminate its most worrisome postwar military imbalance—Soviet conventional preponderance in central Europe—but to shift the stage for future military competition more to the transcentury realm.

Beyond the positive impact of a "deep cut" CFE agreement for the investment strategy we propose, a transformation in U.S. defense investment priorities could also be spurred by the abandonment of the navy's "maritime strategy" and the scaling down of its surface fleet, especially its aircraft carrier task force groups, as well as through a restructuring of the SDI program stressing not a 1990s payoff in BMD but in space combat/denial means. The central focus of the 1990s transcentury weapons program should be to ensure U.S. leadership in "eyes and brains" technologies, especially in battleworthy RSTA systems and ASAT, with PGM and aerospace defense development playing a secondary role.

Despite concern among some within the U.S. planning community that deep reductions in NATO force structure could result in a lowering of the "force to space ratio"—leaving NATO potentially vulnerable to an offensive conducted by a "leaner, meaner" Soviet transcentury force—the arguments for pursuing a "deep cut" CFE agreement are persuasive.[7] While eliminating the prospects for short warning war in Europe (since this would require a large and visible Soviet mobilization process), conventional arms reduction in central Europe could allow NATO to creatively design a theatrewide "covering force" of agile air mobile and motorized ground units, supported by battleworthy RSTA and artillery systems and a large mobilizable reserve, as the leading edge of an effective deterrent to any Soviet effort to reassert Euro-theatre preponderance in the twenty-first century.

Intersecting a fast maturing process of economic and political liberalization in Eastern Europe, a significantly reduced Soviet military presence in that area will likely result in an increase in national government control over defense forces, creating a further formidable obstacle to any future Soviet invasion scenario for Western Europe since this would necessitate a forceful reintroduction of massive Red Army forces onto East European soil.

Even in the absence of a large-scale Soviet defense retrenchment, the United States could undertake a smaller and slower upgrading of its transcentury weapons effort through a diversion of resources from the navy's surface ship programs. The rationale of the "maritime strategy" for the expansion of naval force structure in the 1980s retains little credibility. Moreover, the threat Washington perceives in global theatres has begun to abate, especially in the Middle East/Persian Gulf region, and may wane further if Moscow's defense retrenchment weakens its power projection forces and the "new thinking" in Soviet foreign policy fully matures. At the same time, however, the deterrent and coercive value of U.S. power projection forces for global theatres is under challenge from the escalating flow of advanced contemporary weapons systems into these areas.

Importantly, these two developments argue for a cut in funding for contemporary U.S. power projection forces, especially for the excessive number of planned carrier task forces. While the reduction in the immediate threat weakens the foundation for such funding, the United States in the future is likely to rely less on traditional forces—the surface fleet and light, high quality infantry—for military intervention in global theatres turning instead to an intervention capability that minimizes the exposure of forward deployed forces through the employment of an array of transcentury systems centered about global and theatre RSTA, long-range nonnuclear strike systems, theatre missile defenses, and superior electronic warfare.

One final vehicle we recommend for upgrading the U.S. transcentury weapons effort in the 1990s is the restructuring of the SDI program. As the premier U.S. transcentury weapons program, the Strategic Defense Initiative has been weakened as a result of overambitious objectives and unsupportable outyear costs. Under the weight of these difficulties, the organization's goals have been scaled back to where today its Phase One (1990s) mission centers about the pedestrian objective of disrupting a theoretical Soviet counterforce capability against the land-based leg of the U.S. triad, and again this mission involves great costs.

A more fruitful practical goal for the program during this decade, one that supports our emphasis on augmenting the U.S.'s ability to gain information supremacy in a high technology military environment, would (in the absence of arms control banning their deployment) be the creation by the end of this century of a mobilization base for terrestrially based ASAT weaponry. In this endeavor Washington must remain sensitive to the powerful escalation potential inherent in space combat, and in order to reduce the preemptive instabilities in the deployment of space combat/denial means, it should avoid ASAT deployment in space.

Another harnessable application of SDI efforts is likely to be in the development of tactical ballistic missile defenses and in DEW technologies for combat vehicle defense, both of which may play a role in protecting power projection forces, especially in the harsher military climate emerging in global theatres. We believe that the SDI should also sustain work in its original area of concern—strategic ballistic missile defense—through the construction of a mobilization base to guard against any potential Soviet surge in strategic defenses and as insurance against a limited ballistic missile attack, i.e., a third party or accidental launch.

Any U.S. defense investment strategy for the 1990s will have to ensure the value of what will remain at the center of the country's military deterrent—its strategic nuclear forces. While we propose to protect strategic force accounts from the ill effect of accelerated disinvestment, these accounts will still have to function within tight funding limits and rising unit costs. Within these austere confines, emphasis should be placed on ensuring the survivability of U.S. strategic forces rather than on the countermilitary requirements of holding Soviet land mobile and sea-based strategic forces at risk. Although pressure on the U.S. to invest in more survivable strategic nuclear forces is lessened if one views the improved strategic forces of the U.K., France, and China as part of a de facto multilateral strategic deterrent arrayed against the Soviet Union, U.S. strategic forces will still require substantial investment.[8]

To remain within what may turn out to be generous spending limits that we propose, the United States will confront two alternative investment paths for strategic forces. The first rests upon sustaining a traditional balanced triad that continues to prioritize the modernization of the land-based ICBM force (deployment of the rail mobile MX missile or ample deployments of small ICBMs—SICBMs—on mobile launchers).[9] The second offers a more radical solution, one we are inclined to support. It would deemphasize ICBM modernization while including a limited SICBM program for silo deployment whose mobilization base would offer a hedge against a Soviet antisubmarine warfare breakthrough. This second alternative argues that instead of concentrating resources on the most vulnerable leg of the triad—land-based missiles—greater weight should be given to a bomber force that could also be used in nonnuclear campaigns and which should be protected against submarine-launched cruise missile (SLCM) attack by enhanced aerodynamic surveillance systems developed through a moderately funded air defense initiative program. It would therefore shield funding for the B-2 bomber, if that program should prove technically viable. As with the first alternative, a large Trident II SLBM program would be maintained. The approach that we recommend would therefore allow for the deployment of a bomber and submarine fleet able to assure a strong retaliation capability into the 1990s and beyond.

* * *

The national security environment that the United States will confront in the transcentury era promises to be highly volatile. While the impending revolution in defense technologies holds out the prospect of greater and more

Conclusion

threatening military asymmetries, decades of decline in superpower economic performance call into question the ability of either to develop and exploit the fruits of this revolution.

The Soviet Union enters the 1990s under pressure to face its "economic dimension of security vulnerability" squarely, and the range of paths it may follow in response holds within it disparate national security spending levels, military force structures, and alliance system characteristics. The United States begins the 1990s with unsustainable financial imbalances certain to drain national security expenditures, defense sector spending in particular. If not remedied, these imbalances will lead to a U.S. economy at the turn of the century in no better position to restore its defenses.

To address the challenges of the transcentury national security environment, American policymakers must understand the potent relationship between economic performance and national security. The United States can only ensure its strategic competitiveness in the transcentury era through a successful cycle of adjustment coordinated with its free world trading partners. Failure would mean a widening "economic dimension of security vulnerability" that would not only undermine America's ability to compete in a transcentury weapons environment; it would also inflame security threats internal to the free world issuing from tensions over scarce markets and savings.

Furthermore, the United States must reorient its defense investment strategy toward the construction of a mobilization base for transcentury weapons, a shift whose viability depends on the successful implementation of a cycle of adjustment. Such a transition could be sped if Moscow responds to its own "economic dimension" with a "deep cuts" defense spending policy and if Washington is prepared to exploit this decision by pursuing the elimination of the contemporary force imbalance in Europe through a CFE agreement. Deep cuts in contemporary force funding made possible through such an agreement could allow for the construction of a transcentry weapons R& D base, which in turn would function as a deterrent against any Soviet military breach of this new security arrangement.

If Moscow should reject a "deep cuts" approach, the transformation in U.S. defense investment priorities would be slowed. But even such a slowed transformation would steer the superpower military competition into the qualitative arena where the United States enjoys distinct advantages while also strengthening its ability to respond to any third party challenge that might arise from the diffusion of advanced contemporary military technologies into global theatres.

Appendix A

U.S. Government National Security Outlays, FY1940–88 (Billions 1982 Dollars)

	FY	National Defense	Period Average	Space/ Science	Period Average	International Affairs	Period Average	TOTAL	Period Average
PREWAR REGIME	1940	15.1		0.0		0.4		15.5	
	1941	51.2	80.3	0.0	0.0	1.2	2.9	52.4	83.3
	1942	174.7		0.0		7.2		181.4	
W.W. II REGIME	1943	414.7		0.0		8.7		423.4	
	1944	522.1	467.0	0.3	0.4	10.1	11.8	532.5	479.1
	1945	591.3		0.8		13.8		605.9	
	1946	339.8		0.3		14.5		354.6	
POSTWAR DEMOBILIZATION REGIME	1947	89.9		0.0		35.7		125.6	
	1948	55.8	76.8	0.0	0.2	24.3	29.0	80.1	105.9
	1949	77.4		0.3		31.6		109.3	
	1950	83.9		0.3		24.2		108.4	
CONTEMPORARY REGIME									
Korean War Period	1951	150.2		0.3		20.1		170.7	
	1952	258.9	232.7	0.3	0.3	13.9	12.9	273.1	245.9
	1953	271.5		0.2		10.2		281.9	
	1954	250.0		0.2		7.5		257.7	
Heyday of Strategic Forces	1955	211.0		0.3		10.1		221.4	
	1956	198.5		0.3		10.5		209.3	
	1957	203.5		0.5		13.1		217.1	
	1958	198.3	199.6	0.6	1.9	13.2	12.6	212.1	214.1
	1959	196.0		1.1		11.8		208.9	
	1960	192.1		2.2		11.0		205.3	

Era	Year							
	1961	195.2		3.8		10.8		209.8	
	1962	202.2		6.2		20.3		228.7	
Dawning of Assured Destruction	1963	197.1		10.5		18.3		225.9	
	1964	198.8	192.4	16.7	14.5	16.8	17.6	232.3	224.5
	1965	181.4		16.3		17.6		215.3	
Vietnam War Peak	1966	197.9		21.5		17.9		237.3	
	1967	235.1	229.3	19.3	19.0	17.3	16.9	271.7	265.2
	1968	254.8		16.3		15.6		286.7	
Accelerated Disinvestment	1969	243.4		14.0		12.8		270.2	
	1970	225.6		11.7		11.3		248.6	
	1971	202.7		10.1		10.1		222.9	
	1972	190.9	189.3	9.5	9.5	10.9	11.0	211.3	209.8
	1973	175.1		8.7		8.9		192.7	
	1974	163.3		7.8		11.2		182.3	
	1975	159.8		7.0		12.5		179.3	
	1976	153.6		7.2		10.6		171.4	
Carter Plateau	1977	154.3		7.2		9.7		171.2	
	1978	155.0	158.1	7.0	7.0	10.6	11.6	172.6	176.7
	1979	159.1		6.9		9.8		175.8	
	1980	164.0		6.9		16.4		187.3	
Accelerated Investment	1981	171.4		6.9		14.0		192.3	
	1982	185.3		7.2		12.3		204.8	
	1983	201.3		7.6		11.4		220.3	
	1984	211.3	218.3	7.7	7.8	14.7	12.3	233.7	238.4
	1985	230.0		7.7		14.5		252.2	
	1986	243.7		7.9		12.4		264.0	
	1987	250.3		7.9		10.0		268.2	
	1988	252.9		9.5		9.2		271.6	

Source: Executive Office of the President, Office of Management and Budget, *Historical Tables—Budget of the United States Government, FY90* (Washington, DC: U.S. Government Printing Office, 1989)

Appendix B

U.S. External Balances, 1946–88

	FY	Merchandise Trade ($Billions)	Current Account ($Billions)	Net Exports (Billions 1982 Dollars)	Capital Account ($Billions)	Net Investment Balance ($Billions)
POSTWAR DEMOBILIZA-						
TION REGIME	1946	6.7	4.9	27.0		
	1947	10.1	9.0	42.4		
	1948	5.7	2.4	19.2		
	1949	5.3	0.9	18.8		36.7
	1950	1.1	-1.8	4.7		
CONTEMPORARY REGIME						
Korean War	1951	3.1	0.9	14.6		
Period	1952	2.6	0.6	6.9		
	1953	1.4	-1.3	-2.7		
	1954	2.6	0.2	2.5		
Heyday of	1955	2.9	0.4	0.0		
Strategic	1956	4.8	2.7	4.3		
Forces	1957	6.3	4.8	7.0		37.2
	1958	3.5	0.8	-10.3	-3.6	
	1959	1.1	-1.3	-18.2	-0.9	
	1960	4.9	2.8	-4.0	-6.2	
	1961	5.6	3.8	-2.7	-5.2	
	1962	4.5	3.4	-7.5	-6.0	44.7
Dawning of	1963	5.2	4.4	-1.9	-6.4	
Assured	1964	6.6	6.8	5.9	-8.3	
Destruction	1965	5.0	5.4	-2.7	-6.7	66.8

	Year				
Vietnam	1966	3.8	3.0	-13.7	-2.8
War Peak	1967	3.8	2.6	-16.9	-6.0
	1968	0.6	0.6	-29.7	1.1
Accelerated	1969	0.6	0.4	-34.9	2.3
Disinvest-	1970	2.6	2.3	-30.0	-13.0
ment	1971	-2.3	-1.4	-39.8	-29.0
	1972	-6.4	-5.8	-49.4	-5.3
	1973	0.9	7.1	-31.5	-12.3
	1974	-5.5	1.9	0.8	-10.7
	1975	8.9	18.1	18.9	-22.8
	1976	-9.5	4.2	-11.0	-14.7	58.5
Carter	1977	-31.1	-14.5	-35.5	-20.6
Plateau	1978	-34.0	-15.4	-26.8	-16.4
	1979	-27.5	-1.0	3.6	-14.2
	1980	-25.5	1.9	57.0	-9.7	74.6
Accelerated	1981	-28.0	8.2	49.4	-8.1
Investment	1982	-36.4	-7.0	26.3	11.6
	1983	-67.1	-44.3	-19.9	42.2
	1984	-112.5	-104.2	-84.0	117.8	106.3
	1985	-122.1	-112.7	-104.3	122.3
	1986	-144.5	-133.2	-129.7	108.2
	1987	-160.3	-143.7	-115.7	96.8	140.9
	1988	-127.2	-126.5	-74.9	N.A.	-111.4
						-532.5

Source: Executive Office of the President, *Economic Report of the President, 1989* (Washington, DC: U.S. Government Printing Office, 1989) (for 1946–87 merchandise trade and capital account balances, 1946–80 current account balances, 1946–85 net export balances, and 1980, 1981, 1985 net investment balances); U.S. Department of Commerce, Bureau of Economic Analysis, "Summary of U.S. International Transactions: Second Quarter 1989" (12 September 1989) (for 1988 merchandise trade and capital account balances); U.S. Department of Commerce, Bureau of Economic Analysis, "GNP Second Quarter 1989—Advance" (27 July 1989) (for 1986–88 net export balances); U.S. Department of Commerce, Bureau of Economic Analysis, "U.S. Net International Investment Position, 1988" (29 June 1989) (for 1988 net investment balance); Joint Economic Committee and Council of Economic Advisers, "Economic Indicators, November 1989" (Washington, DC: U.S. Government Printing Office, 1989) (for 1981–88 current account balances).

Appendix C

National Security and Transfer Payments as a Percent of GNP, FY1940–88

	FY	National Defense	Period Avg.	Space/ Science	Period Avg.	Internat'l Affairs	Period Avg.	TOTAL National Security	Period Avg.	Payments to Individuals	Period Avg.
PREWAR REGIME	1940	1.7		0.0		0.0		1.7		1.7	
	1941	5.8	8.5	0.0	0.0	0.1	0.3	5.9	8.8	1.5	1.5
	1942	18.0		0.0		0.6		18.6		1.2	
W.W. II REGIME	1943	37.9		0.0		0.7		38.6		0.9	
	1944	39.2	34.1	0.0	0.0	0.7	0.8	39.9	34.9	0.9	1.4
	1945	39.1		0.0		0.9		40.0		1.0	
	1946	20.0		0.0		0.9		20.9		2.7	
POSTWAR DEMOBILI-ZATION REGIME	1947	5.7		0.0		2.5		8.2		4.0	
	1948	3.7	4.9	0.0	0.0	1.8	2.1	5.5	7.0	3.6	4.1
	1949	5.0		0.0		2.3		7.3		3.8	
	1950	5.1		0.0		1.6		6.7		5.1	
CONTEMPORARY REGIME											
Korean Wa Period	1951	7.5		0.0		1.1		8.6		3.3	
	1952	13.5	12.2	0.0	0.0	0.8	0.7	14.3	12.9	3.2	3.2
	1953	14.4		0.0		0.6		15.0		3.0	
	1954	13.3		0.0		0.4		13.7		3.4	
Heyday of Strategic Forces	1955	11.1		0.0		0.5		11.6		3.7	
	1956	10.2		0.0		0.6		10.8		3.6	
	1957	10.3		0.0		0.7		11.0		3.9	
	1958	10.4	10.1	0.0	0.1	0.7	0.7	11.1	10.9	4.6	4.5
	1959	10.2		0.1		0.6		10.9		4.7	
	1960	9.5		0.1		0.6		10.2		4.8	

Period	Year							
	1961	9.6	0.2		0.6	10.4		5.3	
	1962	9.4	0.3		1.0	10.7		5.2	
Dawning of Assured Destruction	1963	9.1	0.5		0.9	10.5		5.3	
	1964	8.7	0.8	8.4	0.8	10.3	9.9	5.1	5.1
	1965	7.5	0.8		0.8	9.1		4.9	
Vietnam War Peak	1966	7.9	0.9		0.7	9.5		5.0	
	1967	9.0	0.8	8.8	0.7	10.5	10.3	5.4	5.4
	1968	9.6	0.6		0.6	10.8		5.9	
Accelerated Disinvest- ment	1969	8.9	0.5		0.5	9.9		6.1	
	1970	8.3	0.4		0.4	9.1		6.5	
	1971	7.5	0.4		0.4	8.3		7.6	
	1972	6.9	0.3	6.8	0.4	7.5	7.5	8.1	8.2
	1973	6.0	0.3		0.3	6.6		8.2	
	1974	5.6	0.3		0.4	6.3		8.5	
	1975	5.7	0.3		0.4	6.4		10.1	
	1976	5.3	0.2		0.4	5.9		10.6	
Carter Plateau	1977	5.0	0.2		0.3	5.5		10.2	
	1978	4.8	0.2	4.9	0.3	5.4	5.5	9.7	10.0
	1979	4.8	0.2		0.3	5.4		9.5	
	1980	5.0	0.2		0.5	5.7		10.4	
Accelerated Investment	1981	5.3	0.2		0.4	5.9		10.8	
	1982	5.9	0.2		0.4	6.5		11.4	
	1983	6.3	0.2		0.3	6.8		11.9	
	1984	6.2	0.2	6.1	0.4	6.8	6.7	10.8	10.9
	1985	6.4	0.2		0.4	7.0		10.8	
	1986	6.5	0.2		0.3	7.0		10.7	
	1987	6.4	0.2		0.3	6.9		10.6	
	1988	6.1	0.2		0.2	6.5		10.4	

Source: Executive Office of the President, Office of Management and Budget, *Historical Tables—Budget of the United States Government, FY90* (Washington, DC: U.S. Government Printing Office, 1989)

Appendix D
National Security and Transfer Payments as a Percent of U.S. Government Outlays, FY1940–88

	FY	National Defense	Period Avg.	Space/ Science	Period Avg.	Internat'l Affairs	Period Avg.	TOTAL National Security	Period Avg.	Payments to Individuals	Period Avg.
PREWAR REGIME	1940	17.5		0.0		0.1		17.6		17.5	
	1941	47.1	45.9	0.0	0.0	1.1	1.3	48.2	47.2	12.2	11.6
	1942	73.0		0.0		2.8		75.8		5.0	
W.W. II REGIME	1943	84.9		0.0		1.6		86.5		2.1	
	1944	86.7	84.6	0.1	0.1	1.6	2.2	88.4	86.9	1.9	4.2
	1945	89.5		0.1		2.1		91.7		2.4	
	1946	77.3		0.1		3.5		80.9		10.3	
POSTWAR DEMOBILI- ZATION REGIME	1947	37.1		0.0		16.8		53.9		26.2	
	1948	30.6	33.5	0.0	0.1	15.3	14.7	45.9	48.2	30.4	28.7
	1949	33.9		0.1		15.6		49.6		25.9	
	1950	32.2		0.1		11.0		43.2		32.1	
CONTEMPORARY REGIME											
Korean War Period	1951	51.8		0.1		8.0		59.9		22.6	
	1952	68.1	64.7	0.1	0.1	4.0	4.3	72.2	69.1	16.0	17.7
	1953	69.4		0.1		2.8		72.3		14.4	
	1954	69.5		0.1		2.3		71.9		17.8	
Heyday of Strategic Forces	1955	62.4		0.1		3.2		65.7		20.9	
	1956	60.2		0.1		3.4		63.8		21.5	
	1957	59.3		0.2		4.1		63.6		22.2	
	1958	56.8	55.5	0.2	0.5	4.1	3.8	61.1	59.8	25.4	24.5
	1959	53.2		0.3		3.4		56.9		24.7	
	1960	52.2		0.6		3.2		56.0		26.2	

Era	Year	Col1	Col1 Avg	Col2	Col2 Avg	Col3	Col3 Avg	Col4	Col4 Avg	Col5	Col5 Avg
	1961	50.8		1.1		3.3		55.2		28.2	
	1962	49.0		1.6		5.3		55.9		27.1	
Dawning of Assured Destruction	1963	48.0		2.7		4.8		55.5		27.8	
	1964	46.2	45.7	4.1	3.9	4.2	4.5	54.5	54.1	27.2	27.7
	1965	42.8		4.9		4.5		52.2		28.0	
Vietnam War Peak	1966	43.2		5.0		4.1		52.3		27.5	
	1967	45.4	44.9	4.0	4.0	3.5	3.5	52.9	52.4	27.4	27.6
	1968	46.0		3.1		3.0		52.1		27.9	
Accelerated Disinvestment	1969	44.9		2.7		2.5		50.1		31.1	
	1970	41.8		2.3		2.2		46.3		33.1	
	1971	37.5		2.0		2.0		41.5		38.3	
	1972	34.3	33.7	1.8	1.8	2.1	2.1	38.2	37.7	40.3	40.6
	1973	31.2		1.6		1.7		34.5		42.5	
	1974	29.5		1.5		2.1		33.1		44.6	
	1975	26.0		1.2		2.1		29.3		46.2	
	1976	24.1		1.2		1.7		28.7		48.5	
Carter Plateau	1977	23.8		1.2		1.6		26.6		48.0	
	1978	22.8	23.1	1.1	1.1	1.6	1.7	25.3	25.9	46.0	46.8
	1979	23.1		1.0		1.5		25.6		46.3	
	1980	22.7		1.0		2.2		25.9		47.0	
Accelerated Investment	1981	23.2		1.0		1.9		26.1		47.7	
	1982	24.9		1.0		1.6		27.5		47.8	
	1983	26.0		1.0		1.5		28.5		48.9	
	1984	26.7	26.3	1.0	1.0	1.9	1.5	29.6	28.8	46.9	46.9
	1985	26.7		0.9		1.7		29.3		45.0	
	1986	27.6		0.9		1.4		29.9		45.4	
	1987	28.1		0.9		1.2		30.2		46.8	
	1988	27.3		1.0		0.9		29.2		46.9	

Source: Executive Office of the President, Office of Management and Budget, *Historical Tables—Budget of the United States Government, FY90* (Washington, DC: U.S. Government Printing Office, 1989)

Appendix E

National Defense Investment and Procurement as a Percent of U.S. National Defense Expenditures, FY1962–88

	FY	Defense Investment Spending	Period Avg.	Defense Procurement	Period Avg.
	1962	46.3		27.7	
Dawning of	1963	48.9		31.1	
Assured	1964	46.2	45.3	28.1	27.5
Destruction	1965	40.7		23.3	
Vietnam	1966	40.3		24.6	
War Peak	1967	40.6	40.6	26.6	26.5
	1968	41.0		28.4	
Accelerated	1969	41.6		29.0	
Disinvest-	1970	38.4		26.4	
ment	1971	36.4		24.0	
	1972	34.7	35.4	21.6	22.1
	1973	34.4		20.5	
	1974	33.7		19.2	
	1975	32.3		18.5	
	1976	31.8		17.9	
Carter	1977	32.7		18.7	
Plateau	1978	33.0	34.1	19.1	20.3
	1979	35.4		21.8	
	1980	35.4		21.6	
Accelerated	1981	35.8		22.3	
Investment	1982	36.8		23.4	
	1983	39.5		25.5	
	1984	41.7	40.9	27.2	26.1
	1985	43.1		27.9	
	1986	44.4		28.0	
	1987	45.3		28.6	
	1988	43.3		26.6	

Source: Executive Office of the President, Office of Management and Budget, *Historical Tables—Budget of the United States Government, FY90* (Washington, DC: U.S. Government Printing Office, 1989)

Notes

Chapter 1

1. Central Intelligence Agency and Defense Intelligence Agency, "The Soviet Economy in 1988: Gorbachev Changes Course," report submitted to the Subcommittee on National Security Economics of the Joint Economic Committee of the U.S. Congress (14 March 1989), pp. 4–5. The seven technologies evaluated are microprocessors, computer-operated machine tools, minicomputers, main frames, supercomputers, software, and flexible manufacturing systems.

2. See Central Intelligence Agency and Defense Intelligence Agency, "The Soviet Economy Under a New Leader," report submitted to the Subcommittee on Economic Resources, Competitiveness, and Security Economics of the Joint Economic Committee of the U.S. Congress (19 March 1986), pp. 35–37, for Soviet defense spending as a percent of GNP. See Executive Office of the President, Office of Management and Budget, *Historical Tables—Budget of the United States Government, Fiscal Year 1990* (Washington, DC: U.S. Government Printing Office, 1989), pp. 138–40, for FY80–88 average yearly defense spending as a percent of GNP was 6.0 percent.

3. William E. Odom, "Soviet Force Posture: Dilemmas and Directions," *Problems of Communism*, vol. 34, no. 4 (July–August 1985), pp. 6–11; Rebecca Strode, "The Soviet Armed Forces: Adaptation to Resource Scarcity," *The Washington Quarterly* (Spring 1987), pp. 55–69.

4. From FY69 to FY79 U.S. national defense outlays in real dollars shrank by 35.6 percent. *Historical Tables, FY90*, pp. 126–128.

5. "Accelerated investment" refers to a period of positive real growth in national defense spending during which a growing portion of national defense outlays is devoted to defense investment (procurement, RDT&E, and military construction). The percentage of national defense outlays devoted to investment rose from 35.4 percent in FY80 to 45.3 percent in FY87. Defense spending patterns express the opposite trends during periods of "accelerated disinvestment," when real defense spending contracts while the percentage of defense outlays devoted to investment falls each year. Data source: *Historical Tables, FY90*.

6. Advanced Space Combat Systems. Both superpowers will be able to gain military leverage by deploying sophisticated space-borne sensors and navigation and communications systems. The sensors will be critical to the success of any future theatre and/or strategic campaign that involves attacks on mobile targets. This could lead to terrestrial and space-based weapons designed to conduct anti-satellite and

ballistic missile defense missions.

Nonnuclear Transoceanic Attack Systems. Enhanced space defensive weapons technologies may lead to an array of terrestrial attack systems that could include kinetic energy projectiles and high brightness laser weapons, and the successful exploitation of low observable and super "smart" guidance technologies could lead to a variety of very long-range manned and unmanned aerodynamic attack systems.

Theatre Reconnaissance Strike Systems. Theatre warfare may be revolutionized with the deployment of long-range ballistic and cruise missile attack systems coupled with multisensor target acquisition systems. In turn, a wide array of countermeasures would be feasible, including directed energy weapons.

Revolutionary Combat Vehicle Production Techniques. Currently, both superpowers are burdened with rising unit costs of advanced combat vehicles. This may be reversed with the introduction of adaptive and highly automated production lines into advanced vehicle manufacturing.

Chapter 2

1. Central Intelligence Agency, Directorate of Intelligence, "Revisiting Soviet Economic Performance Under Glasnost: Implications for CIA Estimates," Research Paper SOV 88-10068 (September 1988). See p. 12 for a comparison of CIA, official Soviet, and unofficial Soviet economic expert estimates of Soviet economic growth. See also Michael Ellman, "The Macroeconomic Situation in the USSR—Retrospect and Prospect," *Soviet Studies*, vol. 38, no. 4 (October 1986), pp. 530–542.

2. See Paul R. Gregory and Robert C. Stuart, *Soviet Economic Structure and Performance*, 3rd ed. (New York: Harper and Row, 1986), pp. 51–58, and William L. Blackwell, *The Industrialization of Russia: An Historical Perspective* (New York: Crowell, 1970), pp. 55–76, for the period including World War I and its aftermath. See Blackwell, pp. 144–145, for an analysis of the late 1930s Soviet economic slump, p. 149 for the Korean War military build-up's role in economic sluggishness of Stalin's last years, pp. 137–144 for an analysis of the mid-1930s surge in the Soviet economy, and pp. 145–146 for discussion of the slowed defense expansion during the Hitler-Stalin Pact period. See Gregory and Stuart, *Soviet Economic Structure and Performance*, pp. 129–130, for information on the Soviet economic expansion of 1946–50, and pp. 135–136 on the acceleration in economic activity from 1956–60.

3. Gregory and Stuart, *Soviet Economic Structure and Performance*, pp. 77–78, 100–117; Blackwell, *Industrialization of Russia*, pp. 88–131.

4. See Alec Nove, *An Economic History of the USSR*, (New York: Penguin Books, 1976), pp. 144–147, for discussion of the process whereby output growth targets were increasingly raised. See Gregory and Stuart, *Soviet Economic Structure and Performance*, pp. 106–117, for the transfer of resources, and pp. 102–105 for the centralization effort.

5. See Boris Rumer, "Soviet Economy: Structural Imbalances," *Problems of Communism*, vol. 33, no. 4 (July–August 1984), pp. 26–27, for discussion of the rising extraction costs of energy and raw materials. See Folke Dovring, "Soviet Agriculture: A State Secret," *Current History*, vol. 83, no. 495 (October 1984), pp.

326, 338, and Marshall Goldman, *USSR In Crisis: The Failure of an Economic System* (New York: W. W. Norton, 1983), pp. 79–80, for discussion of the Soviet battle to maintain arable land.

6. Ed A. Hewett, *Energy Economics and Foreign Policy in the Soviet Union* (Washington, DC: The Brookings Institution, 1984), pp. 40–41. The extraction costs for oil rose by 237 percent from the 1966–70 period to 1976–80. By 1980, 64 percent of all energy produced in the Soviet Union came from the Urals or areas east of this area, whereas 75 percent of total energy consumption occurred in areas west of the Urals. The transition to energy resources in Soviet Siberia is reflected in the fact that in 1975 only 50 percent of all energy produced in the Soviet Union came from the Urals or areas to the east.

7. Rumer, "Soviet Economy: Structural Imbalances," pp. 26–27.

8. George W. Breslauer, *Khrushchev and Brezhnev as Leaders: Building Authority in Soviet Politics* (London: Allen and Unwin, 1982), pp. 35–36; Blackwell, *Industrialization of Russia*, p. 151.

9. Dovring. "Soviet Agriculture," p. 338; "Irrigation Shrinks Aral Sea," *Washington Post* (5 September 1989). During the 1980s the Aral Sea began to shrink, suggesting that if environmental protection is not administered, it, along with the rivers that flow from it, will all but disappear in the next century.

10. Gertrude E. Schroeder, "The Soviet Economy," *Current History*, vol. 84, no. 504 (October 1985), pp. 311–312; Hewett, *Energy Economics and Foreign Policy*, p. 105. Soviet energy consumption per unit of GNP rose from 12.2 percent to 13.0 percent from 1970 to 1980 while over the same period it declined in the U.S. from 12.7 percent to 9.8 percent and in the E.C., from 6.0 percent to 5.1 percent. See Rumer, "Soviet Economy," p. 27, for the high Soviet metal per unit of output ratio.

11. Dovring, "Soviet Agriculture," p. 325.

12. Goldman, *USSR In Crisis*, p. 83.

13. Gregory and Stuart, *Soviet Economic Structure and Performance*, p. 129.

14. Laurie Kurtzweg, "Trends in Soviet Gross National Product," in *Gorbachev's Economic Plans*, vol. I, Study Papers Submitted to the Joint Economic Committee of the U.S. Congress (Washington, DC: U.S. Government Printing Office, 1987), p. 138. The Soviet agricultural output growth rate plunged to 2.8 percent a year in the 1961–65 FYP before recovering to 3.4 percent in the 1966–70 FYP. But in the 1971–75 FYP it collapsed, contracting by 2.3 percent a year, and from 1976–80 it barely grew, averaging a 0.2 percent advance a year. See Hewett, *Energy Economics and Foreign Policy*, p. 3. The Soviet energy output growth rate fell from 5.7 percent a year from 1961–70 to 5.0 percent in the 1971–75 period and 3.5 percent in the 1976–82 period.

15. Jochen Bethkenhagen, "Commentary," *Gorbachev's Economic Plans*, vol. I, p. 567. Soviet production of oil fell from 616 million tons (m.t.) in 1983 to 613 m.t. in 1984 and 595 m.t. in 1985, marking a recession in the Soviet petroleum sector. See Goldman, *USSR In Crisis*, p. 65, for Soviet grain output from 1971–80, and Central Intelligence Agency and Defense Intelligence Agency, "The Soviet Economy Under a New Leader," a report submitted to the Subcommittee on Eco-

nomic Resources, Competitiveness, and Security Economics of the Joint Economic Committee of the U.S. Congress (19 March 1986), for grain output in 1981. From 1971 when Soviet grain output reached 181 million metric tons (mmt), it fell to 168 mmt in 1972, marking that year's agricultural recession. In 1973—the year after—Soviet grain output mounted a powerful recovery, reaching what was a peak up to that point of 223 mmt. But in 1974 Soviet grain output fell to 196 mmt before plunging to 140 mmt in the agricultural recession of 1975. But again by 1978, grain output hit a new postwar peak of 237 mmt. In 1979, it collapsed to 179 metric tons before rising in 1980 to 189 mmt. In 1981 it fell anew to 158 mmt.

16. Goldman, *USSR In Crisis*, p. 65, and Central Intelligence Agency and Defense Intelligence Agency, "The Soviet Economy In 1988: Gorbachev Changes Course," report submitted to the Subcommittee on National Security Economics of the Joint Economic Committee of the U.S. Congress (14 April 1989). After peaking in 1978 at 237 mmt, Soviet grain output has failed to approach that level again, coming closest in 1987 when it reached 211 mmt. From 1979–88, Soviet grain output averaged only 189 mmt a year.

17. R. Caron Cooper, "Looming Crisis in the Soviet Oil Refinery Sector," *PlanEcon Report*, vol. 5, no. 5 (3 February 1989), p. 1. The Soviet oil industry had, through substantial investment and labor discipline measures, gotten output back up to 624 m.t. in 1987 from a 1985 recession trough of 595 m.t., but in 1988 oil output did not surpass its 1987 level.

18. Dovring, "Soviet Agriculture," p. 323.

19. Ibid., p. 325.

20. Rumer, "The Soviet Economy: Structural Imbalances," p. 29.

21. Breslauer, *Khrushchev and Brezhnev as Leaders*, pp. 23–31.

22. CIA/DIA, "Soviet Economy in 1988," p. 41. The growth rate for Soviet personal consumption per capita fell from 3.9 percent a year during the 1956–60 FYP to 2.5 percent in the 1961–65 FYP. After recovering to 5.0 percent in the 1966–70 FYP, it plunged to 3.0 percent from 1971–75 and 2.0 percent from 1976–80.

23. Gertrude E. Schroeder, "Consumption," in *The Soviet Economy: Toward the Year 2000*, ed. Abram Bergson and Herbert S. Levine (London: Allen and Unwin, 1985), pp. 320–323 (for comparative consumption data), 326 (for time spent in queues).

24. David E. Powell, "The Emerging Health Crisis in the Soviet Union," *Current History*, vol. 84, no. 504 (October 1985), pp. 325–326 (for the Soviet birth rate, infant mortality, and the alcoholism and death rate and alcoholism in the male workforce). From 1955–65 the Soviet infant mortality rate fell steadily, reaching a low in 1971 of 22.9 per 1,000 live births. However, in 1972 it began to rise, hitting 27.9 in 1974. Soon after, the Soviet government stopped publishing official statistics on infant mortality. See also Murray Feshbach, "Population and Labor Force," in Bergson and Levine, *The Soviet Economy*, pp. 80–92 (on the death and birth rates); Aaron Trehub, "New Figures on Infant Mortality in the USSR," *Radio Liberty Research*, RL 438/87 (29 October 1987).

25. Feshbach, "Population and Labor Force," pp. 79–82, 96.

26. Stanley H. Cohn, "Sources of Low Productivity in Soviet Capital Investment," in *Soviet Economy in the 1980s: Problems and Prospects*, Selected Papers submitted to the Joint Economic Committee of the U.S. Congress, Part 1 (Washington, DC: U.S. Government Printing Office, 1983), p. 181. See also Central Intelligence Agency and Defense Intelligence Agency, "Gorbachev's Modernization Program: A Status Report," report submitted to the Subcommittee on National Security Economics of the Joint Economic Committee of the U.S. Congress (19 March 1987), for information on the overamortized state of Soviet capital stock. Soviet equipment is reported to have an average age of 20 years, compared to 10 years in West Germany, France, and Italy, and 12 years in the U.S. On the same point, see also Rumer, "Soviet Economy: Structural Imbalances," pp. 26–28.

27. Robert Leggett, "Soviet Investment Policy in the Eleventh Five-Year Plan," in *Soviet Economy in the 1980s*, Part 2, p. 140 (for the rising capital to output ratio); Schroeder, "The Soviet Economy," p. 312 (for the technological increment to economic growth).

28. Goldman, *USSR In Crisis*, p. 40.

29. Rumer, "The Soviet Economy: Structural Imbalances," pp. 24–29.

30. Gregory and Stuart, *Soviet Economic Structure and Performance*, p. 129.

31. Raymond Hutchings, *Soviet Economic Development*, 2nd ed. (New York: New York University Press, 1982), pp. 74–75. From 1947–50 to 1951–55, the growth rate of Soviet national income was halved. See also Breslauer, *Khrushchev and Brezhnev as Leaders*, pp. 23–24, and Nove, *Economic History of the USSR*, pp. 314–321.

32. Breslauer, *Khrushchev and Brezhnev as Leaders*, pp. 24–34; Nove, *Economic History of the USSR*, pp. 322–332.

33. Nove, *Economic History of the USSR*, pp. 330–332; Gregory and Stuart, *Soviet Economic Structure and Performance*, pp. 130–131.

34. Goldman, *USSR In Crisis*, p. 76. From 1956–60, the early success of the "virgin lands" program propelled Soviet agricultural output up by 40 percent over that of the 1951–55 period.

35. Breslauer, *Khrushchev and Brezhnev as Leaders*, pp. 61–62, 65, 81, 181. Khrushchev forecast that the Soviet per capita economic output and consumer affluence would equal that of the U.S. by 1970. See also Nove, *Economic History of the USSR*, pp. 252–54.

36. "Soviet Economic Performance in 1985: A Recovery That Was Not," *PlanEcon Report*, vol. 2, no. 7 (17 February 1986). From the 1956–60 to the 1961–65 FYP, the Soviet national material product produced growth rate fell from 9.2 to 6.5 percent, the industrial production growth rate fell from 10.4 to 8.6 percent, the agricultural product growth rate dropped from 5.9 to 2.4 percent, the retail sales turnover growth rate declined from 9.4 to 6.0 percent, the gross investment growth rate plunged from 13.0 to 6.2 percent, the industrial labor productivity growth rate fell from 6.5 to 4.6 percent, and the real income per capita growth rate fell from 5.7 to 3.5 percent.

37. Hutchings, *Soviet Economic Development*, p. 80. After a peak output year

in 1962, Soviet agriculture suffered a severe drought and recession in 1963. See also Roy Medvedev, *Khrushchev*, trans. Brian Pearce (New York: Anchor Press/ Doubleday, 1984), p. 226.

38. Breslauer, *Khrushchev and Brezhnev as Leaders*, p. 62. In 1959 Khrushchev unveiled his Seven Year Plan, which called for largescale exploitation of Siberian and Central Asian energy and raw material resources.

39. Carl A. Linden, *Khrushchev and the Soviet Leadership, 1957-64* (Baltimore: Johns Hopkins Press, 1966), pp. 175-82, 203-208; Medvedev, *Khrushchev*, pp. 235-245.

40. CIA/DIA, "Soviet Economy Under a New Leader," p. 3. Soviet real defense spending grew by 50 percent from 1965-75, or by a 4-5 percent annual average.

41. Fyodor I. Kushnirsky, "The Limits of Soviet Economic Reform," *Problems of Communism*, vol. 33, no. 4 (July-August 1984), pp. 33-37.

42. Breslauer, *Khrushchev and Brezhnev as Leaders*, pp. 141-147, 150-152.

43. Sarah Meiklejohn Terry, "Theories of Socialist Development in Soviet-East European Relations," in *Soviet Policy in Eastern Europe*, ed. Sarah Meiklejohn Terry (New Haven: Yale University Press, 1984), pp. 139-147.

44. Harry Gelman, *The Brezhnev Politburo and the Decline of Detente* (Ithaca, NY: Cornell University Press, 1984), pp. 124-126.

45. Paul Marer, "The Political Economy of Soviet Relations With Eastern Europe," in *Soviet Policy in Eastern Europe*, ed. Terry, p. 175.

46. "Soviet Economic Performance in 1985: A Recovery That Was Not," *PlanEcon Report*. From the 1966-70 to the 1971-75 FYP, the growth rate for Soviet national product produced fell from 7.7 to 5.6 percent, for industrial production from 8.5 to 7.4 percent, for agricultural production from 4.2 to 0.8 percent, for retail sales turnover from 8.2 percent to 6.4 percent, for gross investment from 7.6 to 6.9 percent,, and for real income per capita from 5.9 to 4.4 percent. The only index to advance was industrial labor productivity, which grew from 5.8 to 6.0 percent.

47. Breslauer, *Khrushchev and Brezhnev as Leaders*, pp. 204-205.

48. Breslauer, *Khrushchev and Brezhnev as Leaders*, pp. 205-207.

49. Schroeder, "The Soviet Economy," pp. 309-310.

50. Rumer, "The Soviet Economy: Structural Imbalances," pp. 25-26. See also Goldman, *USSR In Crisis*, p. 55 (for assessments of forced savings); Feshbach, "Issues in Soviet Health Problems," in *Soviet Economy in the 1980s*, Part 2, pp. 204-208 (for the decline in workforce health).

51. William T. Lee and Richard F. Staar, *Soviet Military Policy Since World War II* (Stanford: Hoover Institution Press, 1986), p. 10.

52. Alvin Z. Rubenstein, ed., *The Foreign Policy of the Soviet Union*, 3rd ed. (New York: Random House, 1972), pp. 179-193, 209-217.

53. Lee and Staar, *Soviet Military Policy*, p. 21.

54. Harriet Fast Scott and William F. Scott, eds., *The Soviet Art of War: Doctrine, Strategy, and Tactics* (Boulder, CO: Westview, 1982), pp. 17-22.

55. Scott and Scott, *The Soviet Art of War*, pp. 75-76.

56. David Holloway, *The Soviet Union and the Arms Race* (New Haven: Yale University Press, 1983), p. 25. By the mid-1950s the United States enjoyed a three-year lead over the USSR in the development of high yield weapons. See also Lawrence Freedman, *The Evolution of Nuclear Strategy* (New York: St. Martin's, 1983), pp. 77-78. By the end of the Korean War, the United States was able to exploit the mobilization base for nuclear forces constructed during the Truman administration to produce a full range of nuclear weapons as well as strategic and theatre delivery systems.

57. Breslauer, *Khrushchev and Brezhnev as Leaders*, p. 25; Rubenstein, *Foreign Policy of the Soviet Union*, pp. 250-251.

58. Breslauer, *Khrushchev and Brezhnev as Leaders*, p. 27.

59. Lee and Staar, *Soviet Military Policy*, p. 21. From 1955-58, cuts in defense spending were reflected in reduced manpower and the abandonment of Stalin's conventional navy plans while resources were shifted to missiles, electronics, and nuclear weapons.

60. Marer, "The Political Economy of Soviet Relations With Eastern Europe," p. 156.

61. Marer, "The Political Economy of Soviet Relations With Eastern Europe," pp. 156-161.

62. Stephen T. Hosmer and Thomas W. Wolfe, *Soviet Policy and Practice Toward Third World Conflicts* (Lexington, MA: D.C. Heath, 1983), pp. 11-13.

63. Holloway, *The Soviet Union and the Arms Race*, p. 40; Linden, *Khrushchev and the Soviet Leadership*, pp. 90-91 (for Khrushchev's planned force reductions); Medvedev, *Khrushchev*, pp. 141-156 (for Khrushchev's detente effort).

64. Linden, *Khrushchev and the Soviet Leadership*, pp. 114-115.

65. Lee and Staar, *Soviet Military Policy*, p. 21.

66. Linden, *Khrushchev and the Soviet Leadership*, p. 205.

67. Lee and Staar, *Soviet Military Policy*, p. 75.

68. Scott and Scott, *The Soviet Art of War*, p. 159.

69. Ibid., pp. 207-210.

70. Ibid., pp. 207.

71. Paul F. Langer, "Soviet Military Power in Asia," in *Soviet Policy in East Asia*, ed. Donald S. Zagoria (New Haven: Yale University Press, 1982), p. 267.

72. A. A. Grechko, "The Growing Role, Tasks, and Obligations of Young Officers at the Contemporary Stage of Development of the Soviet Armed Forces," *Red Star* (27 November 1969). Here, the Soviet defense minister argues that "much attention is being devoted to the reasonable combination of nuclear rocket weapons with perfected conventional classic armaments, to the capability of units and subunits to conduct combat action under nuclear as well as nonnuclear conditions."

73. Scott and Scott, *The Soviet Art of War*, pp. 241-245.

74. Marer, "The Political Economy of Soviet Relations With Eastern Europe," pp. 171-180.

75. Marie Lavigne, "Soviet Trade With LDCs," in *Gorbachev's Economic Plans,* vol. II, pp. 505–507.

76. Hosmer and Wolfe, *Soviet Policy and Practice,* pp. 42–46.

77. Lee and Staar, *Soviet Military Policy Since World War II,* p. 115.

78. CIA/DIA, "Soviet Economy Under a New Leader," pp. 3, 8.

79. Richard F. Kaufman, "Causes of the Slowdown in Soviet Defense," in *Soviet Economy,* I (1985), pp. 9–31.

80. Marer, "The Political Economy of Soviet Relations With Eastern Europe," p. 175.

81. Hosmer and Wolfe, *Soviet Policy and Practice,* p. 75 (for aid to the nonaligned Third World), 77 (for aid to Cuba and Vietnam).

Chapter 3

1. Abel Aganbegyan, *The Economic Challenge of Perestroika,* ed. Michael Barratt Brown, trans. Pauline M. Tiffen (Bloomington: Indiana University Press, 1988), p. 173. In Novosibirsk, 46 factories and sectors of fifteen enterprises were turned into contract collectives. Average productivity rose 15 percent, or 2.5 times faster than was previously the case. In some units productivity rose by 20–30 percent.

2. See Vladimir Solovyov and Elena Klepikova, *Yuri Andropov: A Secret Passage Into the Kremlin,* trans. Guy Daniels (New York: Macmillan, 1983), pp. 90–120, for a description of the activities of Aliyev and Shevardnadze in the 1970s.

3. See Solovyov and Klepikova, *Yuri Andropov,* p. 120.

4. Rebecca Strode, "The Soviet Armed Forces: Adaptation to Resource Scarcity," *Washington Quarterly* (Spring 1987), pp. 53–69.

5. Blair Ruble, "Romanov's Leningrad," *Problems of Communism* (November–December 1983), vol. 32, no. 6, pp. 36–48.

6. George W. Breslauer, *Khrushchev and Brezhnev as Leaders: Building Authority in Soviet Politics* (London: Allen and Unwin, 1982), p. 239. In his 1981 speech before the Twenty-Sixth Party Congress, Brezhnev abandoned earlier rhetoric championing Western imports, in effect delinking his domestic program from dependence on foreign imports.

7. Breslauer, *Khrushchev and Brezhnev as Leaders,* pp. 237–238. In his speech before the Twenty-Sixth Party Congress, Brezhnev was forced to make a strong pitch for expansion of private plots in agriculture, a point that found resonance in the 1982 Food Program. Zhores Medvedev, *Andropov: An Insider's Account of Power and Politics Within the Kremlin* (New York: Penguin, 1984), p. 15. Andropov allies Shevardnadze and Aliyev came to play leading roles in the promotion of the 1982 Food Program.

8. Medvedev, *Andropov,* pp. 162–168.

9. Alice C. Gorlin, "Soviet Industry and Trade," *Current History,* vol. 83, no. 495 (October 1984), p. 319.

10. Medvedev, *Andropov,* pp. 132–134.

11. Medvedev, *Andropov,* pp. 135–144; Mark R. Beissinger, "The Age of the

Soviet Oligarchs," *Current History*, vol. 83, no. 495 (October 1984), pp. 307, 339.

12. Fyodor I. Kushnirsky, "The Limits of Soviet Economic Reform," *Problems of Communism*, vol. 33, no. 4 (July-August 1984), pp. 39-40; Beissinger, "The Age of Soviet Oligarchs," p. 307-308 (for the introduction of the Andropov reform program at the 1983 Central Committee gathering and the attacks on it); Boris Rumer, "Structural Imbalance in the Soviet Economy," *Problems of Communism*, vol. 33, no. 4 (July-August 1984), p. 25 (for the nature of the Baibakov opposition).

13. Charles Wolf, Jr., "The Costs and Benefits of the Soviet Empire," in *The Future of the Soviet Empire*, ed. Henry S. Rowen and Charles Wolf, Jr. (New York: St. Margin's, 1987), p. 139.

14. Richard Cohen, "China's New Foreign Policy," *Washington/World Intelligence Focus*, vol. 2, no. 9 (September 1985), pp. 20-21.

15. Far Eastern Economic Review, *Yearbook, 1984* (Hong Kong: Far Eastern Economic Review, 1985), p. 285.

16. Nayan Chanda, "The Deep Freeze," *Far Eastern Economic Review* (14 June 1984), pp. 46-48.

17. Dusko Dodor, "Soviet Journal Criticizes China's Policies," *Washington Post* (15 November 1984).

18. Paul Quinn, "Return to Moscow," *Far Eastern Economic Review* (2 August 1984), pp. 24-26.

19. Melvin Croan, "Politics of Division and Detente in East Germany," *Current History*, vol. 84, no. 505 (November 1985), p. 371.

20. "Soviet Economic Performance in 1985: A Recovery That Was Not," *PlanEcon Report*, vol. 2, no. 7 (17 February 1986), pp. 12-15.

21. Wolf, "Costs and Benefits," pp. 129-140.

22. Robert E. Leggett, "Gorbachev's Reform Program: 'Radical' or 'More of the Same,'" *Comparative Ecoonomic Studies*, vol. 29, no. 4 (Winter 1987), p. 33 (for a description of the Gorbachev discipline campaign); Central Intelligence Agency and Defense Intelligence Agency, "The Soviet Economy Under a New Leader," report submitted to the Subcommittee on Economic Resources, Competitiveness, and Security Economics of the Joint Economic Committee of the U.S. Congress (19 March 1986), p. 10; Walter D. Conner, "Social Policy Under Gorbachev," *Problems of Communism*, vol. 35, no. 4 (July-August 1986), pp. 34-35 (for the origins of the anti-alcoholism campaign).

23. Central Intelligence Agency and Defense Intelligence Agency, "Gorbachev's Modernization Program: A Status Report," report submitted to the Subcommittee on National Security Economics of the Joint Economic Committee of the U.S. Congress (19 March 1987), p. 22; Mark R. Beissinger, "The New Leadership and the Soviet Party Congress," *Current History*, vol. 85, no. 513 (October 1986), p. 312.

24. "Gorbachev Urges Plant Retooling," *New York Times* (12 June 1985).

25. Leggett, "Gorbachev's Reform Program," pp. 37-38.

26. Leggett, "Gorbachev's Reform Program," pp. 34-35; "Import Implications of Dramatic Shift in Soviet Investment Strategy in 1986," *PlanEcon Report*, vol. 2, nos. 1-2 (15 January 1986), pp. 1, 4-6.

27. CIA/DIA, "Gorbachev's Modernization Program." The CIA and DIA reported that Soviet defense spending grew by 3.0 percent in 1986, indicating that for the two years 1985–86, the rate of defense spending growth was slightly higher than the rate for recent years, while defense procurement advanced by 3.0 percent a year in 1985–86, well above the average for 1976–84.

28. Richard Cohen, "Can the Soviet Economy Be Revived?" *Washington/World Intelligence Focus*, vol. 2, no. 12 (December 1985), pp. 34–35 (for discussion of Soviet pressure on Eastern Europe during Gorbachev's first year in office); Jackson Diehl, "Bulgaria Beset by Economic Woes," *Washington Post* (8 November 1985); "Bulgarian Economic Performance in 1986 and During the First Quarter of 1987— Record Hard Currency Trade Deficit and Improved Weather Fuel Economic Recovery," *PlanEcon Report*, vol. 3, no. 21 (21 May 1987), pp. 1, 7. This article details the harsh impact of the 7.0 percent cut in volume of CMEA (almost all Soviet) energy exports to Bulgaria as part of the Soviet effort to squeeze the Bulgarian leadership into adopting initiatives to improve energy efficiency.

29. A. D. Horne, "Gorbachev Calls for New Diversity in Eastern Europe," *Washington Post* (8 July 1989) (for Soviet restraints on East German relations with West Germany in 1984); Michael Kraus, "Soviet Policy Toward Eastern Europe," *Current History*, vol. 86, no. 523 (November 1987), pp. 355–356 (for Gorbachev's activity in Eastern Europe from 1985–87).

30. "Developments in Soviet East European Debt to BIS-Area Commercial Banks Between 1974–1988," *PlanEcon Report*, vol. 5. nos. 21–22 (2 June 1989), p. 2.

31. Beissinger, "The New Leadership," p. 311.

32. CIA/DIA, "Gorbachev's Modernization Program," p. 20.

33. Ed A. Hewett, "The June Plenum and Economic Reform," *Plan Econ Report*, vol. 3, no. 30 (23 July 1987).

34. Allen Kroncher, "Political and Economic Aspects of the Draft Law," *Radio Liberty Research*, RL 83/87 (27 February 1987); "Soviet Economic Performance During the First Quarter of 1989: Wages and Inflation Are Out of Control While the Economy Deteriorates Further," *PlanEcon Report*, vol. 5, no. 17 (28 April 1989), p. 5. From the end of March 1988 to the end of March 1989, 3.6 million Soviets entered the private sector. Ben Eklof, *Soviet Briefing: Gorbachev and the Reform Period* (Boulder, CO: Westview, 1989), pp. 101–102. Michael Dobbs, "Gorbachev Sets Sweeping Agricultural Reforms," *Washington Post* (16 March 1989).

35. Eklof, *Soviet Briefing*, pp. 43–59.

36. Eklof, *Soviet Briefing*, pp. 25, 32; Mark R. Beissinger, "Political Reform and Soviet Society," *Current History*, vol. 81, no. 531 (October 1988), p. 318–319.

37. Paul Marentz, "Soviet 'New Thinking' and East–West Relations," *Current History*, vol. 87, no. 531 (October 1988), pp. 311, 346.

38. Marentz, "Soviet 'New Thinking'," p. 309–311.

39. Lawrence T. Caldwell, "United States–Soviet Relations and Arms Control," *Current History*, vol. 86, no. 522 (October 1987), pp. 346–347.

40. "China '86: New Thresholds," *Far Eastern Economic Review* (20 March 1986), pp. 70–78.

41. Phyllis M. Martin, "Peace in Angola?" *Current History*, vol. 88, no. 538 (May 1989), pp. 332, 346-347. The Soviets are described by U.S. State Department officials as eager to reduce in 1988 the $1.0-$1.5 billion in military equipment they had delivered to Angola and this is given as one reason for their willingness to apply pressure on Cuba to become more flexible in negotiations involving prospects for a Cuban troop withdrawal from Angola. "China '88: But Does It Catch Mice?" *Far Eastern Economic Review* (24 March 1988), pp. 56-57. The Soviets organized efforts to bring Prince Sihanouk directly into negotiations with the Heng Samrin government in Cambodia.

42. Beissinger, "The New Leadership," p. 311 (for the expansion of the antialcoholism campaign in 1986); Directorate of Intelligence, Central Intelligence Agency, "USSR: Sharply Higher Budget Deficits Threaten Perestroyka," Research Paper SOV 88-10043U (September 1988), p. 2 (for the impact of the antialcoholism campaign on government revenues).

43. CIA/DIA, "Gorbachev's Modernization Program," p. 12. Soviet fixed investment rose by 7.5 percent in 1986, the highest increase in over a decade and above the 1986 target.

44. "Soviet Economic Performance in 1988: Disappointing Results Are Covered Up By Gross Manipulation of Key Statistics," *PlanEcon Report*, vol. 5, nos. 6-7 (19 February 1989), p. 14. After advancing by 23.3 percent a year from 1981-85, Soviet inventories rose by only 6.5 percent in 1986 before contracting by 1.0 percent in 1987 and 10.0 percent in 1988.

45. Directorate of Intelligence, "USSR: Sharply Higher Budget Deficits," pp. 1-2.

46. Central Intelligence Agency and Defense Intelligence Agency, "Gorbachev's Economic Program: Problems Emerge," report submitted to the Subcommittee on National Security Economics of the Joint Economic Committee of the U.S. Congress (13 April 1988), pp. 14-15.

47. Eklof, *Soviet Briefing*, pp. 94-95.

48. Rudolf Tokes, "Hungarian Reform Imperatives," *Problems of Communism*, vol. 33, no. 5 (September-October 1984), pp. 1-23. Richard Cohen, "China: What's At Stake in China's Economic Modernization," *Washington/World Intelligence Focus*, vol. 2, no. 8 (August 1985), pp. 1-25.

49. Eklof, *Soviet Briefing*, pp. 27-35, 89 (for opposition to political and economic reform); David Remnick, "For Kremlin Co-ops Are Good—To a Point," *Washington Post* (January 8, 1989) (for the increase in taxes on the new private sector).

50. Central Intelligence Agency and Defense Intelligence Agency, "The Soviet Economy in 1988: Gorbachev Changes Course," report submitted to the subcommittee on National Security Economics of the Joint Economic Committee of the U.S. Congress (14 April 1989), pp. 11, 13.

51. *PlanEcon Report* (17 February 1989), p. 9.

52. Directorate of Intelligence, "USSR: Sharply Higher Budget Deficits," pp. 7-12 (for the decision to confront the budget deficit); CIA/DIA, "Soviet Economy in 1988," pp. 13-14, 27-30 (for the postponement of radical perestroika).

53. "Soviets Increase Alcohol Production," *Journal of Commerce* (11 October 1988); "Soviet Economic Performance During the First Quarter of 1989," *PlanEcon Report*, p. 15. During the first quarter of 1989 Soviet state alcohol sales were up 30 percent from their first quarter 1988 level.

54. CIA/DIA, "Soviet Economy in 1988," pp. 23–25; Albert Axebank, "Soviets Map Emerging Steps to Escape Economic Quagmire," *Journal of Commerce* (8 August 1989). Soviet investment in industrial production for 1990 is now targeted to be cut by a huge 30 percent.

55. CIA/DIA, "Soviet Economy in 1988," pp. 12–13, 25.

56. R. Caron Cooper, "Looming Crisis in the Soviet Oil Refinery Sector," *PlanEcon Report*, vol. 5, no. 5 (3 February 1989), p. 2.

57. Data source: United National Conference on Trade and Development, *Handbook of International Trade and Development Statistics, Supplement 1986* (New York: United Nations, 1987). Twenty-six percent of total Soviet imports originated in the developed sector in 1984, and 19.2 percent originated in Western Europe.

58. *PlanEcon Report* (17 February 1989), p. 1.

59. Soviet Premier Puts Debt at $52.7 Billion, Warns Against Borrowing," *Investors Daily* (12 June 1989).

60. "Developments in Soviet and East European Hard Currency Debt to BIS-Area Commercial Banks Between 1974–1988," *PlanEcon Report*, vol. 5, nos. 21–22 (2 June 1989).

61. Blaine Harden, "Hungary Forms New Party," *Washington Post* (8 October 1989).

62. David B. Ottaway, "U.S. Misreads Gorbachev, Official Says," *Washington Post* (10 September 1989).

63. According to some analysts, Moscow has not lessened the strong priority it gives to the continued firm grip on power of its client state governments. See Jeane Kirkpatrick, "So We've 'Won' the Cold War?" *Washington Post* (25 September 1989), who charges that "the Soviet Union continues aid [to its Third World allies] at previous levels."

64. "Soviet Foreign Trade Performance in 1988: Despite 3 Percent Deterioration in Non-Socialist Terms of Trade, Imports Rose By 21 Percent in Dollar Value," *PlanEcon Report*, vol. 5, nos. 13–14 (7 April 1989). Soviet arms shipments to the Third World continued to represent 55.5 percent of total Soviet exports to the Third World in 1988 as they rose by 2 percent over 1987 levels. But in the fourth quarter of 1988, Soviet arms shipments to the Third World dropped precipitously, suggesting to some that Moscow may be moving into a permanently lower range for its foreign military sales.

65. CIA/DIA, "Gorbachev's Economic Program," p. 20; CIA/DIA, "Soviet Economy in 1988," p. 15.

66. CIA/DIA, "Gorbachev's Economic Program," pp. 31–33.

67. Sergei Zanaseikov, "Gorbachev and the Soviet Military," *Comparative Strategy*, vol. 7 (1988), pp. 233–237; Milon Hauner and Alexander Rahu, "New Chief of Soviet General Staff Appointed," *Radio Liberty Research*, RL 546/88 (16 De-

cember 1988). "Lushev is the New Warsaw Pact C-in-C," *Jane's Defense Weekly* (11 February 1989), vol. 11, no. 6. There has been a major generational transition if not purge of the Ogarkov generation of marshals. Of note was the replacement of Marshal Viktor Kulikov (a key player in the 1980-81 Polish crisis) with army General Petr G. Lushev as commander in chief of the Warsaw Pact Joint Armed Forces in February 1989. With Kulikov's retirement, there are no Marshals of the Soviet Union in the Soviet high command for the first time since 1945.

68. Gerhard Weltig, "Has Soviet Military Doctrine Changed?" *Radio Liberty Research*, RL 465/87 (20 November 1987); R. Jeffrey Smith, "Soviets Debate Basic Military Doctrine," *Washington Post* (1 August 1988). See also Dimitri Simes, "The New Soviet Foreign Policy Approach," in *NATO in the 1990s*, ed. Stanley R. Sloan (Washington, DC: Pergamon-Brassey's, 1989), p. 137, for an account of the objections to the concept of "nonoffensive defense" during 1987 and 1988 from members of the Soviet high command.

69. CIA/DIA, "Soviet Economy in 1988," p. 15. See also Alexey Izyumov and Andrey Kortunov, "The Soviet Union in the Changing World," *International Affairs*, no. 8 (August 1988), for examples of the summer 1988 public assault on excessive military spending during the Brezhnev period.

70. Bill Keller, "Gorbachev Tells of Military Cuts," *New York Times* (19 January 1989) (for the initial announcement); R. Jeffrey Smith, "Soviets May Close Military Budget in Fall," *Washington Post* (28 April 1989) (for later clarification).

71. Douglas Clarke, "Gorbachev's Proposed Restructuring of the Soviet Army," *Radio Liberty Research*, RL 544/88 (8 December 1988); Philip A. Karber, "Military Impact of the Gorbachev Reductions," and Philip A. Peterson and Notra Trulock, III, "Equal Security: Greater Stability at Lower Force Levels," in *Beyond Burdensharing—Future Alliance Defense Cooperation*, The Alliance Papers: Proceedings No. 1, ed. William B. Taylor, Jr. (Brussels: U.S. Mission to NATO, April 1989), pp. 101-129, 61-92.

72. CIA/DIA, "Soviet Economy in 1988," p. 18.

73. CIA/DIA, "Soviet Economy in 1988," p. 18-19.

74. Martin Sieff, "Space Funds Shrinking for Soviets," *Washington Times* (28 April 1989). Yeltsin advocated a five-seven year freeze in funding for the space program while campaigning for the first round of elections to the Congress of People's Deputies in March. Sagdeyev told a Washington press conference that the cost of the Soviet space program was "several times bigger than NASA's." In fact, the Soviet space shuttle program has already been subjected to a severe slowdown in development tempo. See Jeffrey M. Lenorovitz, "Low Mission Rate Planned for Soviet Energia Launcher," *Aviation Week and Space Technology* (11 September 1989), vol. 141, no. 11, p. 38. "Next Energia Mission Delayed Until Early 1991," *Aviation Week and Space Technology* (11 December 1989), p. 32, and "Proton Production Cut to Eight Per Year," *Aviation Week and Space Technology* (11 December 1989). Further evidence of a cutback in Soviet space activity is the slowdown in the production of their heavy lift booster, the Proton.

75. Peter Gumbel, "Gorbachev Announces Spending on Soviet Military for First Time," *Wall Street Journal* (31 May 1989). There are wide differences among some

Western analysts as to the absolute size of Soviet defense spending, but the consensus tends to fall around the CIA number. For a critique of the U.S. official estimates as overstatements of Soviet defense spending, see Franklyn D. Holzman, "Politics and Guesswork: CIA and DIA Estimates of Soviet Military Spending," *International Security* (Fall 1989), vol. 14, no. 2, pp. 101–131, and for a contrary view, see John McCain, "A New Soviet Military? Weapons and Budgets," *Orbis* (Spring 1989), vol. 33, no. 2.

76. R. Jeffrey Smith, "House Panel Hears Top Soviet Military Officer," *Washington Post* (22 July 1989).

77. "Soviets to Shrink War Chest," *Washhington Times* (8 June 1989).

78. R. Jeffrey Smith, "House Panel Hears Top Soviet Military Officer," *Washington Post* (22 July 1989).

79. Peter Gumbel, "Gorbachev Announces Spending on Soviet Military for First Time," *Wall Street Journal* (31 May 1989).

80. Molly Moore, "Soviet Naval Cutbacks Reported," *Washington Post* (23 February 1989). Rear Admiral Thomas Brooks, director of Naval Intelligence, reported that the Soviet Union has scaled back its submarine production and reduced its Pacific fleet. See also Peter Almond, "Cheney Cites Dip in Soviet Tank Production," *Washington Times* (25 September 1989).

81. "Soviet Economists Form Group to Fight Inflation," *Journal of Commerce* (8 May 1989).

82. David Remnick, "Economy Faces Crash, Soviet Congress Told," *Washington Post* (9 June 1989); "Yeltsin Warns Poverty Could Spark a Soviet Revolution," *Washington Times* (30 June 1989).

83. "Soviet Economic Performance During the First Quarter of 1989: Wages and Inflation Are Out of Control While the Economy Deteriorates," *PlanEcon Report*, vol. 5, no. 17 (28 April 1989). In the first quarter of 1989 Soviet crime was up 31 percent from its level in the first quarter of 1988. Violent crime was up 40 percent, theft, 51 percent, and theft of private property, 69 percent. See also David Remnick, "Labor Strikes Now Part of Soviet Life," *Washington Post* (14 July 1989).

84. Peter Conradi, Reuters, "Ethnic Violence Could Slam Door on Soviet Glasnost," *Washington Times* (21 June 1989). See also Steven L. Burg, "The Soviet Natonalities Question," *Current History*, vol. 88, no. 540 (October 1989), pp. 341–344, 359–362.

85. "Soviet Reforms Criticized," *Washington Times* (7 July 1989); Agence-France Presse, "Gorbachev Announces $16 Billion Shopping Spree," *Washington Times* (17 July 1989).

86. "Restricted USDA Analysis Says Soviet Farm Reforms Likely To Fall Short," *Inside U.S. Trade* (5 May 1989).

87. CIA/DIA, "Soviet Economy in 1988," p. 21.

88. Mark D. Berniker, "Soviet Economy Faces Emergency, Top Adviser to Gorbachev Claims," *Journal of Commerce* (20 November 1989). This article quotes Soviet economist Nikolai Schmelev as saying that the current Soviet government budget deficit has risen to 13–14 percent of GNP. See David Remnick, "Gorbachev

Upsets the Progressives," *Washington Post* (19 October 1989), for information on the mounting conservative pressure on Gorbachev, and Michael Dobbs, "Soviets to Accelerate Output for Consumer," *Washington Post* (14 December 1989), for a discussion of the Soviet economic measures taken at the end of 1989.

89. "Soviets To Shrink War Chest," *Washington Times* (8 June 1989).

90. "Soviets Would Save Half With Arms Cuts," *Washington Times* (9 August 1989). Marshal Akhromeyev argues that cutting the Soviet defense budget by 50 percent by 1995 would require substantial arms control including an agreement to cut forces in Europe and cut strategic missiles. "Chinese, Soviets Plan Force Cut Talks," *Washington Times* (31 July 1989). Moscow also seeks to win Sino-Soviet force reductions in order to generate savings in the defense sector. See also "Dependable Defense Above All," *Moscow News*, no. 8 (21 February 1988), for indications of opposition to unilateral cuts by senior staff. Ivan Tretyak, chief of the Air Defense Forces, argues that any proposal for Soviet unilateral cuts must be "examined a thousand times over."

91. Stephen Sestanovich, "Communism's Uneasy Generals," *Wall Street Journal* (2 August 1989). Soviet officers have risen as a vocal force promoting law and order themes, and the possibility of a greater role in domestic policing a la the "Tiananmen Square model" cannot be discounted.

92. Aron Katsenelinboigen, "Will Glasnost Bring the Reactionaries To Power?" *Orbis* (Spring 1988); David Remnick, "Russian Nationalists Seek Heritage," *Washington Post* (31 July 1989). See also Alexander Yanov, *The Russian Challenge and the Year 2000*, trans. Iden J. Rosenthal (Oxford: Basil Blackwell, 1987), for discussion of the prospect of a Russian "fascist" counter-reform regime. See Zbigniew Brzezinski, "Post-Communist Nationalism," *Foreign Affairs* (Winter 1989/90), vol. 68, no. 5, for an elaboration of the crisis of nationalism in the Soviet Union and the prospect for increased Great Russian nationalist responses.

93. Examples of advanced Soviet weapons systems that encountered stretchouts and difficulties in moving to production include: the SU-27 interceptor, the Mil-28 helicopter gunship, the TU-160 intercontinental bomber, and the Akula nuclear powered attack submarine. Bill Sweetman, "SU-27 Flanker in Paris, *International Defense Review* (August 1989), vol. 22, pp. 1020–1022; Brian M. Service, "Mi-28 Helicopter: Revelation of the Year," *International Defense Review* (July 1989), vol. 22, pp. 886–887.

94. Michael MccGwire, "Gorshkov's Navy," *U.S. Naval Institute Proceedings* (September 1989), pp. 42–47; "Chernavin Responds," *Proceedings* (February 1989), pp. 44–51. Although Admiral Gorshkov's swan song, "The Navy: Its Role, Prospects for Development, and Employment," published in late 1987, called for vigorous investment in a transcentury class of weapons, its content and tone have been judged "old thinking" and out of phase with the current, less shrill view of the evolution of the "threat" (i.e., the United States). Gorshkov was clearly an advocate of the large "balanced" navy with a sizable surface fleet to support the ambitious "internationalist" Brezhnev-era foreign policy. The new priority set down by admiral, Chernavin overturns the Gorshkov commitment to a balanced fleet. According to Chernavin, "We consider both nuclear and diesel submarines, along with naval aircraft, to be the main forces of our fleet," and "We consider surface vessels to

be forces intended mainly for the defense of our sea boundaries, lanes, and coast."

95. A. D. Baker, III, "The Ivanovs Keep Up," *Proceedings* (August 1989); David Fouquet, "Superpowers 'Moving Toward Maritime Unilateralism', " *Jane's Defense Weekly,* vol. 11, no. 22 (3 June 1989). The very large fleet of Soviet diesel power attack submarines, built in mass during the 1950s and 1960s, has been steadily dwindling. Given current scrapping rates (including first-generation nuclear powered submarines), the overall size of the Soviet submarine fleet may fall from 370 ships (in 1989) to approximately 230, and the surface fleet of large warships may shrink from 300 to 200 ships by the early 1990s. See Norman Friedman, "World Naval Developments—Soviets Are Scrapping Equipment," *Proceedings* (January 1990), pp. 135–136.

96. Given budgetary pressures, the obsolete first generation of strategic surface-to-air missile sites (such as those for the SA-1 and SA-2) are likely to be replaced by a much smaller overall force structure, as the advanced SA-10 and SA-12 systems are deployed for homeland defense. Similarly, there has not been a one for one replacement of older manned interceptor aircraft such as the SU-9/11 and 15 series with contemporary systems such as the MiG-31 and SU-27. Without a "look down–shoot down" capability against small targets like the Tomahawk class cruise missile, the early generation of interceptor systems is useless in area defense. See Aleksey Arbatov, "How Much Defense Is Sufficient," *International Affairs,* no. 4 (April 1989), pp. 31–44, for identification of Soviet air defenses as a likely candidate for future reduction in force structure.

97. The Soviet high command had become increasingly concerned about the military consequences of the "third revolution" in military technology (i.e., transcentury weapons) by the late 1970s. Marshal Ogarkov was the most outspoken advocate of seizing the initiative in this area. This forward-thinking view with its considerable emphasis on historical continuity is found in Makhmut Akhmetovich Gareev, *M. V. Frunze: Military Theorist* (London: Pergamon-Brassey's, 1988). For U.S. assessments suggesting that the Soviets are moving in this direction, see Martin Sieff, "Analysts Doubt Soviet Switch," *Washington Times* (15 August 1989). Former under secretary of Defense for Planning and Resources Dov Zakheim describes what he believes is a Soviet decision to transform their force structure in the European theatre into a leaner and meaner one.

98. The Soviet military is giving serious thought to creating special "artillery and machine gun" divisions optimized to defend fortified zones. See Charles G. Pritchard, "Soviet Fortified Regions—A New 'Cult of Defense'? " *International Defense Review* (July 1989), vol. 22, pp. 895–899.

99. Thomas H. Buckley, *The United States and the Washington Conference, 1921–1922* (Knoxville: University of Tennessee Press, 1970).

100. Professional military interest in pursuit of transcentury weapons rose under former Soviet chief of staff Marshal Nikolai Ogarkov, who strongly promoted a Soviet response to the "third revolution" in warfare, made the case that the nuclear balance between NATO and the Warsaw Pact had reached a stalemate in his often quoted article, "History Teaches Vigilance," *Voyenizdat* (Moscow: April 1985), translated in U.S. Government, Foreign Broadcast Information Service, USSR Report (30 August 1985), and further argued that future defense planning would be

dominated by advanced nonnuclear weapons systems and sensors. For three discussions of the Soviet shift to a nonnuclear strategy, see William Odom, "Soviet Force Posture: Dilemmas and Directions," *Problems of Communism*, vol. 34, no. 4 (July-August 1985); Michael MccGwire, *Military Objectives in Soviet Foreign Policy* (Washington, DC: The Brookings Institution, 1987); and Mary E. Fitzgerald, "Marshal Ogarkov on Modern War: 1977-1985," Center for Naval Analyses, Arlington, VA (March 1986). The tenets of the so-called Ogarkov Doctrine emphasize the transcentury threat. These tenets include: (1) the superpower nuclear balance is in a stalemate; (2) limited and controlled use of nuclear weapons is not feasible; (3) focus of doctrine and design of forces should be on the perfection of nonnuclear theatre combined arms warfighting capabilities; (4) command, control, communications, and intelligence systems and structures should be deployed in peacetime to allow for a rapid transition to a war footing; (5) major efforts to stimulate research and development of weapons technologies that will bring a "revolution" in military affairs should be undertaken. See Notra Trulock, III, "Emerging Technologies and Future War: A Soviet View," in "The Future Security Environment," Report of the Future Security Environment Working Group, Appendix B, submitted to the Commission on Integrated Long-Term Strategy (limited publication by the Department of Defense, October 1988), for a discussion of Soviet views on new military technologies.

101. Responding to concerns about the reliability of East European armies, the Brezhnev era Soviet high command took many measures to insure that the "international" character of the alliance was preserved during wartime, giving to itself command and control hegemony over the command structure of the various East European national armies, a cause of the bitter break between Romania and the USSR. The effectiveness of the Brezhnev arrangement to strengthen control will be shattered by current political developments in Eastern Europe. See Ivan Volgyes, "The Warsaw Pact: Changes In Structure and Function," *Armed Forces and Society*, vol. 15, no. 4 (summer 1989), p. 557, for discussion of the Soviet success in gaining greater control over the national armies of Eastern Europe during 1979-80. See also "Hungary Seized Chance to Counter Romanian Threat," *Jane's Defense Weekly* (9 September 1989), vol. 12, no. 10, p. 436, and "Poland Set To Cut Budget, Force Strength," *Jane's Defense Weekly* (9 September 1989), vol. 12, no. 10, p. 437. See also Jeffrey Simon, *NATO-Warsaw Pact Force Mobilization* (Washington, DC: National Defense University Press, 1988), especially Part I, "National and Warsaw Pact Institutional Developments."

102. "Soviet Military Faces Rise in Minority Conscripts," *Jane's Defense Weekly* (1 October 1988), vol. 10, no. 13, p. 817. The number of military recruits from the Central Asian and Transcaucasian regions grew from 28% in 1980 to 37% in 1989. These demographic changes have led to reports of widespread ethnic tension and violence within the ranks. In addition, the problems arising from the Soviet high command's attempts to reequip with complex weapons a mass mobilization army drawn increasingly from the non-Slavic population has led to public criticism of the poor standards of readiness and training of even allegedly elite ground force units. See "Kozlov is GSFG Forces' New Chief," *Jane's Defense Weekly* (1 October 1989), vol. 10, no. 13, p. 814. See army General Dmitri Sihkorvkov, Moscow Television

Service (15 April 1989), translated in U.S. Government, Foreign Broadcast Information Service, USSR Report (April 19, 1989), p. 117, for an indication of acceptance by some in the Soviet military of the need to improve quality to make up for losses in force structure.

103. Currently, USSR ground forces are structured along a battalion/regiment/division/army/front and theatre hierarchy. Hungary was the first to shift to a brigade/corps structure in which the divisional command echelon was abolished, and evidence suggests the Soviets may view this as a prototype. Under this structure, Warsaw Pact ground forces would be grouped into "corps" that would control a number of combined arms brigades, each brigade being a mixture of armored infantry and armored battalions. Unlike the past more homogeneous force structure heavily biased toward the tank, future corps would be optimized to fight in specific areas of operations. See Major R. H. Pepper and Warrant Officer Second Class P. Leonard, "A Soviet New Model Army?" *International Defense Review* (March 1989), vol. 22, pp. 259–263. See also *Krasnaya Zvesda* (10 February 1989), translated in U.S. Government, Foreign Broadcast Information Service, USSR Report (13 February 1989), pp. 77–81, for an emphatic Soviet General Staff rejection of a territorial militia system and a volunteer professional army.

104. It does not seem extraordinary that the Soviet military and police forces were poorly prepared to deal with serious and sustained civil disorder. The use of paratroopers to suppress demonstrators led to the April 9, 1989, "massacre" at Tbilisi, Georgia, a political disaster for Moscow and a public relations disaster for the Soviet armed forces. By the late summer of 1989 there was an attempt to create specialized riot control units out of the Ministry of the Interior's police force. See "Ethnic Tension Creating Security Problem," *Jane's Defense Weekly* (12 August 1989), vol. 12, no. 6.

105. This would merely accelerate the trend and priorities articulated by Admiral Chernavin.

Chapter 4

1. Richard Cohen, *World Trade and Payments Cycles: The Advance and Retreat of the Postwar Order* (New York: Praeger, 1989), chap. 5, pp. 81–127. *World Trade and Payments Cycles* analyses the four postwar free world trade and payments cycles, each of which can be divided into similar sequences of six phases. In the present work (chapters 4 and 5), the four postwar United States business cycles—which run parallel to the world trade and payments cycles—are analyzed, for which four phases that occur in each are identified.

2. Executive Office of the President, *Economic Report of the President, 1989* (Washington, DC: U.S. Government Printing Office, 1989), p. 397. The U.S. government fiscal deficit in FY82 and FY83 averaged annual rates of growth of over 60 percent—62.1 percent in FY82 and 62.3 percent in FY83.

3. Data source: Organization for Economic Cooperation and Development, *OECD Economic Outlook, December 1987* (Paris: OECD, 1987). The U.S. domestic demand growth rate, after contracting by 1.9 percent in 1982, shot up to average 6.9 percent annual growth in 1983 and 1984.

4. Data source: International Monetary Fund, *International Financial Statistics Yearbook, 1989* (Washington, DC: IMF, 1989), p. 165. In the 1970s the world economic growth rate (which in the *International Financial Statistics (IFS)* publications does not include the majority of East European CPEs and the USSR) advanced at a 3.7 percent annual rate, while in the 1980s (1980-86) it grew at a 2.2 percent annual rate.

5. Cohen, *World Trade and Payments Cycles*, pp. 37-39, 44-47, 62-65.

6. Albert L. Danielsen, *The Evolution of OPEC* (New York: Harcourt, 1982), pp. 69-70, 170.

7. Andrea Boltho, "Growth," in *The European Economy: Growth and Crisis*, ed. Andrea Boltho (Oxford: Oxford University Press, 1982), pp. 25-26.

8. Dennis S. Ippolito, *Congressional Spending*, A Twentieth Century Fund Report (Ithaca, NY: Cornell University Press, 1981), pp. 52-53, 55-56.

9. IMF, *International Financial Statistics Yearbook, 1986* (Washington, DC: IMF, 1986), pp. 346-347, 420-421, 684-685, 690-691. Aside from West Germany, most leading developed sector economies experienced a rise in government fiscal deficit to GNP ratios from the 1959-67 to the 1968-75 business cycles. Whereas the average annual government fiscal deficit to GNP ratio fell from 0.6 to 0.1 percent for West Germany in this period, in the United States it jumped from 0.8 to 1.4 percent, in the U.K. from 1.1 to 2.1 percent and in Japan from 0.8 to 1.5 percent. Data source: U.N. Conference on Trade and Development (UNCTAD), *Handbook of International Trade and Development Statistics, 1986 Supplement* (New York: United Nations, 1987). The current account deficits of nonoil exporting developing nations rose from $10.0 billion in 1970 to $34.6 billion in 1975. While this sector's nominal GNP growth rate rose vigorously, it did not match the pace of expansion in its current account deficit, resulting in a rise in external overindebtedness.

10. See Maxwell Newton, *The Fed: Inside the Federal Reserve, the Secret Power Center That Controls the American Economy* (New York: Times Books, 1983), pp. 212-217, for an account of the shift in U.S. monetary policy in 1979. See Far Eastern Economic Review, *Asia Yearbook, 1980* (Hong Kong: Far Eastern Economic Review, 1981), p. 202, and *Asia Yearbook, 1981* (Hong Kong: FEER, 1982), p. 165, for an account of the transformation in Japanese fiscal policy. See also International Monetary Fund, *World Economic Outlook, October 1988* (Washington, DC: IMF, 1988), pp. 95, 109. The net external borrowing of capital importing developing countries fell from a peak of $123.2 billion in 1981 to $71.6 billion in 1983, and their aggregate current account balance fell from a deficit of $115.8 billion in 1981 to a deficit of only $63.3 billion in 1983. Although this sector's nominal GNP growth rate also weakened, it did not fall, whereas the sector's current account deficit did.

11. Franco Bernabe, "The Labour Market and Unemployment," in *The European Economy*, ed. Boltho, pp. 169-184.

12. Data source: *Economic Report of the President, 1989*. From 1967 to 1975 investment in the U.S. manufacturing sector grew by 66.4 percent while investment in the U.S. mining sector advanced by 343.6 percent. Similarly, from 1975 to 1982 the investment in the U.S. mining sector surged ahead, increasing by 227.6 percent

compared to 124.9 percent for the manufacturing sector. These trends represented a sharp reversal from those that held from 1952–67 when investment in the manufacturing sector rose by 191.3 percent compared to only 24.3 percent in the mining sector.

13. Data source: IMF, *International Financial Statistics Yearbook, 1986.* From the 1959–67 to the 1968–75 business cycle, the developed sector's average GDP growth rate dropped sharply, from 5.0 to 3.3 percent a year. Because the average annual share of investment in GDP from the 1959–67 to the 1968–75 cycle improved only marginally—from 23.8 to 24.1 percent—in the developed sector, the growth rate of investment contracted from the first to the second cycle. In contrast, the developing sector's average GDP growth rate rose from 5.0 percent in the 1959–67 cycle to 6.0 percent in the 1968–75 cycle, while its investment as a share of GDP grew vigorously, from 19.6 to 22.9 percent. As a result, its investment growth rate soared. From the 1968–75 to the 1976–82 business cycle, a similar pattern unfolded.

14. IMF, *World Economic Outlook, October 1988,* pp. 64–96. While the developing sector's GNP continued to grow in the current business cycle, its current account deficit has fallen from an average $12.8 billion from 1970–82 to $3.9 billion from 1983–88, suggesting that the process of overindebtedness is weakening.

15. Data source: IMF, *International Financial Statistics Yearbook, 1989,* for interest rate levels in the 1980s. Data source: OECD, *OECD Economic Outlook, June 1988* (Paris: OECD, 1988). In the first half of the 1976–82 business cycle (that is, from 1976–78), OECD gross nonresidential fixed investment rose by 5.2 percent a year, whereas in the first half of the current business cycle (1983–86) it rose at a 4.9 percent annual rate. When the severely depressed developing sector investment growth rate of the present business cycle is factored in, the entire free world economy investment growth rate for 1983–86 is substantially lower than for the years 1976–78.

16. IMF, *International Financial Statistics, Supplement on Trade Statistics,* Supplement Series No. 15 (Washington, DC: IMF, 1988), pp. 2–3. From 1959–67 the average annual developing sector external deficit was $3.1 billion, from 1968–75 it averaged a $5.0 billion annual surplus, and from 1976–82, a $26.0 billion surplus.

17. IMF, *International Financial Statistics Yearbook, 1986,* pp. 152–153. From 1959–67 to 1968–75, the average GDP growth rate of the world economy dropped from 5.0 to 3.8 percent, whereas over the same period the GDP growth rate of the developing sector rose from 5.0 to 6.0 percent.

18. The Great Depression of the 1930s brought with it a dramatic plunge in primary commodity prices, a development that forced sizable import compression and economic hardship for developing economies. With less ferocity, the depressed nonfood primary commodity prices of the post–Korean War period placed severe limits on the growth of developing sector imports and, hence, on development. In reaction to the difficult domestic economic consequences borne of primary commodity price volatility, developing sector nations in the postwar period have experimented with a number of trade strategies aimed at insulating their domestic economies from the vagaries of primary commodity price fluctuation. Among the tactics developed, two with negative trade diverting consequences have assumed notoriety: (1) import sub-

stitution, which became popular in Latin America, sought to downgrade investment in traditional export sectors in favor of domestic production intended to provide substitutes for imports; and (2) the primary commodity producer cartel, best exemplified by OPEC, able to prop up a particular primary commodity price when necessary by manipulating the dimensions of supply. See Werner Baer, "The Economics of Prebisch and ECLA," pp. 211-214, and Albert O. Hirschman, "The Political Economy of Import-Substituting Industrialization in Latin America," pp. 237-266, in *Latin America: Problems in Economic Development*, ed. Charles T. Nisbet (New York: Free Press, 1969); and Danielsen, *Evolution of OPEC*, pp. 21-67.

19. IMF, *IFS, Supplement on Trade Statistics*, pp. 4-5. The merchandise trade surplus of developing sector oil producers rose from the 1959-67 business cycle, when it averaged $3.4 billion a year, to $27.0 billion a year in the 1968-75 cycle and $92.7 billion in the 1976-82 cycle. Developing sector oil importers experienced the opposite trend. From a merchandise trade deficit of $7.1 billion in the 1959-67 business cycle, this sector's deficit rose to $23.0 billion a year in the 1968-75 cycle and $66.3 billion in the 1976-82 cycle.

20. IMF, *IFS, Supplement on Trade Statistics*, p. 197. From 1982 to 1986, the developing sector's terms of trade plummeted by 25.5 percent. IMF, *International Financial Statistics Yearbook, 1989*, p. 165. The sector's GNP growth rate also plunged, from an average 5.3 percent a year in the 1976-82 cycle to 2.6 percent from 1983-86.

21. IMF, *World Economic Outlook, October 1988*, p. 108. From a postwar peak in 1981 of $125.7 billion, net borrowing by the developing sector fell to a nadir of $21.4 billion in 1988.

22. United Nations, *World Economic Survey, 1955* (New York: United Nations, 1956), p. 52. The U.S. ratio of imports of goods to national income not only declined from 4.3 percent in 1937 to 3.2 percent in 1948, it was far lower than those of West Germany (11.2 percent in 1948), Japan (14.0 percent in 1954), and the U.K. (17.5 percent in 1948). UNCTAD, *Handbook*, pp. 168, 171, 182. In 1970 the share of primary commodities in U.S. imports was just 32.8 percent compared to 50.9 percent for West Germany and 77.2 percent for Japan. For information on the Japanese and German loss of special trade arrangements, see Tatsuro Uchino, *Japan's Post-War Economy: An Insider's View of Its History and Its Future* (Tokyo: Kodansha International, 1983), pp. 17-18, and John Lewis Gaddis, *The United States and the Origins of the Cold War, 1941-47* (New York: Columbia University Press, 1972), pp. 95-173.

23. Klaus Hinrich Hennings, "West Germany," in *The European Economy*, ed. Boltho, pp. 483-485; Chalmers Johnson, *MITI and the Japanese Miracle: The Growth of Industrial Policy, 1925-75* (Stanford: Stanford University Press, 1982), pp. 198-241.

24. W. M. Scammell, *The International Economy Since 1945*, 2d ed. (London: Macmillan, 1983), p. 75.

25. UNCTAD, *Handbook*, pp. 143, 146, 158. In 1970 the percentage of primary commodities in West German exports was 18.3, in Japanese exports 21.4, and in

U.S. exports 32.8. The disparity between West German/Japanese and U.S. percentages of primary commodities in total exports was even more extreme after World War II, when the former required higher levels of primary commodities in imports to compensate for domestic shortfalls and the latter enjoyed higher levels of primary commodity exports because of enhanced exports to Eurasian markets.

26. U.N., *World Economic Survey, 1961* (New York: United Nations, 1962), pp. 64, 67. From 1950 to 1960, the average annual growth rate for manufacturing output was 18.1 percent in Japan and 10.1 percent in West Germany, compared to 3.6 percent in the United States and 3.5 percent in the U.K., and from 1950 to 1960, Japan's share of world manufacturing exports rose from 3.2 to 6.1 percent and West Germany's from 6.1 to 16.9 percent, whereas the U.S.'s fell from 21.7 to 18.7 percent and the U.K.'s from 21.9 to 14.0 percent.

27. Roy Hofheinz, Jr. and Kent E. Calder, *The Eastasia Edge* (New York: Basic Books, 1982), p. 111. In 1978 Japan's relative advantages in labor costs were in full view as it lost only 36 days per 1,000 workers due to strikes, whereas West Germany lost 203, the United States 428, and Italy 720. OECD, *Economic Outlook: Historical Statistics, 1960–87* (Paris: OECD, 1989), p. 63, 70. By 1982 the percentage of Japan's GNP accounted for by social security transfers was just 11.0 percent, compared to 17.6 percent in West Germany and 21.2 percent in the U.K. In 1982 Japan's savings rate was 16.5 percent, while in the United States it was just 8.9 percent.

28. John Bispham and Andrea Boltho, "Demand Management," in *The European Economy*, ed. Boltho, pp. 293–294.

29. Uchino, *Japan's Post-War Economy*, pp. 208–212.

30. Hennings, "West Germany," pp. 393–396.

31. IMF, *International Financial Statistics Yearbook, 1986*, pp. 346–47. Although West Germany's merchandise trade surplus rose from the 1968–75 to the 1976–82 business cycle, its export growth declined from 154.4 to 93.1 percent. The improvement in the trade balance was thus made possible by a huge drop in Bonn's import growth, which fell from 162.5 percent from 1968–75 to 104.3 percent from 1976–82.

32. C. Fred Bergsten, *The Dilemmas of the Dollar: The Economics and Politics of United States International Monetary Policy* (New York: New York University Press, 1975), pp. 91–95.

33. OECD, *World Economic Outlook, April 1988*, p. 189. U.S. net external assets collapsed from a surplus of $129.9 billion in 1981 to a deficit of $274.7 billion in 1986, while Japan's surplus rose from $9.9 billion to $179.3 billion, West Germany's from $20.1 billion to $106.3 billion, and the U.K.'s from $47.6 billion to $162.3 billion.

34. *Economic Report of the President, 1989*, pp. 310–311, 338. From 1939 to 1944, the U.S. economy grew by 92.7 percent in real terms, while from 1929 to 1939 it only grew by 1.0 percent. In 1939 the U.S. personal savings rate stood at 2.6 percent. By 1945 it had risen to 25.1 percent.

35. *Economic Report of the President, 1989*, p. 424, 397. The lowest U.S. merchandise trade surplus over this period was $1.1 billion in 1950, the highest, $10.1

billion in 1947. After FY46, the largest U.S. government fiscal deficit in this period was $6.5 billion during the Korean War in FY53, and over these 12 years the United States registered six fiscal surpluses.

36. Ippolito, *Congressional Spending*, pp. 40–42, 45–47 (on the budget surpluses that followed the Civil War and World War I), and pp. 43–45 (on the 1890s and 1930s budget deficits).

37. Ippolito, *Congressional Spending*, pp. 211–218.

38. Executive Office of the President, Office of Management and Budget, *Historical Tables—Budget of the United States Government, Fiscal Year 1990* (Washington, DC: U.S. Government Printing Office, 1989), pp. 15, 17. U.S. government receipts rose from 14.8 percent of GNP in FY50 to 19.3 percent of GNP in 1952.

39. U.N., *World Economic Survey, 1956* (New York: United Nations, 1957), pp. 17–22.

40. U.N., *World Economic Survey, 1957* (New York: United Nations, 1958), p. 155. From 4.48 percent in 1953, U.S. imports to output rose to 4.75 percent in 1957.

41. Fred L. Block, *The Origins of Interntional Economic Disorder* (Berkeley: University of California Press, 1977), pp. 121–122. Data source: U.N., *World Economic Report, 1951/52* (New York: United Nations, 1952). From 1950 to 1951, West German machinery exports grew by 100 percent while those of the United States rose by only 15.6 percent and the U.K. by 13.6 percent.

42. Scammell, *International Economy Since 1945*, pp. 21–25.

43. Block, *Origins of International Economic Disorder*, pp. 88–99.

44. Scammell, *International Economy Since 1945*, pp. 21–30.

45. U.N., *World Economic Survey, 1957*, pp. 148–149, 153–154.

46. *Historical Tables, FY90*, pp. 15, 125. In FY59, U.S. government receipts fell from $79.6 billion in FY58 to $79.2 billion, while in real terms discretionary domestic spending rose by a staggering 32.6 percent.

47. *Historical Tables, FY90*, p. 125. In FY60 real discretionary domestic spending took a sizable cut, falling by 14.2 percent.

48. *Economic Report of the President*, p. 424; U.N., *World Economic Survey, 1960* (New York: United Nations, 1961), p. 145. U.S. exports rose by a healthy 19.4 percent in 1960. Western Europe's imports rose by a strong 14.0 percent in 1960.

49. David P. Calleo, *The Imperious Economy* (Cambridge: Harvard University Press, 1982), pp. 145–147.

50. Ibid., pp. 20–21.

51. Ibid., pp. 12, 184.

52. Block, *Origins of International Economic Disorder*, pp. 174–77.

53. Martin Wolf, "Managed Trade in Practice: Implications of the Textile Agreements," in *Trade Policy in the 1980s*, ed. William R. Cline (Washington, DC: Institute for International Economics, 1983), pp. 457–459.

54. William R. Cline, "Introduction and Summary," in *Trade Policy in the 1980s*, ed. Cline, pp. 6–10.

55. Data source: OECD, *National Account Statistics, 1986* (Paris: OECD, 1987). The U.K.'s domestic demand growth rate rose from 1.2 percent in 1962 to a peak of 6.6 percent in 1964, Italy's peaked at 7.1 percent in 1963, and France's at 7.3 percent in 1964.

56. IMF, *International Financial Statistics, 1986*, pp. 110, 172. World consumer price inflaton advanced by an average 2.8 percent from 1959–62, by 3.9 percent in 1963, and by 4.6 percent a year from 1963–66. Nonfuel primary commodity prices declined by 1.9 percent from 1958 to 1962, rose by 1.6 percent in 1963, and by 14.1 percent from 1962–66.

57. IMF, *International Financial Statistics, Trade Supplement*, p. 2. From 1959 to 1962, developing sector merchandise imports grew by an average 3.0 percent a year and in 1963–64 by 7.9 percent a year.

58. U.N., *World Economic Survey, 1963* (New York: United Nations, 1964), p. 24.

59. U.N., *World Economic Survey, 1965* (New York: United Nations, 1966), pp. 179–183.

60. Richard T. Froyen, *Macroeconomics: Theories and Policies*, 2nd ed. (New York: Macmillan, 1986), p. 645.

61. See Table 4.4a in Chapter 4.

62. *Historical Tables, FY90*, p. 126. U.S. real defense spending rose by 40.5 percent from FY65 to FY68.

63. IMF, *International Financial Statistics, Supplement on Trade Statistics*, p. 200. From 1968–70, nonfuel primary commodity prices rose by 9.4 percent, food prices by 7.3 percent, and from 1968–71 oil prices (Saudi-Ras Tanura) advanced by 21.8 percent.

64. Ryutaro Komiya, "The U.S.-Japan Trade Conflict: An Economist's View From Japan," in *Japan's Economy: Coping With Change in the International Environment*, ed. Daniel I. Okimoto (Boulder, CO: Westview, 1982), p. 201.

65. C. Fred Bergsten, *Dilemmas of the Dollar*, pp. 330–331; I. M. Destler, *American Trade Politics: System Under Stress* (Washington, DC: Institute for International Economics, 1986), pp. 27–28.

66. U.N., *World Economic Survey*, 1968 (New York: United Nations, 1969), p. 109.

67. *Economic Report of the President, 1989*, p. 390. From 1967 to 1969, the federal funds rate rose from 4.2 to 8.2 percent and the rate for three-month Treasuries jumped from 4.3 to 6.7 percent.

68. *Historical Tables, FY90*, p. 15.

69. *Historical Tables, FY90*, p. 16. The U.S. government fiscal balance fell from a surplus of $3.2 billion in FY69 to a deficit of $23.0 billion in FY71. In addition to weakness in revenues provoked by the 1969–70 recession, the deterioration in the U.S. government budget was the result of a leap in "payments to individuals" outlays, which jumped 28.7 percent in real terms from FY69–FY71.

70. *Economic Report of the President, 1989*, p. 390. The U.S. federal funds rate dropped from 8.2 percent in 1969 to 4.7 percent in 1971; over the same period the rate for three-month Treasuries fell from 6.7 to 4.3 percent.

71. Wilfred Ethier, *Modern International Economics* (New York: W. W. Norton, 1983), pp. 459–461.

72. Ethier, *Modern International Economics*, pp. 459–461, 460–461.

73. Riccardo Parboni, *The Dollar and Its Rivals: Recession, Inflation, and International Finance* (London: Verso, 1981), pp. 83–84.

74. Uchino, *Japan's Post-War Economy*, pp. 189–196.

75. IMF, *International Financial Statistics, Supplement on Trade*, p. 200. From 1971 to 1974 nonfuel primary commodity prices rose by 111.0 percent, food prices by 140.9 percent, and oil prices (Saudi-Ras Tanura) by 420.9 percent.

76. See Table 4.4c in Chapter 4 for data on these developments.

77. Data source: U.S. Department of Commerce, Bureau of Economic Analysis, *The National Income and Product Accounts of the United States, 1929–82—Statistical Tables* (Washington, DC: U.S. Government Printing Office, September 1986). The rise in U.S. agricultural exports in 1973 above the rate experienced for the previous two years was equivalent to 98.6 percent of the improvement in the U.S. merchandise trade balance in 1973.

78. Data source: U.S. Department of Commerce, Bureau of Economic Analysis, *Survey of Current Business* (June 1986). The advance in the U.S. direct investment income balance in 1973 was equivalent to 40.2 percent of the improvement in the U.S. current account balance in 1973.

79. See Table 4.4d in Chapter 4.

80. IMF, *International Financial Statistics, Yearbook 1986*, pp. 152–153, 346–347, 420–421. From the 1968–75 to the 1976–82 business cycle, West Germany's annual merchandise trade surplus rose from $10.6 billion to $18.2 billion, while Japan's climbed from $4.6 billion to $13.3 billion. Over the same period West Germany's average annual GNP growth rate fell from 3.6 to 2.3 percent, and Japan's from 7.0 to 4.5 percent.

81. See Table 4.4a in Chapter 4.

82. IMF, *International Financial Statistics, Trade Supplement*, p. 201. In 1976–77, nonfuel primary commodity prices rose by 20.0 percent while oil prices (Saudi-Ras Tanura) jumped by 14.7 percent.

83. See Table 4.4a in Chapter 4.

84. Komiya, "The U.S.-Japan Trade Conflict," p. 201.

85. U.N., *World Economic Survey, 1976* (New York: United Nations, 1978), pp. 21, 22, 25; U.N., *World Economic Survey, 1977* (New York: United Nations, 1978), pp. II21–II24.

86. See Table 4.4b in Chapter 4 for data on these developments.

87. Data source: IMF, *International Financial Statistics Yearbook, 1986*. In 1977–78, the U.S.'s effective exchange rate dropped by 9.0 percent.

88. Scammell, *International Economy Since 1945*, pp. 211–212.

89. See Table 4.4c in Chapter 4.

90. IMF, *International Financial Statistics, Trade Supplement*, p. 201. From 1978 to 1980 nonfuel primary commodity prices rose by 28.1 percent and food prices by 26.7 percent, and from 1978 to 1981 oil prices (Saudi-Ras Tanura) advanced by 156.7 percent.

91. IMF, *International Financial Statistics Yearbook, 1986*, p. 111. From 1978 to 1980, world consumer price inflation increased from 9.6 to 15.7 percent.

92. See Table 4.4c in Chapter 4 for data on these developments.

93. Data source: *The Natonal Income and Product Accounts of the United States, 1929–82*. The rise in U.S. agricultural exports in 1979 above their pace for the previous two years was equivalent to 26.5 percent of the improvement in the U.S. merchandise trade balance in 1979. Data source: *Survey of Current Business* (June 1986). The increase in the net U.S. direct investment income balance in 1979 was the equivalent of 74.3 percent of the improvement in the U.S. current account balance.

94. See Table 4.4d in Chapter 4.

95. See Amos A. Jordan and William J. Taylor, Jr., *American National Security: Policy and Process*, revised ed. (Baltimore: Johns Hopkins University Press, 1984), pp. 60–66, for economic constraints on U.S. defense spending in the 1950s. *Historical Tables, FY90*, p. 126. U.S. national defense spending contracted by 4.3 percent in real terms in FY69.

96. *Historical Tables, FY90*, pp. 126, 128. From FY69 to FY79, "payments to individuals" outlays rose by 114.5 percent in real terms, whereas national defense outlays declined by 34.6 percent in real terms.

97. Jordan and Taylor, *American National Security*, pp. 62–63. See Takafusa Nakamura, *The Postwar Japanese Economy—Its Development and Structure*, trans. Jacqueline Kaminski (Tokyo: University of Tokyo Press, 1983), pp. 35–40, for a description of the "reverse course" policy.

98. John Lewis Gaddis, *Strategies of Containment: A Critical Appraisal of Postwar American Security Policy* (Oxford: Oxford University Press, 1982), p. 82.

99. Jordan and Taylor, *American National Security*, p. 68.

100. Data source: Office of the Assistant Secretary of Defense (Comptroller), *The National Defense Budget Estimates for FY87* (Washington, DC: U.S. Government Printing Office, May 1986). The average annual TOA (total obligational authority) for strategic forces rose from 10.7 to 43.2 FY86 billion dollars from the postwar demobilization regime (FY47–50) to the Korean War period (FY51–54). Data source: *Historical Tables, FY90*. Funding for Atomic Energy Defense rose from 0.4 FY82 billion dollars in FY50, the last year of the postwar demobilization regime, to 0.8 FY82 billion dollars in FY54, the last year of the Korean War period. See Thomas B. Cochran, William M. Arkin, and Milton M. Hoening, *Nuclear Weapons Databook—Volume I: U.S. Nuclear Forces and Capabilities* (Cambridge, MA: Ballinger, 1984), pp. 6–11. When SAC was established in 1946, it could call on 148 B-29s. By 1948, SAC had 500 aircraft, including the improved B-50 and the first true transoceanic-range bomber, the B-36. With its production greatly accelerated by the

onset of the Korean War, the B-47 medium-range bomber was operational by 1951. Having a relatively modest combat radius, the B-47s required forward bases in Eurasia and a large support fleet of aerial tankers. The Korean War also stimulated the development of the all-jet B-52, which was deployed in operational units in 1955, by which time the fleet of B-47s had reached 1,500 aircraft.

101. U.S. forces in Europe took on three roles: to provide local protection for the forward deployed air base infrastructure of SAC, to provide a direct defense capability that became increasingly nuclearized, and to act as "hostages" to increase the credibility of the U.S. extended deterrent.

102. John Spanier, *American Foreign Policy Since World War II* (New York: Praeger, 1962), pp. 144-145; Jordan and Taylor, *American National Security*, pp. 67-68.

103. In 1946 the U.S. nuclear stockpile consisted of nine unassembled variants of the Nagasaki "fat man" fission weapon, growing to 13 in 1947 and fifty in 1948. The late 1940s stagnation in weapons design, largely a product of budgetary austerity, ended with the rapid expansion of nuclear weapons design and production facilities during the Korean War. See Thomas B. Cochran, William M. Arkin, Robert S. Norris, et al., *Nuclear Weapons Data Book—Volume II: U.S. Nuclear Warhead Production* (Cambridge, MA: Ballinger, 1987), pp. 2-15. See also Chuck Hansen, *U.S. Nuclear Weapons—The Secret History* (New York: Orion, 1988), pp. 31-41, for a description of this expansion. Of profound strategic consequence to the Soviets was President Truman's November 1950 decision, taken at the height of the Chinese intervention into Korea, to press ahead with development of a thermonuclear weapon.

104. With SAC's deployment of the B-52 bomber during the late 1950s, the importance of the forward bases in Eurasia faded as anything but bases for tanker aircraft, as it was acknowledged that forward deployed nuclear armed aircraft were becoming increasingly vulnerable to counterforce attacks. See Edward S. Quade, ed., *Analysis for Military Decisions* (Chicago: Rand McNally, 1966), pp. 24-63, for a description of the seminal RAND Corporation analyses that led to this shift. See Thomas W. Wolfe, *Soviet Power and Europe, 1945-1970* (Baltimore: Johns Hopkins University Press, 1970), pp. 160-194, for a history of the evolution of Soviet forces in Europe during the 1950s.

105. Data source: *Historical Tables—Budget of the United States Government, Fiscal Year 1988* (Washington, DC: U.S. government Printing Office, 1987). From FY58 to FY62, real national defense research and development outlays soared by 152.9 percent.

106. Russel F. Weigley, *The American Way of War: A History of United States Military Strategy and Policy* (Bloomington: Indiana University Press, 1977), pp. 442-444. Initially, the Kennedy administration became enamored with various concepts of nuclear counterforce operations to deal with the expanding Soviet transoceanic nuclear capability. Interest was encouraged by the recognition that the Soviet long-range missile build-up lagged far behind the alarmist intelligence forecasts of the late 1950s. Administration drift toward a workable "damage limiting" nuclear warfighting capability reached a peak with Defense Secretary Robert McNamara's spring 1962 speech in Ann Arbor, Michigan, outlining the concept of strategic nu-

clear warfare in which cities might be spared early attack. This "no cities" doctrine was roundly denounced by Khrushchev, who feared that the Kennedy administration was preparing to exploit the U.S. nuclear build-up, which had commenced in the late 1950s in response to Khrushchev's earlier efforts to build a mobilization base for Soviet strategic forces.

107. Data source: *The National Defense Budget Estimates for FY87*. From FY63 to FY66, Defense Department TOA for general purpose forces rose from 34.4 to 42.1 percent to total DOD TOA.

108. Weigley, *American Way of War*, pp. 444–445; Alain C. Enthoven and K. Wayne Smith, *How Much Is Enough? Shaping the Defense Program, 1961–1969* (New York: Harper and Row, 1971), pp. 172–196. By the mid-1960s McNamara came to consider the effort to deploy a credible "damage limiting," i.e., efficient counterforce and aerospace defense, capability very costly and ultimately unworkable. The prospect that the Soviets would deploy MIRVed and ground mobile ICBMs convinced him that the army could not provide a cost-effective defense and that the USAF would be unable to locate and destroy large numbers of the land mobile forces. Ironically, the Soviet program to deploy a land mobile ICBM faltered with the technically flawed SS-14 and SS-15 programs. The Soviets would not successfully deploy a land mobile ICBM until the mid-1980s, with the SS-24 and SS-25.

109. Gaddis, *Strategies of Containment*, pp. 198–236.

110. Data source: U.N., *World Economic Survey, 1959* (New York: United Nations, 1960), for 1952–59; IMF, *International Financial Statistics Yearbook, 1986*, for 1960–67. U.S. net private capital outflows, which averaged $1.7 billion a year from 1952–59, rose to average $5.4 billion a year from 1960–67.

111. *Historical Tables, FY90*, pp. 132–136.

112. Ibid., pp. 136–138.

113. IMF, *International Financial Statistics Yearbook, 1986*, pp. 686–687.

114. *Historical Tables, FY90*, pp. 136–138.

115. Ippolito, *Congressional Spending*, p. 21. In 1975, uncontrollable U.S. government outlays had risen to 73.0 percent of total outlays. By 1981 they had jumped further to account for 76.0 percent.

116. *Historical Tables, FY90*, pp. 124–128.

117. Ibid., pp. 55–56, 128–129.

118. John Newhouse, *War and Peace in the Nuclear Age* (New York: Knopf, 1989), p. 206.

119. See David N. Schwartz, *NATO's Nuclear Dilemma* (Washington, DC: The Brookings Institution, 1983). Fearing that his country's geostrategic interests might be compromised during the SALT II negotiations, West German Chancellor Helmut Schmidt raised the issue of the Soviets' new SS-20 IRBM in the fall of 1977. He argued that NATO had to respond to the SS-20 buildup at the very time transoceanic, i.e., strategic nuclear weapons were being constrained by the United States and USSR. This prompted the Carter administration, after some expressions of reluctance, to consider various counterdeployment options, leading to the decision to deploy the ground mobile Pershing II ballistic and the Gryphon ground-launched cruise missiles. See also Newhouse, *War and Peace in the Nuclear Age*, p. 309.

120. Newhouse, *War and Peace in the Nuclear Age*, p. 285–291, for an account of President Carter's interest in the technical and operational problems with strategic nuclear C^3I and the evolution toward a more "flexible" nuclear employment posture, embodied in PD-59.

Chapter 5

1. *Economic Report of the President, 1989* (Washington, DC: U.S. Government Printing Office, 1989). In 1968 personal consumption represented 59.4 percent of GNP. By 1980 this percentage had undergone a secular increase, rising to 62.8 percent of GNP. Never falling below its 1968 level in the intervening years, it reached a peak of 63.8 percent in 1976. Net nonresidential fixed investment represented 4.1 percent of GNP in 1968. It suffered a secular decline, falling to 3.2 percent of GNP in 1980. After rising too 4.4 percent of GNP in 1969, it dropped to a low of 2.2 percent in 1976.

2. Executive Office of the President, *Economic Report of the President, 1985* (Washington, DC: U.S. Government Printing Office, 1985), pp. 26, 27; U.S. Congress, Congressional Budget Office, "The Economic Outlook," A Report to the Senate and House Committees on the Budget, Part I (February 1984), p. 45. From FY82–84, the tax rate for individuals was cut by 23.0 percent, while depreciation allowances for business were liberalized and investment tax credits were enacted. Executive Office of the President, Office of Management and Budget, *Historical Tables—Budget of the United States Government, Fiscal Year 1990* (Washington, DC: U.S. Government Printing Office, 1989), p. 25. In part as a result of the supply-side tax program, U.S. government receipts from individual income taxes rose by only $3.0 billion in FY83, while corporate tax receipts plummeted by $24.1 billion.

3. *Economic Report of the President, 1989*, p. 338. The U.S. personal savings rate in FY47 was 3.1 percent and in FY87, 3.2 percent.

4. *Economic Report of the President, 1989*, p. 310. In 1983 personal consumption rebounded, accounting for 84.1 percent of GNP growth, while nonresidential fixed investment continued to fall, representing a negative 4.6 percent of GNP growth.

5. Organization for Economic Cooperation and Development, *OECD Economic Outlook, June 1988* (Paris: OECD, 1988), p. 177. From 1982 when U.S. domestic demand contracted by 1.9 percent, it boomed to average an annual 6.9 percent in 1983–84. The recovery in the domestic demand growth rate of the rest of the developed sector was far weaker. For the OECD outside of the U.S., the domestic demand growth rate rose from 0.8 percent in 1982 to only an average 2.2 percent in 1983–84.

6. Stephen Marris, *Deficits and the Dollar: The World Economy At Risk* (Washington, DC: Institute for International Economics, 1985), pp. 19–22.

7. U.S. Department of Commerce, Bureau of Economic Analysis, "U.S. Net International Investment Position, 1988" (29 June 1989). From a surplus of $140.9 billion in 1981, the U.S. net investment balance with the rest of the world tumbled to a deficit of $378.3 billion in 1987. In 1988 the deficit grew to $532.5 billion.

8. Data source: Executive Office of the President, *Economic Report of the Pres-*

ident, 1988 (Washington, DC: U.S. Government Printing Office, 1988); *Historical Tables, FY89*. The U.S. net investment income surplus with the rest of the world grew as a percentage of GNP from a 1959–67 average of 0.7 percent to a 1968–75 average of 1.4 percent. But from 1976–82, the average fell to 1.0 percent and from 1983–87, to 0.6 percent. The U.S. government's net interest outlay deficit has grown as a percentage of GNP over the business cycles. From 1.2 percent in the 1959–67 cycle, it grew to 1.4 percent in the 1968–75 cycle, 2.2 percent in the 1976–82 cycle, and 3.0 percent from 1983–87.

9. International Monetary Fund, *International Financial Statistics Yearbook, 1986* (Washington, DC: IMF, 1986), p. 684.

10. United Nations, U.N. Conference on Trade and Development (UNCTAD), *Handbook of International Trade and Development Statistics, 1986 Supplement* (New York: United Nations, 1986), p. 3.

11. *Economic Report of the President, 1989*, pp. 308, 424.

12. U.N., *IFS Yearbook, 1986*, pp. 347, 421, 685. From a surplus of $6.3 billion in 1981, West Germany's capital other than reserves balance turned to a deficit of $0.3 billion in 1982, $5.9 billion in 1983, and $11.0 billion in 1984. Japan's capital other than reserves balance turned from a deficit of $1.6 billion in 1981 to a deficit of $16.2 billion in 1982, $21.3 billion in 1983, and $36.6 billion in 1984. The U.K.'s balance turned from a surplus of $1.7 billion in 1982 to a deficit of $7.5 billion in 1983 and $18.3 billion in 1984.

13. United Nations, *World Economic Survey, 1985* (New York: United Nations, 1985), p. 57. In 1983 off-shore banking and the developing sector combined suffered a net $18 billion capital outflow to the U.S. In 1984 this figure rose to $40.0 billion. *Economic Report of the President, 1989*, p. 429. In 1984 the U.S. net investment surplus sank to $8.5 billion.

14. IMF, *IFS Supplement on Trade Statistics*, Supplement Series, No. 15 (Washington, DC: IMF, 1988), p. 201. From 1982–84, nonfuel primary commodity prices rose by just 8.4 percent, compared to 20.0 percent from 1975–77. From 1982–84, oil prices (Saudi-Ras Tanura) declined by 14.9 percent, while from 1975–77 they rose by 14.6 percent.

15. *Economic Report of the President, 1989*, p. 391. From February to August 1984, the federal funds rate rose from 9.59 to 11.64 percent, while three-month Treasury rates increased from 9.03 percent in February to 10.49 percent in August 1984.

16. Executive Office of the President, *Economic Report of the President, 1986* (Washington, DC: U.S. Government Printing Office, 1986), pp. 63–65.

17. *OECD Economic Outlook, May 1986*, pp. XVIII, 70–75.

18. C. Fred Bergsten and William R. Cline, "Trade Policy in the 1980s: An Overview," in *Trade Policy in the 1980s*, ed. William R. Cline (Washington, DC: Institute for International Economics, 1983), pp. 66–72.

19. Japan Economic Institute of America, *Yearbook of U.S.-Japan Economic Relations in 1982* (Washington, DC: Japan Economic Institute of America, 1983), pp. 45–46.

20. Joan Seaburg, "Hill Skeptics Doubt Japan's Sincerity," *Washington Post* (31 July 1985); Robert Manning, "Retreat From Reason," *Far Eastern Economic Review*, vol. 125, no. 33 (16 August 1984), pp. 55–57.

21. Rudiger Dornbusch, "The Road to Economic Recovery," background paper, *Report of the Twentieth Century Fund Task Force on International Debt* (New York: Priority Press, 1989), pp. 37–47.

22. UNCTAD, *Handbook of International Trade and Development Statistics in 1986*, pp. 5, 7. From 1981 to 1984, Latin America's imports fell by 35.6 percent and Africa's by 22.4 percent.

23. IMF, *IFS Supplement on Trade, 1988*, p. 201; In 1985 nonfuel primary commodity prices contracted by 13.0 percent, whereas oil prices (Saudi-Ras Tanura) fell by 2.5 percent.

24. Dornbusch, "Road to Economic Recovery," pp. 69–70 (for an examination of the Baker Plan); Norman A Bailey and Richard Cohen, *The Mexican Time Bomb* (New York: Priority Press, 1987), pp. 35–38 (for events leading up to the Mexican balance of payments difficulties in 1985).

25. OECD, *Historical Statistics, 1960–87* (Paris: OECD, 1989), pp. 98–99.

26. *OECD Economic Outlook, June 1988*, p. 88. The statistics reveal a substantial leap in Japan's public works expenditures in FY87–88.

27. IMF, *IFS Yearbook, 1989*, p. 117 (for nonfuel primary commodity prices); *OECD Economic Outlook, June 1989*, p. 156 (for oil prices—spot market). From 1986–88, nonfuel primary commodity prices rose by 34.0 percent, but oil prices fell marginally, by 2.6 percent.

28. Richard Cohen, *World Trade and Payments Cycles: The Advance and Retreat of the Postwar Order* (New York: Praeger, 1989), pp. 247–248.

29. IMF, *IFS Trade Supplement, 1988*, p. 201 (for nonfuel prices); OECD Economic Outlook, June 1988, p. 156 (for oil prices—spot market). In 1986 nonfuel primary commodity prices fell by 3.8 percent, while spot market oil prices for refined product plunged by 40.7 percent.

30. *Economic Report of the President, 1989*, p. 424. The U.S. merchandise trade balance deteriorated by $8.5 billion in 1985; it worsened by $22.4 billion in 1986.

31. IMF, *International Financial Statistics, April 1988* (Washington, DC: IMF, 1988), pp. 228, 298. Whereas West Germany's merchandise trade surplus increased by $6.2 billion in 1985, it surged ahead by $27.2 billion in 1986, and while Japan's merchandise trade surplus rose by $11.7 billion in 1985, it jumped by $36.8 billion in 1986.

32. IMF, *International Financial Statistics, April 1988*, pp. 520–521. From the first quarter of 1985 to the fourth quarter of 1987, the dollar's effective exchange rate depreciated by 35.3 percent.

33. *Economic Report of the President, 1989*, p. 425. While private foreign investment in the U.S. continued to rise in 1986, foreign official investment surged ahead. After falling by $1.2 billion in 1985, foreign official investment in the U.S. exploded in 1986, recording a surplus of $35.5 billion. In 1987 the latter surplus registered $45.0 billion, but private investment in the U.S. fell by $19.2 billion.

34. Hobart Rowen, "Paris Talks Restored Cooperation," *Washington Post* (25 February 1987); *OECD Economic Outlook, December 1987*, p. 73.

35. *Economic Report of the President, 1989*, p. 391. From February to October 1987, the federal funds rate jumped from 6.10 to 7.29 percent while the three-month Treasury rate advanced from 5.45 percent in January to 6.40 percent in October 1987.

36. IMF, *World Economic Outlook, April 1988* (Washington, DC: IMF, 1988), pp. 41–52.

37. *Economic Report of the President, 1988*, pp. 39–44.

38. Data source: IMF, *IFS Yearbook, 1986* (for 1962–64, 1971–73, and 1977–78); *OECD Economic Outlook, June 1989* (for 1986–88). For Japan the central government fiscal deficit to GNP ratio rose from 1962 when it was 0.3 percent to 0.8 percent in 1963 and 1.1 percent in 1964. Similarly, the percentage rose from 1971 when it was 0.2 percent to 1.6 percent in 1972 and 1973. From 1977 the rate rose from 6.1 to 6.6 percent in 1978. But in Phase Three of the current business cycle, the percentage has fallen from 3.0 percent in 1986 to 2.0 percent in 1987 and 1.7 percent in 1988. Whereas the percentage of central government deficit to GNP rose for the second-tier West European economies in Phase Three of the 1959–67, 1968–75, and 1976–82 business cycles, in the current cycle it has dropped. In 1986 the U.K. central government deficit to GNP ratio was 2.1 percent. In 1987 it fell to 1.3 percent and in 1988 it turned in a 1.0 percent surplus. France's was 2.3 percent in 1986 and 1987, before it fell to 1.4 percent in 1988. Italy's was 12.8 percent in 1986, dropping to 11.6 percent in 1987 and 11.7 percent in 1988. The only leading developed sector economy to experience a worsening central government budget deficit to GNP ratio in the beginning of Phase Three of the current business cycle was West Germany, as its ratio rose from 1.2 percent in 1986 to 1.4 percent in 1987 and 1.7 percent in 1988.

39. *OECD Economic Outlook, June 1989*, p. 179. From 1971 when the non-U.S. OECD domestic demand growth rate was 3.9 percent, it soared to 5.3 percent in 1972 and 7.2 percent in 1973. From 1977 when the non-U.S. OECD domestic demand growth rate was 2.2 percent, it jumped to 3.2 percent in 1978 and 4.7 percent in 1979. From 1986 when the non-U.S. OECD domestic demand growth rate was 3.1 percent, it rose to 4.2 percent in 1987 and 5.3 percent in 1988, a leap smaller than that from 1977–79 or 1971–73. Data source: U.S. Department of Commerce, Bureau of Economic Analysis, *National Income and Product Accounts of the United States, 1929–82—Statistical Tables* (Washington, DC: U.S. Government Printing Office, 1986); U.S. Department of Commerce, Bureau of Economic Analysis, "U.S. International Transactions" (15 June 1988 and 12 September 1988); *Economic Report of the President, 1989*. While from the fourth quarter of 1972 through the third quarter of 1973 the growth of U.S. agricultural exports above recent historical rates accounted for 140.0 percent of the improvement in the U.S. merchandise trade balance and while from the second quarter of 1978 through the fourth quarter of 1978 it accounted for 104.7 percent of the advance in the U.S. merchandise trade balance, from the first quarter of 1988 through the third quarter of 1988, it only accounted for 15.7 percent of the improvement in the U.S. merchandise trade balance.

40. Data source: U.S. Department of Commerce, *Survey of Current Business* (June 1981 and June 1986); Bureau of Economic Analysis, Department of Commerce, "U.S. International Transactions" (15 June 1988 and 12 September 1989); *Economic Report of the President, 1989*. In 1973 the advance in U.S. direct foreign investment income as a percent of current account balance improvement was 55.0 percent, in 1979 it was 88.2 percent, and in 1988, only 8.0 percent.

41. Data source: U.S. Department of Commerce, *Survey of Current Business* (June 1977) (for 1973); *Economic Report of the President, 1988* (for 1979); U.S. Department of Commerce, Bureau of Economic Analysis, "U.S. Net International Investment Position, 1988" (29 June 1989) (for 1987 and 1988). In 1973 the U.S. net investment surplus was $61.9 billion and in 1979, $94.5 billion. In 1987 it registered a deficit of $378.3 billion, and in 1988 the deficit reached $532.5 billion.

42. The author estimates that by the end of Phase Three of the current business cycle, the U.S. merchandise trade deficit will still be no lower than $90 billion, the current account deficit no lower than $100 billion, and the net investment deficit somewhere in the range of $600–700 billion.

43. *OECD Economic Outlook, June 1988*, p. 23. Especially in Phase One of the current business cycle, West German and Japanese fiscal policies turned decidedly contractionary. As a result, Japan's central government fiscal deficit as a percentage of GNP fell from 5.2 percent in 1982 to 4.9 percent in 1983 and 4.0 percent in 1984. West Germany's dropped from 2.1 percent in 1982 to 1.6 percent in 1983 and 1.3 percent in 1984.

44. Nigel Gault, "The Outlook for the U.S. Current Account Deficit," testimony before the Joint Economic Committee of the U.S. Congress (13 September 1988). Gault's baseline projection without adverse trends shows the U.S. merchandise trade and current account balances beginning to worsen in 1990. By 1995 the merchandise trade deficit will have grown to $184 billion and the current account deficit to $288 billion.

45. See Jacques S. Gansler, *Affording Defense* (Cambridge, MA: MIT Press, 1989), p. 171, for a discussion of structural disarmament. U.S. Army procurement expenditures increased by 147.4 percent from the 1977–80 period to the peak of the Reagan build-up (1982–85) for armored fighting vehicles, while the actual quantity only increased 30 percent. For tactical aircraft, while procurement increased by 75.4 percent during this time frame, the quantity of tactical aircraft only rose by 8.8 percent.

46. By the close of the Reagan administration, efforts to reach the navy's core planning requirement of 600 ships had faltered. Fiscal pressure on the navy's force structure became manifest with the early retirement of 16 early generation ASW frigates (most were transferred to foreign navies during 1989). During the first year of the Bush administration, these cuts in force structure were followed by the retirement of two battleships and a further 23 frigates and destroyers. See John F. Morton, "The U.S. Navy in 1988," *U.S. Naval Institute Proceedings* (May 1989), pp. 154–165, for a discussion of the fiscal pressure on the navy. This process of early decommissioning continued under the Bush administration with the retirement of an additional 32 guided missile destroyers. See also "U.S. Ships Due to Be Decommissioned," *International Defense Review*, vol. 22 (September 1989), p. 1271.

47. For an account of the evolution of anxiety about the "window of vulnerability," see John Prados, *The Soviet Estimate—U.S. Intelligence Analysis and Russian Military Strength* (New York: Dial, 1982), pp. 200–201. On U.S. concern about the U.S.-Soviet nuclear balance during the early Reagan years, see Alexander M. Haig, Jr., *Caveat—Realism, Reagan, and Foreign Policy* (New York: Macmillan, 1984), pp. 218–237.

48. Data source: Office of the Assistant Secretary of Defense (Comptroller), *National Defense Budget Estimate for FY87* (Washington, DC: Office of the Assistant Secretary of Defense (Comptroller), May 1986). During the period of accelerated disinvestment (FY69–76), strategic forces TOA as a percent of total DOD TOA averaged 9.0 percent. From FY81–86—during the period of accelerated investment—it averaged only 8.5 percent, slightly higher than during the Carter plateau period (FY77–80) when it averaged 7.8 percent.

49. See John M. Collins, *U.S.-Soviet Military Balance, 1980–85* (Washington, DC: Pergamon-Brassey's, 1985), pp. 61–63, for a descripton of the evolution of strategic employment doctrine from the Nixon to the Reagan administrations.

50. *Report of the President's Commission on Strategic Forces* (Washington, DC, Government Printing Office, April 1983). The Scowcroft Commission's report tended to discount the significance of the vulnerability of the Minuteman missile and formulated the concept of the land mobile single warhead ICBM, which became the Midgetman, or small ICBM, program. See John Newhouse, *War and Peace in the Nuclear Age* (New York: Knopf, 1989), pp. 358–359, for an account of the Scowcroft Commission's conclusion that the "window of vulnerability" was overstated and its recommendation for deployment of 100 MX missiles in Minuteman silos, contrary to Carter administration support of mobile and hardened basing for the MX. More recently the Reagan administration under secretary for Defense, Fred C. Ikle, stated that the issue of land-based missile vulnerability was overblown. See "The Ever-Present Danger—Fred C. Ikle on Changing Threats to Our Freedom," interview by Adam Meyerson, *Policy Review* (Summer 1989), no. 49, pp. 7–12.

51. See David Isenberg, "The Reagan Doctrine: Why a Good Offense Is Not the Best Defense," in *Collective Defense or Strategic Independence? Alternative Strategies for the Future,* ed. Ted Galen Carpenter (Lexington, MA: Lexington Books, 1989), pp. 176–178, for the origins of the doctrine.

52. See Lawrence T. Caldwell, "United States–Soviet Relations and Arms Control," *Current History,* vol. 86, no. 522 (October 1987), pp. 307–308, regarding Gorbachev's concessions leading up to the INF agreement.

53. Similarly, the Bush administration's commitment during 1989 to ambitious goals for U.S. space exploration implies immense future costs, although during the Reagan and early Bush periods real growth in space, science, and technology outlays averaged less than 1.0 percent a year. See "The Cost of Freedom," *The Economist* (7 October 1989), pp. 105–106, for discussion of budget pressures on NASA. See also William J. Durch, *The Future of the ABM Treaty,* Adelphi Papers 223 (London: International Institute for Strategic Studies, 1987), for a review of the debate over the status of the ABM Treaty during the Reagan administration.

54. Since the Kennedy administration there has been a thrust in U.S. defense

policy that has sought to reduce the requirement for the early U.S. resort to nuclear weapons during a NATO/Warsaw Pact war. See Bernard Brodie, *War and Politics* (New York: Macmillan, 1973), pp. 396-400. This thrust has led to an effort to raise the nuclear threshold by building a robust nonnuclear defense capability for NATO, an effort central to U.S. Army plans and programs. See also Carl H. Builder, *The Masks of War—American Military Styles in Strategy and Analysis* (Baltimore: Johns Hopkins University Press, 1989), pp. 138-142. The Air/Land Battle doctrine is built around the notion that NATO should be prepared to conduct a sustained nonnuclear campaign in Europe in the event of a Warsaw Pact invasion.

55. See David Hobbs, *NATO and the New Technologies* (Lanham, MD: University Press of America, 1989), pp. 45-46, for a discussion of the difficulties NATO has and will have in attempting to translate the FOFA concept into operational reality.

56. See F. J. West, Jr., "Maritime Strategy and NATO," *Naval War College Review* (November 1985), regarding the implications of the "Maritime Strategy." For a critique of the strategy, see John J. Mearsheimer, "A Strategic Misstep—the Maritime Strategy and Deterrence in Europe," *International Security*, vol. 11, no. 2 (Fall 1986), pp. 3-57.

57. *Historical Tables*, FY90, pp. 97, 109, 130. Defense investment declined from 45.3 to 43.3 percent of total defense outlays in 1988 while procurement fell from 28.6 to 26.6 percent of total defense outlays. In FY89 real national defense outlays are anticipated to fall by 1.1 percent, and in FY90 by 2.2 percent.

58. David E. Rosenbaum, "Sizing Up Cuts to the Military Budget," *New York Times* (1 January 1990).

59. Benjamin F. Schemmer, "Army Volunteers Five Division Cuts by 1994 to be Remolded as a 'Contingency Army,'" *Armed Forces Journal International* (January 1990), p. 14, and "Air Force, Navy Offer Fighter Wings, Carriers in Budget-Pruning Exercise," *Armed Forces Journal International* (January 1990), p. 15.

Chapter 6

1. Strobe Talbott, ed., *Khrushchev Remembers: The Last Testament* (Boston: Little Brown, 1974), pp. 19-53. Enthusiasm for the thesis that guided weapons would totally dominate the future high technology battlefield has surfaced a number of times since the late 1950s. Khrushchev was an early and forceful proponent of this view. He initiated policies to scrap the postwar Soviet Navy commitment to a large surface fleet and focused resources on new technologies such as long-range ballistic missiles and lighter missile-equipped armored vehicles in place of the main battle tank (MBT). A more recent example of great enthusiasm for guided weapon technology, in this case PGMs, can be found in Albert Wohlstetter, Fred Ikle, et al., *Discriminate Deterrence, Report by the Commission on Integrated Long-Term Strategy* (Washington, DC: U.S. Government Printing Office, January 1988). See Peter A. Wilson, "Battlefield Guided Weapons: The Big Equalizer," *U.S. Naval Institute Proceedings* (February 1975), pp. 18-25, for an early discussion of the potential "revolutionary" change that precision guided munitions might have on the future battlefield.

2. David Isby, *Weapons and Tactics of the Soviet Army*, fully revised ed. (London: Jane's Publishing Co., Inc., 1988), chap. 13. The Lebanon campaign demonstrated the importance of the military leverage won from the capacity to rapidly gain information dominance, in this case through battleworthy RSTA sensors and the exploitation of drone surveillance vehicles. Syria suffered a humiliating defeat with the destruction of its forward deployed mobile surface-to-air missile units and an aerial loss ratio of 83 to 1. The results of this high technology combined arms campaign deeply shocked the Soviet High Command and led to a major shake-up in the organization of the aerospace defense forces during the mid-1980s.

3. David Hobbs, *NATO and the New Technologies* (Lanham, MD: University Press of America, 1989), pp. 45–46.

4. Khrushchev was just one of many postwar politicians who sought technological panaceas for military insufficiencies. Like Eisenhower, he saw long-range nuclear armed missiles as a cheap means for providing a credible deterrence and coercive posture, but he went beyond Eisenhower's position to press for the wholesale replacement of units equipped with manned combat vehicles. Contemporary examples of the technological quick-fix orientation include the "competitive strategies" approach considered by the Reagan administration's Office of the Secretary of Defense, which promotes a "low cost" investment in new PGMs as a means of defeating the USSR's quantitative advantage in armored fighting vehicles. For the debate on competitive strategies, see Sam Cohen, "Can Smart Bombs Save the West? Don't Think They Can't Be Outwitted," and David M. Abshire, "Use Them Instead of a New Lance," *Wall Street Journal* (21 June 1989). For a critique of technological panacea solutions, see Steven L. Canby, "The Quest for Technological Superiority—A Misunderstanding of War?" in *The Changing Strategic Landscape, Part III*, Adelphi Papers 237 (London: International Institute for Strategic Studies, Spring 1989).

5. Rolf Hilmes, *Main Battle Tanks—Developments in Design Since 1945*, trans. Richard Simpkin (London: Brassey's Defence Publishers, 1987). In constant dollars, the M-1 battle tank costs approximately 2.5 times that of the preceding generation. See p. 72 for weight increase of MBT, p. 91 for cost increase of MBT, p. 92 for increase in complexity from second generation (Leopard I) to third generation (M-1 class) MBT.

6. During the late 1950s, the enthusiasm for the surface-to-air missile rose as the U.K. came to believe that the air defense missile would impose such severe attrition rates on combat aircraft as to make it unnecessary to develop a new generation of them. Similar views were held by many U.S. and Soviet experts. The presence of surface-to-air missiles had an immense impact on aircraft design, compelling the addition of expensive electronic warfare capabilities. Further, the USAF and USN began to design strike "packages" in which only a small number of aircraft carried ordinance and the rest participated in suppression by electronic and direct attack means. By the end of the Vietnam War the air force needed three support aircraft for every one attack aircraft for missions against heavily defended targets in North Vietnam. See Jeffrey Ethell and Alfred Price, *One Day In a Long War, May 10, 1972, Air War, North Vietnam* (New York: Randon House, 1989), Chapter 3. This

led to even more sophisticated penetrating aircraft designs, which now include low observable (stealth) technologies. With this competition has come rising unit costs for both combat aircraft and surface-to-air missiles. A similar process of measure and countermeasure has been at work between surface ships and antiship guided missile designers. After the shock of the sinking of the Israeli destroyer *Elat* by a Soviet designed antiship missile in the 1967 Arab-Israeli War, navies of the world invested massively in close-in defense systems and electronic countermeasures to render ineffective this new generation of robot weapons. Again, this competition has fueled a steady rise in costs of surface ships and antiship guided missiles.

7. The strategic bombing campaigns of World War II, Korea, and Vietnam demonstrated the problem of targets that would not "stay dead." Further, one of the operational problems of contemporary stand-off weapons is that a large portion of their weight is tied up in propulsion, fuel, and airframes, and as a result many have modest high explosive warheads. This means that the guided weapon must hit hardened targets precisely to have a meaningful military effect. For instance, technical analysis has suggested that a nonnuclear campaign in the European theatre would require more than 10,000 long-range PGMs, a number generated in part by the requirement to reattack reconstituted targets. These large inventory demands prompted proponents of long-range PGMs to press for a major reduction in their unit costs. For a discussion of these issues, see "The Future of Containment: America's Options for Defending Its Interests on the Soviet Periphery," Report of the Offense-Defense Working Group Prepared for the Commission on Integrated Long-Term Strategy, Prepublication Draft (limited publication by the Department of Defense, September 1988), Chapter 3.

8. Advanced airborne wide-area surveillance platforms are vulnerable to electronic and direct attack. Already very costly, only a small fleet can be purchased, rendering each platform a very lucrative as well as a comparatively easy target for long-range surface-to-air missiles or manned interceptors. To improve their military resilience would radically drive up their already high unit costs. See Hobbs, *NATO and the New Technologies*, pp. 29–30, for a description of airborne ground surveillance radars. These systems are also vulnerable to attack at their operating bases on the ground, a weakness that points to a new generation of airborne sensors that relies on a "bistatic" concept in which the airborne receiver is physically separated from the radar transmitter, allowing the airborne antenna to receive signals without radiating telltale energy. This suggests that the future airborne sensors will have to become more stealthy and operate primarily in a passive mode. A similar phenomenon occurred in antisubmarine warfare technology. All major navies had been relying increasingly on passive sonars to detect submarines, but more recently the advances in submarine quieting have compelled reintroduction of very low frequency active sonars employing techniques in which the sound source of the active sonar is in a separate platform, e.g., a helicopter, from the detecting array, e.g., a surface warship.

9. In particular, the PGM/RSTA combination has the potential to radically devalue the military worth of the main battle tank and the tactical fighter bomber, weapons that symbolize the institutional raison d'etre of contemporary armies and

air forces. If asymmetrically deployed by NATO, survivable RSTA platforms coupled with tens of thousands of PGMs could paralyze the offensive potential of the Warsaw Pact, affording a technological solution to the Soviet quantitative advantage in the Euro-theatre. Similarly, a unilateral deployment of space and airborne RSTA systems coupled with a large inventory of antiship missiles could overturn the contemporary naval balance. See Timothy Garden, *The Technology Trap—Science and the Military* (London: Brassey's Defence Publishers, 1989), pp. 113–114, for the relationship between guided weapons effectiveness and surveillance capability.

10. See John Lewis Gaddis, *The Long Peace: Inquiries Into the History of the Cold War* (New York: Oxford University Press, 1987), especially pp. 195–214, for a discussion of the evolution of Soviet attitudes toward the "sanctuary" status of reconnaissance satellites.

11. Camouflage, concealment, and deception (CC&D) methods have been gaining greater appreciation within the U.S. military in the face of the rising threat of PGMs. The air force became most active during the 1980s in utilizing these technologies. The Soviet military has also given *maskirovka* (their term for CC&D) heavy emphasis. For a discussion of the Soviet commitment to *maskirovka* as stimulated by the "third revolution" in warfare, see Christopher Donnelly, *Red Banner— The Soviet Military System In Peace and War* (Coulsdon, Surrey: Jane's Information Group, 1988), especially chap. 2.

12. See J. Richard Vyce and John W. Hardy, "Adaptive Optics: Potential for Verification," in *Arms Control Verification—The Technologies That Make It Possible*, ed. Kosta Tsipis, David W. Hafemeister, and Penny Janeway (Washington, DC: Pergamon-Brassey's, 1986), pp. 97–103, for a description of adaptive optic technology used to develop staring sensors that would operate at high and geosynchronous orbit. See Ronald J. Ondrejka, "Imaging Technologies," in *Arms Control Verification*, ed. Tsipis, Hafemeister, and Janeway, pp. 92–96, for a discussion of the use of advanced technologies to combine information from sensors acquiring it from different parts of the spectrum. See William D. O'Neil, "Winning the ASW Technology Race," *Proceedings* (October 1988), pp. 86–91, for a description of efforts already underway to develop software for pattern recognition and advances that are also likely in the development of software for detection of mobile land targets.

13. See Edward H. Kolcum, "First USAF/McDonnell Douglas Delta 2 Launch Begins New Military Space Era," *Aviation Week & Space Technology* (20 February 1989), pp. 18–19, for a description of the first successful launch of an operational variant of the NAVSTAR Global Positioning System. Barring further launch difficulties, the air force plans to have a constellation of 21 satellites operational by the end of 1992 able to provide three-dimensional accuracy within 10 to 20 meters, an invaluable aid for designers of long-range cruise and ballistic missile systems.

14. Ashton B. Carter, "Communications Technologies and Vulnerabilities," in *Managing Nuclear Operations*, ed. Ashton B. Carter, John D. Steinbruner, and Charles A. Zraket (Washington, DC: The Brookings Institution, 1987), pp. 217–281.

15. Lt. Commander Marcus M. Urioste, USNR, "Where is the SSN Going?" *Proceedings* (October 1988), pp. 109–112.

16. For a discussion of the relationship between improved satellite reconnaissance capabilities and the interest in ASAT options, see Paul B. Stare's "Nuclear Operations and Antisatellites," in *Managing Nuclear Operations*, ed. Carter, Steinbrunner, and Zraket (Washington, DC: The Brookings Institution, 1987), pp. 679–703. See also Adm. William A. Owens, USN, and Commander James A. Moseman, USN, "The Maritime Strategy: Looking Ahead," *Proceedings* (February 1989), pp. 24–32.

17. See Commander Robert B. Shields, Jr., USN, "Emerging Deterrence Technologies," *Proceedings* (October 1988), pp. 126–131, for a discussion of the U.S. Navy's interest in ASAT. See General Crosbie E. Saint, USA, "CINCUSAREUR Places High Priority on ASAT," *Armed Forces Journal International* (September 1989) p. 40, for a contemporary argument in favor of a U.S. ASAT capability. See Garden, *The Technology Trap*, pp. 130–32, for a discussion of the increased importance of space combat means in future warfare.

18. For a survey of ASAT technology that flows from the technology investment strategy at the Office of the Strategic Defense Initiative, see U.S. Congress, Office of Technology Assessment (OTA), *Strategic Defenses—Ballistic Missile Defense Technologies: Anti-Satellite Weapons, Countermeasures, and Arms Control* (Princeton, NJ: Princeton University Press, 1986), especially the "Executive Summary" of the second part, pp. 3–21. See also OTA, *SDI: Technology, Survivability, and Software*, OTA-ISC-353 (Washington, DC: U.S. Government Printing Office, May 1988), especially chap. 5, "Ballistic Missile Defense Technology: Weapons, Power, Communications, and Space Transportation," and Paul B. Stares, *Space and National Security* (Washington, DC: The Brookings Institution, 1987), pp. 73–119.

19. OTA, *Strategic Defenses*, pp. 49–75.

20. "Surikov: How We'll Counter SDI," *Jane's Defense Weekly* (16 July 1988).

21. See Douglas Barrie, "Funding Cuts 'Serious Blow'," *Jane's Defense Weekly* (5 August 1989), p. 198, for a statement on the impact of budget cuts on the SDI program; also John A. Adam, "Star Wars In Transition," *IEEE Spectrum*, Journal of the Institute of Electrical and Electronics Engineers, vol. 26, no. 3 (March 1989), pp. 32–38.

22. The issue of air defense was raised early in the national debate over the SDI program. Critics raised the possibility of a "by-pass" strategy in which the Soviets would invest heavily in cruise missiles. This criticism and the rapid deployment of a new Soviet bomber (Bear H) armed with a Tomahawk class cruise missile (AS-15) prompted the creation of the small Air Defense Initiative program to explore some next-generation surveillance sensors for countering low observable aircraft and missiles. By the end of the 1980s both the U.S. and the USSR had deployed long-range first-generation low observable cruise missiles. With the banning of the long-range ground-launched cruise missile has come a renewed debate about whether to restrain long-range sea-launched cruise missiles. See Rose E. Gottemoeller, *Land-Attack Cruise Missiles*, Adelphi Papers 226 (London: International Institute for Strategic Studies, Winter 1987/8). Second-generation low observable aerodynamic strike vehicles that are close at hand are the advanced cruise missile and the B-2 bomber, encompassing innovations that suggest that designers of future air defense systems face a difficult task in developing reliable surveillance and tracking systems. See

also Bill Sweetman, *Stealth Bomber—Invisible Warplane, Black Budget* (Osceola, WI: Motorbooks International, 1989), for a discussion of the B-2. He notes that the payoff of "stealth" is not invisibility but the radical reduction that it renders in the effective range of contemporary radars (especially medium/high frequency fire control systems). For a discussion of new near-term and possible medium-term Soviet long-range aerodynamic attack systems and possible US air defense responses, see Peter A. Wilson, "Is the Air Defense Problem By-Passing the SDI?" in *Security Implications of SDI*, ed. Jeffrey Simon (Washington, DC: National Defense University Press, 1990).

23. For a discussion of the use of directed energy weapons in direct defense of a high value platform, see Lieutenant John P. Spencer, USN, "Designing a Destroyer for the 21st Century," *Proceedings* (October 1988) pp. 138–143. See also R. M. Ogorkiewicz, "Countermeasures for Tanks Beating Smart Munitions," *International Defense Review*, vol. 22 (January 1989), pp. 53–57.

24. See Jacques S. Gansler, "How To Improve the Acquisition of Weapons," in *Reorganizing America's Defense—Leadership In War and Peace*, ed. Robert J. Art, Vincent Davis, and Samuel P. Huntington (Washington, DC: Pergamon-Brassey's 1985), chap 19, for a discussion of "structural disarmament."

25. *Deterrence In Decay: The Future of the U.S. Defense Industrial Base*, CSIS Report (Center for Strategic and International Studies: Washington, DC, May 1989).

26. See A. D. Baker, III, "The Ivanovs Keep Up," *Proceedings* (August 1989), pp. 53–57, for a discussion of the Soviet experience with naval structural disarmament. See also Norman Polmar, "The Soviet Navy—Continuing Warship Construction," *Proceedings* (January 1990), pp. 132–134.

27. Mark Hewish, "Unmanned Aerial Vehicles, Part 1: European Programs," *International Defense Review*, vol. 22 (April 1989), pp. 449–457, and Bill Sweetman, "Unmanned Aerial Vehicles, Part 2: Developments in the U.S.," *International Defense Review*, vol. 23 (May 1989), pp. 599–604.

28. UAVs have also been exported to a variety of users. The United States has exported to Egypt the Model 324 Scarab long-range reconnaissance drone that has a range payload characteristic similar to the now-banned Tomahawk class ground-launched cruise missle. Such drones have the potential for being transformed into long-range unmanned bombardment systems. For a description of the family of long-range drones developed by the U.S. firm Teledyne Ryan, see J. R. Wilson, "The Teledyne Ryan Aeronautical Family of RPVs," *International Defense Review*, vol. 23 (May 1989), p. 603.

29. Gerard Turbe, "Upgrading Older Main Battle Tanks (MBTs): From Dream to Reality," *International Defense Review*, vol. 21 (October 1988), pp. 1278–1288; "Updating Older Combat Aircraft: A Fiercely Contested Market," *International Defense Review*, vol. 21 (December 1988), pp. 1587–1593.

30. Steven Zaloga, "Ballistic Missiles in the Third World," *International Defense Review*, vol. 21 (November 1988), pp. 1423–1427. See also Leonard Spector, *The Undeclared Bomb* (Cambridge, MA: Ballinger, 1988), pp. 25–66. For the Middle Eastern powers, the military utility of ballistic and cruise missiles is substantial, and with access to contemporary inertial guidance and space navigation systems, non-

superpower ballistic missiles will develop far greater accuracies sufficient to make point targets vulnerable to regional bombardment. The current generation of the region's tactical ballistic missiles comprises inaccurate V-2 class city bombardment weapons. With the use of new navigation systems, Middle Eastern armed forces may acquire the next generation and be able to efficiently attack civilian targets with high explosive warheads. Opponents of Israel, facing its clearly superior air force, will find this class of weapons most attractive since they do not require highly trained flight crews. Ballistic missile technologies have been pouring into the region (most dramatic has been the Chinese decision to sell Saudi Arabia the 3,000-kilometer range CSS-2 intermediate-range ballistic missile) and are likely to be followed by the spread of cruise missile technologies. Following the Iran-Iraq war's shattering of the no-first-use ban on chemical weapons, the major Islamic states also appear to be acquiring biochemical arsenals, efforts that have recently been linked to the quasi-public acknowledgment of the Israeli nuclear weapons program. On the subcontinent, India long ago demonstrated its ability to produce nuclear bombs, has test fired a short-range tactical ballistic missile, the Prithvi, and in the summer of 1989 successfully tested its Agni intermediate-range ballistic missile. Pakistan is focusing its missile effort (with likely Chinese assistance) on shorter range weapons through its Haft program. Israel is currently developing (with U.S. assistance) the Arrow antitactical ballistic missile. In turn, Iraq has the Faw-1 program. Given the rapid proliferation of ballistic missiles, regional powers can be expected to seek an active defense capability. In addition, by the end of the 1990s low earth orbit ASAT capabilities could have widely proliferated in the region. The United States is providing Israel (through its Arrow program) appropriate guidance technology for low earth orbit interceptors. Other potential ASAT capable states include India, Pakistan, Iran, Iraq, and Saudi Arabia. All of these military states may well have a strong interest in denying low earth reconnaissance over their territory during a regional war.

31. With the rising "entry price" for military intervention, both superpowers will search for intervention means that are politically and militarily acceptable and play to their technological advantage over potential regional opponents. These will include the extensive use of space-based RSTA and long-range precision deep strike weapons to influence the course of a future conflict, as both nations become increasingly reluctanct to expose ground troops to the threat of attack or to deploy surface warships near the coastline of a regional opponent heavily armed with antiship missile systems. The classic form of intervention—deployment of a relatively small number of high quality ground troops—will become increasingly anachronistic for the greater Middle East, further motivating the superpowers to invest in costly new technologies. See also Peter A. Wilson, "The Marine Corps in 1985," *Proceedings* (January 1976), pp. 31–38, and Peter A. Wilson, "The Marine Corps in 1995," *Proceedings* (November 1985), pp. 60–61, for discussions of the implications of diffusion of advanced weapons technology on the doctrine, structure, and weapons investment of the USMC.

32. Karl Kaiser, "Non-Proliferation and Nuclear Deterrence," *Survival*, vol. 31, no. 2 (March/April 1989); Hans Binnendijk, "NATO's Nuclear Modernization Dilemma," *Survival*, vol. 31, no. 2 (March/April 1989).

33. See Paul Beaver, ed., *China In Crisis* (Surrey, U.K.: Jane's Information Group, 1989), pp. 109–113, for an estimate of the PRC's nuclear forces that places their size and quality substantially above earlier estimates.

Chapter 7

1. Data source: United Nations, U.N. Conference on Trade and Development (UNCTAD), *Handbook of International Trade and Development Statistics, 1986* (New York: United Nations, 1987). In 1984, 26.0 percent of the Soviet Union's imports came from the developed sector and 19.2 percent from Western Europe. In 1984, 68.0 percent of China's imports came from the developed sector and 31.3 percent came from Japan. In 1984, 4.1 percent of the Soviet Union's imports came from the U.S. and Canada, while 18.8 percent of China's came from these sources.

2. See U.S. Department of State, "The European Community Prepares to Complete a Single Market by 1992" (5 July 1988), and "Canadian Trade Policy: The Anatomy of a Trade Deal," *The Economist* (22 October 1988), pp. 77–78.

3. C. Fred Bergsten, *America In the World Economy: A Strategy for the 1990s*, (Washington, DC: Institute for International Economics, November 1988), pp. 71–72, 150–56.

4. Abraham Lowenthal, "The United States and South America," *Current History*, vol. 87, no. 525 (June 1988), pp. 4, 42; Howard J. Wiarda and Ieda Siqueria Wiarda, "The United States and South America: The Challenge of Fragile Democracy," *Current History*, vol. 88, no. 536 (March 1989), pp. 114–16.

5. U.S. Congress, Congressional Budget Office, "Effects of a Constrained Budget on U.S. Military Forces," staff working paper (March 1989). This study reveals the immense problems that will confront U.S. defense planners in the 1990s as a result of rising unit costs for defense machinery. Assuming zero real growth in the U.S. national defense budget authority from FY89–94, defense planners would have to cut air force tactical wings from the projected 23 to 15 in 1994, carrier battle groups from 15 to 10, and army divisions from 18 to 12 in order to protect defense investment budget authority proposed in the last Reagan budget for FY89–94 from collapse. If force structure were to be maintained according to plan by 1994—i.e., 23 air force tactical wings, 15 carrier groups, and 18 army divisions—the 27 percent growth in procurement anticipated in the last Reagan budget by 1994 would plunge to only 3.0 percent and defense R&D would drop from a planned 3.0 percent increase to a contraction of 4.0 percent. Under conditions of negative real growth in budget authority for defense over the FY89–94 period, the implications of structural disarmament for force structure and defense investment become even more severe. See also U.S. Congress, Congressional Budget Office, "Operations and Support Costs for the Department of Defense" (July 1988). This study analyses upward pressures on future O&M costs driven by the requirements of operating and maintaining the defense machinery produced as a result of 1980s accelerated investment.

6. See James R. Kurth, "The Military-Industrial Complex Revisited," in *1989–90 American Defense Annual*, ed. Joseph Kruzel (Lexington, MA: Lexington Books, 1989), pp. 195–215, for a discussion of the likely resistance the U.S. defense industry prime contractors would put up to a "Copernican revolution" that calls for a

transition away from manned combat vehicles to the transcentury weapons of PGMs and RSTA systems. See Mark E. Morrow, "FY90-91 Budget Indicates Shifting Congressional Priorities," in *Armed Forces Journal International* (September 1989), pp. 11-12, for a summary of the political and institutional struggles ignited by Secretary of Defense Cheney's 1989 program cuts.

7. Concern about the possible "destabilizing" consequences of reduced forward NATO forces was explored in the influential study by James A. Thomson and Nanette C. Gantz, *Conventional Arms Control Revisited: Objectives In the New Phase* (Santa Monica, CA: RAND, 1987). See also James A. Thomson, "An Unfavorable Situation: NATO and the Conventional Balance," in *The Changing Strategic Landscape*, International Institute for Strategic Studies, Adelphi Papers 236, Part II (London: International Institute for Strategic Studies, Spring 1989), pp. 72-102.

8. See Peter A. Wilson, "The Geostrategic Risks of SDI," in *Star Wars and European Defense,"* ed. Hans Gunter Brauch (London: Macmillan, 1987), pp. 352-368, for a discussion of the emergence of a multilateral nuclear deterrent "gridlock." An important element of the multilateral nuclear deterrent system is the ability of all parties to threaten to use theatre-range nuclear weapons as the "first salvo." This suggests that the United States should try to ensure that some of its theatre nuclear forces remain on the European continent after a CFE agreement. Given West German reluctance to deploy a mobile short-range missile, this smaller nuclear deterrent posture might reside in a modest vertical landing fighter bomber fleet equipped with a stand-off missile (i.e., the AV-8B Harrier II with a variant of the SRAM-II ASM).

9. See David M. Abshire and Stanley Harrison, cochairmen, "Defense Economics for the 1990s: Resources, Strategies, and Options," Report by the Center for Strategic and International Studies and the Potomac Foundation (Washington, DC: Center for Strategic and International Studies, April 1989), p. 31, for a "school solution" favoring strong investment in mobile land-based ICBM forces.

Bibliography of Data Sources

U.S. Government

Executive Office of the President. *Economic Report of the President*. Washington, DC: U.S. Government Printing Office. Published annually, year of the title date.

———. Office of Management and Budget. *Historical Tables—Budget of the United States Government*. Washington, DC: U.S. Government Printing Office. Published annually, year before the title date.

U.S. Department of Commerce. Bureau of Economic Analysis. *National Income and Product Accounts of the United States, 1929–82—Statistical Tables*. Washington, DC: U.S. Government Printing Office, September 1986.

———. *Survey of Current Business*. Published monthly.

———. "U.S. International Transactions." Published annually.

———. "U.S. Net International Investment Position, 1988." 29 June 1989.

U.S. Department of Defense. Office of the Assistant Secretary of Defense (Comptroller). "The National Defense Budget Estimates for FY87." Washington, DC: U.S. Government Printing Office, May 1986.

United Nations

United Nations. United Nations Conference on Trade and Development (UNCTAD). *Handbook of International Trade and Development Statistics, 1986 Supplement*. New York: United Nations, 1987.

———. *World Economic Survey*. New York: U.N. Published annually, year following the title date (called *World Economic Report* prior to 1955).

International Monetary Fund (IMF)

International Monetary Fund. *International Financial Statistics Yearbook* and *International Financial Statistics* monthly reports (IFS). Washington, DC: IMF. Yearbooks published annually, year of the title date.

———. *International Financial Statistics, Supplement on Trade Statistics*, Supplement Series No. 15. Washington, DC: IMF, 1988.

———. *World Economic Outlook*. Washington, DC: IMF, published biannually in April and October.

Organization for Economic Cooperation and Development (OECD)

Organization for Economic Cooperation and Development. *OECD Economic Outlook*. Paris: OECD, published annually, year of the title date.

———. *OECD Outlook: Historical Statistics, 1960–87*. Paris: OECD, 1989.

General Agreement on Tariffs and Trade (GATT)

General Agreement on Tariffs and Trade. *International Trade*. Geneva: GATT, published annually, year following the title date.

Selected Bibliography

Abshire, David M., and Stanley Harrison, cochairmen. "Defense Economics for the 1990s: Resources, Strategies, and Option." Report by the Center for Strategic and International Studies and the Potomac Foundation. Washington, DC: The Center for Strategic and International Studies, April 1989.

Aganbegyan, Abel. *The Economic Challenge of Perestroika*. Ed. Michael Barratt Brown. Trans. Pauline M. Tiffen. Bloomington: Indiana University Press, 1988.

Art, Robert J., Vincent Davis, and Samual P. Huntington, eds. *Reorganizing America's Defense—Leadership In War and Peace*. Washington, DC: Pergamon-Brassey's, 1985.

Bailey, Norman A., and Richard Cohen. *The Mexican Time Bomb*. New York: Priority Press, 1987.

Beaver, Paul, ed. *China In Crisis*. Surrey, U.K.: Jane's Information Group, 1989.

Bellamy, Chris. *The Future of Land Warfare*. New York: St. Martin's, 1987.

———. *Red God of War—Soviet Artillery and Rocket Forces*. London: Brassey's Defense Publishers, 1986.

Bergson, Abram, and Herbert S. Levine, eds. *The Soviet Economy: Toward the Year 2000*. London: Allen and Unwin, 1985.

Bergsten, C. Fred. *America In the World Economy: A Strategy for the 1990s*. Washington, DC: Institute for International Economics, 1988.

———. *The Dilemmas of the Dollar: The Economics and Politics of United States International Monetary Policy*. New York: New York University Press, 1975.

Blackwell, William L. *The Industrialization of Russia: An Historical Perspective*. New York: Thomas Y. Crowell, 1970.

Block, Fred L. *The Origins of International Economic Disorder*. Berkeley: University of California Press, 1977.

Boltho, Andrea, ed. *The European Economy: Growth and Crisis*. Oxford: Oxford University Press, 1982.

Brauch, Hans Gunter, ed. *Star Wars and European Defense*. London: Macmillan, 1987.

Breslauer, George W. *Khruschev and Brezhnev As Leaders: Building Authority In Soviet Politics*. London: Allen and Unwin, 1982.

Brodie, Bernard. *War and Politics*. New York: Macmillan, 1973.

Buckley, Thomas H. *The United States and the Washington Conference, 1921–1922.* Knoxville: University of Tennessee Press, 1970.

Builder, Carl H. *The Masks of War—American Military Styles In Strategy and Analysis.* Baltimore: Johns Hopkins University Press, 1989.

Calleo, David P. *The Imperious Economy.* Cambridge: Harvard University Press, 1982.

Carpenter, Ted Galen, ed. *Collective Defense or Strategic Independence? Alternative Strategies for the Future.* Lexington, MA: Lexington Books, 1989.

Carter, Ashton B., John D. Steinbruner, and Charles A. Zraket, eds. *Managing Nuclear Operations.* Washington, DC: The Brookings Institution, 1987.

Central Intelligence Agency, Directorate of Intelligence. "Revisiting Soviet Economic Performance Under Glasnost: Implications for CIA Estimates." SOV 88-10068. September 1988.

———. "USSR: Sharply Higher Budget Deficits Threaten Perestroyka." SOV 88-10043U. September 1988.

Central Intelligence Agency and Defense Intelligence Agency. "Gorbachev's Economic Program: Problems Emerge." Report submitted to the Subcommittee on National Security Economics of the Joint Economic Committee of the U.S. Congress. 13 April 1988.

———. "Gorbachev's Modernization Program: A Status Report." Report submitted to the Subcommittee on National Security Economics of the Joint Economic Committee of the U.S. Congress. 19 March 1987.

———. "The Soviet Economy Under a New Leader." Report submitted to the Subcommittee on Economic Resources, Competitiveness, and Security Economics of the Joint Economic Committee of the U.S. Congress. 19 March 1986.

———. "The Soviet Economy in 1988: Gorbachev Changes Course." Report submitted to the Subcommittee on National Security Economics of the Joint Economic Committee of the U.S. Congress. 14 April 1989.

Center for Strategic and International Studies. *Deterrance In Decay: The Future of the U.S. Defense Industrial Base.* Washington, DC: CSIS, May 1989.

Cline, William R., ed. *Trade Policy In the 1980s.* Washington, DC: Institute for International Economics, 1983.

Cochran, Thomas B., William M. Arkin, and Milton M. Hoenig. *Nuclear Weapons Databook—Volume I: U.S. Nuclear Forces and Capabilities.* Cambridge: Ballinger, 1984.

Cochran, Thomas B., William M. Arkin, Robert S. Norris, and Milton M. Hoenig. *Nuclear Weapons Databook—Volume II: U.S. Nuclear Warhead Production.* Cambridge: Ballinger, 1987.

Cochran, Thomas B., William M. Arkin, Robert S. Norris, and Jeffrey I. Sands. *Nuclear Weapons Databook—Volume IV: Soviet Nuclear Weapons.* Grand Rapids, MI: Harper and Row, 1989.

Cohen, Richard. *World Trade and Payments Cycles: The Advance and Retreat of the Postwar Order.* New York: Praeger, 1989.

Collins, John M. *U.S.-Soviet Military Balance, 1980–85*. Washington, DC: Pergamon-Brassey's, 1985.

Congressional Budget Office. U.S. Congress. "Effects of a Constrained Budget on U.S. Military Forces." Staff Working Paper. March 1989.

———. "Operations and Support Costs for the Department of Defense." July 1988.

Danielsen, Albert L. *The Evolution of OPEC*. New York: Harcourt, 1982.

Deitchman, Seymour J. *Military Power and the Advance of Technology*, 2nd ed. Boulder, CO: Westview, 1983.

Destler, I. M. *American Trade Politics: System Under Stress*. Washington, DC: Institute for International Economics, 1986.

Donnelly, Christopher. *Red Banner—The Soviet Military System In Peace and War*. Surrey, U.K.: Jane's Information Group, 1988.

Durch, William J. *The Future of the ABM Treaty*. Adelphi Papers 223. London: International Institute for Strategic Studies, 1987.

Edmonds, Robin. *Soviet Foreign Diplomacy—The Brezhnev Years*. Oxford-York: Oxford University Press, 1983.

Eklof, Ben. *Soviet Briefing—Gorbachev and the Reform Period*. Boulder, CO: Westview, 1989.

Enthoven, Alain C., and K. Wayne Smith. *How Much Is Enough? Shaping the Defense Program, 1961–1969*. New York: Harper and Row, 1971.

Ethier, Wilfred. *Modern International Economics*. New York: W. W. Norton, 1983.

Far Eastern Economic Review. *Asia Yearbook*. Hong Kong: Far Eastern Economic Review Ltd. Published annually the year following the title date.

Freedman, Lawrence. *The Evolution of Nuclear Strategy*. New York: St. Martin's, 1983.

Froyen, Richard T. *Macroeconomics: Theories and Policies*, 2nd ed. New York: Macmillan, 1986.

Gaddis, John Lewis. *The United States and the Origins of the Cold War, 1941–47*. New York: Columbia University Press, 1972.

Gaddis, John Lewis. *Strategies of Containment: A Critical Appraisal of Postwar American Security Policy*. Oxford: Oxford University Press, 1982.

Gaddis, John Lewis. *The Long Peace: Inquiries Into the History of the Cold War*. Oxford: Oxford University Press, 1987.

Gansler, Jacques S. *Affording Defense*. Cambridge, MA: MIT Press, 1989.

Garden, Timothy. *The Technology Trap—Science and the Military*. London: Brassey's Defence Publishers, 1989.

Gareev, Col. Gen. Makhmut Akhmetovich. *M. V. Frunze: Military Theorist*. London: Pergamon-Brassey's, 1988.

Gelman, Harry. *The Brezhnev Politburo and the Decline of Detente*. Ithaca, NY: Cornell University Press, 1984.

Goldman, Marshall I. *USSR In Crisis: The Failure of an Economic System*. New York: W. W. Norton, 1983.

Gottemoeller, Rose E. *Land-Attack Cruise Missiles*. Adelphi Papers 226. London: International Institute for Strategic Studies, Winter 1987/8.

Gregory, Paul R., and Robert C. Stuart. *Soviet Economic Structure and Performance*, 3rd ed. New York: Harper and Row, 1986.

Haig, Alexander M., Jr. *Caveat—Realism, Reagan, and Foreign Policy*. New York: Macmillan, 1984.

Hansen, Chuck. *U.S. Nuclear Weapons—The Secret History*. New York: Orion Books, 1988.

Hewett, Ed A. *Energy Economics and Foreign Policy In the Soviet Union*. Washington, DC: The Brookings Institution, 1984.

Hilmes, Rolf. *Main Battle Tanks—Developments In Design Since 1945*. Trans. Richard Simpkin. London: Brassey's Defence Publishers, 1987.

Hobbs, David. *NATO and the New Technologies*. Lanham, MD: University Press of America, 1989.

Hofheinz, Roy, Jr., and Kent E. Calder. *The Eastasia Edge*. New York: Basic Books, 1982.

Holloway, David. *The Soviet Union and the Arms Race*, 2nd ed. New Haven: Yale University Press, 1984.

Hosmer, Stephen T., and Thomas W. Wolfe. *Soviet Policy and Practice Toward Third World Conflicts*. Lexington, MA: D. C. Heath, 1983.

Hutchings, Raymond. *Soviet Economic Development*, 2nd ed. New York: New York University Press, 1982.

International Institute for Strategic Studies. *The Changing Strategic Landscape*. Adelphi Papers 236. London: International Institute for Strategic Studies, 1989.

Ippolito, Dennis S. *Congressional Spending*. A Twentieth Century Fund Report. Ithaca, NY: Cornell University Press, 1981.

Isby, David C. *Weapons and Tactics of the Soviet Army*. Fully rev. ed. London: Jane's Publishing Co., 1988.

Japan Economic Institute of America. *Yearbook of U.S.-Japan Economic Relations in 1982*. Washington, DC: Japan Economic Institute of America, 1983.

Joffe, Ellis. *The Chinese Army After Mao*. Cambridge: Harvard University Press, 1987.

Johnson, Chalmers. *MITI and the Japanese Miracle: The Growth of Industrial Policy, 1925-1975*. Stanford, CA: Stanford University Press, 1982.

Joint Economic Committee. U.S. Congress. *Gorbachev's Economic Plans*. Volumes I and II. Study papers submitted to the Joint Economic Committee of the U.S. Congress. Washington, DC: U.S. Government Printing Office, 1987.

―――. *The Soviet Economy In the 1980s: Problems and Prospects*. Parts 1 and 2. Selected papers submitted to the Joint Economic Committee of the U.S. Congress. Washington, DC: U.S. Government Printing Office, 1983.

Jordan, Amos A., and William J. Taylor, Jr. *American National Security: Policy and Process*, rev. ed. Baltimore: Johns Hopkins University Press, 1984.

Kruzel, Joseph, ed. *1989–1990 American Defense Annual*. Lexington, MA: Lexington Books, 1989.

Lee, William T., and Richard F. Staar. *Soviet Military Policy Since World War II*. Stanford, CA: Hoover Institution Press, 1986.

Lin, Chong-Pin. *China's Nuclear Weapons Strategy*. Lexington, MA: Lexington Books, 1988.

Linden, Carl A. *Khrushchev and the Soviet Leadership, 1957–1964*. Baltimore, MD: Johns Hopkins University Press, 1966.

MccGwire, Michael. *Military Objectives In Soviet Foreign Policy*. Washington, DC: The Brookings Institution, 1987.

Macksey, Kenneth. *Technology In War*. New York: Prentice Hall, 1986.

Mandelbaum, Michael. *The Nuclear Question*. London: Cambridge University Press, 1979.

Marris, Stephen. *Deficits and the Dollar: The World Economy At Risk*. Washington, DC: Institute for International Economics, 1985.

Medvedev, Zhores A. *Andropov: An Insider's Account of Power and Politics Within the Kremlin*. New York: Penguin Books, 1984.

Medvev, Roy. *Khrushchev*. Trans. Brian Pearce. New York: Anchor Press/Doubleday, 1984.

Nakamura, Takafusa. *The Postwar Japanese Economy—Its Development and Structure*. Trans. Jacqueline Kaminski. Tokyo: University of Tokyo Press, 1983.

Newhouse, John. *War and Peace In the Nuclear Age*. New York: Knopf, 1989.

Newton, Maxwell. *The Fed: Inside the Federal Reserve, The Secret Power Center that Controls the American Economy*. New York: Times Books, 1983.

Nisbet, Charles T. *Latin America: Problems In Economic Development*. New York: Free Press, 1969.

Nove, Alec. *An Economic History of the USSR*. New York: Penguin Books, 1976.

Office of Technology Assessment, U.S. Congress. *SDI: Technology, Survivability, and Software*. Washington, DC: U.S. Government Printing Office, May 1988.

———. *Strategic Defenses—Ballistic Missile Defense Technologies: Anti-Satellite Weapons, Countermeasures, and Arms Control*. Princeton, NJ: Princeton University Press, 1986.

Okimoto, Daniel I., ed. *Japan's Economy—Coping With Change In the International Environment*. Boulder, CO: Westview, 1982.

Parboni, Riccardo. *The Dollar and Its Rivals: Recession, Inflation, and International Finance*. London: Verso, 1981.

Pipes, Richard. *Survival Is Not Enough*. New York: Simon and Schuster, 1984.

Prados, John. *The Soviet Estimate—U.S. Intelligence Analysis and Russian Military Strength*. New York: Dial, 1982.

President's Commission on Strategic Forces (the Scowcroft Commission). *Report of the President's Commission on Strategic Forces*. Washington, DC: U.S. Government Printing Office, April 1983.

Quade, Edward S., ed. *Analysis For Military Decisions*. Chicago: Rand McNally, 1966.

Rowen, Henry S., and Charles Wolf, Jr., eds. *The Future of the Soviet Empire*. New York: St. Martin's, 1987.

Rubenstein, Alvin Z., ed. *The Foreign Policy of the Soviet Union*, 3rd ed. New York: Randon House, 1972.

Scammell, W. M. *The International Economy Since 1945*, 2nd ed. London: Macmillan, 1983.

Schwartz, David N. *NATO's Nuclear Dilemma*. Washington, DC: The Brookings Institution, 1983.

Scott, Harriet Fast, and William F. Scott. *The Soviet Art of War: Doctrine, Strategy, and Tactics*. Boulder, CO: Westview, 1982.

Simon, Jeffrey, ed. *NATO-Warsaw Pact Force Mobilization*. Washington, DC: The National Defense University, 1988.

Sloan, Stanley R., ed. *NATO In the 1990s*. Washington, DC: Pergamon-Brassey's, 1989.

Solovyov, Vladimir, and Elena Klepikova. *Yuri Andropov: A Secret Passage Into the Kremlin*. Trans. Guy Daniels. New York: Macmillan, 1983.

Spanier, John. *American Foreign Policy Since World War II*. New York: Praeger, 1962.

Spector, Leonard. *The Undeclared Bomb*. Cambridge, MA: Ballinger, 1988.

Staar, Richard F. *Communist Regimes In Eastern Europe*, 4th ed. Stanford, CA: Hoover Institution Press, 1984.

Stares, Paul B. *Space and National Security*. Washington, DC: The Brookings Institution, 1987.

Steinbruner, John D., ed. *Restructuring American Foreign Policy*. Washington, DC: The Brookings Institution, 1989.

Sweetman, Bill. *Stealth Bomber—Invisible Warplane, Black Budget*. Osceola, WI: Motorbrooks International, 1989.

Talbott, Strobe, ed. *Khrushchev Remembers: The Last Testament*. Boston: Little Brown, 1974.

Taylor, William B., Jr., ed. *Beyond Burdensharing—Future Alliance Defense Cooperation*. The Alliance Papers: Proceedings No. 1. Brussels, Belgium: United States Mission to NATO, April 1989.

Terry, Sarah Meiklejohn, ed. *Soviet Policy In Eastern Europe*. New Haven: Yale University Press, 1984.

Thomson, James A., and Nanette C. Gantz. *Conventional Arms Control Revisited: Objectives In the New Phase*. Santa Monica, CA: RAND Corporation, 1987.

Tsipis, Kosta, David W. Hafemeister, and Penny Janeway, ed. *Arms Control Verification—The Technologies That Make It Possible*. Washington, DC: Pergamon-Brassey's, 1986.

Twentieth Century Fund Task Force on International Debt. *Report of the Twentieth Century Fund Task Force on International Debt*. New York: Priority Press, 1989.

Uchino, Tatsuro. *Japan's Post-War Economy: An Insider's View of Its History and Its Future*. Tokyo: Kodansha International Ltd., 1983.

Weigley, Russell F. *The American Way of War: A History of the United States Military Strategy and Policy*. Bloomington: Indiana University Press, 1977.

Wohlstetter, Albert, Fred Ikle, et al. *Discriminate Deterrence*. Report by the Commission on Integrated Long-Term Strategy. Washington, DC: U.S. Government Printing Office, January 1988.

Wolfe, Thomas W. *Soviet Power and Europe, 1945–1970*. Baltimore: Johns Hopkins University Press, 1970.

Yanov, Alexander. *The Russian Challenge and the Year 2000*. Trans. Iden J. Rosenthal. Oxford, U.K.: Basil Blackwell, 1987.

Zagoria, Donald S., ed. *Soviet Policy in East Asia*. New Haven: Yale University Press, 1982.

Index

Abalkin, Leonid, 63, 69
Abasha, 46, 47
Afghanistan, 99; costs of war in, for USSR, 66, 49, 50, 53, 55, 63, 66, 78, 81; Reagan Doctrine in, 176, 177; Soviet invasion of, 5, 42, 48, 65, 137, 151; Soviet withdrawal from, 81, 85, 86
Africa, 50, 78, 164
Aganbegyan, Abel, 9, 46, 63, 69
Air Defense Forces, Soviet. *See* PVO
Air Defense Initiative, 189, 204
Air Force, U.S., 178, 180
Air/Land Battle, 177
Akhromeyev, Sergei, 84
Aliyev, Geidar, 46, 47, 50, 64
Andropov, Yuri, 5, 59, 60, 69, 153; ascension of, 45; and China, 50; discipline campaign of, 49, 53, 57; economic policy impact of, 52, 58; economic strategy of, 44, 56
Angola, 42, 48, 63, 66, 176
Antisatellite weapons, 187, 188, 202, 203
Antitank guided missile, 183–184
Arab-Israeli War, 133
Arkhipov, Ivan, 51, 60
Armenia, 92
Army, U.S., 177, 178, 180
Austria, 100
Azerbaijan, 46, 47, 92
Azeri model, 46, 64

B-2 bomber, 175, 180, 204
Baibakov, Nikolai, 49, 58, 59
Baker Plan, 164
Baker, James, III, 162, 164
Ballistic Missile Defense, 187, 188–189, 202, 203. *See also* Strategic Defense Initiative
Baltic States, 87
Bekaa Valley, 47
Beveridge System, 114
Black Monday, 170
Bogomolev, Oleg, 63, 70
Bonn Summit, 166
Brezhnev Doctrine, 77
Brezhnev, Leonid, 5; ascension of, 44, 45; Doctrine, 77; Economic program of, 26, 27, 28; Gorbachev opposition to program of, 58; military spending under, 37, 41, 43, 84, 96; opposition to, 44, 45, 47–49, 65, 66; Tashkent speech on China, 50; Trust in Cadres policy, 46; Tula Doctrine, 41, 80
Budget deficit. *See* U.S. government budget, deficit of
Budget Summit, 167, 178–179
Bukharin, Nikolai, 64
Bulgaria, 39, 59–60, 77
Bush, George, 179, 196, 201
Business cycles, free world, 103, 105, 106–110, 111; in 1990s, 171, 195; national macroeconomic policy

Business cycles (*Continued*)
  differences in, 114; phases of, 124–128
Byelorussia, 87

C³I (command, control, communications, and intelligence), 98, 100
Cambodia, 43, 66, 78
Canada, 166, 199
Capital flows, cross-border, 119, 157, 199
Carter, Jimmy, 134, 136, 138, 151, 162, 174, 175
Caspian Sea, 14
Ceausescu, Nicolae, 78
Chebrikov, Victor, 44
Cheney, Richard, 179, 201
Chernavin, Vladimir N., 96
Chernenko, Konstantin, 49, 50–51, 53, 56, 58, 60
China, 90, 144; Andropov policy towards, 50–51; Brezhnev policy towards, 48; Chernenko policy towards, 51; Gorbachev policy towards, 56, 60, 66; nuclear arsenal, 193; reforms in, 50, 58, 64, 69, 83, 88, 94; role in 1990s, 198, 204; and USSR, 33, 35, 38–39, 40, 81, 94
CIA, estimates of Soviet defense spending by, 4, 79, 81, 84–86, 89
Civil War, 122
CMEA (Committee for Mutual Economic Assistance), 2, 39, 51, 198. *See also* Eastern Europe
Cold War, 33, 102, 140
Common Agricultural Policy, 129
Contract Responsibility System, Chinese, 64
Conventional Forces in Europe Agreement, 82, 97–98, 99, 202, 205

Counterforce, 146
Cuba, 40, 42, 50, 53, 78, 176
Cuban missile crisis, 36, 37
Czechoslovakia, 27, 39, 59, 87, 81

Defense spending. *See* Soviet defense spending; U.S. defense spending
Deng Xiaoping, 99
Detente, 27, 36, 150
Developing sector, 109, 110, 111–112, 130, 157; debt crisis in, 163–164, 166, 170, 198
Directed energy weapons, 188, 189, 203
Dollar gap, 123–124
Dollar, U.S., 118, 121, 123–124; depreciation in Phase Three, 125; devaluation by Nixon, 132–133, 152; in 1960s, 147; in 1961, 129; in 1968, 132, 149; in 1977–78, 136; in 1980s, 157, 159, 162; in 1985, 75; in 1986–87, 166; in 1985–88, 168

East Germany, 50, 51, 59, 60, 81; reform in, 78
Eastern Europe: and Chernenko, 51; economic fragility of, 39, 43, 49, 50, 55, 77; and Gorbachev, 56, 58–59, 62–63, 68, 76–78; hard currency imports of, 28, 42, 48; 1960s reforms in, 27; 1989 revolutions in, 89, 177, 180; in 1990s, 198–199, 202; Soviet alliance with, 33, 34; Soviet military presence reduced in, 98–100; Soviet trade relations with, 35, 40, 42, 48, 53–55. *See also* individual countries
Economic dimension of security vulnerability, 31, 194; defined, 2; for U.S.: 102, 104, 137, 138,

140–141, 148–150, 153, 172, 179, 180, 194–196, 200, 205; for USSR: 31, 33, 34, 37, 43, 44, 48, 56, 57, 59–60, 63, 76, 90, 92, 94, 137, 177, 205; Gorbachev attitude toward, 59–60
Economic primitivization: of free world economy, 110; of USSR, 20, 29, 41, 43, 53, 56, 59, 73, 74, 89
Egypt, 36, 40
Eisenhower, Dwight D., 128, 144
Estonia, 58
Ethiopia, 42
European Community, 100, 197, 199
European Economic Community, 129, 131
Exoatmospheric reentry vehicle interceptor, 187, 188

Federal Reserve Board, 128, 130; in late 1960s, 132; in 1981–82, 153; in 1984, 161; in 1986, 166; in 1987, 167
Finland, 100
Five-Year Plan: growth rate contraction in successive, 2, 9; Sixth, 23; Seventh, 24; Eighth, 26; Twelfth, 59, 66, 73; Thirteenth, 64, 89; Twelfth-Fourteenth, 56
Flexible response, 38, 146
Floating exchange rate regime, 136
Follow On Forces Attack, 177–178
Ford, Gerald R., 138
Franc zone, 113
France, 113, 117, 142, 193, 204

GATT, 129, 195, 199
Georgia (USSR), 46, 47, 48, 58, 92

Germany: potential threat to USSR of unified, 94; prospects for unified, 100. *See also* East Germany; West Germany
Glasnost, 45, 63, 64, 66, 84, 85, 96
GLONASS, 186
Gold, 133
Gorbachev, Mikhail: ascension of, 56; attitude toward "economic dimension," 59–60; and China, 56, 60, 66; and defense spending, 56–57, 59, 80–82, 84, 86, 89, 97; downgrading of professional military by, 80; early program, 49, 56–63; and its failure, 66–69; economic retrenchment by, 70–72; radicalization of, 44–45, 64, 66; task confronting, 5, 9, 11. *See also* Eastern Europe, and Gorbachev; Glasnost; New Thinking; Perestroika, under Gorbachev
Gorshkov, Sergei, 80, 96
Gosplan, 49, 58, 59
Gramm-Rudman-Hollings law, 161, 178
Great Depression, 111, 114, 120, 149
Great Society, 106, 131, 149
Greece, 142
Grenada, 55, 176
Grishin, Victor, 49, 58
Ground-launched cruise missile, 55, 176
Group of Seven, 166

Hitler-Stalin Pact, 11
Hungary, 51; economic reforms in, 39, 46, 50, 58, 69, 88; exports to USSR of, 59; hard currency debt of, 40, 77; Soviet troop pull-out from, 81

Import substitution, 113, 123
Indochina, 42, 48, 50, 66
INF (Intermediate-Range Nuclear Forces) Agreement, 65, 81, 85, 176, 177
Inflation, free world: inflation/output dilemma, 106, 111, 112, 114, 119, 124, 134; in 1960s, 109, 130; in 1970s, 109, 133, 135; in 1979–81, 137; in 1980s, 157, 159, 161, 166, 167; in 1990s, 171; Phase Three rise in, 127. *See also* Petroleum, world price of; Primary commodities, price of; Soviet economy, inflation; U.S. economy, inflation
Intercontinental ballistic missiles, 35, 36, 144, 146, 150, 176, 204
Interest rates, free world, 198, 110, 155, 167
Intermediate-range missiles, 55, 65, 151, 176. *See also* Pershing II; SS20 *International Life journal*, 51
Iran, 142, 151
Iran-Iraq war, 137
Iraq, 192
Israel, 183, 191, 192
Italy, 113, 117, 142

Japan, 191; biases, economic policy, 114, 134, 197; commodity composition of trade, 112; economic performance, early postwar, 114–116, 142; economic advantages, 121; export emphasis, 113, 114; financing of U.S. deficits, 160; 1976 expansion in, 135; as protectionism target, 131, 135, 163, 166; role in 1987–88, 166, 167; role in 1990s, 171, 195, 197; and Smithsonian Agreement, 133
Johnson, Lyndon B., 106, 130–131, 132, 146, 148, 149, 173

Kazakhstan, 14
Kennedy Round, 129
Kennedy, John F., 119, 124, 125, 128–129, 131, 132, 133, 136, 162, 154; defense policy of, 146
KGB, 45, 46, 47
Khrushchev, Nikita: early confidence of, 24–26, 28; economic program of, 83; military doctrine of, 144, 184; ouster of, 26, 44, 80, 92; military opposition to, 84; military spending policies of, 34–38; and Nomenklatura, 46; vs. Malenkov, 23, 34
Korean War, 33, 34, 84, 95, 140; defense spending during, 173; effect on primary commodity prices, 106, 111; effect on NATO, 144; effect on Soviet economy, 22, 23, 35; effect on Soviet defense spending, 148; effect on U.S. economy, 120, 121, 122, 123, 124; effect on U.S. defense spending, 143, 148
Kosygin, Alexei: economic program of, 26, 37, 72; heirs to reforms of, 46, 47; ouster of, 27; reforms of, 27, 45, 58; downgrading of, 44
Kulikov, Victor, 80
Kunaev, Dinmukhamed, 58

Labor, free world: costs of, 106, 110, 113; in 1980s, 168; in 1990s, 171; mobility of, 110; productivity of, 110; strike wave, 106; wage explosion, 106, 131

Laos, 78
Latin America, 164, 199
Learn From Hungary campaign, 48
Lebanon, 183, 191
Lehman, John, 178
Leningrad model, 47
Liberman, Evsei, 46
Libya, 176
Ligachev, Yegor, 44, 49, 69, 89
Long cycle, 2; causes, 11; in free world economy, 105, 110, 111; in U.S., 105, 149, 153, 194, 197; in USSR, 9, 11–12, 20–21, 24, 28, 30, 37, 43, 44, 56, 60, 63, 66, 72, 83, 90, 92, 94, 177, 194
Long-range cruise missiles, 186, 189
Long-Term Agreement on Cotton, 129
Louvre Accords, 166, 167

Malenkov, Gregorii: conflicts with Khrushchev, 23–26, 34; defense cuts of, 34; economic program of, 23–26, 72, 83; military opposition to, 84; ouster of, 23, 44, 80, 92
Manchuria, 66
Marine Corps, U.S., 180
Maritime strategy, 177, 178, 202
Marshall Plan, 35, 123, 142
Massive retaliation, 144
Mexico, 164
Middle East, 35, 40, 106, 127, 192, 203
Military doctrine. *See* Soviet Union, military doctrine of; United States, military doctrine of
Minuteman missiles, 150
MIRVs, 150
Moldavia, 87

Mongolia, 50, 51, 60, 66, 78, 81
Multi-Fiber Arrangement, 166
Mutually Assured Destruction, 146
MX missiles, 204

Nakasone, Yasuhiro, 163
National security spending regimes, 140–152
NATO, 38, 39, 55, 65, 82, 90, 97, 99, 184; militarization of, 144; role in 1990s, 202
NAVSTAR, 186
Navy, Soviet, 80, 96, 98, 100
Navy, U.S., 175, 177, 178, 191, 202
NEP (New Economic Policy), 9, 12, 30, 88, 94
New Deal, 114, 122, 131, 149
New Economic Mechanism (Hungarian), 40, 88, 94
New Protectionism, 129, 131, 135, 163, 166, 170, 199
New Thinking, 63, 65, 66, 76, 78, 80, 203
Nicaragua, 43, 63, 78
Nixon, Richard M., 130, 131, 132, 133, 136, 138, 162
NMP (national material product), 2, 9, 56
Nomenklatura, 46, 47, 49
Nonoffensive defense, 80, 95, 98
North Korea, 35, 78
Novosibirsk Institute, 46
Novosibirsk model, 46, 47, 51, 63, 66, 69, 70
NSC-68, 143, 146
Nuclear weapons, 39, 41, 55; early U.S. advantage in, 34, 143–144; potential role of space for, 185; spread of, 192; Soviet development of, 37

OECD, 2
Ogarkov, Nikolai, 5, 44, 50;

Ogarkov, Nikolai (*Continued*)
conflict with Brezhnev regime, 47; demotion of, 55, 80; rebellion in professional military led by, 84
OPEC, 106, 112, 127, 133, 161, 164, 166, 167. *See also* Petroleum, world price of
Orderly marketing agreements, 163
Overindebtedness, 106, 109, 110; of non-U.S. developed sector, 118; of second-tier West European economies, 117; of U.S., 119, 121, 155, 158, 170

Payments to individuals outlays, 122, 128, 130, 132, 135, 139, 148, 149, 159, 180
Peaceful coexistence, 34, 65
Perestroika, 46; early versions of, 27, 44; under Andropov, 44, 49, 50; under Chernenko, 51; moderate, under Gorbachev, 56, 58, 62; radical, under Gorbachev, 45, 63, 66; effects of radical, 68–69; radical in decline, 71, 83, 89; future prospects for, 92, 93, 94
Pershing II missiles, 55, 176
Persian Gulf, 106, 127, 137, 167, 203
Petroleum: CMEA trading price of, 42; Soviet exports of, 48; Soviet industry recession in, 52–53; Soviet output of, 73; world price of, 27, 40, 50, 54, 61, 75, 106, 112, 124, 127, 134, 161, 164, 166; 167, 169, 171
PGM (precision guided munitions), 98, 177, 180, 183–192, 202
Phases of the business cycle, 124–128. *See also* Business cycles
Phobos-2, 82

Plaza Accords, 162, 163, 164
Poland, 40, 43, 49, 56, 59, 77
Poseidon submarine, 150
Primary commodities, price of, 110; in 1960s, 130, 131; in 1968–81, 106, 110; in 1970s, 133, 134, 135; in 1979–81, 137; in early 1980s, 161; in 1980s, 157, 164; in 1986, 166; in 1987–88, 164, 167; in 1990s, 198; Korean war effect on, 106; Phase Three rise of, 127
PVO, 96, 97, 98, 100

Reagan Doctrine, 55, 176
Reagan, Ronald, 138, 153, 162, 163, 164, 166; defense build-up of, 172–181, 191; Doctrine, 55, 176; and SDI, 189; supply-side initiative of, 5, 6, 103, 119, 154, 159
Recessions: *see* U.S. recessions
Red Army, 33, 45, 202
Robot weapons, 191
Rogers Plan, 178
Rogers, Bernard, 177
Romania, 40, 78
Romanov, Gregorii, 44, 47, 58
RSTA (reconnaissance, surveillance, and target acquisition), 98, 100, 177, 183–192, 202, 203
Ryzhkov, Nikolai, 89, 99, 100, 181, 202

Sagdeyev, Raold, 82, 85
Sakharov, Andrei, 64
SALT I Agreement, 37, 151
SATCOM, 186
Saudi Arabia, 164, 166
Schmelev, Nikolai, 69, 86
Scowcroft Commission, 176
Shah of Iran, 137

Shevardnadze, Eduard, 46, 58, 65
Siberia, 87
Slyunkov, Nikolai, 64
Smithsonian Agreement, 133, 136, 138, 166
Soft landing, economic, 170
Solidarity labor movement, 77
Soviet defense spending, 22, 24, 26, 28, 29, 30; alternative futures, 83; estimates of, 84–86, 87, 89; Gorbachev, under, 56–57, 59, 79–82; in 1950s–1960s, 34–37; in 1970s, 39–41, 47, 138; in 1980s, 43–44, 47, 50, 53, 62–65; in 1989–91, 86–90; long-term projections, 90–95, 191; Ryzhkov's deep cuts proposal, 89–90; surges, 11; threat regimes, 31–32
Soviet economy: agricultural sector, 14–16, 20, 22, 24, 28, 47, 48, 50, 51, 52, 64, 67, 73, 75, 88; commodity composition of trade, 40; defense industry conversion, 88; extensive mode of development, 11, 20–21, 26; fixed capital in, 19–20; food deficits, 106, 127, 130, 133, 137; hard currency borrowing, 61; hard currency imports, 27–28, 40, 48, 75, 198; industry, investment in, 22, 29, 59, 67–68, 71–72, 87, 89; inefficiency of, 15; inflation, 66, 67, 68, 70–71; intensive mode of development, 11, 26; Korean War, effects of, 22, 23, 35; personal consumption, 17–18, 22, 23, 29, 45, 53, 60, 66, 67, 69, 71, 86–89; population growth, 18; price reforms (1967), 27, 46; price reforms (1987), 64, 71; primary commodity and energy sectors, 14–16, 20, 24, 28, 29, 41, 52 54, 56, 59, 61, 73; privatization and marketization attempts, 50, 51, 58, 64, 69, 88, 89, 93; productivity of labor, 29, 53, 56, 60, 66–67, 72, 87; scissors crisis, 12; service sector, 50, 51, 64, 69; trade deficit, 66, 67, 68, 70, 87; War Communism, 9; workforce in, 16–17, 18. *See also* Eastern Europe, Soviet trade relations with; Economic dimension of security vulnerability, USSR; Economic primitivization, USSR; Five-Year Plan; Long cycle, USSR; NEP; NMP; Soviet defense spending; Stalinist economic principles
Soviet Institute for Space Research, 82
Soviet Union: alcoholism in, 18, 29, 56, 67, 71, 87; alliance system, economic and military aid to, 35, 39, 42, 53, 76, 78; coal miners strike, 87, 89; crime rate, 87; military doctrine of, 33, 38, 39, 80, 95–101; nationalist disturbances, 87, 92, 93; post-World War II expansionism, 142; space program, 35, 39, 79, 82, 85, 89, 101, 187, 189. *See also* Glasnost; New Thinking; Soviet defense spending; Soviet economy; names of individual leaders
Space, military use of, 185–189. *See also* Soviet Union, space program; Strategic Defense Initiative
Special trade arrangements, 112, 113, 195, 199
Sputnik, 36, 144, 185

SS-20, 50, 55, 65, 81, 151
Stagflation, 109
Stalin, Joseph, 9, 35, 65; economic system, principles of, 12. *See also* NEP
START negotiations, 97, 201
Sterling zone, 113
Strategic Air Command, 143, 144
Strategic Defense Initiative, 55, 97, 175, 177, 187, 188, 189, 202, 203
Strategic Rocket Forces, 41
Structural disarmament, 190–192, 200
Submarine-launched ballistic missiles, 146, 151, 204
Suez crisis, 124
Superministries, 58
Surplus disposal program, 124
Sweden, 100
Syria, 40, 183

Tank, main battle, 98, 180, 183–184, 189, 191
Third Revolution in warfare, 98, 187
Third World debt crisis, 164, 170. *See also* Developing sector
Tikhonov, Nikolai, 51, 58, 59
Transcaucasus region, 46, 87, 100
Transcentury weapons, 6, 184–192, 199–200, 205; Soviet prospects for, 97, 99, 100; U.S. efforts in, 177, 178, 180
Trident II missiles, 204
Truman Doctrine, 142
Truman, Harry S., 142, 143, 146
Trust in Cadres program, 46
Tula Doctrine, 41, 80
Turkey, 142

U-2 incident, 36
Ukraine, 14, 87

United Kingdom, 117; biases, economic, 114; commodity composition of trade, 113; financing of U.S. deficits, 160; nuclear arsenal, 193; pound devaluation, 132; role in 1990s, 204
United States: early strategic advantage of, 34, 143; military doctrine of, 38, 55, 143–144, 146, 175, 177. *See also* U.S. defense spending; U.S. economy
U.S. defense spending, 6; from 1940s–1970s, 139; in late 1940s, 122, 142–143; in 1950s, 120, 121, 143–144; in 1960s, 38, 131, 144–147, 148; in 1970s, 132, 137–138, 148, 150–151, 153, 181; in 1980s, 55, 103, 154, 172–181, 191; in 1990s, 172, 178, 179–181, 194, 195, 197, 200–201, 204; national security spending regimes, 140–152. *See also* United States, military doctrine of
U.S. domestic demand: in 1950s, 120, 123; in 1960s, 131; in 1970s, 133, 135, 151; in 1980s, 104, 157, 159, 162; in 1990s, 104, 128, 197
U.S. economy: advantages of, 118, 120; biases, economic, 104, 111, 114, 134, 149, 195, 196; commodity composition of trade, 112, 113, 118, 134; early postwar performance, 143; economic growth in 1950s, 121; economic growth in 1950s–1980s, 118; economic growth in 1980s, 104, 155; economic growth in 1990s, 104; inflation in 1960s, 130–131; inflation in 1970s, 133; inflation in 1980s,

103–104, 119, 157, 159, 161, 170; productivity and competitiveness, 120, 121, 129, 155–157; recoveries in Phase One, 124; recovery in 1959, 128; recovery in 1976, 135; recovery in 1983–84, 104, 160. *See also* Dollar; Economic dimension of security vulnerability, U.S.; Long cycle, U.S.; U.S. recessions; Overindebtedness, U.S.; U.S. domestic demand; U.S. defense spending; U.S. government budget

U.S. external balances: recoveries in Phase Three, 127; in 1950s, 120, 123, 124; in 1960s, 130, 131, 132, 147, 149; in 1970s, 118, 132, 134, 135, 151, 137; in 1980s, 104, 118–119, 157, 161, 170–172; in 1987–88, 164–169; in 1990s, 104, 127, 179. *See also* overindebtedness, U.S.

U.S. government budget, deficit of: in 1890s–early twenty first century, 122; in 1940s–1950s, 120, 122; in 1960s, 131, 132; in 1976, 135; in 1980s, 104, 155, 159, 161, 171; in 1987–88, 164; in 1990s, 104, 179; means of financing, 138–139; in Phase Three, 127. *See also* Overindebtedness, U.S.; Payments to individuals outlays

U.S. recessions, 119, 120, 121, 125, 128; in 1949 and 1958, 122; in 1954, 122, 124; in 1960, 128; in 1967 (growth recession), 130; in 1969–70, 132; in 1975, 134; in 1981–82, 137, 153

U.S.-Canada Free Trade Agreement, 199

USA-Canada Institute, 69
Ustinov, Dmitri, 80
Uzbekistan, 87, 92

Van Tien Dung, 51
Vietnam, 40, 42, 50, 51, 53, 78
Vietnam War, 131, 146, 148–149, 150, 176; U.S. defense spending during, 173–174
Vladivostok, 66
Voluntary restraint agreement, 163

Wall Street, 167
War Communism, 9
Warsaw Pact, 80, 82, 90, 97, 178
Washington Naval Agreement (1922), 98
Weinberger, Caspar, 175, 176
West Germany, 51, 60, 133; biases, economic, 114, 134, 135, 198; commodity composition of trade, 112; competitiveness and export emphasis, 113, 123; economic advantages of, 121, 133; economic performance of, 114–117; financing of U.S. deficits, 160; in 1976, 135; in 1987–88, 164, 166; in 1990s, 195, 198
Window of vulnerability, 151, 175, 176
World War I, 122
World War II, 31, 109, 113, 114, 122, 140, 142, 154

Yakovlev, Alexander, 64
Yazov, Dmitri, 82
Yeltsin, Boris, 82, 86

Zero option, 176

About the Authors

Richard Cohen is the author of *World Trade and Payments Cycles: The Advance and Retreat of the Postwar Order* (Praeger, 1989) and coauthor (with Dr. Norman A. Bailey) of *The Mexican Time Bomb* (Twentieth Century Fund, 1987). He directs his own economics consulting firm, Washington/World Analysts, and is the economic analyst for the Washington Defense Research Group on its projects for the U.S. government and Los Alamos National Laboratories. Formerly chief analyst for Colby-Bailey Associates, he received his B.A. degree from Queens College, New York.

Peter A. Wilson is a consultant to the RAND Corporation and Los Alamos National Laboratories (through the Washington Defense Research Group) dealing with national security issues. He teaches a seminar at the MITRE Institute and has taught at the Foreign Service Institute of the Department of State. Former member of the Department of State Policy Planning Staff (1978–81) and an analyst in the CIA's Office of Strategic Research (1975–78), he has written numerous articles on national security matters, including two coauthored with Richard Cohen in *Comparative Strategy*. Others include "The Marine Corps in 1995," in *U.S. Naval Institute Proceedings;* "The Geostrategic Risks of SDI," in *Star Wars and European Defense* (Macmillan, 1987), and "Future U.S. Reinforcement Options," in *NATO-Warsaw Pact Force Mobilization* (National Defense University Press, 1988). He holds a B.A. from Princeton University and an M.A. from the University of Chicago.

For Product Safety Concerns and Information please contact our EU representative GPSR@taylorandfrancis.com
Taylor & Francis Verlag GmbH, Kaufingerstraße 24, 80331 München, Germany

www.ingramcontent.com/pod-product-compliance
Lightning Source LLC
Chambersburg PA
CBHW070554300426
44113CB00010B/1255